SHAKESPEARE IN PRODUCTION

MUCH ADO ABOUT NOTHING

to focus wholly on the
issues and trends in the
QUEEN MARC successive reinterpretations of
the **CORSTOR** cultural and ideological contexts. Gender issues
are central highlights in striking ways the changing constructions of womanhood in performances from Shakespeare's time to the
present.

A commentary along the New Cambridge edition of the text recreates
in lively detail interpretations of each passage in a variety of British,
American, Canadian and other productions, including film and television
versions. A full introduction examines these and other, controversial aspects
of the play, such as the problematic relation of its dark and comic elements, in
a wide range of performances.

An essential resource for students, teachers, actors and directors, this is an
illuminating book for all theatregoers.

SHAKESPEARE IN PRODUCTION

SERIES EDITORS: J. S. BRATTON AND JULIE HANKEY

This series offers students and researchers the fullest possible stage histories of individual Shakespearean texts.

In each volume a substantial introduction presents a conceptual overview of the play, marking out the major stages of its representation and reception. In this context, no single approach to the play can be described as more 'authentic' than any other. The extrapolations of Tate, the interpretations of Dryden, the upholstering of Charles Kean and the strippings-down of Marowitz are all treated as ways of reading and rewriting Shakespeare's text and understood in terms of contemporary audiences, tastes and sensibilities.

The commentary, presented alongside the New Cambridge edition of the text itself, offers detailed, line-by-line evidence for the overview presented in the introduction, making the volume a flexible tool for further research. The editors have selected interesting and vivid evocations of settings, acting and stage presentation and range widely in time and space.

The plays of Shakespeare are a particularly rich field for such treatment, having formed a central part of British theatrical culture for four hundred years. Major stage productions outside Britain are also included, as are adaptations, film and video versions.

ALREADY PUBLISHED
A Midsummer Night's Dream, edited by Trevor R. Griffiths

FORTHCOMING VOLUMES
Antony and Cleopatra, edited by Richard Madelaine
The Tempest, edited by Christine Dymkowski
Hamlet, edited by Robert Hapgood
Macbeth, edited by John Wilders
Julius Caesar, edited by James Rigney

MUCH ADO
ABOUT NOTHING

EDITED BY

JOHN F. COX

Senior Lecturer in English, Avondale College,
New South Wales

PUBLISHED BY THE PRESS SYNDICATE OF THE UNIVERSITY OF CAMBRIDGE
The Pitt Building, Trumpington Street, Cambridge CB2 1RP, United Kingdom

CAMBRIDGE UNIVERSITY PRESS
The Edinburgh Building, Cambridge CB2 2RU, United Kingdom
40 West 20th Street, New York, NY 10011–4211, USA
10 Stamford Road, Oakleigh, Melbourne 3166, Australia

© Cambridge University Press, 1997

First published 1997

Printed in the United Kingdom at the University Press, Cambridge

Typeset in 10/12.5 Monotype Ehrhardt, in QuarkXpress^{TM} [SE]

A catalogue record for this book is available from the British Library

Library of Congress cataloguing in publication data

Shakespeare, William, 1564–1616.
Much Ado About Nothing / edited by John F. Cox.
p. cm. – (Shakespeare in Production)
Includes bibliographical references and index.
ISBN 0 521 47163 X (hardback) – ISBN 0 521 59822 2 (paperback)
1. Shakespeare, William, 1564–1616. Much Ado About Nothing.
2. Shakespeare, William, 1564–1616 – Stage history. 3. Shakespeare,
William, 1564–1616 – Dramatic production. 4. Shakespeare, William,
1564–1616 – Film and video adaptations. 5. Women in literature.
6. Comedy. I. Cox, John F. II. Title. III. Series.
PR2828.A2C69 1997
822.3′3 – dc21 96–51102 CIP

ISBN 0 521 47163 X hardback
ISBN 0 521 59822 2 paperback

CONTENTS

ILLUSTRATIONS

SERIES EDITORS' PREFACE

It is no longer necessary to stress that the text of a play is only its starting-point, and that only in production is its potential realised and capable of being appreciated fully. Since the coming-of-age of Theatre Studies as an academic discipline, we now understand that even Shakespeare is only one collaborator in the creation and infinite recreation of his play upon the stage. And just as we now agree that no play is complete until it is produced, so we have become interested in the way in which plays often produced – and pre-eminently the plays of the national Bard, William Shakespeare – acquire a life history of their own, after they leave the hands of their first maker.

Since the eighteenth century Shakespeare has become a cultural construct: sometimes the guarantor of nationhood, heritage and the status quo, sometimes seized and transformed to be its critic and antidote. This latter role has been particularly evident in countries where Shakespeare has to be translated. The irony is that while his status as national icon grows in the English-speaking world, his language is both lost and renewed, so that for good or ill, Shakespeare can be made to seem more urgently 'relevant' than in England or America, and may become the one dissenting voice that the censors mistake as harmless.

'Shakespeare in Production' gives the reader, the student and the scholar a comprehensive dossier of materials – eye-witness accounts, contemporary criticism, promptbook marginalia, stage business, cuts, additions and rewritings – from which to construct an understanding of the many meanings that the plays have carried down the ages and across the world. These materials are organised alongside the New Cambridge Shakespeare text of the play, line by line and scene by scene, while a substantial introduction in each volume offers a guide to their interpretation. One may trace an argument about, for example, the many ways of playing Queen Gertrude, or the political transmutations of the text of *Henry V*; or take a scene, an act or a whole play, and work out how it has succeeded or failed in presentation over four hundred years.

For, despite our insistence that the plays are endlessly made and remade by history, Shakespeare is not a blank, scribbled upon by the age. Theatre history charts changes, but also registers something in spite of those changes. Some productions work and others do not. Two interpretations may be entirely different, and yet both will bring the play to life. Why? Without setting out to give absolute answers, the history of a play in the theatre can often show where the energy and shape of it lie, what has made it tick, through many permutations. In this way theatre history can find common ground with literary criticism. Both will find suggestive directions in the introductions to these volumes, while the commentaries provide raw material for readers to recreate the living experience of theatre, and become their own eye-witnesses.

J. S. Bratton
Julie Hankey

This series was originated by Jeremy Treglown and published by Junction Books, and later by Bristol Classical Press, as 'Plays in Performance'. Four titles were published; all are now out of print.

ACKNOWLEDGEMENTS

This book was made possible by a visiting lectureship at Newbold College, Berkshire, England, arranged conjointly with my home institution, Avondale College, Australia. I am most grateful for the generous research grants provided by both Newbold College and the Avondale Foundation. I should like to thank the series editors, Professor J. S. Bratton and Julie Hankey, for their counsel and encouragement, and copyeditor Margaret Berrill for her careful attention to detail. I also wish to thank the following for permission to reproduce the illustrations: Bodleian Library, Oxford (illustration 1), reproduced from the frontispiece of Wenman's 1778 acting edition, shelfmark Mal.B.340 (26); The Board of Trustees of the Victoria & Albert Museum (2, 3, 4, 5, 6); Mrs E. T. M. Craig and Mrs J. Taylor (the Edward Gordon Craig Estate) and the Bibliothèque Nationale, Paris (7); Birmingham Repertory Theatre Limited (8); Mr David Ball, the Angus McBean Estate (9, 11); the Theatre Museum, London, courtesy of the Trustees of the Victoria & Albert Museum (10); Shakespeare Centre Library, Stratford-upon-Avon: Thomas Holte Collection (12) and Joe Cocks Collection (13); Mr Chris Davies (14).

EDITOR'S NOTE

Notes on cuts and textual alterations are based on the relevant promptbook or printed acting version (see bibliography), and are not individually referenced. Unless otherwise indicated, comments on Eyre's 1971 RSC production, the 1984 BBC/Time–Life television production, and Branagh's 1993 film are based on my own observations.

The playtext used is *Much Ado About Nothing*, ed. F. H. Mares, 1988 (New Cambridge Shakespeare).

ABBREVIATIONS

L *Lady*
Lacy T. H. Lacy acting edition,
c.1858
LC *London Chronicle*
LDP *Liverpool Daily Post*
LE *Liverpool Echo*
LJ *Liverpool Journal*
LL *The Law Against Lovers,*
1662
Lloyd's *Lloyd's Weekly London*
Newspaper
LS *The London Stage 1660–1800,*
ed. W. Van Lennep *et al.*
LSC *Leamington Spa Courier*
LTR *London Theatre Record*
MA *Morning Advertiser*
ManC *Manchester Courier*
MC *Morning Chronicle*
MCT *Middlesex County Times*
MET *Manchester Examiner and*
Times
MG *Manchester Guardian*
MH *Morning Herald*
MN *Morning News*
MP *Morning Post*
MS *Mirror of the Stage*
MSC *Manchester Sunday Chronicle*
NC *News Chronicle*
NEP *Nottingham Evening Post*
NEW *New English Weekly*
NMM *New Monthly Magazine*
NR *New Republic*
NS *New Statesman*
NSN *New Statesman and Nation*
NT National Theatre, London
NY New York
NYDT *New York Daily Tribune*
NYH *New York Herald*
NYHT *New York Herald Tribune*
NYM *New York Magazine*
NYP *New York Post*
NYr *New Yorker*
NYSF New York Shakespeare
Festival
NYT *New York Times*
O *Observer*

Or *Oracle*
OT *Oxford Times*
OUDS Oxford University Dramatic
Society
Oxberry Oxberry acting edition, 1823
p Code for promptbooks not
listed in Shattuck, *The*
Shakespeare Promptbooks (see
promptbooks in bibliography)
PA *Public Advertiser*
pbk(s) promptbook(s)
PhI *Philadelphia Inquirer*
PI *Plays International*
PMG *Pall Mall Gazette*
PP *Plays and Players*
pr. photo production photograph
PW *Pictorial World*
Q Quarto edition of *Much Ado,*
1600
RA *Rugby Advertiser*
RHC *Record-Herald,* Chicago
RSC Royal Shakespeare Company
RST Royal Shakespeare Theatre,
Stratford-upon-Avon
RTC Renaissance Theatre
Company
s Code for promptbooks listed
in Shattuck, *The Shakespeare*
Promptbooks (see
promptbooks in bibliography)
Saker Saker acting edition, 1878
SC *Shakespearean Criticism,*
Detroit, Gale Research
Sc *Scotsman*
SCL Shakespeare Centre Library,
Stratford-upon-Avon
SCN *Sutton Coldfield News*
SF Shakespeare Festival
SH *Stratford-upon-Avon Herald*
Sk *Sketch*
SMT Shakespeare Memorial
Theatre, Stratford-upon-
Avon
Soc *Society*
SP *Shakespeare Pictorial*
Sp *Spectator*

PRODUCTIONS

The following is a selective chronological list of productions of *Much Ado About Nothing*. The 'leading personnel' column lists actors of Beatrice and Benedick and, where indicated, directors or managers. In entries grouping performances from more than one year, the dates in the left column and the venue(s) in the right refer to performances by the first person in the entry; subsequent names in the entry are the Beatrice(s) and/or Benedick(s) associated with the first person's performances. Venues are in London unless identified otherwise.

Date(s)	Leading personnel	Venue(s)
1598 or –9 to 1642?		Curtain?, Globe, Blackfriars
Winter 1612–13		Two court performances
1662 (*LL*)		Lincoln's Inn Fields
1721	Cast included Lacy Ryan, James Quin, Letitia Cross, Anna Seymour, Jane Giffard	Lincoln's Inn Fields
1737, 1739	**Thomas Chapman** **Elizabeth Bincks/Vincent**	CG
1737, 1741 (*UP*)	**Catherine Clive** (Liberia) **James Quin** (Protheus)	DL
1746	**Lacy Ryan, Hannah Pritchard**	CG
1748–9, 1753–63, 1765–76	**David Garrick** Hannah Pritchard 1748–9, 1753–6; Hannah Pritchard Jr 1756–63 (1761–3 as Mrs Palmer); Jane Pope 1762, 1765–75; Frances Abington 1775–6	DL
1774–5	**John Lee** Ann Barry 1774; Mary Bulkley 1775	CG
1775–6, 1783, 1785–9, 1797–8	**Frances Abington** David Garrick 1775–6; John Henderson 1783, 1785; Joseph Holman 1786; William Lewis 1787–9, 1797–8	DL 1775–6; CG 1783, 1785–9, 1797–8
1777, 1779, 1787–9, 1793–4, 1797–8, 1803, 1806–7	**William Lewis** Mary Bulkley 1777; Jane Pope 1779; Frances Abington 1787–9, 1797–8; Harriet Esten 1793–4; Louisa Brunton 1803; Julia Glover 1806–7; Nanette Johnston 1807	CG (except 1779); DL 1779

xiv

Date(s)	Leading personnel	Venue(s)
1778–81, 1783–5	John Henderson Jane Pope 1778–9; Elizabeth Younge 1779–81, 1784; Frances Abington 1783, 1785	DL 1778–9; CG 1779–81, 1783–5
1783, 1787	**Thomas King** Frances Kemble 1783; Elizabeth Farren 1787	DL 1783; Haymarket 1787
1786–7, 1812	**Joseph Holman** Frances Abington 1786; Anne Brunton 1787; Agnes Holman 1812	CG 1786–7; Park, NY 1812; Chestnut, Philadelphia 1812
1787	**Matthew Browne, Mary Bulkley**	Haymarket
1787, 1789	**Lewis Hallam, Elizabeth Morris**	John Street, NY 1787; Southwark, Philadelphia 1789
1788–90, 1792–3, 1797–9, 1801–2	**John Philip Kemble** Elizabeth Farren 1788–90, 1792–3, 1797; Dorothy Jordan 1798–9, 1801–2; Ann Biggs 1799	DL 1788–90, 1797–9, 1801–2; DL company at King's 1792–3
1796–7, 1802	**John Hodgkinson, Elizabeth Johnson**	John Street, NY 1796–7; Park, NY 1802
1797, 1809, 1813, 1816–17, 1822, 1824, 1827, 1838	**Thomas Cooper** Anne Merry (nee Brunton) 1797; Lydia Kelly 1824, 1827	New, Philadelphia 1797; John Street, NY 1797; Park, NY 1809, 1817, 1824, 1827; Chestnut, Philadelphia 1813, 1816–17, 1822; Charleston 1838
1798–9, 1801–4, 1807–8	**Dorothy Jordan** J. P. Kemble 1798–9, 1801–2; William Barrymore, Haymarket 1798; John Powell 1799; Charles Kemble 1803; Robert Elliston 1804, 1807–8	DL 1798–9, 1801–4, 1807–8; Haymarket 1798
1803, 1811–12, 1817–18, 1820, 1823–7, 1829–36, 1840	**Charles Kemble** Dorothy Jordan 1803; Nanette Johnston 1811–12; Maria Kemble 1811, 1818; Elizabeth Brunton 1817; Emma Wensley 1820; Eliza Chester 1823–6; Frances Jarman 1827; Maria Foote 1829–30; Frances (Fanny) Kemble 1831–4; Harriette Taylor 1835; Helena Faucit 1836; Louisa Nisbett 1840	DL 1803; CG 1811ff. America 1832–3, 1833–4; Haymarket 1835

Date(s)	Leading personnel	Venue(s)
1804, 1806–8, 1812–13	**Robert Elliston** Dorothy Jordan 1804, 1807–8; Maria Duncan 1806; Elizabeth Edwin 1812–13	DL
1804	**William Warren, William Wood,** managers	Chestnut, Philadelphia
1809–11	**Benjamin Wrench, Elizabeth Edwin**	DL company at Lyceum
1823, 1828–9, 1836–7, 1842–4, 1845–6, 1849–50, 1852–4, 1856–9	**James W. Wallack** Agnes Gilfert (nee Holman), NY 1823; Lydia Kelly, NY 1828–9; Clara Fisher, Boston 1828; Josephine Clifton 1836; Sarah Hildreth 1837; Helena Faucit 1842; Emma Brougham 1844; Charlotte Cushman 1845; Mary (Fanny) Stirling 1845–6; Louisa Nisbett 1849; Mary Warner 1850; Laura Keene 1852; Sarah Conway 1854; Rosa Bennett 1854; Josephine Hoey 1856, 1858	Park, NY 1823, 1828–9, 1843–4; Chestnut, Philadelphia 1823; Tremont, Boston 1828; National, NY 1836–7; Haymarket 1842, 1849–50; Princess's 1845–6; Boston 1846; Wallack's, NY 1852–4, 1856, 1858–9; Brougham's Bowery, NY 1857
1823	**Vincent de Camp**	Park, NY
1824–31	**Lydia Kelly** Stanley 1824–5; Thomas Cooper 1824, 1827; James Caldwell, NY 1828–9; James Wallack, NY 1828–9; James Barton, NY 1831	Park, NY 1824–9, 1831; Chestnut, Philadelphia 1828, 1830–1
1826, 1828, 1837	**George Barrett** Agnes Gilfert 1826, 1828; Ellen Tree 1837	Bowery, NY 1826, 1828; Park, NY 1837
1828–30	**James Caldwell** Lydia Kelly 1828–9; Clara Fisher 1830	Park, NY
1830, 1832, 1848	**John Cooper** Louisa Mordaunt 1830; Harriette Taylor 1832; Anne Barrett 1848	Haymarket 1830, 1832; Princess's 1848
1830, 1840, 1843, 1847–8, 1849	**Louisa Mordaunt/Nisbett** John Cooper 1830; Charles Kemble 1840; William Macready 1843; Benjamin Webster 1847–8; James Wallack 1849	Haymarket 1830, 1847–8, 1849; CG 1840; DL 1843
1833, 1836	**Frederick Vining** Elizabeth Yates (nee Brunton) 1833; Harriette Taylor 1833; Ellen Tree 1836	Haymarket
1835, 1837–8	**William Abbott** Lydia Phillips 1835; Josephine Clifton 1837; Ellen Tree 1838	Park, NY

Date(s)	Leading personnel	Venue(s)
1836, 1842–3, 1858, 1874, 1879	**Helena Faucit** Charles Kemble 1836; James Wallack 1842; William Macready 1843; Charles Dillon 1858; William Creswick 1874; Barry Sullivan 1879	CG 1836; Haymarket 1842, 1874; DL 1843; Lyceum 1858; SMT 1879; various provincial theatres
1836, 1837–9, 1845–6, 1850, 1852, 1858–9, 1861, 1865	**Ellen Tree/Kean** Frederick Vining 1836; J. K. Mason, NY 1837; George Barrett, NY 1837; James Murdoch, NY 1838; William Abbott, NY 1838; John S. Balls 1839; Charles Kean 1845–6, 1850, 1852, 1858–9, 1861, 1865	Haymarket 1836, 1850; Park, NY 1837–9, 1845–6; National, Boston 1837–8; Chestnut, Philadelphia 1845; Princess's 1852, 1858–9; DL 1861; Broadway, NY 1865
1838, 1845–7, 1857	**James Murdoch** Ellen Tree 1838; Eliza Bland 1845; Fanny Wallack 1847; Sallie St Clair 1857	Park, NY 1838, 1845–6; Broadway, NY 1847; Burton's, NY 1857
1839	**Henry Marston, Mary (Fanny) Stirling**	DL
1840, 1843–4, 1845, 1849–50, 1852	**Charlotte Cushman** Peter Richings 1840; William Macready 1843; George Vandenhoff 1844; James Wallack 1845; Charles Couldock 1849–50	Park, NY 1840, 1843–4; Princess's 1845; Broadway, NY 1849–50; Brougham's Lyceum, NY 1852
1840, 1848	**Peter Richings** Charlotte Cushman 1840; Fanny Wallack 1848	Park, NY 1840; Broadway, NY 1848
1842–4, 1846, 1847–8, 1850, 1852, 1853	**George Vandenhoff** Emma Brougham 1843; Mrs H. Hunt 1844; Charlotte Cushman 1844; Charlotte Barnes 1846; Fanny Wallack 1847; Mary Farren 1848; Marie Duret 1850; Catherine Sinclair 1852; Jane Reynolds 1853	Park, NY 1842–4, 1846; Broadway, NY 1847–8; Astor Place, NY 1850; Brougham's Lyceum, NY 1852; Boston Theatre 1852; Haymarket 1853
1843, 1851	**William Macready** Louisa Nisbett 1843; Helena Faucit 1843; Charlotte Cushman, NY 1843; Mary Warner 1851	DL 1843; Haymarket 1851; Park, NY 1843
1844	**James Anderson, Clara Ellis**	Park, NY
1845–6, 1850, 1852, 1858–9, 1861, 1865	**Charles and Ellen Kean**	Park, NY 1845–6; Chestnut, Philadelphia 1845; Haymarket 1850; Princess's 1852, 1858–9; DL 1861; Broadway, NY 1865

Date(s)	Leading personnel	Venue(s)
1846–7, 1848–50, 1855–6	Edward L. Davenport Anna Cora Mowatt 1846–7, 1848–50; Fanny E. Davenport 1855–6	Park, NY 1846–7; Princess's 1848; Marylebone 1849; Olympic 1850; Broadway, NY 1855; Brougham's Bowery, NY 1856
1847–8	Benjamin Webster, Louisa Nisbett	Haymarket
1848–54, 1858	Samuel Phelps, manager Henry Marston 1848–54, 1858; Fanny Cooper 1848–9, 1852, 1854; Isabella Glyn 1850; Fanny Vining 1851; Emma Fitzpatrick 1851; Jane Young 1853, 1858	Sadler's Wells
1850, 1852, 1873–4, 1877	William Creswick Elizabeth Ponisi 1850; Fanny Cooper 1850; Isabella Glyn 1852; Miss Carlisle 1873; Emily Fowler 1874; Helena Faucit 1874	Surrey 1850, 1852; Holborn 1873; Crystal Palace 1874; Haymarket 1874; Australian tour 1877
1854, 1867, 1873–4	Sarah Conway James Wallack 1854; Frederick Conway 1867, 1873; Frank Roche 1874	Wallack's, NY 1854; Park, Brooklyn 1867, 1873–4
1855, 1867, 1870, 1873	Frederick Conway Eloise Bridges 1855; Sarah Conway 1867, 1873; Mary Scott-Siddons 1870	Broadway, NY 1855; Park, Brooklyn 1867, 1870, 1873
1856	Laura Keene, George Jordan	Laura Keene's, NY
1857	Belton, Julia Barrow	Burton's, NY
1857–8, 1863, 1868	Henry Howe Catherine Sinclair 1857–8; Amy Sedgwick 1858; Jane Young 1858; Louisa Angel 1863; Mary Scott-Siddons 1868	Haymarket
1858, 1866	Charles Dillon Helena Faucit 1858; Kate Reignolds 1866	Lyceum 1858; Broadway, NY 1866
1858	James W. Wallack Jr, Ann Wallack	Niblo's Garden, NY
1858	Barry Sullivan, Fanny Morant	Burton's, NY
1859, 1866	Walter Lacy Jane Reynolds 1859; Louisa Herbert 1866	Haymarket 1859; St James's 1866
1865	George Boniface, Kate Newton	Bowery, NY
1867, 1874, 1881	Henry Neville Kate Terry 1867; Emily Fowler 1874; Hortense Rhea 1881	Adelphi 1867; Olympic 1874; Gaiety 1881

Date(s)	Leading personnel	Venue(s)
1869	Lester Wallack, Rose Eytinge	Wallack's, NY
1869	Augustin Daly, manager D. H. Harkins, Mary Scott-Siddons	Daly's, NY
1871, 1873, 1876–7, 1879, 1889–90	Edwin Booth Bella Pateman 1871, 1873; Clara Jennings 1876–7; Elizabeth Bowers 1879; Helena Modjeska 1889–90	Booth's, NY 1871, 1873, 1879; Lyceum, NY 1876–7; Broadway, NY 1889; Harlem Opera House, NY 1889; Academy of Music, Brooklyn 1890
1874	Adelaide Neilson, John H. Barnes	Lyceum, NY
1875, 1880	Ada Cavendish Hermann Vezin 1875; Samuel Piercy 1880	Gaiety 1875; Park, Brooklyn 1880
1878	Edward Saker	Alexandra Theatre, Liverpool
1879–80	Barry Sullivan Rose Eytinge, Haymarket 1879; Helena Faucit, SMT 1879; Ellen Wallis, SMT 1879; Miss Masson, SMT 1880	Haymarket 1879; SMT 1879–80
1881	Edward Compton, Virginia Bateman	SMT
1882–3	William Harris, Hortense Rhea	Park, Brooklyn
1882–3, 1884–5, 1887, 1891, 1893,–4,–5	Henry Irving, Ellen Terry	Lyceum 1882–3, 1884, 1887, 1891, 1893,–4,–5; Edinburgh, Glasgow, Liverpool 1883; North America 1884–5
1886, 1891	Lawrence Barrett, Minna Gale	Park, Brooklyn 1886; Broadway, NY 1891
1886	Fanny L. Davenport, John H. Barnes	Union Square, NY
1886, 1888–9	Louis James, Marie Wainwright	Criterion, Brooklyn 1886; Fifth Avenue, NY 1888; Star, NY 1889
1888–92, 1900	Helena Modjeska Eben Plympton 1888; Edwin Booth 1889–90; Otis Skinner 1892	Fourteenth Street, NY 1888; Park, Brooklyn 1888, 1891; Broadway, NY 1889; Harlem Opera House, NY 1889; Academy of Music, Brooklyn 1890; Union Square, NY 1892; Garden,

Date(s)	Leading personnel	Venue(s)
		NY 1892; American circuit 1900
1891,–4,–7, 1901, 1905–11, 1913–14	**Frank Benson**, manager Frank and Constance Benson 1891,–4,–7, 1901, 1905–6, 1908–9, 1911; Frank Benson 1913–14; Henry Ainley, Edith Wynne-Matthison 1907, Robert Loraine 1909–10; Violet Vanbrugh 1910–11, 1913; Fred Terry, Julia Neilson 1911; Dorothy Green 1914	SMT all years listed; Coronet 1908
1892–3, 1904–5, 1911, 1913	**Julia Marlowe** Henry Jewett 1893; Edward Sothern 1904–5, 1911, 1913	Park, Brooklyn 1892–3; American circuit 1904–5, 1911, 1913
1895, 1904, 1916–17	**Ben Greet**, manager Mary Kingsley, Frank Rodney 1895; Ben Greet, Edith Wynne-Matthison 1904; Sybil Thorndike 1916–17; Jerrold Robertshaw, SMT 1916; William Stack, Old Vic 1916; Terence O'Brien, Old Vic 1917	SMT 1895, 1916; Metropole 1904; Old Vic 1916–17
1896–7	**Augustin Daly**, manager Ada Rehan, Charles Richman	Daly's, NY
1898	**George Alexander, Julia Neilson**	St James's
c.1900	**Charles Hanford, Marie Drofnah**	Washington
1900–1, 1917	**Richard Flanagan**, manager May Harvey, Cooper Cliffe 1900–1; Marie Wilson, Norman Partridge 1917	Queen's, Manchester
1903–4	**Edward Gordon Craig**, director Ellen Terry 1903–4; Oscar Asche 1903; Matheson Lang 1903–4	Imperial 1903; tour 1904
1903, 1908	**Charles Fry, Olive Kennett**	Royalty 1903; Court 1908
1904	**William Poel**, director Rita Jolivet, Victor Dougall	Court Theatre and various London halls
1904	**William Morris, Jessie Milward**	Princess's, NY
1904–5, 1911, 1913	**Edward H. Sothern, Julia Marlowe**	American circuit
1905	**H. Beerbohm Tree, Winifred Emery**	His Majesty's
1909–10	**B. Iden Payne**, director Mona Limerick, Ian Maclaren	Gaiety, Manchester

Date(s)	Leading personnel	Venue(s)
1910	**Clive Currie**, director Mabel Mannering, H. A. Saintsbury	Court
1911	**Eade Montefiore**, director Alice Crawford, Frederick Worlock	Coronet
1912	**H. A. Saintsbury**, director H. A. Saintsbury, Leah Bateman-Hunter	Court
1912–13	**Annie Russell, Frank Reicher**	Empire, NY
1914	**Patrick Kirwan**, director Arthur Bourchier, Margaret Halstan	SMT
1914	**Shakespeare Stewart**, director Hutin Britton, Patrick Kirwan	Old Vic
1914–15, 1922–3, 1927, 1931	**Dorothy Green** Frank Benson 1914; Randle Ayrton 1915; Baliol Holloway 1922–3; Wilfrid Walter 1927; John Gielgud 1931	SMT 1914, 1922–3, 1927; Coronet 1915; King's, Hammersmith 1923; Old Vic 1931
1916–17, 1927	**Sybil Thorndike** William Stack 1916; Jerrold Robertshaw 1916; Terence O'Brien 1917; Lewis Casson 1927	Old Vic 1916–17; SMT 1916; Old Vic at Lyric, Hammersmith 1927
1918	**George Foss**, director Mary Sumner, Ernest Milton	Old Vic
1919	**Nugent Monck**, director	Maddermarket, Norwich
1919–20	**Conal O'Riordan, Barry Jackson**, directors. Margaret Chatwin, D. A. Clarke-Smith	Birmingham Repertory Theatre
1920	**Fred Terry, Violet Farebrother**	King's, Hammersmith
1920, 1922–3, 1925–7, 1929, 1930, 1933–4	**W. Bridges-Adams**, director Ethel Warwick, Murray Carrington 1920; Dorothy Green 1922–3, 1927; Baliol Holloway 1922–3, 1934; Florence Saunders, James Dale 1925; Madge Titheradge, Henry Ainley, New 1926; Wilfrid Walter 1927,–29,–30; Dorothy Massingham 1929; Fabia Drake 1930, 1933; George Hayes 1933; Dorothy Black 1934	SMT all years except 1926; King's, Hammersmith 1923; New 1926
1921–2, 1925, 1937, 1945	**Robert Atkins**, director Florence Buckton, Rupert Harvey 1921–2; Marie Ney 1925; Ion Swinley, Neil Porter	Old Vic 1921–2, 1925; The Ring, Blackfriars 1937; SMT 1945

Date(s)	Leading personnel	Venue(s)
	1925; Margaretta Scott, Jack Hawkins 1937; Claire Luce, Antony Eustrel 1945	
1924	**Beatrice Wilson**, director Athene Seyler, Nicholas Hannen	Strand
1926	**Henry Jewett, Eve Walsh Hall**	Boston Repertory Theatre
1926	**Arthur Rosson**, director Helene Costello, Raymond Griffith	Silent film, USA
1926–7	**Andrew Leigh**, director Edith Evans, Baliol Holloway 1926; Sybil Thorndike, Lewis Casson 1927	Old Vic 1926; Old Vic at Lyric, Hammersmith 1927
1930		Hull Playgoers' Society
1931	**Harcourt Williams**, director Dorothy Green, John Gielgud	Old Vic, Sadler's Wells
1934	**Henry Cass**, director Mary Newcombe, Maurice Evans	Old Vic, Sadler's Wells
1934	**Hugh Hunt**, director	Maddermarket, Norwich
1936, 1939, 1941	**B. Iden Payne**, director Barbara Couper, James Dale 1936; Vivienne Bennett, Alec Clunes 1939; Margaretta Scott, George Hayes 1941	SMT
1938–40, 1945, 1949	**Donald Wolfit**, director Donald Wolfit, Rosalinde Fuller 1938–40; Rosalind Iden 1945, 1949	Touring productions; Kingsway 1940; Winter Garden 1945
1946	**Fabia Drake**, director Renee Asherson, Robert Donat	Aldwych
1947	**Hugh Hunt**, director Rosalie Crutchley, Clement McCallin	Bristol Old Vic; Embassy
1949–50, 1952, 1955, 1959	**John Gielgud**, director Anthony Quayle 1949; John Gielgud 1950,–52,–55,–59; Diana Wynyard 1949, 1952; Peggy Ashcroft 1950, 1955; Margaret Leighton 1959	SMT 1949–50; Phoenix 1952; SMT, Palace and European tour 1955; Lunt–Fontanne, NY 1959
1952	**Antony Eustrel**, director Antony Eustrel, Claire Luce	Music Box, NY
1956–7	**Denis Carey**, director Barbara Jefford, Keith Michell	Old Vic
1957	**John Houseman, Jack Landau**, directors Katharine Hepburn, Alfred Drake	ASF, Stratford, Conn.

Date(s)	Leading personnel	Venue(s)
1958	**Douglas Seale**, director Googie Withers, Michael Redgrave	SMT
1958	**Robert Norton, Nina Foch**	Video/teleplay, USA
1958, 1961	**Michael Langham**, director Christopher Plummer 1958, 1961; Eileen Herlie 1958; Geraldine McEwan 1961	Stratford, Ontario 1958; RST 1961
1961	**Joseph Papp**, director Nan Martin, J.D. Cannon	NYSF, Central Park, NY
1964	**Allen Fletcher**, director Jacqueline Brookes, Philip Bosco	ASF, Stratford, Conn.
1965–7	**Franco Zeffirelli**, director Robert Stephens 1965–7; Maggie Smith 1965–6; Joan Plowright 1967	NT 1965–7; BBC-TV 1967
1968–9	**Trevor Nunn**, director Janet Suzman, Alan Howard	RST 1968; Aldwych 1969
1970	**Toby Robertson**, director Sylvia Syms, John Neville	Prospect Theatre Company: Edinburgh Festival and tour
1971	**Ronald Eyre**, director Elizabeth Spriggs, Derek Godfrey	RST; Aldwych
1971	**William Hutt**, director Jane Casson, Kenneth Welsh	Stratford, Ontario
1972–3	**Joseph Papp**, producer; **A. J. Antoon**, director. Kathleen Widdoes, Sam Waterston	NYSF, Central Park, NY 1972; Winter Garden, NY 1972–3; CBS-TV 1973
1973	**Frank Dunlop**, director Denise Coffey, Andrew Robertson	Young Vic
1975	**John Milligan**, director Rita Litton, Dennis Lipscomb	Champlain SF, Burlington, Vermont
1975	**Michael Finlayson**, director Alice Altvater, Wayne Alexander	Odessa Globe, Texas
1975, 1977	**John Bell**, director Anna Volska, Peter Carroll	Nimrod, Sydney
1976	**James Edmondson**, director Jean Smart, Allen Nause	Oregon SF, Ashland
1976–7	**John Barton**, director Judi Dench, Donald Sinden	RST 1976; Aldwych 1977

Date(s)	Leading personnel	Venue(s)
1978	**Duncan Ross**, director Megan Cole, Harry Groener	Seattle Repertory Theatre
1979	**Mario Siletti**, director Susanne Egli, Julian Bailey	National Shakespeare Co., NY: touring production
1979	**Terence Knapp**, director Rumi Matsumoto, Noriaki Teraizumi	Kinokuniya Theatre, Tokyo
1980	**Howard Davies**, director Charlotte Cornwell, Kenneth Colley	RSC touring production; Warehouse
1980	**Robin Phillips**, director Maggie Smith, Brian Bedford	Stratford, Ontario
1980	**Jerry Turner**, director Barbara Dirickson, Mark Murphey	American Conservatory Theatre: Geary Theatre, San Francisco
1981	**Peter Gill**, director Penelope Wilton, Michael Gambon	NT
1981	**Ian Talbot**, director Kate O'Mara, Gary Raymond	Open Air, Regents Park
1981	**Edward Berkeley**, director Lisa Banes, John Glover	National SF, San Diego
1981	**Jay Broad**, director Shannon Eubanks, James Donadio	Alabama SF, State Theatre, Anniston
1982–5	**Terry Hands**, director Sinead Cusack, Derek Jacobi	RST 1982; Barbican 1983; American tour 1984–5
1983	**Dennis Bigelow**, director Joan Stuart-Morris, Wesley Grant	Oregon SF, Ashland
1983	**Jean-Pierre De Decker**, director Magda Cnudde, Jef Demedts	Nederlands Toneel Gent, Ghent, Belgium
1984	**Stuart Burge**, director Cherie Lunghi, Robert Lindsay	BBC/Time–Life TV production
1985	**John Neville-Andrews**, director Mikel Lambert, Roderick Horn	Folger Theatre, Washington
1987	**John Neville**, director Tandy Cronyn, Richard Monette	Stratford, Ontario
1988	**Di Trevis**, director Maggie Steed, Clive Merrison	RST
1988	**Judi Dench**, director Samantha Bond, Kenneth Branagh	RTC touring production; Phoenix

Date(s)	Leading personnel	Venue(s)
1988	**Gerald Freedman**, director Blythe Danner, Kevin Kline	NYSF, Central Park, NY
1989	**Elijah Moshinsky**, director Felicity Kendal, Alan Bates	Strand
1990–1	**Bill Alexander**, director Susan Fleetwood, Roger Allam	RST 1990; Barbican 1991
1992	**Michael Kahn**, director Kelly McGillis, David Selby	Shakespeare Theatre, Washington
1992	**Alexandru Darie**, director Marie Francis, James Simmons	Oxford Playhouse
1993	**Matthew Warchus**, director Janet McTeer, Mark Rylance	Queen's
1993	**Kenneth Branagh**, director Kenneth Branagh, Emma Thompson	Film: Samuel Goldwyn Company, Renaissance Film Production
1996	**John Bell**, director John Bell, Anna Volska	Playhouse, Sydney Opera House
1996	**Michael Boyd**, director Siobhan Redmond, Alex Jennings	RST

INTRODUCTION

A play in production is a dynamic, living thing that generates fresh meanings in the very process of performance. The script which leaves the author's hand becomes a pre-text for the creativity of players, designers and directors. Its meaning is never fixed. Each age refashions the play to some extent in its own image, inscribing in productions something of the cultural attitudes, conflicts and ideologies of the time. The performance of a play produces in turn ideological constructions which reinforce or challenge contemporary norms. The production history of *Much Ado About Nothing* enables us to recover the meanings generated in performances of different periods and to analyse their cultural significance. The way a particular culture has appropriated the play reveals something of the nature of that culture. Production history is thus, among other things, a record of cultural change.

The study of *Much Ado* in performance offers particularly rewarding insights into some of the changing constructions of gender between the Renaissance and the present day. Gender issues are prominent and contentious in the play, and at critical periods the trends in its production and reception are excellent indicators of shifting gender attitudes. Beatrice especially unsettles conventional norms of gender difference. Changing tendencies in the representation of this role provide striking evidence of parallel changes in society's conceptions and expectations of womanhood.

Analysis of a variety of performances focuses and clarifies a range of key production decisions applicable to *Much Ado*. These include whether the play is to be viewed primarily as a happy comedy or as a problematic, unsettling work; how to manage the uneasy relationship between its comic and darker elements, and how much weight to give to each; the prominence to be given to the Hero–Claudio story; whether or not to play Claudio sympathetically; how traumatic to make the broken wedding; and how to manage the tension between this episode and the reconciliations of the final act.

A further set of decisions relates to the play's social milieu. What kind of society is it, and how will its social codes be made accessible to the audience? What social status will be given to each of the characters? How prominent are patriarchal values, aristocratic and courtly values, military values, or other social modes, and will such values be subjected to challenge? To what extent will hierarchies of power and privilege be endorsed or subverted? Is Don Pedro unproblematically benevolent, or is there a dangerous edge to his power? How disturbing a threat is Don John? How will the play's conflicting gender ideologies be represented? What significance will be attached to the pervasive eavesdropping, equivocation, deception and intrigue in the play? How much weight will be given to subordinate figures such as Dogberry and Borachio? Will challenges to the conventional order be neutralised or contained at the end, or remain potential sources of instability?

Other important decisions include whether to stage the play in a style of predominant artifice or naturalism; whether to leave the stage space unlocalised or to suggest a social context by the choice of specific period and location; how to give significance to the pervasive theatricality in the play and to emblematic sequences such as the masquerade; the relative weight to give to the play's disparate dramatic and stylistic modes.

Some of the cardinal choices relate to Beatrice and Benedick, traditionally the central focus of the play in performance. Will a developing fascination between them be implied from the beginning? How much will be made of the hints that Beatrice has been emotionally hurt in an earlier relationship with Benedick? How combative or playful is their 'merry war' (1.1.45–6)? How will their scepticism be balanced against their capacity for sympathy and commitment? Benedick has been played with varying blends of soldierliness and refinement, bluffness and gallantry, vanity and depth; Beatrice with different combinations of scorn and merriment, aggression and pleasantry, wit and sensibility. How powerful and independent is she? To what extent is her female assertiveness a threat to the male-dominated world of the play? Is she finally subsumed within the patriarchal order, or does she give a temporary glimpse, albeit in an imagined comic world, of possibilities for transcending conventional gender limitations? The following pages explore the variety of ways in which players have approached these and other

One of the most illuminating aspects of the study will be to explore the varying interpretations which players have given to specific passages in the play. For instance, the 'Kill Claudio' sequence (4.1.248–316) at the end of the broken wedding has long been regarded as one of the most sensitive episodes in *Much Ado*. The commentary documents the great variety of ways in which players have negotiated this sequence, particularly the critical moment of Beatrice's 'Kill Claudio' (279). In most productions there is a precarious balance between serious and comic as Beatrice utters these words and Benedick replies, and the audience reaction is not always easy to gauge. Beatrice is taut with outrage at the atrocity suffered by Hero, yet the extravagance and surprise of her demand are potentially comic. At Benedick's reply the release of tension often draws laughter as well. Irving and Ellen Terry usually played the lines without laughter, but not in every performance

(*St James's Gazette*, 6 Jan. 1891). A laugh came regularly in Bridges-Adams's productions (Sprague and Trewin, *Shakespeare's Plays*, 75). Gielgud and Diana Wynyard forestalled it by subduing 'the humour of the love declaration so that Beatrice's sudden murderous entreaty [could] be received not as a climax threatening anticlimax but as a deepening of the lovers' new-found seriousness' (*T*, 22 July 1955). Gielgud and Peggy Ashcroft allowed the laughter to surface, as have many other acclaimed performers. Too big a laugh, however, may leave the audience unprepared for the tautness of Beatrice's next response ('You kill me to deny it, farewell' (281)); but if only a few titters surface, the audience may feel uneasy, as if the laugh were inappropriate.

In addition to exploring the potential meanings of specific passages, the study will also investigate the broad cultural significance of major developments in the production of *Much Ado*. Parallels between the performance of the play and literary trends in certain periods, for example, indicate relationships between theatre and the wider culture. In the nineteenth and early twentieth centuries the stage and literary criticism shared a similar interest in the psychology of character. Later, the fashion for formalist aesthetics showed itself in the attention given by stage and critics to matters of style and structure. Directors such as Bridges-Adams and Gielgud sought to represent *Much Ado* as a coherent work of art ending in harmony and reconciliation. In the postmodern era greater attention has been paid to the contrarieties, tensions and ideological conflicts in the play, and to unresolved elements in its conclusion, resulting in a more disturbing play than formerly. Production history demonstrates the inevitability of such reshaping as each generation approaches the play from fresh cultural perspectives. The play is continually being made again, and each revival is the guarantee of its continued life.

Much Ado in the Renaissance theatre

The first performance of *Much Ado* probably occurred late in 1598 or early in 1599 (see Chambers, *Shakespeare*, I.79). It was a popular play, remaining in the repertoire until the closure of the theatres by parliament in 1642. Beatrice and Benedick early became the central stage interest: the play was called 'Benedicte and Betteris' in one of two references to court performances in the Lord Treasurer's accounts of 1613 (Malone Society *Collections*, VI.55–6); and Charles I wrote 'Benedik and Betrice' by the title of the play in his copy of the Second Folio edition (1632). A reference to Beatrice and Benedick in the 1624 edition of Burton's *Anatomy of Melancholy* assumes that readers were well acquainted with the play. Its popularity is impressively attested in Leonard Digges' verses prefacing the 1640 edition of Shakespeare's poems:

> let but *Beatrice*
> And *Benedicke* be seene, loe in a trice
> The Cockpit Galleries, Boxes, all are full.

In addition to the comic appeal of Beatrice and Benedick, the provocative treatment of gender issues in *Much Ado* must have been central to its impact in the Renaissance theatre. Gender issues were particularly prominent in the ideological ferment of late sixteenth- and early seventeenth-century England. An extensive and controversial literature on the nature of women and their position in society flourished during the period (see Woodbridge, *Women in the English Renaissance*; K. Henderson and B. McManus, *Half Humankind*), and gender issues figured conspicuously in the drama of the time. The Renaissance stage gave extraordinary attention to independent, assertive or unruly women who transgressed conventional norms of femininity. One reason for the remarkable interest in gender in the early modern period was that traditional gender ideologies appear to have been under strain. Conventionally, women were supposed to be silent, gentle, passive and submissive. But in the late sixteenth and early seventeenth centuries there was a consciousness of widening rifts between ideology and actual behaviour (Amussen, *Ordered Society*, 103, 119, 122; Woodbridge, *Women in the English Renaissance*, 135, 171–2; Underdown, 'Taming of the scold', 116–36; Wrightson, *English Society*, 95). Not least of the ideological contradictions of Shakespeare's time was the presence on the English throne of a woman who projected an equivocal male–female identity, problematising traditional definitions of womanhood and 'womanly' roles (see Marcus, 'Shakespeare's comic heroines, Elizabeth I, and the political uses of androgyny', 137–45). In the late Elizabethan and Jacobean periods, the destabilising of traditional gender ideology appears to have inflamed anxieties about the erosion of the social order associated with unsettling changes in the political, religious, social, economic and intellectual life of the nation (Amussen, *Ordered Society*, 122–3; Underdown, 'Taming of the scold', 116–36). While a few extraordinary women were admired for their 'manly' accomplishments (King, *Women of the Renaissance*, 191), in the general society of England assertive, independent, loquacious and insubordinate women were frequently regarded with disquiet, as threats to be contained (Wiesner, *Women and Gender*, 252–5; Underdown, 'Taming of the scold', 120). Comic drama was a means of sublimating such anxieties through laughter, though the comic response also induced, paradoxically, a fascination with the transgressive behaviour, as the Renaissance reception of *Much Ado* illustrates.

The conflict of opposing gender ideologies in *Much Ado* would have held particular significance for contemporary audiences. In the patriarchal society of the play, masculine loyalties are regulated by conventional codes of honour and camaraderie and a sense of superiority to women. Assumptions that women are by nature prone to inconstancy are expressed in repeated jokes on cuckoldry, and partly explain Claudio's readiness to believe the slur against Hero. On the other hand, the stereotype of women's inconstancy is deconstructed in Balthasar's song, which represents men as the deceivers, the inconstant ones, and women as the sufferers: 'The fraud of men was ever so' (2.3.63). The fraud of men and their mistreatment of women are seen at their most ruthless in the events leading to Claudio's repudiation of Hero, the pain of which brings into question the social codes which have made such an event possible.

Beatrice disrupts the conventional gender polarities of the period. As a woman she exhibits the assertiveness, intelligence, verbal dexterity and strength of personality which had traditionally been associated with masculinity. The gender disruption was doubly acute on the Renaissance stage, where female roles were played by male actors. Yet Beatrice's position as a woman is ambiguous. In a male-oriented world she is a formidable contender, urging Hero to defy her father if she dislikes his choice of a husband, and putting even Benedick on his mettle; yet she also recognises that in a male-dominated society there are powers a woman cannot exercise: 'Oh God that I were a man!' she cries as she burns to avenge Hero (4.1.294–5).

In *Much Ado* the elements challenging conventional gender stereotypes exist in sharp tension with expressions of traditional patriarchal ideology, often voiced by Benedick himself. One of Benedick's roles in the play is that of the witty stage misogynist voicing male anxieties about women's sharp tongues and proneness to sexual lightness. Renaissance audiences familiar with this convention would have enjoyed the comedy of the witty misogynist meeting his match in an articulate, assertive woman. The ideological power play of this contest undoubtedly brought new pungency and suspense to the perennial stage interest of the battle of the sexes. Robert Burton's reference to couples that 'are harsh and ready to disagree, offended with each others carriage, like Benedict and Betteris in the Comedy' (*Anatomy of Melancholy*, 1624 edn, 3.2.2.4) suggests that the 'merry war' may have been played on the Renaissance stage in somewhat quarrelsome vein.

Beatrice and Benedick stand in equivocal relation to the romantic conventions of mediaeval and Renaissance literature. Though they profess to disdain these conventions, they do not remain wholly outside them: Benedick tries to sing love songs, and Beatrice frames her resolve to tame her 'wild heart' to his 'loving hand' (3.1.112) in the conventional language of romantic surrender, that is, of female submission. Audiences familiar with the conventions would have appreciated the double inversion in their commitment to love: for Beatrice, capitulation to a man; for Benedick, a breach of male solidarity. The conflict of ideologies continues to the end of the play. Beatrice is silenced as Benedick, albeit playfully, stops her mouth with a kiss, and the final sequence is given to the men, still jesting about women's inconstancy. But Beatrice's containment is equivocal: her last witty dialogue with Benedick suggests that she will not be silenced in marriage. Beatrice and Benedick were in many ways cultural anomalies, and audiences clearly found their lively transgression of gender norms comic and provocative.

The Hero–Claudio story evidently appealed to the Renaissance consciousness as well: seventeen variants of the legend have been traced in the period (*SC*, 8.2). Males no doubt saw in it an image of silent, submissive womanhood; females an image of women's sufferings. The play's parody of the English country constabulary was no doubt highly enjoyed, particularly at the opening performances when Dogberry was played by the famous stage jester William Kemp. Kemp and Richard Cowley, who played Verges, are named in the speech headings of the examination scene in the first quarto edition of 1600. When Kemp left the Lord Chamberlain's Company of players early in 1599, the role of Dogberry probably passed to his successor, Robert Armin (Chambers, *Elizabethan Stage*, II.300). While the watch scenes provided broad humour, the play's wit and repartee would also have appealed to more sophisticated members of the audience, ensuring the play's continued popularity with the predominantly aristocratic and courtly patrons of the Caroline theatre. In an age highly conscious of power and politics, the relations of power and subversion centring on Don Pedro and Don John gave further interest.

Much Ado was perhaps first performed at the Curtain in Shoreditch, an outdoor amphitheatre which the Lord Chamberlain's Company probably used as a temporary playhouse while the Globe Theatre was being built. The play presumably became part of the repertoire at the Globe Theatre (opened autumn 1599) and later at the Blackfriars, an indoor playhouse which the company used in addition to the Globe from 1608–9.

The play was well adapted to theatres whose staging conventions were mainly non-naturalistic. In the Renaissance theatres the absence of scenery, except perhaps for a few movable properties, ensured the primacy of the spoken word, important in a play with so much verbal elaboration. Location was indicated, if at all, by word or gesture ('hither ... in the orchard' (2.3.3–4), 'here upon the church bench' (3.3.73–4), 'under this penthouse' (86)). The unlocalised stage space gave actors and audiences flexibility to alternate between naturalistic and conventionalised modes with greater freedom than on stages where expectations of verisimilitude are imposed by pictorial mounting. The absence of scene changes also allowed continuous action from one episode to the next, highlighting juxtapositions which are blurred by scene breaks. For example, Don John's exit in 1.3 was followed at once by the disparaging discussion of him in the opening lines of 2.1.

The non-naturalistic staging conventions of the Renaissance theatre would have heightened awareness of the play as performance, an important effect in a comedy which foregrounds masking, theatricality, the acting of roles, and the uncertain boundaries between illusion and reality. The staging conventions included direct address to the audience in soliloquies and asides, the assumption that actors may be inaudible or invisible to others on stage, and the assumption that masquerade disguises are impenetrable or partly transparent. The boys playing the female roles were assumed to be women while still recognised as boys; in the street and tomb scenes darkness was assumed on stages lit continuously by daylight (at the Globe) or candlelight (at the Blackfriars); and the pressures of the repertory system must have imposed some degree of conventionalisation on the acting. The artifices of these staging conventions accorded well with the elements of artifice in the play: its elaborate verbal conceits, its contrivances of plot (e.g. the gulling of Benedick and Beatrice), and the conventionalisation of the Hero–Claudio story. In the social relations of Leonato's house there is nearly always an overlay of artifice, of disingenuousness; witty indirection is a mark of social sophistication.

Despite the absence of scenery, performances involved considerable spectacle. The ornately carved and painted decor of the theatres, with hangings across the rear of the stage which may have included tapestries and cloths painted with emblems (Hattaway, *Elizabethan Popular Theatre*, 27), formed a visual counterpart to the ornate verbal texture of the play. Costuming was lavish, and *Much Ado* gave plenty of opportunity for its display. The large Globe stage was well suited to the spectacular treatment of festive or ceremonial scenes such as the arrival, masquerade, wedding, and final sequences, and to a vigorous display of violence at the arrest of Borachio and Conrade. (On Renaissance playhouses and staging see Gurr, *Shakespearean Stage*, 115–211; Foakes, 'Playhouses and players', 1–52; Dessen, 'Shakespeare and the theatrical conventions of his time', 85–100).

The popularity of *Much Ado* in the first half of the seventeenth century ended in 1642 with the suppression of the theatres by parliament. After the restoration of the monarchy in 1660 and the relicensing of theatrical companies by royal patent, Beatrice and Benedick returned to the stage in much-altered form in an adaptation by William Davenant.

Davenant's *The Law Against Lovers*

In *The Law Against Lovers*, performed at Lincoln's Inn Fields in 1662, Davenant adapted Beatrice and Benedick as characters in a Restoration play based partly on characters and situations from Shakespeare's *Measure for Measure*. Benedick, transformed into a Restoration libertine, leads a faction in opposition to Angelo's rigid enforcement of the law against lovers, staging an insurrection in an attempt to free Claudio and Julietta, who have been imprisoned for transgressing this law. In Davenant's play Benedick is Angelo's brother, Beatrice Angelo's ward and cousin to Julietta. As in *Much Ado*, Beatrice and Benedick engage each other in a 'merry war', their initial disdain of matrimony and professed antipathy to each other not quite concealing a growing mutual attraction.

Davenant's experience in the pre-Commonwealth theatre would have made him aware of the popularity of Beatrice and Benedick, and of the taste for witty repartee and the love game/duel already apparent among the more sophisticated theatregoers of the pre-Commonwealth period. Davenant rightly assessed that these dramatic modes would also appeal to Restoration audiences drawn largely, though not entirely, from a privileged and courtly elite. They were in fact to become central features of Restoration comedy. In *The Law Against Lovers* Davenant added greatly to the repartee and love intrigue in his sources. Despite the parallels between the Beatrice–Benedick relationship in Davenant's play and Shakespeare's, Davenant borrowed little more than a hundred lines of actual dialogue from *Much Ado*. In *The Law Against Lovers* the repartee between Beatrice and Benedick is often harsher than in *Much Ado*, and Davenant accommodated his audience's taste for the salacious with much more bawdy dialogue than in Shakespeare's play.

In *The Law Against Lovers*, as in many Restoration comedies and in the aristocratic and courtly strata of Restoration society, libertinism, sexual cynicism and misogyny were common male attitudes. In the conflict between the libertinism of Benedick's faction and the moralistic rigour of Angelo, audiences of the time may well have detected parallels with the recent clash of Cavalier and Puritan values in England: 'Restoration playwrights and audiences habitually interpreted plays in terms of contemporary politics' (Taylor, *Reinventing Shakespeare*, 23).

Davenant's Beatrice anticipates the witty, impudent, assertive women of Restoration comedy. She has something of the libertine spirit of the age, irreverent and worldly wise, with a touch of cynicism, though lacks the deftness and sparkling lightness of some of the witty heroines of the period. The calculated double-speak in many of her remarks about Benedick (the barbed half-compliment, the gibe half hinting fascination) are typical of Restoration comedy, as is her habit of masking her feelings for him with postures of semi-indifference. Her coquetry with Lucio anticipates the sex intrigue in the plays of the period.

The Restoration distaste for romantic comedy (Pepys, *Diary*, 29 Sep. 1662, 6 Jan. 1663, 20 Jan. 1669; *LL* 5.515–20) no doubt determined Davenant's rejection of the Hero–Claudio content of *Much Ado*, though the Hero story is echoed in Beatrice's plea for Benedick to defend the cause of her wronged cousin (Julietta). There are also several references to the wrongs and griefs suffered by women, a theme later popularised in the pathetic drama of the late seventeenth and early eighteenth centuries. The Restoration saw the first appearance of actresses in the English theatre, and the four prominent female roles in *The Law Against Lovers* (Beatrice, Isabella, Julietta and Viola, Beatrice's young sister) allowed Davenant to display his actresses to advantage.

The play had only limited success, with three known performances, all in 1662. Pepys thought it 'a good play and well performed' (*Diary*, 18 Feb. 1662), enjoying especially the singing and dancing of the actress who played Viola (Moll Davis?). Jacques Thierry and Will Schellincks, Dutch visitors who attended the theatres frequently during their stay in London in 1661–2, considered it the best play they had seen in England (Seaton, *Literary Relations*, 334), though another playgoer wrote that Davenant had merely cobbled together 'two good Playes to make one bad' (Hotson, *Commonwealth and Restoration Stage*, 247).

The early eighteenth century; Miller's *The Universal Passion*

Interest in Shakespearean comedy, which had declined sharply during the late seventeenth century, revived gradually during the early eighteenth, with a significant resurgence in the late 1730s. The first known performance of *Much Ado* since the pre-Commonwealth period was in 1721, at Lincoln's Inn Fields. The play was again revived in 1737, 1739 and 1746.

Meanwhile, in 1737 there appeared at Drury Lane an adaptation of *Much Ado* entitled *The Universal Passion*, by James Miller. Miller's adaptation included most of the incidents in *Much Ado* augmented with content from Molière's *La Princesse d'Elide* and a few lines from Shakespeare's *The Two Gentlemen of Verona* and *Twelfth Night*. The characters Liberia and Protheus in *The Universal Passion* derive mainly from Beatrice and Benedick; Bellario and Lucilia are based partly on Claudio and Hero, partly on Molière's Princesse and her lover Euryale.

The years between the Restoration and 1737 had seen marked changes in theatrical taste. The increasing bourgeois presence in late seventeenth-century audiences, attacks by Collier and others on the alleged immorality of the theatre, pressures by women for reform of the drama, and changes in the general cultural climate had all contributed to a gradual shift in theatrical fashions, including a new moral and didactic emphasis in drama, a reduction of bawdy, a taste for sentiment and sincerity, the emergence of a drama of pathos centred on women's sufferings at the hands of men, and a strong interest in romantic plays endorsing mutual love and marriage. All these tendencies are evident to some degree in *The Universal Passion*.

Whereas Davenant had rejected the Hero–Claudio content of *Much Ado*, Miller expanded it as the central focus of his play, and sought to enhance its interest and plausibility. The pallid Hero was transformed into the mettlesome Lucilia. By borrowing from Molière, Miller made the relationship of both his leading couples begin with scorn and disdain and end in marriage. This arrangement doubled the possibilities for witty raillery, still popular in comedy, and the neat parallelism between the two couples satisfied the neoclassical principles of order, proportion and symmetry which the age admired. Miller also amplified the Hero–Claudio story to satisfy the neoclassical criteria of probability, consistency and clarity voiced by critics such as Dryden, Rymer and Gildon. Miller gave the Don John figure a plausible motive for slandering Lucilia, and made Bellario a more sincere and sympathetic character than Claudio in *Much Ado*. In *The Universal Passion* Bellario is more reluctant than Claudio to believe the slanders against his betrothed, shows sorrow at the broken wedding, and when the plot against Lucilia is unmasked, is stricken with grief and remorse, averse to accepting a substitute bride. In the final scene Lucilia is reluctant to take Bellario until persuaded by his sincere contrition. Miller's omission of Claudio's jesting speeches in the fifth act of *Much Ado* heightened the impression of Bellario's sincerity. Bellario's moral earnestness in the later scenes, tending towards sentimentality, highlighted the cultural shift which had occurred since Restoration comedy, where a mask of studied insincerity was a sign of social sophistication.

The changes to Beatrice and Benedick were less marked. In contrast with the nineteenth-century tendency to soften and refine the representation of Beatrice, Miller's Liberia, played by Catherine Clive, was sometimes harsher and more scornful than her Shakespearean counterpart. The attempt to conflate content from two sources involved an inconsistency between Liberia's anti-romantic stance and a speech, based on Molière, in which she reproves Lucilia for scorning her lovers (p.8). Quin, whose wit was inclined towards the scornful (Foote, *Passions*, 24; Victor, *History*, II.68), played Protheus with more '*Severity* and *Flout* … than *Mirth* or *Pleasantry*' (*Daily Journal*, 5 Mar. 1737).

The moral expectations of the period were reflected in Miller's dedicatory epistle and prologue, both of which proclaimed the play's 'strict Regard' to 'Decency and good Manners'. The central theme of love's power, even over those who had scorned it, was reinforced in the parallels between the two leading couples, in accordance with the age's expectation that plays should demonstrate a clear moral purpose throughout. The audience was meant, despite cynical songs and jests and a debunking epilogue, to see love and marriage vindicated at the end. The challenge to conventional gender attitudes represented by Liberia and Lucilia was offset by the play's moral and by its recurrent expression of gender stereotypes: that women are inferior to men (p.17), that they find men irresistible (pp. 2, 17), that women's 'natural' destiny and duty is to surrender to love (p.44), that ideal womanhood is 'virtuous, genteel, good-natured' (p.36).

As in most eighteenth- and nineteenth-century productions of *Much Ado*, the Leonato figure received dignified and sympathetic treatment in Miller's adaptation, an effect no doubt enhanced by the acting of Millward, who excelled 'in characters where distress is rendered venerable by age, and dignified by superiority of rank' (Davies, *Garrick*, 1.26). The name Porco for the constable and the assignment of the role to Harper, 'a lusty fat man' (*ibid.*, 1.34), was consistent with the recurrent stage tradition of a corpulent Dogberry.

The Universal Passion enjoyed a measure of stage success, with ten performances in 1737 and a revival in 1741. It was strongly cast, and favoured 'with New Scenes and Habits' at a time when stock scenery and costumes sufficed for most plays (press cutting, 2 Mar. 1737, BL). *The Daily Journal* (5 Mar. 1737) exemplified a growing regard for Shakespeare in its comment, however, that in Miller's adaptation Shakespeare had been 'most miserably hacked and defaced'.

The Garrick era

Under David Garrick's management at Drury Lane (1747–76) Shakespeare's plays enjoyed a notable resurgence of popularity, *Much Ado* being one of Garrick's favourites. He staged it more often than any other Shakespearean comedy. Under his management only three plays in the Drury Lane repertoire were performed more frequently (*LS*; Pedicord, *Theatrical Public*, Appendix C; Burnim, *Garrick*, 174). Garrick's productions of *Much Ado* were swift, lively and entertaining, with Benedick and Beatrice the dominant interest. *The Theatrical Review* (1, 1771, 91) considered 'the under Parts ... very immaterial'. 'As to *Pedro*', wrote Francis Gentleman, 'if he looks like a nobleman, any decent delivery will do for his dialogue' (Bell); 'there is nothing in the part [of Claudio] which requires, or could shew great abilities' (*DrC* 2, 1770, 319); Don John is 'as unaccountable, and as unimportant a scoundrel, as we have met with' (Bell). Average playing times for *Much Ado*, excluding entr'acte entertainments, were only one hour fifty-two minutes (Brownsmith, *Time-Piece*, 68). About 17 per cent of the text was cut (Bell). The primary emphasis was on the acting rather than the background, since Garrick used stock scenery for most of his Shakespearean productions (*Letter to David Garrick*, 1769, 26; Boaden, *Kemble*, I.21–2). The players wore contemporary fashions of their own choice.

Garrick represented Benedick as a light-hearted, vivacious, somewhat eccentric humorist (Wilkes, *General View*, 259–60; *Court Miscellany*, Nov. 1765, 278; *TR*, Feb. 1763, 79–80). He played the part with exceptional ease, lightness and animation (Lichtenberg, *Visits*, 2, 6–7, 14), often emphasising his comic points with starts and other 'extravagant attitudes' (Cibber, *Theophilus Cibber*, 55–6), though he became more graceful and less extravagant in his maturity (Davies, *Garrick*, II.99). Benedick was one of his most preferred roles; some thought it his best comic part (*DrC*, 2, 1770, 318).

Garrick and the actresses at Drury Lane played the 'merry war' with the utmost vigour, as a competition for supremacy in wit. While the sportive nature of the contest was not forgotten, the combative element was very prominent. Hannah Pritchard, who played Beatrice opposite Garrick's Benedick from 1748 to 1756, sustained the contest aggressively. For all Garrick's spirit, he was often 'hard put to it ... to return the Ball of Repartee to her' (Victor, *History*, III.124). The wit was 'beat to and fro between them with as much celerity as if it were a game of battledore and shuttlecock' (Murphy, *Garrick*, I.154). 'Every scene between them was a continual struggle for superiority; nor could the audience determine which was the victor' (Davies, *Garrick*, I.164). Yet the 'spirit' and 'vigour' of her sallies were balanced with mirth and pleasantry (Wilkinson, *Patentee*, II.257; *Gray's Inn Journal*, 29 Sep. 1753; Wilkes, *General View*, 286; Davies, *Garrick*, II.179). Murphy said that when she resigned the part to her daughter in 1756, 'the play lost half its value' (*Garrick*, I.156).

Jane Pope, whose forte was in low comic parts, took over the role in 1762, playing it with spirit and pertness (*Theatrical Biography*, I.52; Hawkins, *Miscellanies*, 26). Then in Garrick's final season (1775–6) the role passed to Frances Abington, whose pre-eminence in the part was widely acclaimed. After Garrick's retirement she played the role at Covent Garden from 1783 to 1789, and again in 1797–8. Abington represented Beatrice as a high-born lady of fashion with an incisive wit. 'There was a keenness in her utterance of sarcasm, which cannot be conceived by those who never saw her Beatrice ... "Every word stabbed"' (Gilliland, *Dramatic Mirror*, II.627). Her repartee had the intellectual edge of the brilliant

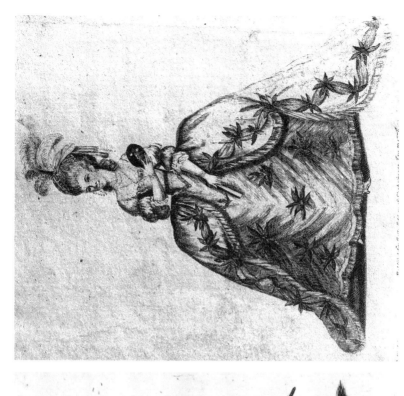

1 and 2 David Garrick as Benedick (2.3) and Frances Abington as Beatrice (5.4). The Garrick engraving, published in Wenman's 1778 acting edition, bore the caption: 'Ha! the Prince & Monsieur Beu! I will hide me in the Arbour.'

conversationalist (Lichtenberg, *Visits*, 33; *Deutsches Museum*, May 1778, 435ff.). Boaden, citing her Beatrice, thought her 'the most brilliant satirist of her sex' (*Kemble*, 1.83). Her raillery combined tartness with pleasantry (*ibid.*); it had 'all the force of sprightliness, judiciously separated from ill-nature' (*PA*, 22 Jan. 1785). Her performance was noted for its buoyancy and ease: 'the spirits of Beatrice were all afloat'; and 'the wit flowed so spontaneously, that it seemed all her own' (*PA*, 3 Nov. 1785, 8 Nov. 1787). Whereas Pritchard's Beatrice had manners of the middling sort (Davies, *Garrick*, 11.178–9) and Pope's a touch of the commonplace (Hawkins, *Miscellanies*, 26; *Theatrical Biography*, 1.50, 52), Abington gave the role an air of high breeding and modish elegance (*MC*, 26 Apr. 1783; *MP*, 3 Nov. 1785; Boaden, *Kemble*, 1.83), setting an expectation until at least the end of the century that Beatrice should be represented as a fine lady. *The Green-Room Mirror* (p. 57) caricatured her Beatrice as 'Comedy in the chariot of Fashion' (see illustration 2).

The dramatic critics of the Garrick period enjoyed the aggressive vigour of Pritchard's Beatrice, the pertness of Pope's, and the incisiveness of Abington's, without questioning, as many nineteenth-century reviewers were to do, whether such qualities were appropriate in a woman. In the Garrick period critics were less interested in issues of gender definition than in the social status which the actress's manners gave to Beatrice.

Garrick was not particularly concerned with the psychological subtleties of the play. Descriptions of his production give little hint of a latent attraction between Benedick and Beatrice in the early scenes, as in most nineteenth-century performances. According to Murphy, Don Pedro's scheme 'makes the first impression on *Benedick* in favour of *Beatrice*'; it is 'on a sudden revolution of sentiment' that they are 'enamoured of each other' (*Garrick*, 1.154–5).

The praise of Abington's Beatrice, on the other hand, confirms the high premium the period placed on wit. The comic aspects of the play appealed most strongly to reviewers of the time; the Victorian concern to demonstrate the fundamental seriousness of Beatrice and Benedick was foreign to the Garrick era. Nor were the critics of the Garrick period much concerned, as most in the nineteenth century were, to demonstrate proclivities for feeling in Beatrice and Benedick. Gentleman described their dialogue at the end of the broken wedding (4.1) primarily as a piece of comedy, 'a pretty entertaining declaration of mutual affection' by 'whimsical lovers', and dismissed their intimate colloquy in 5.2 as 'a very unimportant conference' (*DrC* 2, 1770, 315, 317). One of the most significant features of the post-Garrick period was to be an increasing attention to the emotional as well as the comic dimensions of *Much Ado*.

The post-Garrick years and the transition to the nineteenth century

The last quarter of the eighteenth century and the first two decades of the nineteenth were a time of major cultural change, paralleled by significant changes in the performance of *Much Ado*. The traditions of the Garrick period were continued by Pope and Abington as Beatrice and by Henderson and Lewis as Benedick. Meanwhile new approaches to these roles were being developed by Elizabeth Younge, Elizabeth Farren and Dorothy Jordan as Beatrice, and by John and Charles Kemble and Robert Elliston as Benedick.

The growing importance of feeling and sensibility in the culture was paralleled by an emerging tendency to represent Beatrice and Benedick as characters of sensibility as well as of wit. Players and critics in the Kemble era also began to give more prominence than formerly to the serious elements in *Much Ado*. The performance and reception of Beatrice began to alter in parallel with broad changes in gender expectations in the culture.

Elizabeth Younge, who played Beatrice from 1779 to 1784, and Elizabeth Farren, who played the role from 1787 to 1797, lacked Abington's incisiveness, but followed her example in representing Beatrice as a refined lady of fashionable elegance (*Gz*, 1 Jan. 1780; *Monthly Mirror* 3, 1797, 236–8). Whereas in 1780 a reviewer had commented on the difficulty of uniting 'a character of humour so strongly drawn as that of Beatrice, with the easy, elegant ... manners of the real gentlewoman' (*Gz*, 1 Jan. 1780), by the following decade it was affirmed that 'the sprightly wit and genteel repartee' of Beatrice and Benedick 'savours more of the manners of our Augustan age' than of Shakespeare's (*Thespian Magazine*, Jan. 1793, 57).

Younge and Farren gave Beatrice a softer, warmer sensibility than previous actresses, Younge also conveying the sense of a deeper seriousness beneath the gaiety (*MC*, 10 Jan. 1784; *PA*, 10 Jan. 1784; *WR*, 10 Dec. 1789). Farren softened Beatrice's wit towards a playful, good-humoured merriment (*MC*, 26 Jan. 1788; *WR*, 10 Dec. 1789). These developments anticipated major tendencies in the nineteenth-century interpretation of the role.

The changing conceptions of Beatrice also began to colour the dramatic criticism of the period. Whereas reviewers of the Garrick era had enjoyed sharp, aggressive Beatrices, there were now critics who believed that Beatrice 'is always to be admired for her amiable, as well as brilliant qualities' (*PA*, 3 Nov. 1785). Whereas Abington had once attracted almost universal admiration, *The Public Advertiser* (9 Jan. 1784) now declared a preference for Younge, saying that Abington lacked 'apparency of heart'. *The Morning Chronicle* (10 Jan. 1784) considered that the feeling Younge brought to the role made her Beatrice 'an entire portrait of the woman being represented'. Reviewers also began to note 'tenderness' and 'feeling' in the representation of Hero (*Or*, 3 Nov. 1792; *WR*, 3 Nov. 1792), and to focus on Beatrice's 'love' and 'tender concern' for her cousin at the broken wedding (*PA*, 22 Jan. 1785; *Or*, 7 Oct. 1797). 'The too sarcastic levity, which flashes out in the conversation of Beatrice, may be excused', wrote Steevens, on account of her solicitude for Hero (intro. to Bell, 1788). On the other hand *The Oracle* argued that the new style of performance gave inadequate emphasis to the sharpness in Beatrice (19 Sep. 1793, 13 Nov. 1794), protesting that Farren was 'not the Beatrice of Shakespeare, nor waspish enough by half' (2 Nov. 1792).

From 1798 to 1808 the leading Beatrice on the London stage was Dorothy Jordan, who played the part with a hearty joyousness, an exuberant sense of fun, and a sense of effortless spontaneity (*EC*, 30 Sep.–2 Oct. 1823; *Tatler*, 18 Feb. 1831; intro. to Cumberland, 7). She lacked the refined manners of Abington and Farren (Boaden, *Kemble*, I.391), but went further than any previous actress in presenting Beatrice as a woman of sensibility as well as of wit (*T*, 5 Nov. 1804; *C*, 16 Nov. 1807), and in softening the raillery to a 'pleasant archness', a sportive good-humour (*BWM*, 14 Oct. 1798; *C*, 16 Nov. 1807; *Star*, 14 Jan. 1808). Elizabeth Edwin, who succeeded her in the role at Drury Lane (1809–13), also played it with a mixture of merriment and sensibility, 'flash[ing] her wit about her like beamy corruscations [*sic*] of the fancy' (*MH*, 26 Jan. 1810). Julia Glover (CG 1806–7) and Maria Duncan (DL 1806) reverted to earlier styles, playing the part with satirical wit, Duncan also displaying something of the fashionable elegance of late eighteenth-century Beatrices (Boaden, *Kemble*, I.84; Hunt, *Critical Essays*, 171–2, 175).

In the acting of Benedick, John Henderson and William Lewis carried on the Garrick tradition of a light-hearted, vivacious representation. Henderson, who played the part in London from 1778 to 1785, modelled his performance very closely on Garrick's (Boaden, *Siddons*, II.48; Boaden, *Kemble*, I.248–9), though his touches of 'reflective, sententious' humour in the soliloquies (*Gz*, 1 Jan. 1780) anticipated the Kemble era as well. Lewis, who acted Benedick from 1777 to 1807, played the part with mercurial gaiety and animation (*T*, 7 Oct. 1797; *London Magazine*, Jan. 1820, 66): 'the jests and repartees flew from his lips with the most perfect *éjouement*', and 'the flash of [his] eye carried the jest along with it' (intro. to Cumberland, 6–7).

John Kemble, who played Benedick at Drury Lane from 1788 to 1802, departed from the Garrick school by suggesting an underlying dignity and seriousness in the role and an air of gentlemanly refinement (Robson, *Playgoer*, 38; Pollock, *Macready*, 130). He spoke the lines with precision, point and intelligence (Lamb, *Art of the Stage*, 82; *MP*, 28 Nov. 1789), but was too stiff and formal for comedy (*Gz*, 1 May 1788; *WR*, 3 Nov. 1792; Hunt, *Critical Essays*, 6; Boaden, *Kemble*, I.22; Boaden, *Siddons*, II.48–9); his style 'bore too sententious and declamatory an aspect', and there was more scorn than gaiety in his jests (*ibid.*; Hazlitt, *English Stage*, 459–60). In 1803 he resigned the part to his brother Charles, who was to become one of the most notable Benedicks in the history of the play.

John Kemble's major importance in the production of *Much Ado* lay not in his acting but in his text and stage business, which established the basic patterns for the development of the play's performance traditions in the nineteenth century. Kemble's acting text was in some respects a further development of Garrick's. Kemble cut about one-fifth of the original play. He also interpolated at the end of 4.1 a sequence of dialogue between Beatrice and Benedick adopted, with variations, in productions throughout the nineteenth century. John Kemble's influence in the history of *Much Ado* was most fully realised in the productions of his brother Charles, discussed in the next section.

Meanwhile Robert Elliston was playing Benedick at Drury Lane (1804–13) with 'something of the fire and vivacity' of Lewis, tempered with the Kembles' capacity for dignity, gentility and seriousness (intro. to Cumberland, 7; Hunt, *Critical Essays*, 74–5; *DA*, 5 Nov. 1804). Leigh Hunt observed that whereas Lewis excelled 'in all the lighter parts' of Benedick, Elliston was stronger 'in the more earnest and impassioned': 'in Elliston you have more of the frank soldier, more of the man of rank, more of the resolute lover; in Lewis you have more of the airy gallant, of the careless hey-day fellow, of the merry soul who turns everything into a jest: when Benedick's manner is serious or when his humour acquires an additional dryness from gravity, you are intent upon the forceful style of Elliston … Lewis, it must be confessed, has no seriousness at all' (*E*, 3 Jan. 1808).

In the English theatre of the period, Don Pedro, Claudio and Leonato were typically characterised as aristocratic gentlemen with manners befitting their rank and breeding. While not all actors and critics viewed Claudio sympathetically, it was widely expected that he should show a sincere sorrow in the final act, *The Morning Herald* (26 Jan. 1788) suggesting that his witticisms here 'should seem not as an effusion of gaiety, but as an effort to forget the feelings which prey upon his heart'. The tradition of a venerable and dignified Leonato was continued. Dogberry was played chastely by Quick (CG 1777–94), but exaggerated by Munden (CG 1797–1811) to the point of buffoonery (*MC*, 16 Oct. 1777; *UM* 9, 1808, 45), a broadening of style no doubt encouraged by the vast enlargement of London's leading theatres in the 1790s. Thorough ensemble work was not yet realised (Goede, *Stranger*, 11.242), and costuming for the play was still largely a matter of individual choice.

Much Ado entered the American repertory in the 1780s, Lewis Hallam and Elizabeth Morris playing Benedick and Beatrice in 1787 (New York) and

1789 (Philadelphia), followed by John Hodgkinson and Elizabeth Johnson (NY, 1796–7, 1802). Between 1797 and 1838 Thomas Cooper played Benedick in New York and other centres such as Boston, Philadelphia, Baltimore and Charleston. The tendency of the period to soften the role of Beatrice and highlight her capacity for feeling was no doubt exemplified in the performances of Anne Merry (1797, 1801), an actress noted for tenderness and pathos. William Warren and William Wood presented the play in Philadelphia from 1804 in a version similar to Kemble's (83). English dramatic traditions continued to influence the American theatre through acting editions and promptbook copies, as well as via the many players who crossed the Atlantic in both directions during the nineteenth century. Joseph Holman of Covent Garden and his daughter were the first visiting English players (1812) to include *Much Ado* in their repertoire (production records in Odell, *Annals*; Seilhamer, *American Theatre*; Pollock, *Philadelphia Theatre*; James, *Old Drury*. See also Shattuck, *Shakespeare on the American Stage*, I.22, 37; Kolin, *Shakespeare in the South*, 104–5).

The Charles Kemble era

The Kemble tradition in *Much Ado* came to full flower in Charles Kemble's productions between his brother John's retirement in 1817 and his own in 1836. During this period all except seven London performances of *Much Ado* were under Charles Kemble's direction. He performed the play in America in the 1832–3 and 1833–4 seasons, chose it for his retirement performance in 1836, and played Benedick for the last time on his return to the stage for a brief series of royal command performances in 1840. *The Theatrical Observer* (2 Oct. 1823) judged Charles Kemble's *Much Ado* one of the most attractive productions of the period. The staging arrangements were a further development of John Kemble's. There was now more attention to visual effect than in earlier productions of the play, with rich costumes and scenery 'not unsuited to the old pomp of Italian noble life' (*LC*, 29 Nov.–1 Dec. 1817). As in Garrick's productions, the opening setting was a court before Leonato's house (Bell, Kemble edns). The costume descriptions in Cumberland's acting edition suggest some uniformity of style in the men's clothes (jacket, trunks, pantaloons, plumed hat, boots, sword), but the women still appear to have worn whatever they chose. The production moved at a somewhat leisurely pace compared with Garrick's, with performance times, including breaks, of about three hours (Oxberry, viii).

Charles Kemble's *Much Ado* exhibited a more inward psychological interest in character and motivation than the Garrick tradition, a development which paralleled similar trends in the literature and criticism of the early nineteenth century. Performers now hinted a latent fascination between Beatrice and Benedick early in the play. In parallel with the temper of the times, the mutual commitment of Beatrice and Benedick in the fourth act was managed with a warmer, more romantic touch than formerly. There was a strong tendency to idealise Benedick and Beatrice in the direction of early nineteenth-century stereotypes of gentility and womanhood.

In contrast with the rollicking waggishness of Garrick and Lewis, Charles Kemble as Benedick mingled buoyancy and good humour with the polished ease and elegance of the gentleman of distinction (*TO*, 1 Oct. 1824; *MP*, 10 Oct. 1827, 2 June 1835; *MH*, 18 Feb. 1831; *Sp*, 26 Dec. 1836; *EC*, 9 Apr. 1840; *A*, 11 Apr. 1840). His was 'a *modest* richness of humour … not an overstrained indulgence in mirth', blending 'refinement and delicacy with mirth and spirit' (press cutting, 31 Dec. 1836, TM; Marston, *Recent Actors*, I.132). He played the part with a touch of dry whimsy (*Theatrical Inquisitor* 6, 1815, 423). 'In sally and repartee there was the nicest precision and point, which yet seemed spontaneous, and a vein of light but ceremonious courtesy in the strife which suggested the grace of accomplished fencers as well as the glitter of the foils' (Marston, *Recent Actors*, I.132). He gave a new subtlety to the role, a minute attention to 'the finer and more fleeting shades of character, the more graceful and delicate manifestations of feeling' (Butler, *Journal*, I.184). There was a strong element of idealisation in his performance, 'a general air of the graceful and romantic' (*E*, 5 Feb. 1815), a note of chivalric gallantry (*CJ*, 24 Oct. 1835). He showed beneath the mirth of Benedick a capacity for seriousness, honour and nobility, especially in the second half of the play (intro. to Cumberland, 6–7; *MC*, 24 Dec. 1836; *JB*, 12 Apr. 1840; *A*, 11 Apr. 1840), though even here 'there was a vein of arch, sly humour running through the whole' (*CJ*, 19 Feb. 1831). Some preferred the airy gusto of Lewis's Benedick (*EC*, 30 Sep.–2 Oct. 1823; *E*, 20 Feb. 1831), George Daniel arguing that Charles Kemble was 'too elaborately elegant' in the part (intro. to Cumberland, 6–8), though others thought Lewis had not enough depth and seriousness for the role (*MH*, 26 Jan. 1810; *E*, 3 Jan. 1808; Robson, *Playgoer*, 62–3).

Kemble's representation of Benedick as a gentleman and man of honour was paralleled in much of the dramatic criticism of the first half of the nineteenth century. The writer of Oxberry's introduction saw Benedick as a compound not only of 'wit' and 'drollery', but also of 'generosity and bravery' (p.iii). Dolby urged that the wit of Benedick and Beatrice was 'not inconsistent with the best energies of the heart' (Dolby, iii–iv). Critics increasingly praised Benedick's dignity and seriousness in the church and challenge sequences (4.1, 5.1), some viewing these as his most significant attributes (e.g. *T*, 31 Oct. 1839; *JB*, 12 Apr. 1840). The changing temper of the age was

3 and 4 The idealisation of Beatrice and Benedick: Eliza Chester as
Beatrice and Charles Kemble as Benedick.

evident in some reviews valuing seriousness more highly than wit, *John Bull* (12 Apr. 1840) affirming that Benedick and Beatrice were 'made for better things than breaking jests', another critic praising the way Charles Kemble's Benedick '*rose* [my emphasis] from the humorous gentleman to the nerved and noble man of honour' (*MS*, 21 Apr. 1823, 108).

The idealising tendencies of the period were especially evident in the representation of Beatrice. Eliza Chester (1823–6), Maria Foote (1829–30) and Fanny Kemble (1831–4) softened, sweetened and ennobled Beatrice, refining her wit to a playful banter, and portraying her as a woman of feeling whose 'true' depth of sensibility is revealed in the second half of the play. *The Examiner* (5 Oct. 1823) thought Eliza Chester 'the mildest of all the fair Lady Disdains we have beheld'. She tempered the frankness of Beatrice, seeming to apologise 'for the naughty things that in the rapid race of wit slip from her tongue' (*TO*, 17 Apr. 1823). Some objected that she lacked the 'poignancy and ardour ... of invective', 'the keen and predominant intellectuality' needed in the role (*MS*, 21 Apr. 1823; *E*, 21 Apr. 1823), though Crabb Robinson was more pleased by her performance than by 'any comic actress for many years' (*Diary*, 101).

Maria Foote softened the role even further, almost neutralising the pungent lines by her 'well-bred playfulness' and 'charming sweetness of manner' (*T*, 16 Dec. 1829; *NMM*, 1 Jan. 1830). While some reviewers endorsed Foote's idealisation of the character, *The Dramatic Magazine* (1 Jan. 1830) argued that her manners were too delicate and refined for 'the masculine gaiety of Beatrice'. Leigh Hunt's view was ambivalent:

> Miss Foote's Beatrice is the Beatrice of the drawing-room of 1829; it is oily, and gentle, and tender, and lady-like (according to the dogmas of modern gentility). The tart and verjuice speeches of Signor Leonato's niece trip over her tongue like delicate compliments, instead of coming off with a twang as though that active little member had been astringed with the rough lees of new port, tartaric acid, and alum ... In short, she has *none* of 'the Devil', and into this character Beatrice was within an ace of sinking. (*E*, 20 Dec. 1829)

Fanny Kemble played the role with subtlety and refinement, highlighting the sensibility of Beatrice in the later scenes. The tendency of the age to idealise the role and to foreground feeling is evident in the reviews, critics admiring the actress's 'depth of feeling and earnestness' in the broken-wedding scene, where it was said she gave 'fit utterance to all that nobleness which can fitly dignify woman and inspire man' (*G&T*, 18 Feb. 1831; *NMM*, 1 Mar. 1831). 'Her seeming antipathy to Benedick was but the effect of her suppressed sympathy' (*Sp*, 19 Feb. 1831).

The remarkable transformations in the stage image of Beatrice since the time of Garrick were symptomatic of major changes which had occurred in the cultural construction of womanhood since the mid-eighteenth century. The attempts to accommodate Beatrice to nineteenth-century models of femininity produced strains and disagreements in the dramatic criticism of the period. While some critics idealised Beatrice as an image of noble womanhood, others could not agree, pointing to qualities in the character which they found incompatible with nineteenth-century concepts of femininity. Hazlitt struck the idealising vein in a *Times* review (29 Nov. 1817):

Beatrice is in truth a noble creature; all that she says and does is referable to an innate sense of power ... a dignity of manner that is never compromised ... Her temper is open, warm, and unsuspecting: when she believes that she is really loved, she does not trifle with the passion she has raised, and in her grief and indignation at the fate of her unfortunate friend, forgets her power, her love, and all the world besides.

'That exquisite heroine [Beatrice]', wrote another critic, 'is the true representative of the peculiarities of the female character: her wit, keen and intellectual, is yet delightfully feminine' (*NMM*, 1 May 1823). Others, however, found the character more difficult to accept. Anna Jameson criticised the 'touch of insolence', the 'slight infusion of the termagant' in Beatrice. 'It required a profound knowledge of women', Jameson wrote, 'to bring such a character within the pale of our sympathy', adding that an independent temper, a satiric wit, disdain of marriage and possession of power 'are more becoming to the masculine than to the feminine character'. While admitting that Beatrice does in the end show a 'feminine heart', she accepted the character only with considerable strain (*Characteristics of Women*, 1.129ff.). In an age which idealised Shakespeare's conception of womanhood, numerous writers found Beatrice an embarrassment. She was an example of so much that the ideal nineteenth-century woman was not: aggressive, insubordinate, verbal, sharp-tongued, scornful, bawdy, formidable. *The Morning Post* (21 Oct. 1835) described her as 'that most difficult character'. She 'has more wit and pertness than good breeding', wrote John Taylor (*Records*, 1.414). Thomas Campbell called her 'an odious woman', 'a tartar', whose faith in her cousin's innocence scarcely atoned for her otherwise 'disagreeable' character (*Shakespeare*, xlvi).

The strains which Beatrice imposed on the critics surfaced in passages highlighting the contradictions within the character. 'Though her speech be bitter, her heart is affectionate' (intro. to Cumberland, 5). Her 'generous indignation at the slander cast upon Hero tends ... to heighten our admiration of her character, which has previously appeared somewhat open to a suspicion of insensibility and shrewishness' (intro. to Oxberry, iv). 'In almost any other hands than Shakespeare's', wrote Leigh Hunt, 'Beatrice would have sunk into a mere virago, and might almost have deserved being unsexed for the purpose of kicking. But then, with all her wantonness of tongue, she has a loving heart ... and a generous affection for her injured cousin, the lovely Hero' (*E*, 20 Dec. 1829).

For nineteenth-century critics, the antithesis between the sharp-tongued Beatrice and 'the lovely Hero' focused the contradiction at the heart of the play's representation of womanhood. Nineteenth-century reviewers repeatedly praised Hero's quietness, gentleness, grace and softness, as well as her modesty and passivity, sweetness and delicacy, feeling and pathos. 'How charmingly do the soft and noble qualities of Hero's more staid and quiet nature contrast with the headstrong, yet sparkling gaiety of Beatrice', wrote a reviewer of Charles Kean's 1858 production (press cutting, 18 Dec. 1858, St Marylebone Public Library). Anna Jameson even suggested that Hero is 'the sentimental heroine of the play' (*Characteristics of Women*, 1.129ff.). Hazlitt had likewise suggested that 'Hero is the principal figure', and Beatrice and Benedick 'the principal *comic* characters' (*Characters of Shakespear's Plays*, 183, my emphasis). The problem was that on stage Beatrice was unquestionably the dominant figure. Nineteenth-century audiences were thus confronted by two heroines from different dramatic traditions, the more prominent of the two being the less worthy in their eyes. The 'solution' was to make Beatrice 'worthy' of her dominant stage role by seeking to reshape her according to contemporary ideals of womanhood. John Kemble's acting text had relieved one of the difficulties by cutting much of the bawdy in Beatrice's dialogue, but the part still had to be manipulated into shape with some care. Thus Elizabeth Brunton 'softened down the rudeness of the author', so that the lines 'might be enjoyed with unmingled pleasure' (*MP*, 29 Nov. 1817). 'To give the living picture of an almost unbridled wit, without grossly violating feelings of delicacy and good taste', wrote *The Theatrical Observer* (17 Apr. 1823), requires 'the most skilful … acting'.

It was indicative of the altered critical and cultural climate of the period that whereas in the 1780s the satiric sharpness of Abington's Beatrice had been admired, in 1832 John Taylor disparaged Abington's incisiveness as 'perhaps a vulgar quality' (*Records*, 1.419). *The Spectator* (1831) now thought the soft and ardent Beatrice of Fanny Kemble close to 'the ideal nature' of the character. It was Beatrice's capacity for earnest feeling that most attracted Romantic critics. Some suggested (the idea became a commonplace of Victorian criticism) that Beatrice's comic aspect is a 'mask' which she 'throws aside' to display the 'depth of feeling and earnestness' of her essential nature (*G&T*, 18 Feb. 1831). One reviewer of Charles Kemble's final performance in *Much Ado* went so far as to censure Louisa Nisbett for making Beatrice 'too exclusively comic for so deep and earnest a character' (*Sp*, 11 Apr. 1840).

Charles Kemble and his daughter Fanny were received with great acclaim as Benedick and Beatrice on their American tours of 1832–3 and 1833–4. James Wallack also acted Benedick with distinction in both America and England between 1823 and 1859. He played the part with a bold dashing vivacity, representing the character as a 'careless light-hearted soldier' breathing an air of 'self-satisfied, triumphant ease' (*ST*, 28 Apr. 1850; *E*, 5 Apr. 1845). 'He was everywhere at once', wrote William Winter, '… and dazzled the observer with the opulence of his enjoyment. He was alive to the tip of his fingers' (Matthews and Hutton, *Actors and Actresses*, III.66–7). Yet there was also a grace and gallantry in his performance (Faucit, 'Female characters', 209). In England *The Sunday Times* (28 Nov. 1853, 5 Oct. 1859) thought him the best Benedick since Charles Kemble. Between 1824 and 1831 the leading Beatrice on the American stage had been Lydia Kelly, said to have acted the role in a 'hearty and buoyant, if somewhat masculine' style (Odell, *Annals*, III.249). In the 1830s *Much Ado* was also performed at the Haymarket Theatre, London, under the direction of John Cooper (1830, 1832) and Frederick Vining (1833, 1836). Vining and Wallack modelled their acting texts and stage business closely on Kemble's (S12, S8).

The period brought little change in the representation of Don Pedro, Claudio and Leonato. William Warren in America played an 'incomparable' Dogberry (Winter, *Memories*, 30). In England Emery acted the role (1812–18) with a superior, self-satisfied air (Hunt, *Critical Essays*, 112); Blanchard (1820–31) with an amusing gravity, apparently unconscious of his stupidity (*T*, 16 Dec. 1829; *TO*, 16 Dec. 1829); Farren (1823–40) with 'a sharpness that gave the appearance of intention to his blunders' (*T*, 8 Apr. 1840). For much of the nineteenth century Don John was conventionalised as a melodramatic stage villain. Among the minor roles one of the finest performances was Keeley's Verges (1823–32), a little man in 'the dotage of senility … with enough perception to give a fatuous gleam of intelligence'. When seconding Dogberry's remarks he disguised his own dulness by affecting to ponder before giving his assent with an air of self-importance (Marston, *Recent Actors*, II.99–101).

Victorian productions from Macready to Irving

The major productions of *Much Ado* in the Victorian period were mounted in a style of increasingly spectacular pictorial realism, the more sumptuous revivals creating a romanticised world in which aristocratic and courtly values were idealised with unprecedented style and splendour. Macready's *Much Ado* (DL 1843) was more splendidly mounted and stage-managed than any previous production of the play: 'an air of Italian grandeur and elegance pervaded every scene' (*Sp*, 25 Feb. 1843). Macready made Leonato's house a mansion, but Kean and Irving made it a palace.

In Victorian productions the opening setting for *Much Ado* typically showed the columned portico of Leonato's house at one side with a garden overlooking the town and harbour of Messina. The masquerade and final scenes (2.1, 5.4) were most frequently set in an arched or columned banqueting hall, sometimes lit by candelabra and looking out over a moonlit garden.

The gulling scenes (2.3, 3.1) were staged in an ornamental garden, Lester Wallack (1869) adding a fountain spraying water. Kean provided an Italianate street scene for the watch (3.3). Irving's street was backed by a river with boats at the quayside, house lights reflecting in the water, and a tower at one side with a bell tolling eleven. For the church scene (4.1) Macready featured an altar backed by three pointed arches, Kean (1858) an arched and colonnaded chapel, Lester Wallack and Irving a cathedral (see below). The examination scene (4.2) was typically staged in a prison. Charles Kean (1858) set the Don John scenes (1.3 and 2.2) on a columned terrace overlooking the grounds of Leonato's house. Kean's final scene was a massive colonnaded hall. Towards the end of the Victorian period there was an increasing tendency to use solidly built pieces of scenery in conjunction with painted flats (pbks; scene designs and illustrations; *ILN*, 19 Mar. 1859; *NYT*, 8 Feb. 1869; *Time*, Nov. 1882, 957–9; *CJ*, 14 Oct. 1882; *BDA*, 28 Feb. 1884; *NYH*, 14 Nov. 1884; *Daily Star*, Montreal, 3 Oct. 1884; Hatton, in Brown, *Effective Theatre*, 199).

One difficulty of representational mounting in productions of *Much Ado* is that the expectations of realism created by the settings run counter to the artifice and conventionalisation of much in the play itself. Elaborate pictorialism also tends to diminish the primacy of the actor and of the spoken word, a significant limitation in a play where verbal artifice is as prominent as in *Much Ado*. The spoken word was cut heavily in some of the more spectacular Victorian productions to allow for time-consuming scene changes and elaborate staging effects. Macready cut about 17 per cent of the text (about the same as Garrick, and 3 per cent less than the Kembles); Charles Kean cut nearly a quarter, Saker almost a third. Irving cut about 20 per cent in 1882, but about 28 per cent in 1887. Some managers advertised spectacle as an interest in its own right, claiming their productions to be 'authentic' representations of Italian life in the early sixteenth century, the period chosen for the play in most Victorian productions.

In an age that looked for organic unity in works of art, Macready, Kean, Phelps, Irving and others gave more detailed attention than most previous managers to coherence of design. There was now more uniformity of costuming: from Macready on the male characters were generally dressed in early sixteenth-century styles, though female characters typically wore adaptations of contemporary fashions. Beatrice and Benedick were the central focus of productions, but the leading managers sought high standards of performance from the entire cast. They also gave more detailed planning than before to grouping and stage movement, achieving impressive *ensemble* and crowd effects in some of the major scenes. Macready used thirty-two supers for the arrival of Don Pedro (1.1.70 SD), and for the masquerade at least eighty-two supers and musicians in addition to the characters. The masquerade crowd was constantly in motion: lords and ladies in masks and festive garments, pages, servants with ewers and goblets of wine, people dancing between the sequences of dialogue (pbks; *MP*, 25 Feb. 1843; Pollock, *Macready*, 131–2). In Irving's masquerade the revellers seemed numbered by the hundred, richly costumed lords, ladies and attendants moving gracefully in picturesque groupings, pages running about in childish games, a constantly varying crowd remarkable for the apparent diversity of purpose among its individuals (*GN*, 30 Aug. 1883; *BDA*, 28 Feb. 1884; *NYH*, 14 Nov. 1884). Irving's staging effects were time-consuming, however, his *Much Ado* taking almost four-and-a-quarter hours on the opening night, though this was later reduced by about twenty minutes (*MA*, 12 Oct. 1882; Hatton, in Brown, *Effective Theatre*, 199). Macready's performances were much swifter, with average times about 10 per cent shorter than Charles Kemble's (S15, S16, S19). Charles Kean's 1858 performance times (including scene breaks) averaged about two hours forty-five minutes, slightly longer than Macready's (S26). As mounting became more elaborate and expensive, many managers found it efficient to replace the traditional repertory system, in which a different play was scheduled each night, with continuous runs of a single production. In 1882–3 Irving's *Much Ado* achieved a record run of two hundred and twelve consecutive performances.

During the Victorian period stage and critics showed a strong psychological interest in motivation and character development. With the exception of Macready, most leading players of the period indicated early in *Much Ado* a latent fascination between Beatrice and Benedick, suggesting that theirs was no settled antipathy to marriage, but merely a professed disdain. In accordance with the theatrical temper of the age, Victorian productions tended to sentimentalise romantic moments such as the confession of love at the end of the church scene, and to give a touch of melodrama to the Don John scenes and the broken wedding. The mannered sententiousness of the Kemble school gave way to more naturalistic acting styles.

The Theatre Regulation Act of 1843 ending the patent theatres' monopoly of spoken drama allowed Shakespeare's plays to be performed in a wider variety of venues than formerly. Between 1843 and 1880 *Much Ado* was played in at least fourteen different London theatres. Transatlantic visits also became a feature of the period: Ellen and Charles Kean, Macready, Dillon, Sullivan, Irving and Ellen Terry played *Much Ado* on visits to America; James Wallack, George Vandenhoff and E. L. Davenport appeared as Benedick on both sides of the Atlantic; Charlotte Cushman, Anna Mowatt, Catherine Sinclair, Rose Eytinge and Mary Scott-Siddons played Beatrice on visits to Britain.

Macready's Benedick was altogether different from the buoyant, polished,

5 William Charles Macready as Benedick (2.3).

graceful performance of Charles Kemble. Macready made Benedick a testy, saturnine character with a hard, dry, caustic humour 'dashed with sardonic bitterness' (*Sp*, 25 Feb. 1843; *MP*, 25 Feb. 1843; *A*, 4 Mar. 1843; *Lloyd's*, 26 Jan. 1851). His comedy was often somewhat overstrained, one critic reporting that 'he clutched at drollery, as Macbeth at the dagger, with convulsive energy' (*JB*, in Archer, *Macready*, 137). His Benedick was 'no "married man" got up after the fashion of foregone conclusion' (*CJ*, 4 Mar. 1843), but 'as savage in his contempt of the sex as a misanthrope' (*A*, 4 Mar. 1843), his initial disdain of matrimony no lightly affected posture, but a settled conviction (press cutting, BL). His interpretation depended on a sudden and ludicrous change of attitude in the arbour scene (2.3), where he found 'the theory of a whole life knocked down by one slight blow' (*T*, 24 Jan. 1851). In the early scenes he adopted an 'indulgent and half-careless air' towards Beatrice, 'as of one … a little cynical through experience, who, nevertheless, good-naturedly consented to trifle and *badiner* with a lady for her amusement'. He 'sometimes forg[ot] his light role in serious thought, and then, rousing himself, return[ed] apologetically to his recreation' (Marston, *Recent Actors*, 1.86). Macready's acting text, derived largely from the Kemble tradition, strongly influenced the productions of Charles Kean, Irving and other Victorian actor-managers, and his elaborate mounting of the play, with its emphasis on historical and pictorial realism, largely set the style for the production of *Much Ado* in the second half of the century.

Charles and Ellen Kean performed *Much Ado* in England and America between 1845 and 1865. Kean's most finished production of the play (Princess's, 1858) was splendidly mounted, though less sumptuously than his spectacular productions of *Henry V*, *Henry VIII*, *Richard II*, *A Midsummer Night's Dream* and *The Winter's Tale* (pbks; *MC*, 22 Nov. 1858). In his *Much Ado* the dramatic interest was given priority over spectacle (*BLL*, 28 Nov. 1858), and there was less parade of antiquarianism than in some of his other Shakespearean revivals (*Era*, 21 Nov. 1858). Ellen and Charles Kean were the most admired Beatrice–Benedick partnership between the Kemble era and Irving and Ellen Terry. At their best they combined a more than ordinary vitality with courtliness and refinement, playing with spirit and point yet with a touch of romantic idealisation (*Gl*, 22 Nov. 1858; *T*, 30 Jan. 1861; *MP*, 30 Jan. 1861). The male gender attitudes of the period were apparent in Kean's Benedick, his scepticism in the early scenes seeming 'less the result of dislike to the sex than of pride which forbids him to sue to woman' (*ST*, 17 Mar. 1850). Ellen Kean's Beatrice, a performance surpassing her husband's Benedick, will be discussed in the next section, together with other Beatrices of the Victorian period.

Samuel Phelps's productions of *Much Ado* at Sadler's Wells (1848–58) were notable for their *ensemble* work, attention to detail and unity of effect (*MA*, 18 Nov. 1848). They were also impressively mounted (*ST*, 19 Nov. 1848; engraving, TM). In these performances Henry Marston played a spirited, graceful Benedick somewhat after the manner of Charles Kemble (*WN*, 21 Dec. 1850; *ST*, 21 Nov. 1858).

During the 1840s and 1850s James Wallack's Benedick won acclaim in both America and England. Other Benedicks in these decades included Walter Lacy, Henry Howe and William Creswick in England, James Murdoch in America, and Edward L. Davenport and George Vandenhoff, who appeared in the role on both sides of the Atlantic. Davenport and Lacy played the part in a lively, debonair style not unlike James Wallack's (*TJ*, 4 Oct. 1849; *Era*, 9 Oct. 1859; *ST*, 9 Oct. 1859; *MA*, 13 Nov. 1859); Vandenhoff and Howe gave vigorous, soldierly interpretations (*MA*, 29 Nov. 1853; *DN*, 8 Sep. 1857; *MP*, 7 Apr. 1863).

James Wallack staged *Much Ado* frequently during his management at Wallack's, New York (1852–9), mounting the play with more than usual care, even magnificence (Odell, *Annals*, VIII.416). In the mid-Victorian period *Much Ado* was performed in a variety of New York theatres, including Burton's (1857–8) and Daly's (1868–9), and was also popular in other theatrical centres of the country.

In 1869 Lester Wallack staged the play at Wallack's Theatre with a splendour rarely seen in American Shakespearean productions to that time (Odell, *Annals*, VIII.417). Pedestals, pillars, balconies and urns were represented in the 'round' (*NYT*, 8 Feb. 1869). Authentic arms of the early sixteenth century were obtained at considerable effort and expense. *The New York Times* (8 Feb. 1869), however, questioned the need for such elaborateness. Lester Wallack gave a romantic colouring to Benedick, mingling buoyancy and dash with the grace and refinement of the gentleman (Towse, *Sixty Years*, 101; Winter, *Memories*, 109, 112). The Beatrice was Rose Eytinge. Edwin Booth staged the play at Booth's Theatre, New York, in 1871. He disliked the role of Benedick, preferring tragic parts or villains (Shattuck, *Shakespeare on the American Stage*, I.140; *NYT*, 8 Mar. 1871), but persisted with it during the 1870s, playing it again opposite Helena Modjeska's Beatrice on their tour of 1889–90. Fanny Davenport staged a well-mounted *Much Ado* in New York in 1886.

Meanwhile, in England, Edward Saker presented a spectacular *Much Ado* at the Alexandra Theatre, Liverpool, in 1878. The production was overweighted by lavish mounting and a strong antiquarian emphasis, the programme drawing attention to spectacles such as 'the return of the Italian and Spanish noblemen with their battalions', masked revels at the end of the first act and dances in the second, an interpolated tableau of 'the lady at the balcony' (3.2), and two wedding processions (in 4.1 and 5.4). There were six interpolated songs by choral ensembles. To make way for such diversions Saker cut the text heavily, deleting the whole of 1.2, 3.4, 5.2 and 5.3.

Much Ado was chosen in 1879 for the opening performance at the Shakespeare Memorial Theatre, Stratford-upon-Avon, with Helena Faucit as Beatrice and Barry Sullivan as Benedick. The play was to become one of the most popular at Stratford, F. R. Benson's company presenting it in fourteen Memorial Theatre festivals between 1891 and 1914. Benson staged the play simply, with beautifully painted scenes (watercolour reproductions, SCL).

The summit of nineteenth-century achievement in the representation of *Much Ado* was Henry Irving's splendid production at the Lyceum Theatre, London, 1882. After an initial record run at the Lyceum in 1882–3, the production was taken to Edinburgh, Glasgow and Liverpool (1883) and to North America (early 1884). A repeat run at the Lyceum (mid-1884) was followed by a second North American tour (1884–5). In 1887 and 1891 the production was revived at the Lyceum, where it was repeated briefly in 1893, 1894 and 1895. In splendour of spectacle, minute attention to detail, superb ensemble and overall quality of acting it was unsurpassed in the nineteenth century, and became the benchmark for *Much Ado* performances until well into the twentieth. Vincent Sternroyd typified the critical reception when he described it as 'the most completely satisfying entertainment I have ever known in any theatre' (in Saintsbury and Palmer, *We Saw Him Act*, 232).

The production, however, was clearly of its time. An idealised romantic aura suffused and softened the performance. The dominant mood was one of romantic happiness, with only passing emphasis on the darker elements in the play (*LE*, 27 Sep. 1883; Dickins, *Forty Years*, 43). 'An air of ease, wealth, beauty and romance was shed over everything' (*Henry Irving. A Short Account*, 104). The atmosphere of Leonato's house was 'sumptuous and stately' (*PW*, 21 Oct. 1882). In their 'gorgeous, bejewelled costumes of silk and satin', the characters looked 'as if they had stepped out of pictures by … masters of the Italian Renaissance' (*T*, 12 Oct. 1882; *BLL*, 14 Oct. 1882). 'The murmur of music constantly pervade[d] the action, stealing on gradually and fading away at intervals' (*Std*, 13 Oct. 1882; *Spirit of the Times*, NY, 5 Apr. 1884). Irving used an orchestra, a chorus of singers, a military band for the arrival sequence (1.1.70ff.), and an organ for the church scene (4.1) (*Spirit of the Times*, NY, 5 Apr. 1884; pbks). Over six hundred people were employed in the production (*Time*, Nov. 1882, 961), and every detail of the action was embroidered with illustrative by-play (Archer, *Irving*, 98). Some thought only the excellence of the acting saved the play from being 'overweighted with upholstery and wardrobe' (*T*, 12 Oct. 1882; *ST*, 15 Oct. 1882).

The crowning spectacle was William Telbin's church scene (illustration 6), which *The Pictorial World* (21 Oct. 1882) described as distancing 'everything of the kind that has been attempted on the English stage'. Massive columns were built out thirty feet high and three feet nine inches in diameter on bases five feet square. The great wrought iron gates were each twelve feet

6 The church scene (4.1), Lyceum, 1882.

high and four feet wide (*Time*, Nov. 1882, 959–60). The effect was one of 'solemn grandeur' (*MP*, 12 Oct. 1882). As the curtain rose the sound of choir and organ burst forth triumphantly, then the organ subsided to a soft reed stop as acolytes in crimson soutanes and white surplices took their places at the altar with candles, torches and burning censers, and brown-robed vergers bearing halberds spread across the rear of the stage (*Time*, Nov. 1882, 959–60; *Th*, 1 Nov. 1882; *MP*, 12 Oct. 1882; *GN*, 30 Aug. 1883; Hatton, in Brown, *Effective Theatre*, 200; Stoker, *Irving*, 1.101). Stringed music announced the entry of the bridal party, along with scores of brilliantly costumed guests and attendants, crossing themselves, genuflecting to the altar, and whispering as they dispersed about the stage (s47; *Th*, 1 Nov. 1882; *Std*, 13 Oct. 1882; *GN*, 30 Aug. 1883; Williams, in Saintsbury and Palmer, *We Saw Him Act*, 236).

While most critics were lavish in their praise, some argued that the effect was overdone, the eye 'well-nigh overwhelmed by the mass of colour and detail' (*DT*, 6 Jan. 1891; Fitzgerald, *Irving*, 149; *LE*, 27 Sep. 1883). Percy Fitzgerald thought the state and publicity of the occasion brought out strikingly the trauma of the young bride; but he also observed that the Beatrice–Benedick dialogue at the end seemed out of character with the solemn setting (*Irving*, 193, 149). The problem stemmed from the apparent realism of the cathedral and its ritual; with non-illusionistic staging there is no discordance.

Irving bowdlerised the play more extensively than previous managers, making Beatrice and Benedick seem more refined and less earthy than in the full text. He restored the monument scene (5.3), traditionally cut since the eighteenth century, but insisted, much against Ellen Terry's wishes, on retaining a modified version of Kemble's interpolated dialogue at the end of the church scene. The Dogberry scenes were heavily cut, seeming out of character with the prevailing romantic idealisation: 'the audience, whose eyes had been filled by the radiance of a succession of sumptuous Sicilian costumes, failed to sympathise with the sudden and ungenial contrast presented by a troop of purely Elizabethan municipals' (*ILN*, 21 Oct. 1882).

Irving and Ellen Terry gave a largely romanticised interpretation of the Beatrice–Benedick relationship. They took the view that the pair were 'unconsciously in love with each other from the first' (*A*, 7 June 1884), suggesting in their opening encounter a fascination verging towards mutual esteem (*Std*, 6 Jan. 1891), and foregrounding pleasantry more than sharpness in the bouts of repartee (*Th*, 1 Nov. 1882, 295–6; *T*, 6 Jan. 1891). They also suggested, in the manner of the Kemble tradition, a certain nobility and seriousness beneath the cover of jest (*Th*, 1 Nov. 1882, 295; Howard, *Dramatic Notes*, *1882*, 52).

Irving's Benedick was whimsical, sardonic, slightly eccentric, 'fond of sagacious rumination' (Winter, *Irving*, 63; *Th*, 1 Nov. 1882, 300; *EP*, NY, 14 Nov. 1884), but always had an air of distinction (Williams, in Saintsbury and Palmer, *We Saw Him Act*, 235). He represented Benedick as well past his youth (*WD*, 15 Oct. 1882), a bit brusque and crusty at times (*T*, Philadelphia, 12 Dec. 1884; *NY Mirror*, 5 Apr. 1884), but amiable nevertheless (*Boston Post*, 28 Feb. 1884). In the early scenes he reacted to Beatrice with 'good-natured, half-amused tolerance' (*T*, 24 Oct. 1882), receiving her sallies 'in a modest and careless spirit, as if … they did not affect him half as much as she imagines' (*DC*, 12 Oct. 1882). His own thrusts were 'accompanied by a humorous suggestion of half-conscious exaggeration' (*Graphic*, 21 Oct. 1882). There was 'a certain moral and mental exaltation in his ideal of the part', a romantic colouring which caused William Winter to question whether Irving gave his audience Shakespeare's Benedick or 'a glorification of it' (*Irving*, 61). Ellen Terry regretted that he was too deliberate and finicking to allow her Beatrice the pace it needed (*Life*, 162), though his performance became freer and brighter as it matured (*ibid.*, 229; *SR*, 18 June 1887; *Era*, 8 July 1893). In 1887 *The Morning Post* (14 June) still thought, however, that his Benedick seemed 'not so much a spontaneous creation as a piece of ingenious artifice'. Ellen Terry's Beatrice is discussed in the next section.

In Victorian productions aristocratic and courtly values continued to colour the representation of other major figures in the play. Tradition suggested an urbane and dignified Leonato, a princely Don Pedro, and a problematic Claudio whose gentility must by all means be repaired by sincere and regretful behaviour in the final act. The marginalisation of Don John was accepted as natural. In Irving's production these roles were refreshingly individualised. William Terriss made Don Pedro a genial gallant, with a hearty buoyancy to his princely dignity (*Soc*, 14 Oct. 1882; *WD*, 15 Oct. 1882; Howard, *Dramatic Notes, 1882*, 52; *Th*, 1 Nov. 1882, 302–3). Fernandez's Leonato was hale, vigorous and full of humour when the comedy required (*DT*, 12 Oct. 1882; *Soc*, 14 Oct. 1882). Forbes-Robertson showed a Claudio reluctant at first to doubt Hero's faithfulness (s47); but he also 'put a touch of Leontes' into the role, 'a subtle indication of consuming and insanely suspicious jealousy' (Terry, *Memoirs*, 172). He made Claudio's youth and impulsiveness seem partly to condone his behaviour (*Ac*, 21 Oct. 1882). Glenny gave more weight to Don John than in previous nineteenth-century productions, playing the part with 'cold, calm malice' (*MP*, 12 Oct. 1882), but with the gentlemanliness of the Spanish *caballero* (*ILN*, 28 Oct. 1882). Dogberry was seriously underplayed in Irving's production. The most notable Dogberry of the Victorian period had been Henry Compton

(DL 1843; Princess's, 1845, 1848; Olympic, 1850; Haymarket, 1853–63), who had acted the role with a 'dry', 'imperturbable stupidity', 'dogmatic and self-satisfied', speaking with solemn, pompous dignity, 'serenely unconscious' of his own absurdity (*MP*, 6 Oct. 1859; Marston, *Recent Actors*, II.110; *MA*, 8 Sep. 1857; *DT*, 7 Apr. 1863).

Constructions of Beatrice in the Victorian period

While there was considerable variety in the representation of Beatrice in the Victorian period, the dominant tendency was to soften and refine the role in the direction of nineteenth-century conceptions of womanhood, with significant emphasis on the character's capacity for feeling. Something of the range of interpretation may be seen in the performances of the three most notable Beatrices on the stage in the early Victorian period: Helena Faucit, Louisa Nisbett and Ellen Tree/Kean.

Helena Faucit was schooled in the part by Charles Kemble, playing it for his farewell to the stage in 1836. Her last performance of the role was also a significant occasion, the opening of the Shakespeare Memorial Theatre at Stratford-upon-Avon in 1879. Helena Faucit idealised Beatrice as a noble woman of deep and sensitive feeling, with a capacity for tenderness, spirituality and seriousness (Faucit, 'Female Characters', 203–31). 'That she [Beatrice] had a soul, brave and generous as well as good, it was always my aim to show', she wrote. 'With all her sportive and somewhat domineering ways, she is every inch the noble lady, bearing herself in a manner worthy of her high blood and courtly breeding' (*ibid.*, 209). Faucit softened Beatrice's wit in the direction of playfulness (*ibid.*, 204), representing it as 'but the cloak to a warm, tender, and generous heart' (*ST*, 21 Mar. 1858), her raillery 'tempered by passing through a soul of goodness' (*Liverpool Journal*, 2 May 1846). Her performance had the grace and refinement, the closely studied detail, subtle nuances and high finish of the Kemble school (*MH*, 16 Mar. 1858; *MET*, 8 June 1850; *ILN*, 10 Dec. 1874; *ManC*, 11 Apr. 1866; *Ac*, 19 Dec. 1874), but her merriment was somewhat subdued: 'her repartees [were] given with too much elaboration and ha[d] the effect of carefully studied replies, rather than impromptu flashes of wit' (*ST*, 21 Mar. 1858). She excelled in the later scenes, where she portrayed Beatrice as a character of earnestness and deep feeling (*ibid.*; *LDP*, 16 Dec. 1870).

Louisa Nisbett performed the role at the Haymarket in 1830, 1847 and 1849, at Covent Garden in 1840, and in Macready's 1843 production at Drury Lane. Like Dorothy Jordan earlier in the century, Nisbett played Beatrice with hearty comic energy and buoyant, infectious mirth (*MP*, 8 Apr. 1840; Marston, *Recent Actors*, II.152, 156). 'The joyousness of Mrs Nisbett's acting', wrote *The Sunday Times* (7 Oct. 1849), 'draws the sting from the sharp wit of Beatrice, and renders that a playful jest which might otherwise seem a galling sarcasm.' However, she lacked the subtlety, refinement, depth and feeling of Faucit's Beatrice (*Kidd's*, 11 Apr. 1840; *A*, 4 Mar. 1843; Marston, *Recent Actors*, ii.156). *The Standard* (23 Feb. 1858) regretted that she did not do justice to what it termed the 'serious element' of the character (cf. *Sp*, 11 Apr. 1840). Nisbett was most admired in the raillery of the early scenes, Faucit in those sequences later in the play where Beatrice's capacity for feeling is most fully revealed. Faucit's conception of the role was thought to be the more noble.

Ellen Tree/Kean balanced some of the opposite qualities of Faucit and Nisbett, playing Beatrice with a combination of wit, feeling and merriment much admired by critics of the time. Her Beatrice won great acclaim in America in 1837–9; then after her marriage to Charles Kean, she played *Much Ado* with him in America in 1845–6, in London between 1850 and 1861, and again in America in 1865. She conveyed the point and sparkle of the repartee 'with a brilliancy of touch' which 'light[ed] up the stage like an embodiment of quick jumping wit' (*ILN*, 10 July 1852; *BLL*, 11 July 1852), though she retained at the same time 'a womanly grace and delicacy' (*Std*, 22 Nov. 1858). Beatrice's 'impatience of control, her vivacity of disposition, her quickness, sharpness, and fine sense of ridicule were all perfectly delineated', but she also gave the part a 'spirituality and refinement' (*ST*, 17 Mar. 1850). Her railleries were 'not the playful emanations of a youthful imagination, but the pointed, clever, hard-hitting *bon mots* of a satirical and gifted woman of the world' (*DT*, 22 Nov. 1858); yet there was no malice or shrewishness (*DN*, 12 Mar. 1850); 'feminine sensibility' was 'intimately blended with the true spirit of comedy' (*ST*, 28 Nov. 1858). *The Morning Post* (22 Nov. 1858) said she 'avoid[ed] the vulgar error of tasting [the wit] too palpably'. For all the 'animated point', there was 'a ladylike energy' in her raillery; she showed 'the amiable goodness which lurks under the merry defiance' (*Std*, 12 Mar. 1850). The 'slight sharpness' was 'tempered by the good breeding of the woman of the world' (*DN*, 31 Jan. 1861); 'every movement denote[d] the polish of the best society' (*Gl*, 22 Nov. 1858). 'What grace, what spirit, what infinite wit, what playful mischief, what boldness, what perfect dignity ... and yet withal what a gentle heart', wrote the *Era* critic (21 Nov. 1858). Most importantly from the Victorian perspective, she showed 'the loving, generous nature surging up' through the comic crust, 'the fine, lofty spirit of the noble lady' (*MC*, 22 Nov. 1858). Several critics thought hers the finest Beatrice they had seen or were likely to see (*Gl*, 12 Mar. 1850; *DN*, 12 Mar. 1850; *Stage Manager*, 14 Mar. 1850; *MA*, 22 Nov. 1858; *O*, 21 Nov. 1858; Ireland, *Records*, ii.183–4).

Victorian critics tended to analyse performances of Beatrice in terms of two antithetical qualities, wit and feeling. Her intellect and wit were perceived as masculine qualities, her feeling as a feminine quality. *The Critic* (27 Nov. 1858) typified Victorian attitudes when it referred to 'the masculine mind mixed with the feminine feeling' of Beatrice. The Victorians were uncomfortable with Beatrice's wit, *The Morning Advertiser* (28 Nov. 1853) regretting that Shakespeare had portrayed Beatrice 'more as a wit than a woman'. So much masculinity in a woman was unpleasant and inappropriate. *The Weekly Dispatch* (7 Oct. 1849) called Beatrice's raillery 'the repulsive part of the character', contrasting it with her 'better and more feminine traits'. These were most fully revealed in the second half of the play, the Victorians admiring especially Beatrice's soliloquy in the garden (3.1.107–16) and her 'womanly' feelings in the broken-wedding scene (4.1). In the broken-wedding sequence 'where the intellect predominates less and the feeling more', Amy Sedgwick was reported to have given 'impressive utterance to all that nobleness which can fitly dignify woman' (*MP*, 23 Feb. 1858).

The difficulty was reconciling the wit and feeling within the one character. 'Of Beatrice', stated Helena Faucit, 'I cannot write with the same full heart, or with the same glow of sympathy, with which I wrote of Rosalind.' While she admired the sensibility of Beatrice in the later part of the play, she was troubled by the 'keen edge' of her wit ('Female characters', 203). *The Morning Advertiser* (8 Sep. 1857) referred to Beatrice as 'this most difficult and most extraordinary portraiture of female character', an idea repeated by numerous reviewers perplexed by the complex of apparently contradictory elements in the character. 'It requires great delicacy of treatment to make Beatrice altogether attractive', wrote *The Spectator* (3 Aug. 1867), 'for it is not generally brilliancy that is most admired in women.'

The actresses of Beatrice most strongly approved in the period were those who accommodated the role towards nineteenth-century ideals of womanhood while preserving to some degree the liveliness of the repartee. It was not enough to reveal the 'womanly' sensibility of Beatrice in the later scenes only; the 'womanliness' had somehow to be intimated in the early scenes as well. In Ellen Kean's performance, 'the womanly character of Beatrice' was 'never lost sight of for an instant, even in the wildest sallies of her wayward wit' (*MC*, 12 Mar. 1850). She 'perfectly underst[ood] the masculine mind mixed with the feminine feeling' (*Critic*, 27 Nov. 1858), and 'made the woman the interpreter of the wit' (*WD*, 28 Nov. 1858). 'Feminine delicacy is one of the attributes of woman's character which Miss Tree is not willing to dispense with', wrote the American journalist William Leggett; 'and while other actresses give the utmost sharpness and acerbity to every sarcasm and jest that Beatrice utters, we find Miss Tree occasionally delivering a repartee with a downcast air and softened tone, that shows her innate sense of the propriety of Shakespeare's admonition, not to overstep the modesty of nature' (*Spirit of the Times*, 6 Sep. 1845). The reviewer's assumptions about the 'nature' of ideal womanhood are symptomatic of Victorian gender ideology.

Critics attempting to accommodate Beatrice to the period's ideals of femininity often suggested that the 'womanly' sensibility revealed in the second half of the play was her essential nature, and the witty raillery only a temporary front through which glimpses of her 'real' self are intermittently disclosed. Despite her 'provoking wit', wrote *The Sunday Times*, (18 Nov. 1858), Beatrice 'is a true woman at heart'. Thus Amy Sedgwick showed 'behind the mask of a gay mockery the gentle spirit of a woman' (*E*, 27 Feb. 1858). Rose Eytinge's 'bantering and badinage' were also described as 'but the transparent veil of the loving and charming woman' (press cutting in S21). *The Standard* (12 Mar. 1850) wrote of 'the amiable goodness which lurks under the merry defiance' of Beatrice, George Fletcher of 'the profound seriousness which lies beneath all the superficial levity' (*Shakespeare*, 243), *The Morning Chronicle* (12 Mar. 1850) of 'the womanly character of Beatrice, which breaks ... through the garment of masking and mockery when the serious interest of the piece develops itself'. 'Beatrice', wrote C. C. Clarke, 'possesses a fund of hidden tenderness beneath her exterior gaiety and sarcasm' (*SC*, 8.25).

The transformation of Beatrice into a woman acceptable to Victorian tastes required some refining of the character: 'A refinement of manner', argued *The Globe* (22 Nov. 1858) 'is necessary to modify that vigour of language which now appears coarse.' Though spirited as Beatrice, Ellen Kean 'kept down the boisterousness of mirth that would have shocked the notions of modern fine ladies' (*Critic*, 27 Nov. 1858). Kate Terry, too, never allowed her wit 'to forget the restrictions of good taste' (*WD*, 4 Aug. 1867). A common strategy to make Beatrice's raillery more palatable to Victorian audiences was to represent her sallies as the innocent outflow of youthful high spirits (*WD*, 28 Nov. 1858, 8 Apr. 1866; *Gl*, 27 Apr. 1875). As long as the wit seemed playful or mischievous, the repartees could be thrust home with some vigour without appearing malicious or ill-natured. Isabella Glyn, acting the role with the naturalism of a playful girl (*WN*, 12 Oct. 1850), could afford to throw her barbs at Benedick 'with more than ordinary force, making them hit harder and faster', as if she were delighted with the sportiveness of the encounter (*T*, 7 Oct. 1850). Louisa Herbert's sallies, on the other hand, were thought not mirthful enough to avoid the impression of coldness and ill nature (*WD*, 8 Apr. 1866).

Most Victorian actresses succeeded in subduing the sharpness in Beatrice to a considerable extent, softening, sweetening and refining the role in the direction of contemporary ideals of womanhood. Anna Mowatt (NY 1846–7; London, 1848–50) performed the part with a 'playful and coquettish' merriment, 'her sweet tinkling laugh [ringing] through the house like a silver bell' (*TJ*, 4 Oct. 1849; *MA*, 13 Jan. 1848). She played the later scenes with tenderness and 'poetic feeling' (*Tallis's*, 11). Catherine Sinclair's 'genial and harmonising' interpretation (NY 1852; Haymarket, London, 1857–8) represented Beatrice as a 'loveable' woman 'of true heart and sympathy' (*WD*, 13 Sep. 1857), giving the impression that Beatrice's 'wit and waywardness' were simply the innocent outflow of youthful energies (*ibid.*; *MA*, 8 Sep. 1857). Amy Sedgwick's Beatrice (Haymarket 1858), more buoyant and vivacious than Sinclair's, also showed a womanly tenderness and sympathy (*MH*, 16 Mar. 1858; *WD*, 28 Feb. 1858). Louisa Angel's performance (Haymarket 1863), however, was much too 'honeyed' (*MP*, 7 Apr. 1863). Kate Reignolds (Broadway Theatre, NY, 28 Nov. 1866) combined a mischievous merriment with grace, elegance, vivacity, and 'a vein of earnest and tender sentiment' (Winter, in Odell, *Annals*, VIII.158). Rose Eytinge (Wallack's, NY, 1869) also gave a softened rendering, *The New York Times* (8 Feb. 1869) reporting that her 'wit and vivacity ... have nothing cruel in them; they are society manners. Her heart is generous.' Adelaide Neilson (Lyceum, NY, 1874) 'acted Beatrice in a refined, spirited, tender way, and with all a woman's gentleness, ardor and coquettishness', though 'deficient in the steely vivacity and diamond sparkle of intellect' which the critic looked for in the role (*Tribune*, NY, 20 Oct. 1874). Kate Terry (Adelphi, 1867) gave the repartees an intellectual edge (*ST*, 28 July 1867; *DN*, 28 Aug. 1867), but *The Times* (26 July 1867) reported that 'the charm of the woman asserted itself throughout'. Ada Cavendish (Gaiety, London, 1875; Park Theatre, Brooklyn, 1880) represented Beatrice as 'a woman of refinement' with 'a heart' (*ST*, 2 May 1875), with sparkle and vigour in her raillery, and brightness in her wit (*DT*, 27 Apr. 1875; *Era*, 2 May 1875).

However, not all Victorian actresses played the role in this vein. Fanny Stirling (DL 1839; Princess's, 1845–6) acted Beatrice as 'a pert lady ... who uttered every witticism with a sort of shrewish snap – a very *pizzicato* person' (*T*, 31 Oct. 1839). Charlotte Cushman (NY 1840, 1843–4, 1849–50, 1852; London 1845) gave a rather hoydenish performance (*Sp*, 5 Apr. 1845), 'hit[ting] Benedick as though her wit were a bludgeon' (*E*, 5 Apr. 1845). *The Spectator* (5 Apr. 1845) said there was too much 'masculine energy' in her style. Mary Warner (Haymarket, 1850–1) was also thought to lack 'the necessary feminine quality', making the wit too vehement and vigorous (*MP*, 23 Apr. 1850). Laura Keene (NY, 1852, 1856), too, was rather severe (Winter, *Memories*, 46). Jane Reynolds (Haymarket, 1853, 1859) played Beatrice as 'a haughty, inappeasable beauty', 'now all scorn, anon all tenderness' (*MP*, 6

Oct. 1859). Emily Fowler (Olympic, 1874) spoke with 'animated impertinence' (cutting, 21 Feb. 1874, BPL), showing little sensibility even in the
later scenes (*MA*, 18 Feb. 1874). Critics tended to be unenthusiastic about
such performances.

Of all the actresses who sought to refashion Beatrice in the image of nineteenth-century womanhood, none so drew the hearts of the theatrical public
as Ellen Terry. Her Beatrice was one of the most admired performances in
the history of the play. Merriment was its soul and keynote (*Th*, 1 Nov. 1882,
299); it seemed to radiate sunshine (Agate, *Theatre Talks*, 43). There was an
airy grace and lightness, a mischievous playfulness in her manner (*ECG*, 28
Aug. 1883; *SR*, 21 Oct. 1882; *Soc*, 14 Oct. 1882), which seemed 'the inim-
itable overflow of a joyous disposition' (*W*, NY, 1 Apr. 1884). Beatrice is a
'pleasant-spirited lady', she wrote; the repartee, which can easily 'be made to
sound malicious and vulgar', should be spoken 'as the lightest raillery, with
mirth in the voice, and charm in the manner' (*Lectures*, 83–4). As she
matured, her performance gained in brilliance and strength. 'I must make
Beatrice more *flashing* at first', she wrote in 1891, 'and *softer* afterwards. This
will be an improvement upon my old reading of the part' (*Life*, 230). *The
Sketch* (19 July 1893) noted that whereas formerly 'the whole pitch of her
performance was of a light-hearted, merry girl', so that her 'Kill Claudio'
came as something of 'a shock and surprise', now 'she offers a stronger, more
passionate woman'. However, her interpretation was probably always softer
and gentler than Ellen Kean's.

Terry's annotations to her copy of Fletcher's *Studies of Shakespeare* (1847)
indicate that her view of Beatrice shared elements of the idealising tradition
which Helena Faucit had inherited from Charles Kemble. 'Not a look, not a
gesture', wrote Cecil Howard of Terry's Beatrice, 'which does not idealise
the part' (*Dramatic Notes, 1882*, 52). 'All the charm and spirit of noble and
refined womanhood' were exemplified (*PhI*, 19 Mar. 1884). Throughout her
performance flashes of deeper feeling broke through the surface lightness
(cutting, Fitzgerald's Irving scrapbooks, VIII.23), her gaiety from time to
time giving way to 'a faint and beautiful touch of spirituality' (*Boston
Gazette*, 2 Mar. 1884), a 'lambent pathos' (*W*, NY, 6 Apr. 1884). The later
scenes revealed most fully her 'generous warmth of womanly affection' (*SR*,
18 June 1887), but there was tenderness even in her raillery (*Evening Bulletin*,
Philadelphia, 19 Mar. 1884; *Times*, Philadelphia, 19 Mar. 1884; *SR*, 10 Jan.
1891); 'her mockery [was] but a mask to the tender heart beneath' (*ST*, 15
Oct. 1882). Her words, no matter how harsh, 'seemed always sheathed in
velvet' (*PhI*, 19 Mar. 1884).

Some critics observed that this was not quite the Beatrice of Shakespeare.
'Every point does not *stab* quite as certainly as it should', commented Dutton

Cook (cutting, Fitzgerald's Irving scrapbooks, VII.45). 'The sharpness of Beatrice's tongue is lost in Miss Ellen Terry's radiant and sympathetic womanhood' (*T*, 6 Jan. 1891). 'Miss Terry presents a more lovely and tender woman than the Beatrice of the comedy', wrote William Winter. 'She permeates the raillery of Beatrice with an indescribable charm of mischievous sweetness. The silver arrows of her pungent wit have no barb' (*Irving*, 65). 'The result', said *The Boston Daily Advertiser* (28 Feb. 1884), is a Beatrice 'obviously more feminine and gentle than Shakespeare intended' – a Beatrice 'reconstructed on a nineteenth-century plan'.

So persuasive was her representation, however, that many reviewers seemed unaware of the extent of the reconstruction. Some acclaimed her performance as the definitive interpretation of the role, 'the very Beatrice that Shakespeare drew', 'the perfect embodiment of the ideal Beatrice' (*Th*, 1 Dec. 1881; *Quiz*, Glasgow, 31 Aug. 1883; cf. *Soc*, 14 Oct. 1882; *BWM*, 16 Oct. 1882; *Boston Post*, 28 Feb. 1884; *A*, 19 Jan. 1891). Some even declared her representation an improvement on the original: 'the character gains in womanly charm something more than it loses in absolute truth to the text' (*Tribune*, Chicago, 16 Jan. 1885; cf. *NYDT*, 14 Nov. 1884; *SR*, 10 Jan. 1891; St John, *Terry*, 51). 'The Beatrice of Miss Terry is positively ideal', affirmed *The Athenaeum* (10 Jan. 1891); 'its womanliness ... involves the apotheosis of the sex' (cf. *DC*, 12 Oct. 1882; *Liverpool Mercury*, 27 Sep. 1883; *MP*, 2 June 1884; *Evening Telegraph*, Philadelphia, 19 Mar. 1884).

The womanliness of Terry's Beatrice differed in important respects, however, from some of the more spiritualised literary and artistic idealisations of womanhood in Victorian aesthetic. In the male-authored literature of the period the image of the angelic woman was a recurrent stereotype of ideal femininity: sweet, gentle and tender, demure and deferential, passive, contemplative, self-deprecating, with an all-but disembodied purity: Patmore's *Angel in the House* was a striking example (Gilbert and Gubar, *Madwoman in the Attic*, 17–27). A further set of idealisations was seen in the languid, wistful, slightly mystical representations of women in some of the paintings of Dante Gabriel Rossetti, John Everett Millais, Edward Burne-Jones and others. In contrast with these reductive stereotypes, Terry's Beatrice asserted a lively physical presence: she bubbled with merriment and vitality, revelled in the self-dramatisation of her role, delighted in her own femininity. While exemplifying some of the softness and sweetness, tenderness and grace of the literary and artistic ideals, she was also 'the very incarnation of light-hearted mirth' (*SR*, 21 Oct. 1882). There was 'an exquisite, effervescent petulance' in her performance (*W*, 14 Jan. 1891), a 'freedom from conventional restraint' (*BET*, 28 Feb. 1884), a 'recklessness and abandon' in her high spirits (*Toronto World*, 10 Oct. 1884; cf. *MA*, 14 June 1887). 'She revel[led] in the part' (*PW*,

21 Oct. 1882), had 'so much … enjoyment of herself' (*MN*, Chicago, 16 Jan. 1885). In contrast with the delicate, etherealised, slightly disembodied femininity which had been the stage legacy of the ballerina Taglioni, Terry's Beatrice was 'not elfish, but heartily and wholly human' (*MP*, 14 June 1887), her enjoyment an expression of 'high animal spirits stimulated by a quick intellect' (*Evening Telegraph*, Philadelphia, 19 Mar. 1884). And as the responses of male reviewers ('alluring', 'tantalising', 'fascinating', 'seductive') implied, her *jouissance* in the role was at least partly a manifestation of radiant sexuality. The stage, and the role of Beatrice, liberated Terry to dramatise an image of femininity that was sensuous, articulate, lively and self-assertive. Her performance, with its unsettling hints of freedom, was acceptable and admired not only because it included the comfortable qualities of softness, tenderness, nobility and grace (the revered stereotypes of Victorian womanhood), but also and more significantly because audiences discovered her *jouissance* to be so infectiously pleasurable. Her performance was enjoyed partly because it gave access to a range of emotional responses often inhibited in Victorian society outside the theatre.

The role of Beatrice also became for Ellen Terry a means of venting anger at the constriction and mistreatment suffered by women in a male-dominated society. She was not the first Victorian actress to discover such resentment in the role. At the words 'Oh that I were a man!' (4.1.292), Helena Faucit, too, had felt keenly the frustration of a woman's powerlessness (Faucit, 'Female characters', 222). Terry uttered Beatrice's outrage at Claudio's rejection of Hero as a conscious protest against the wrongs suffered by all subjected women. 'Notice', she observed indignantly, 'that all the men, except the Friar, are inclined to think there must be something in Claudio's accusation!' (*Lectures*, 89). 'Women who have fought the heart breaking battle against prejudice in any age do not need to be told what it is that "kills" Beatrice … and Benedick has enough understanding and sympathy to realise what is at stake – it is not for one woman's whim but for the honour of all womanhood that he is to fight' (MS lecture, Ellen Terry Museum).

Terry's Beatrice thus bore an ambiguous relationship to the gender stereotypes of Victorian patriarchal culture, her performance partly assimilating, partly deconstructing and transcending the type-images of the period. 'Her raillery, even at its most daring, ha[d] always a certain reserve of dignity' (*SR*, 18 June 1887). 'Playful abandon and decorous modesty [were] harmoniously blended' (*Globe*, Toronto, 10 Oct. 1884). She was 'brilliant in her daring sallies' (*PhI*, 19 Mar. 1884), 'brimming with merriment and wit, but with a womanly tenderness and sympathy as well' (*Times*, Philadelphia, 19 Mar. 1884). This mix of contradictory qualities contributed to the richness and complexity of her performance, which became something of an icon in its time, establishing a benchmark for the stage representation and dramatic criticism of the role until well into the twentieth century.

Meanwhile, Helena Modjeska was developing a reputation as the foremost Beatrice on the American stage, delighting audiences in the part for nearly two decades after her appearance in the role in 1888. 'She delivered her witty speeches with a snap and sprightliness that ma[de] you fairly tingle, and with a grace and charm … unspeakable', throwing over the whole a 'mantle of distinction and high breeding' (*BET*, 27 Mar. 1888). She, too, revelled in the fun of Beatrice (*ibid.*, 22 Jan. 1890), though Towse thought her raillery too sweet and playful, 'conceived too persistently in the mood of girlish merriment'. But in the dialogue with Benedick at the end of the broken wedding he thought her intermingling of pity, love and scorn brilliant. 'Of all the Beatrices I have seen', he wrote, 'she was one of the very best' (*Sixty Years*, 271–2).

It is by now obvious that most Victorian criticism of Beatrice perceived the role from a male perspective, from the standpoint of an ideal of womanhood imagined almost wholly in terms of qualities pleasing to men. In much of the criticism there was an implicit assumption that the highest and noblest role for a woman is to surrender romantically to a man; hence the approving emphasis on Beatrice's loving surrender to Benedick. In discussions of Beatrice's raillery, on the other hand, male anxieties about female autonomy surfaced frequently in the form of ambivalent attitudes to lively and articulate women. 'Whilst we admire the briskness and wit, the more than womanliness, on the stage', commented *Lloyd's Weekly* (12 Sep. 1857), 'we can but think [*sic*] how very unpleasant it would be in one's own suburban neat villa residence.'

Pictorial realism post-Irving

The period 1896–1905 saw lavish revivals of *Much Ado* by Daly and Sothern in America, and by Alexander, Flanagan and Tree in England. The sumptuous pictorialism of these productions was partly an attempt to emulate Irving, partly a reflection of the fashion for elaborate decor in late Victorian and Edwardian culture. But the dangers of excessive decoration were becoming apparent, especially in the productions of Alexander, Flanagan and Tree, where heavy mounting and a plethora of stage business threatened to overweight the acting and stifle the comedy. In the first decade of the twentieth century experiments with new staging methods were already under way, and would eventually lead to a new fashion for simpler, mainly non-illusionist production.

At Daly's Theatre, New York, 1896, the play was opulently staged with a single setting for each act and a heavily cut text: 1.2, 3.4, 3.5 and 5.3 were cut entirely, and the examination scene (4.2) was transposed to follow the street scene (3.3). The opening setting was a colonnaded hall overlooking Leonato's garden and the city of Messina (Daly acting edition). Ada Rehan and Charles Richman played Beatrice and Benedick. Rehan presented a spirited, though haughty and scornful Beatrice, 'somewhat over-robust and broad in humour' (Towse, *Sixty Years*, 361; *RHC*, 28 Sep. 1904; Daly, *Life*, 604). 'She delivered her thrusts with a deliberation and serious intent which almost conveyed a sense of malignity' (Towse, *Sixty Years*, 361), imparting 'a bitterness, not to say a rudeness', to the repartee (*NYP*, 24 Dec. 1896). Her performance included an impressive 'outburst of passion' at the end of the broken wedding (Winter, intro. to Daly acting edition, 9).

Sothern's productions (1904–5, 1911, 1913) were also richly mounted, with much inventive stage business. The settings and acting text were similar to Irving's, though Sothern cut the monument scene (5.3) and in 1904–5 restored much of the Dogberry content cut by Irving. The church scene (1911) featured a great rose window (s63). Sothern played a courtly Benedick with a touch of cynicism and burlesque (*RHC*, 28 Sep. 1904; Winter, *Memories*, 440–1). Julia Marlowe as Beatrice foregrounded feeling and softened the wit towards playful amiability, though she gave more edge to the raillery as she matured in the role (Shattuck, *Shakespeare on the American Stage*, II.256, 263; Winter, *Memories*, 460).

In George Alexander's production (St James's Theatre, 1898) the lavish mounting became something of an end in itself, the souvenir booklet suggesting that 'the play finds its unity not in character or plot, but as a picture of Renaissance Italian life' and that a primary objective of the production was to unroll 'a whole panorama of life in Messina' (pp.22, 36). Some critics found the production 'overpowering in its elaboration', the embellishments tending to stifle the play's liveliness (*Era*, 19 Feb. 1898; *St James's Gazette*, 17 Feb. 1898). The opening set, a Sicilian piazza enclosed with buildings, looked somewhat crowded on the smallish stage (photo, TM). The massive arches and columns of the interior sets looked ponderous; and the weight of fabric in the women's dresses must have impeded movement (photos in TM, UBTC, BPL, *Sk*, 23 Mar. 1898). 'It was magnificent', wrote W. G. Robertson, one of Alexander's scene designers, 'but *Much Ado About Nothing* ought not to be magnificent, but merely bright, sunny, gay. A glimpse of blue sky and a lick of distemper would have better suggested the atmosphere' (*Time Was*, 264). 'Shakespeare', suggested *The Sketch* (23 Feb. 1898), 'might well have asked whether his plays need so much sugar.'

Alexander's genial, romantic Benedick (*O*, 20 Feb. 1898; *Ac*, 26 Feb. 1898) and Julia Neilson's light, coquettish Beatrice (*Sk*, 23 Feb. 1898; *SR*, 26 Feb. 1898) appeared on the verge of falling in love from the first, their anti-romantic disdain underplayed to a point that almost neutralised the jest of Don Pedro's proposal to bring them together (Crosse, 'Performances', 1.156; *Sk*, 23 Feb. 1898). Fred Terry added a touch of spirit with a hearty, jovial Don Pedro (*DC*, 17 Feb. 1898), and H. B. Irving introduced a streak of sardonic humour to Don John (*Idler*, Apr. 1898, 339). The underweighting of the Dogberry scenes, as at the Lyceum (*DC*, 17 Feb. 1898), allowed even greater prominence to the romanticising tendencies and prevailing aristocratic ethos of the production.

Richard Flanagan's production (Queen's, Manchester, 1900–1, 1917) included diversions in the manner of Edward Saker. The performance commenced with Berlioz's 'Beatrice and Benedick' overture; the street scene (3.3) featured citizens gathering round a fountain to sing an evening prayer; and the church scene was cut in two to make room for a tableau of high mass, the choir performing the Kyrie from Palestrina's *Missa assumptu est Maria* while the play waited (*St*, 22 Feb. 1917; *MG*, 22 Jan. 1900). Yet 'the dialogue', according to C. E. Montague, 'was given with a good deal of the special kind of gusto, the air of delighted preoccupation in bouts of exquisite talking for talk's sake, that the play requires' (*MG*, 22 Jan. 1900).

Tree's production (His Majesty's, 1905) aimed to express what its manager conceived as the 'luxury', 'profusion and riotous extravagance' of the Renaissance in sixteenth-century southern Europe (souvenir programme). The audience was 'almost satiated with colour and movement' (*DE*, 25 Jan. 1905), with at least ten different settings and a profusion of resplendent costumes. The opening scene highlighted the transition from a martial to a courtly milieu with an *al fresco* banquet on the battlements, the guests, including a captain in complete steel, attended by servants and singing minstrels (s69; *Std*, 25 Jan. 1905). Seventy-seven players' names are recorded in the production documents (UBTC), and each of the main characters had three to five costume changes (programme; costume designs, UBTC). An offstage orchestra and chorus provided incidental music (*T*, 25 Jan. 1905; music plot, s68). The masquerade was magnified almost into a carnival, with revellers fantastically disguised, some as *commedia dell'arte* characters, some as figures from pagan festivals, and others as grotesque beasts disporting themselves between the sequences of dialogue (s68–9; costume designs, UBTC; *DG*, 25 Jan. 1905). After Hero and Claudio's betrothal there was more revelry and dancing, which seemed like 'a divertissement dragged in partly for spectacular effect' (*Onlooker*, 11 Feb. 1905). At the end of 2.2 there was a five-minute orchestral 'intermezzo' punctuated by sounds of nature and human activity to illustrate the passage from night to morning (s69; souvenir programme; Shaw, *Dying Tongue*, 11). Edward Gordon Craig suggested that whereas Irving had generally made spectacle subservient to dramatic effect, Tree enjoyed spectacle for its own sake (*Irving*, 94–6).

His lavish embroidery of the play provoked considerable critical unease. 'One's mind was too much occupied by the allurements of accessories to appreciate fully the charm of the play', reported *Modern Society* (4 Feb. 1905). The play was buried 'in a suffocating mass of decoration', said *The Daily News* (25 Jan. 1905). According to G. B. Shaw, Tree 'took unheard-of pains to manufacture "business" to help out scenes that positively bristle[d] with missed Shakespearian points'. 'He is always papering the naked wall, helping the lame dog over the stile … abhorring a vacuum, and filling it with the treasures of his own ingenuity and imagination and fun, and then generously giving our Shakespear the credit' (*Dying Tongue*, 6, 4). Tree cut about a quarter of the text, interpolating many phrases, interjections and snippets of dialogue of his own; there were three interpolated songs (s69). The invented business included much comic exaggeration. 'The text', said *The World* (31 Jan. 1905), 'is to him not so much a canvas as a sort of nucleus, around which he spins and weaves a wholly new, iridescent, dazzling, grandiose work of art.' Such upholstering meant long, slow performances: on the opening night the play lasted four hours, including forty-five minutes of waits (*T*, 25 Jan. 1905; Crosse, *Playgoing*, 37). 'The joyousness, which is the keynote of the comedy, was overwhelmed by the gorgeousness of the frame' (*Ac*, 28 Jan. 1905).

The production gave more than usual prominence to the Hero–Claudio relationship, which was developed with some sentimentality (souvenir programme; *Ac*, 28 Jan. 1905; *A*, 28 Jan. 1905). The romantic mood of Hero and Claudio's betrothal tended to suffuse the rest of 2.1, set in the moonlit orchard with fairy lanterns in the branches and the scent of orange blossom wafting into the audience (s68–9; *SpT*, 28 Jan. 1905). To the influence of this atmosphere, commented *The Globe* (25 Jan. 1905), 'Beatrice and Benedick must inevitably succumb', their wit blurred by the pervading romantic languor. The production exploited to the full the melodramatic potential of the broken wedding (s69), Viola Tree 'illustrat[ing] the shock of youth and innocence with … wounded wonder and havoc of soul' (*DC*, 29 Apr. 1905).

Tree's Benedick was built on a bold contrast between the soldier of the early scenes and the lover of the later part of the play (*Std*, 25 Jan. 1905). He presented Benedick at first as a 'big, bluff, overbearing kind of man' (*MSC*, 29 Jan. 1905), somewhat coarse of manner and rough of speech (*Weekly Tribune*, 5 Feb. 1905), attacking the part vigorously with 'shout and Falstaffian swagger' (*DC*, 25 Jan. 1905). On becoming a lover he developed a new civility and polish and a lighter touch to his humour (*Sheffield Telegraph*,

25 Jan. 1905; *Playhouse*, 28 Jan. 1905). In the early scenes he gave little hint of the possibility of a later transformation (*Truth*, 2 Feb. 1905), seeming more at home as the blunt soldier than as the polished Cavalier (*W*, 31 Jan. 1905). Winifred Emery played Beatrice largely after the manner of Ellen Terry, highlighting the sweeter, merrier side of the character, though with some touches of scorn (Crosse, 'Performances', III.160; *T*, 25 Jan. 1905; *A*, 28 Jan. 1905).

In Tree's production 'scene painters, costumiers, dancers, subordinates, came first – the actors second' (*Ac*, 28 Jan. 1905). *The Annual Register* (147, 1905, 100) thought the performance 'suffered considerably from over-staging and under-acting', *The Daily News* (11 Feb. 1905) that the scenic arrangements overwhelmed the drama. With the *Athenaeum* (28 Jan. 1905) calling guardedly for simpler settings and *The Sketch* (1 Feb. 1905) for greater continuity of action, the time seemed ripe for experiment with new staging methods.

William Poel and Edward Gordon Craig had already demonstrated simpler, non-illusionist alternatives which were to revolutionise the staging of Shakespeare. The new methods were adopted only gradually, however, the traditions of pictorial realism lingering concurrently for some years. In the early twentieth century there were modest pictorial productions of *Much Ado* in London by Greet (1904, 1916–17), Benson (1908), Montefiore (1911), Ayrton (1915), Foss (1918) and Fred Terry (1920). At the Gaiety, Manchester (1909), Iden Payne staged the play with simple representational scenery, alternating built scenes with neutral front curtains (Mazer, *Shakespeare*, 114). At Stratford-upon-Avon *Much Ado* was presented in traditional style until 1916. In America pictorial realism lingered in the productions of Annie Russell (NY, 1912–13) and Henry Jewett (Boston, 1926).

Change and experiment in the first half of the twentieth century

The early twentieth century saw the evolution of Shakespearean production methods towards simpler, suggestive staging, the reaction away from the heavy mounting of the late nineteenth century led initially by William Poel and Edward Gordon Craig. Poel urged a return to Elizabethan staging principles, advocating intimacy between players and audiences, non-scenic mounting and continuous action. To demonstrate these principles he produced Renaissance plays, including *Much Ado* (1904), on a replica of an Elizabethan stage which he mounted in existing theatres or halls. A platform stage was extended into the auditorium, flanked by painted flats representing the galleries of an Elizabethan theatre (Court Theatre programme, 19 Mar. 1904; *DC*, in Headlam, *Shakespeare*, 8; Mazer, *Shakespeare*, 69). There was no set scenery, only movable properties to suggest locations. Draperies were hung against the architectural façade, and the stage was lit from above with a uniform white light in imitation of the daylight in Elizabethan outdoor theatres. Poel did not completely abandon Edwardian theatrical practice, however, setting curtains between the stage pillars to mask the shifting of properties between scenes (Mazer, *Shakespeare*, 60). Players and musicians were dressed in brightly coloured Elizabethan costumes, and Elizabethan music was performed on virginal, lute, viols and cithern. Poel trained his actors to speak 'trippingly', with rapid, lightly stressed delivery. Texts were lightly cut, and stage business was simple (S57; Headlam, *Shakespeare*, 1–9).

Some reviewers became convinced that Poel's principles offered a valid alternative to conventional scenic realism (*DM*, 23 Apr. 1904; *MP*, 23 Apr. 1904; *Truth*, in Headlam, *Shakespeare*, 12), G. B. Shaw commenting that 'we are less conscious of the artificiality of the stage when a few well-understood conventions, adroitly handled, are substituted for attempts at an impossible scenic verisimilitude' (*T*, 2 June 1905). However, it is arguable that Poel's depiction of an Elizabethan theatre on the stage was itself a kind of representationalism (Mazer, *Shakespeare*, 69). Poel's influence was limited initially by the austerity of his staging methods and the antiquarian tendency of his work, which did little to bridge the gap between Renaissance conventions and the responses of modern audiences; but in subsequent years the principles of continuous action, swift, lightly stressed speech, lightly cut texts and simple staging were widely adopted in Shakespearean productions, including the *Much Ado* revivals of Barry Jackson, Robert Atkins, Andrew Leigh, Harcourt Williams and W. Bridges-Adams. In the 1920s and 1930s the influence of Poel's Elizabethanism was also seen in the frequent use of pillared architectural sets and Elizabethan costumes.

Unlike Poel, Edward Gordon Craig placed great importance on scenic art in the theatre, developing simplified methods of suggestion and stylisation as an alternative to the detailed pictorial realism of the major Victorian and Edwardian theatres. Whereas Poel saw Shakespearean production primarily in terms of faithfulness to a historical model, Craig stressed the function of the director as creative artist and interpreter (*Art of Theatre*, 147, 153–5, 175). His settings achieved their effects impressionistically, by the simplest of means. In his *Much Ado* (Imperial, 1903) the hall in Leonato's house was formed by tapestry curtains hung between five Tuscan pilasters (Craig, *Gordon Craig*, 175); the garden was suggested by arched hedges against a 'luminous' blue backcloth, with a vine-clad trellised pavilion in the centre (*W*, 26 May 1903; scene design, V&A). The church scene (see illustration 7) was acclaimed as one of Craig's most impressive creations. A backdrop of grey curtains was folded and skilfully lit to suggest the columns of a lofty

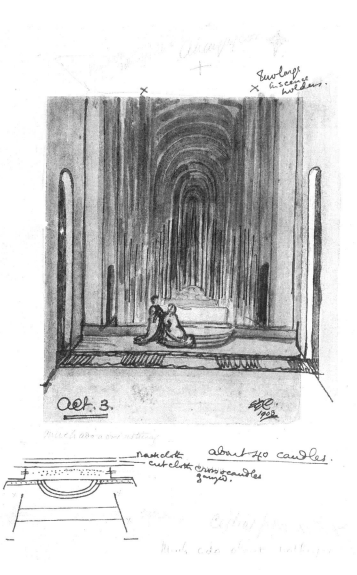

7 Edward Gordon Craig's preliminary sketch for the church scene (4.1),
Imperial Theatre, 1903.

nave (*Ac*, 6 June 1903, 563), or rather 'the dim atmosphere in which the walls
are lost' (*PMG*, 25 May 1903). Blue light glimmered through a narrow vertical cut in the centre of the backdrop, suggesting a stained-glass window at the
far end of a cathedral (*W*, 26 May 1903). In places the drapes were painted
with 'a varnished pattern that sparkled in the dim light', suggesting mosaics

(Craig, *Gordon Craig*, 175; *W*, 26 May 1903). 'A great altar, crowded with enormous candlesticks', was set on 'a long platform, reached by four wide steps' (Craig, *Gordon Craig*, 175–6).

> High over the altar hung a giant crucifix, part of it disappearing into the shadows above ... The only illumination in this dimly lit 'church' came from an imaginary stained-glass window above the proscenium arch that cast a great pool of light upon the floor below ... The characters were only lit when they entered the acting area which was the pool of coloured light; outside it, they too became silhouettes like the columns.   (*ibid.*)

The angle of divergence of the beam of light suggested a source far above the proscenium arch, creating an extraordinary sense of height and space (*PMG*, 25 May 1903). Even reviewers sceptical of Craig's *avant-garde* methods were astonished at the effect of this scene, Max Beerbohm judging it 'incomparably finer than any other attempt ... to suggest a cathedral on the stage' (*SR*, 30 May 1903). Barry Jackson, who was himself to become a leader in innovative staging, saw Craig's church scene as 'clearly indicating that it was possible to attain sheer beauty of setting without recourse to precise detail of architecture or landscape' (*SS* 8, 1955, 77). Craig's *Much Ado* was something of a compromise, however, between scenic innovation and traditionalism in other areas of production. The venture was financed by his mother, Ellen Terry, who also played Beatrice. Desperate to recoup her losses on Craig's earlier production of *The Vikings*, she insisted on 'the *old* play, and the *old me* in it', with an acting text similar to Irving's (Craig, *Gordon Craig*, 174; P-1903b). One benefit of the compromise was to demonstrate the compatibility between Craig's scenic methods and traditional acting styles (Mazer, *Shakespeare*, 102).

While the English theatre was slower than its German and Russian counterparts to follow Craig's example, directors gradually found ways of synthesising ideas drawn from Poel and Craig with elements of traditional theatre practice. Simplified, suggestive, stylised settings became common in Shakespearean productions from the 1920s on. One effect was to give greater prominence to the actors than had been usual on the cluttered stages of heavily mounted traditional productions. The movement away from the illusionist conventions of the late nineteenth-century theatre had stemmed partly from a recognition of incompatibilities between those conventions and Shakespeare's dramaturgy. The artifice and conventionalisation in Shakespearean comedy were better served by elements of stylisation in the staging than by an attempted theatrical realism (see Mazer, *Shakespeare*, 30–48). The stage's potential for illusion was in any case quickly surpassed by the motion picture. The development towards simplified stage settings was also part of a broader aesthetic movement in the early twentieth century away from the heavy decorative styles of the late nineteenth century towards cleaner, simpler decor and architecture.

One of the most innovative productions of *Much Ado* in the early twentieth century was directed by Conal O'Riordan and Barry Jackson at the Birmingham Repertory Theatre in 1919–20. The play was staged with a permanent unlocalised set, using strong primary colours and bright lighting to suggest a dominant tone of hard brilliance (a striking departure from the softening and romanticising trend of productions in the Irving tradition). The set was a platform across the stage reached by a flight of steps beneath a central pillared arch; a ground row of stylised trees suggested a garden; a cross indicated a church. The floor was a chessboard of black and white, the costumes various shades of yellow and red, except for a 'waspish black and yellow Don John' (Jackson, *SS* 8, 1955, 78). The contrast of strong primary colour against the white set, black and white stage, and brilliant blue of the cyclorama 'evoked a general effect of almost violent brightness' emphasising the gaiety and animation of the comedy (*ibid.*; Matthews, *Birmingham Repertory Theatre*, 134; *BP*, 5 May 1919; photo, BRT archives). The acting was consistent with the visual effect, Clarke-Smith giving Benedick a 'hard veneer of brilliance', Margaret Chatwin playing Beatrice with a front of shrewishness beneath which the pleasantry was still visible (*BP*, 5 May 1919).

A similar bold departure from representationalism was seen in Robert Jones's designs for a production of *Much Ado* commissioned by the New York Theatre Guild in 1925, but cancelled at dress rehearsal stage. The actors were to wear scarlet and gold costumes against a background of yellow and orange screens (Larson, *Scene Design*, 75, 208; Speaight, *Shakespeare*, 171–2).

A combination of architectural sets with movable properties or stylised pictorial elements to suggest locations was a common feature of *Much Ado* productions in the 1920s and 1930s. Beatrice Wilson and the Fellowship of Players (Strand, 1924) used such a set in a production described as 'all gold and blue and glowing with Renaissance light' (*DC*, 29 Sep. 1924; *St*, 2 Oct. 1924). At the Maddermarket Theatre, Norwich, 1934, Hugh Hunt used an Elizabethan-type stage façade, in the lower part of which he set a scenic backdrop of a formal garden overlooking the sea (*Eastern Daily Press*, 20 Mar. 1934).

The simplicity and flexibility of the new staging methods proved especially congenial at the Old Vic, London, with its tight budgetary constraints and repertory schedules. At the Old Vic in 1921 Robert Atkins, a disciple of Poel, extended a platform over the orchestra pit, constructed a false

8 Beatrice in caustic mood: Margaret Chatwin, Birmingham Repertory Theatre, 1919–20.

proscenium with stage doors in the pediments, and lit the stage from above. Leonato's garden was suggested by stylised shrubbery, and the expense of an elaborate church scene was saved by imagining the chancel in the auditorium, Hero and Claudio facing the audience before a simple screen of black and gold. The Don John and watch scenes were played before curtains (Isaac, *Greet*, 150; *New Age*, 29 Sep. 1921; cutting, TM).

One of the finest representations of the play in this period was Harcourt Williams's production at the Old Vic in 1931. A simple pillared setting (*MP*, 17 Mar. 1931) gave primary focus to the actors and their dialogue. The play was performed with subtlety and style as 'a courtly and joyous masque moving to the orchestration of good talk' (*TT*, 28 Mar. 1931). The production foregrounded the comic and joyous elements in *Much Ado*, subduing the darker passages, and forestalling questions of plausibility by highlighting the play's artifice (*DT*, 17 Mar. 1931; *MP*, 17 Mar. 1931; *T*, 17 Mar. 1931). John Gielgud as Benedick and Dorothy Green as Beatrice played together with unusual lightness and gaiety (*DT*, 17 Mar. 1931). Green acted Beatrice with particular sensitivity and intellectual refinement (*Era*, 18 Mar. 1931), delivering the polished prose with point, lightness, and a 'keen sense of the finer shades of wit' (*SH*, 28 Apr, 18 Aug. 1922; *BG*, 21 Apr. 1927); Gielgud played Benedick as 'a slight, mocking wasp of a man', slightly conceited, and 'most lovable in his unexpected, almost clumsy bursts of feeling' (*L*, 26 Mar. 1931; *ST*, 22 Mar. 1931).

Between 1920 and 1934 W. Bridges-Adams directed *Much Ado* in Stratford-upon-Avon and London, combining simplicity of staging with a more picturesque production style than was current at the Old Vic. Continuous action was achieved through a combination of permanent or semi-permanent architectural features and shifting pictorial elements. The formal, stylised settings were more austere than those in the Irving tradition, but visually richer than the spare stage settings for *Much Ado* at the Old Vic and elsewhere in the 1920s. The visual impact was enhanced by picturesque groupings and rich costuming (*BM*, 19 May 1925, 24 Apr. 1929). Trewin recalled with pleasure Bridges-Adams's 'high aristocratic treatment of the play' (*Donat*, 169): he 'soothed the comedy along' with a stylishness and 'courtly ease' (Kemp and Trewin, *Stratford Festival*, 148) which looked back in some degree to the Lyceum productions, and forward to the elegant Gielgud revivals of the 1950s. Whereas O'Riordan and Jackson at the Birmingham Repertory Theatre had underlined the harder, more brilliant elements of the play, in Bridges-Adams's performances the 'harsh tones' were 'softened' and 'the pleasant lights highlighted' (*St*, 23 Apr. 1925), the tensions and dissonances in the play smoothed over to achieve an effect of coherence and harmony (*TT*, 5 Mar. 1926).

Iden Payne adopted a modified Elizabethanism for his 1936 Stratford production of *Much Ado*, constructing over the stage a roof supported by two pillars, backed by a triple-arched and curtained false proscenium within which scenery was set. In 1939 and 1941 he used pictorial settings for the play, as did Atkins at Stratford in 1945 (pr. photos).

Among the more interesting experiments in Elizabethanism was Robert Atkins's bare-stage production at the Ring, Blackfriars, 1937, aimed at demonstrating that Shakespeare could hold a modern audience without the help of scenery. A platform backed by an inner stage and balcony was thrust deep into the audience, which surrounded it on three sides. Critics were impressed by the intimacy between players and audience.

In contrast with the rather fusty Elizabethanism of some provincial productions of the period, the Hull Playgoers' Society in 1930 contemporised the play with an *avant-garde* modern dress revival complete with plus-fours and bowler hats, red-tabbed staff officers, cocktails and foxtrots, typewriters, telephones, sporting newspapers and cigarette lighters, and a prince 'interrupted in a round of golf by ... a fatuous Inspector of Police in present-day uniform' (*Hull Daily Mail*, 27 Mar. 1930). A less satisfactory experiment was the attempt at the Old Vic in 1934 to 'remove the play from any definite time or place' (programme) by mixing Elizabethan and Regency costume styles. Critics were also taken aback by elements of caricature in the production, Don John and his men stalking about with stylised movements to a pizzicato from the band (*SunPic*, 11 Nov. 1934; *O*, 11 Nov. 1934), and the designer (David Ffolkes) attempting a visual counterpart to the comic topsy-turvydom of the watch scenes with a cartoon backdrop of a 'cobwebby steeple' and rooftops on which 'cavorted' cats and 'mickey mice' against a sky with 'drunken constellations' (*ST*, 11 Nov. 1934; *SunPic*, 11 Nov. 1934; *Ind*, 17 Nov. 1934). London was not yet ready for such irreverence with Shakespeare.

One of the most imaginative revivals of the immediate post-war period was the Bristol Old Vic production of 1947, directed by Hugh Hunt. In this modern-dress production Hunt conceived the arrival of Don Pedro and his men in terms of the return of soldiers to civilian life at the end of World War II. Benedick was contemporised as 'a sort of subaltern a bit above himself', Beatrice as a woman 'not quite sure of her powers of looking emancipated' (*TT*, 14 June 1947). Don Pedro's party were uniformed as Italian army officers and Don John as a sinister member of the Fascist black-shirt militia (Marshall, *Producer*, 176; *Star*, 3 June 1947). The watch, however, were thoroughly English, including members of the local Home Guard with their rifles, Dogberry entering as an air-raid warden on a bicycle (*BEP*, 9 Apr. 1947). The play was set romantically in the courtyard garden of Leonato's house overlooking the sea. The soldier–girl friend slant sacrificed some of the style and artifice of traditional performances, simplifying the play in the direction of a modern romance story; but the production also brought a freshness and contemporaneity to the sex rivalry and banter (*WDP*, 9 June 1947; *BEW*, 9 June 1947; *TT*, 14 June 1947; *MG*, 4 June 1947). 'The lively, imaginative production', commented *The Stage* (5 June 1947), '… almost convinced one that here is a new version of the play rather than a presentation of the original text embellished only by new clothes.'

In the acting of *Much Ado*, the period from the early twentieth century to the 1940s was characterised more by good ensemble work than by outstanding individual achievements, though there were memorable performances by Edith Evans and Dorothy Green as Beatrice, and by John Gielgud and others as Benedick. Many performances of Beatrice were still coloured by traditions inherited from the nineteenth century, reviewers tending to admire actresses like Julia Neilson (SMT 1911), who 'drew aside the thin gossamer covering of mirth and showed a Beatrice full of tender, womanly feeling' (*BG*, 2 May 1911), or Mary Newcombe (Old Vic, 1934), who reportedly 'gave the character its true basis of feminine sympathy and generosity' (Williamson, *Old Vic*, 7). The view was still widespread that feeling was womanly, wit and intellect were not; and some observers still found the tension between wit and 'womanliness' in Beatrice 'difficult' (e.g. *SH*, 4 Aug. 1916; Isaac, *Greet*, 66). Some actresses challenged such attitudes, Margaret Chatwin (BRT, 1919–20) presenting a more caustic Beatrice than usual (see illustration 8). Edith Evans (Old Vic, 1926) acted the part in the style of Congreve's Millamant, with the emphasis on wit and artifice rather than 'womanly' sensibility (*DN*, 17 May 1926). Sybil Thorndike (Old Vic company, Lyric, Hammersmith, 1927) played a robust and redoubtable Beatrice with an imperious wit and formidable disdain, giving full weight to bawdy lines cut in Victorian productions (*DSk*, 22 Nov. 1927; *DN*, 23 Nov. 1927; Crosse, *Playgoing*, 52). Cathleen Nesbitt (Regent's Park, 1939) acted the role with vigorous wit, 'her method of making points – and every one a bull's eye – reveal[ing] a nimble intelligence and great physical energy, but nothing of the heart' (*NEW*, 22 June 1939). Reviewers tended to find such interpretations less appealing than those of the more amiable Beatrices of the time, one critic confessing that 'in our present society the epigrammatic lady is not popular' (*SH*, Aug. 1916), another declaring that 'a Beatrice who hides her essential moonshine behind a barrage of fireworks is no true woman' (*NEW*, 22 June 1939). Demeaning gender stereotypes were all too commonly voiced by the male reviewers of the period, though a few argued that Beatrice's intellect, wit and incisiveness were seriously undervalued by 'softened' stage interpretations of the role (e.g. *WG*, 21 Jan. 1905; *NEW*, 6 Dec. 1934).

In contrast with Irving's deliberate, sardonic, slightly crusty Benedick, several actors in the first half of the twentieth century performed the role with a virile, debonair gallantry reminiscent of James Wallack. Fred Terry (SMT 1911; King's, Hammersmith, 1920) played a bold, dashing, light-hearted Benedick, 'exuding *bonhomie*' (*BG*, 2 May 1911; *O*, 16 May 1920; Haddon, *Green Room*, 47), modulating between hearty bluffness and delicate banter, with a depth of feeling in the later scenes (*BM*, 9 Oct. 1920; *BP*, 2 May 1911; *St*, 20 May 1920). James Dale (SMT 1925, 1936) combined sparkling lightness with an initial suggestion of soldierly swagger, encompassing a whole range of tones from the breezy to the sardonic (*Oxford Chronicle*, 26 June 1925; Crosse, 'Performances', IX.112; *BP*, 19 May 1925; *YP*, 24 Apr. 1936). Henry Ainley's performance (New Theatre, 1926) included soldierly swagger and a gentler, whimsical humour (*Punch*, 17 Feb. 1926; *SR*, 6 Feb. 1926); his Benedick was always a man of distinction (*SR*, 6 Feb. 1926). Maurice Evans (Old Vic, 1934) played a dashing Benedick with a 'fine flamy humour' (Williamson, *Old Vic*, 6; *NEW*, 6 Dec. 1934). Donald Wolfit, who toured the play in London and the provinces between 1938 and 1949, gave a vigorous, gallant impersonation, light hearted, with a turn of philosophical humour (Williamson, *Old Vic*, 6; *BM*, 29 Nov. 1938; *O*, 25 Feb. 1940).

The first half of the twentieth century brought greater variety than before to the representation of some of the other roles. Eric Maxon (SMT 1927, 1929–30, 1934) played Don Pedro with traditional poise and elegance (*SH*, 26 Apr. 1929), but Ralph Richardson (Old Vic, 1931) added a touch of mischievous irresponsibility (*Era*, 18 Mar. 1931; *TT*, 28 Mar. 1931); and Donald Wolfit (SMT 1936) turned the prince into a light-hearted young gallant (*T*, 24 Apr. 1936; *BED*, 24 Apr. 1936). Maurice Colbourne (SMT 1922–3, 1925) tried to palliate Claudio's behaviour with a touch of boyish petulance (Crosse, 'Performances', IX.114); Patrick Troughton (Aldwych, 1946) gave him a native gentleness, steering a course between the 'sympathetic and odious' (Crosse, 'Performances', XIX.33). Harcourt Williams (Aldwych, 1946) played a harassed rather than venerable Leonato (*St*, 24 Oct. 1946). David Read (SMT 1945) made Don John a cripple (*SP*, Apr. 1945), a concept consistent with his crooked nature which gave fresh point to the references to 'one Deformed' (3.3.103, 5.1.273–4). Dogberry emerged from his partial eclipse under Irving, Alexander and Tree, with memorable performances by George Weir (SMT 1891–1908), Stanley Lathbury (SMT 1922–3, 1927, 1933), Randle Ayrton (SMT 1925), George Hayes (Old Vic, 1925), Hay Petrie (Old Vic, 1927), and Roy Byford (SMT 1929–30, 1934). Directors increasingly explored the theatrical possibilities of the smaller scenes and characters.

Whereas nineteenth- and early twentieth-century dramatic criticism had tended to focus primarily on character analysis, by the 1930s reviewers were also showing a stronger aesthetic interest in style and structure, a trend which paralleled the development of literary formalism. Matters of structure, style and aesthetics would become especially significant in John Gielgud's productions of *Much Ado* in the 1950s, as well as in the theatrical and literary criticism of that decade.

Much Ado mid-century

At Stratford-upon-Avon the predominant mood of *Much Ado* production in the mid-twentieth century was picturesque, romantic and harmonising. The revivals of John Gielgud (1949–59) and Douglas Seale (1958) invited a response partly in terms of game-like romantic fantasy (Gielgud, *Stage Directions*, 39). In the austere post-war economic climate of Britain, the beauty and predominant joyousness of these productions held great appeal. Their festive, harmonious endings chimed with the emphasis in much of the critical writing of the period on the importance of reconciliation, renewal and restored harmony in the closing scenes of Shakespeare's comedies. In the late 1950s Houseman and Landau (Stratford, Connecticut, 1957), Seale (Stratford-upon-Avon, 1958) and Langham (Stratford, Ontario, 1958) departed from the dominant trend of previous *Much Ado* production by setting the play in periods other than the Renaissance, a practice which became frequent during the rest of the century.

Gielgud's *Much Ado* was set in the high Renaissance of fourteenth-century Italy. Hailed by Trewin and others as 'the definitive revival of our time' (*BP*, 23 Nov. 1955; cf. *Drama* 25, 1952, 14; *TW*, Sep. 1955, 8), the production achieved in its day a classic status similar to Irving's. It opened at Stratford in 1949 with Anthony Quayle and Diana Wynyard as Benedick and Beatrice, was repeated at Stratford in 1950 with Gielgud and Peggy Ashcroft in these roles, and was revived in London in 1952 with Gielgud and Wynyard; in 1955 it toured Britain and Europe with Gielgud and Ashcroft in the leading roles, and was staged in New York in 1959 with Gielgud and Margaret Leighton. Reviewers acclaimed its stylishness and finesse, its subtlety, its superb acting and ensemble, its smoothness and rhythmic flow: 'I have never known', wrote Trewin, 'a revival of more silken-streaming grace' (*BP*, 23 July 1955).

The play was interpreted in exceptionally light and buoyant style (*MG*, 8 June 1950; *T*, 12 Jan. 1952), suggesting 'a post-Renaissance man's imagining of an artificial, Italianate, purely Renaissance comedy of manners' (*Public Opinion*, 30 June 1950). The dominant mode was one of elegant artifice,

9 The examination scene (4.2), Shakespeare Memorial Theatre, Stratford-upon-Avon, 1949. George Rose (Dogberry), John Slater (Borachio), William Squire (Verges), Harold Kasket (Sexton), Paul Hardwick (Conrade), and the watchmen.

10 Harmonious grouping: John Gielgud's production, Phoenix Theatre, London, 1952. Margaret (Penelope Munday), Hero (Dorothy Tutin), Beatrice (Diana Wynyard), Ursula (Margaret Wolfit).

11 'Daughter, remember what I told you ...' (2.1.48). Patriarchal admonition, Shakespeare Memorial Theatre, Stratford-upon-Avon, 1955. Anthony Nicholls (Leonato), Judith Stott (Hero).

highlighting the play's verbal ingenuities and the contrivance of its design. Mariano Andreu's opulent settings and costumes drew attention to their theatricality, foregrounding the theatricality in the play itself. The ingenious scene changes created an effect of elaborate contrivance, the scenes 'emerging from one another as by Oriental magic' (*Year's Work in the Theatre,*

1949–50, 56). The opening garden set was transformed into an interior by the movement of hinged screens; for the first watch scene (3.3) two pillared porticoes slid away to reveal a street with a penthouse, which later opened to become the interior of the church (Gielgud, *Stage Directions*, 40).

The production created a strong sense of artistic unity (*Sp*, 18 Jan. 1952). Gielgud regarded *Much Ado* as a 'splendidly organised play': 'Everything counts', he said at the launching of the 1952 revival; 'I have only realised with this production how closely knit the play really is' (*St*, 24 Jan. 1952). Such an emphasis paralleled the interest in structural cohesion in the literary criticism of the time. The privileging of the artificial, game-like elements in the performance eased acceptance of the play's conventionalisations and forestalled questions about plot improbability (*MG*, 14 Jan. 1952; *Sp*, 18 Jan. 1952); but the impression of coherence was achieved at the expense of the darker elements in the play. The performance passed 'from gaiety to gloom and back as in a sunlit garden where the noon is momentarily troubled by a passing cloud' (*TT*, 19 Jan. 1952). The festive ending was melded into harmony by subduing those elements which resist accord: 'A fig for Don John!' wrote Ivor Brown; 'Hey-nonny is the mood; hey-nonny is the victory' (*O*, 13 Jan. 1952). The grace and romantic harmonies of the production were in the tradition of Irving and Bridges-Adams, though unlike Irving, Gielgud gave significant weight to the watch scenes, allowing their earthy robustness to balance the refinement of the dominant high comedy (*LSC*, 3 Apr. 1949; *TT*, 10 June 1950).

Gielgud, Wynyard and Ashcroft suggested an awakening love between Beatrice and Benedick from the start: in their raillery there was 'a delicacy of suppressed affection' (*O*, 13 Jan. 1952). They were perhaps too quickly and obviously in love (*MG*, 14 Jan. 1952), with a consequent minimising of dramatic surprise (*TT*, 19 Jan. 1952), their 'cross-talk to conceal affection' assuming the character of a game-like device 'to postpone the happy ending' (*Sp*, 18 Jan. 1952; *ThN*, 19 Jan. 1952).

Gielgud was widely acclaimed as the best Benedick since Irving. He played the role more as the courtier than the soldier, poised, sophisticated, suave, urbane (*NSN*, 17 June 1950; *Punch*, 23 Jan. 1952; *SH*, 6 Oct. 1950; *T*, 7 June 1950), with a hint of vanity in his dapper appearance and in the slight hauteur of his manner, offset by constant touches of self-mockery (*Truth*, 16 June 1950; *SQ* 2, 1951, 75; Hayman, *Gielgud*, 209). His wit was light, pointed, subtle, intellectually refined (*SH*, 6 Oct. 1950; *SSc*, July 1950, 499; *BP*, 10 June 1950; Kemp, broadcast typescript, 14 June 1950, BPL); he seemed 'to flick home his speeches with a supple turn of the fencer's wrist', each word 'cut to the flashing facet' (*JLW*, 23 June 1950; *SH*, 9 June 1950). There was also an air of ironic detachment, a knowing, slightly introspective quality in his humour (*TT*, 19 Jan. 1952; *Sp*, 29 July 1955; Findlater, *Player Kings*, 195). In 1955 he tried to make the part more soldierly, entering in leather doublet and thigh boots, with a swagger and slight touch of gruffness, but found that this 'went against the grain' (*NS*, 30 July 1955; *GH*, 8 Nov. 1955; Gielgud, *Actor*, 135–6; Findlater, *Player Kings*, 195).

Peggy Ashcroft and Diana Wynyard also played with lightness and refinement, in the gentle tradition of Beatrice passed down from the late nineteenth century. Wynyard was 'poised and controlled' (*DT*, 12 Jan. 1952), though 'perhaps a little too placid for the spiked wit of Beatrice' (*Vogue*, 11 Mar. 1952). 'She is especially good', wrote Anthony Cookman, 'in the way her voice seems to pause and hover for an instant after what is very like a compliment before alighting with a little pounce on just the word she had wanted to turn the compliment into an insult' (*T&B*, 23 Jan. 1952). The Ashcroft–Gielgud interchanges were deft and pointed, with a 'quick, darting intelligence' and a finesse that often persuaded critics to accept finely bred graciousness in place of a blunter, more vigorous tone (Kemp, broadcast typescript, 14 June 1950, BPL; *BG*, 7 June 1950; *MG*, 8 June 1950; *NSN*, 17 June 1950; *JLW*, 23 June 1950), though Ashcroft also included touches of girlish freshness and gaucherie (*SH*, 9 Dec. 1955; *T*, 22 July 1955; Ashcroft, in Cook, *Women in Shakespeare*, 32–3). Philip Hope-Wallace wished for a more astringent Beatrice (*GW*, 22 June 1950). While Ashcroft's Beatrice had a keener edge in 1955 (*NS*, 30 July 1955), *The Financial Times* (22 July 1955) thought it still 'carrie[d] a tinge of decorum where one might expect a mettlesome Renaissance heroine to be more plainly ribald in attack'.

Gender attitudes inherited from the nineteenth century coloured many of the reviews, the *Tribune* (16 June 1950) describing Ashcroft's Beatrice as 'radiant' with 'quintessential femininity'; *The Sketch* (30 Jan. 1952) noting with approval that Wynyard's Beatrice 'had a woman's heart as well as a flashing mind'. *The Manchester Guardian* (14 Jan. 1952) commented that while 'the text may give us a tarter Beatrice than this … there is much gain in a Beatrice who is so little the shrew and so much the woman of feeling'. T. C. Worsley, on the other hand, thought 'something altogether robuster, grittier, earthier would be more appropriate' (*NSN*, 17 June 1950).

Claudio was imagined as young, impetuous and inexperienced (Gielgud, *Stage Directions*, 37; *MG*, 21 Apr. 1949), Don Pedro as genial and debonair (*SH*, 22 Apr. 1949; *MA*, 23 Jan. 1952), Leonato as urbane and patriarchal (*TW*, June 1949, 30; *St*, 17 Jan. 1952). The frequent stage convention of a corpulent Dogberry was seen perhaps at its most extreme in the mountainous, self-important Dogberry of George Rose (see illustration 9), surveying the world 'through half-closed eyes with magisterial oblivion' (*BG*, 20 Apr. 1949), his 'megaphonic' Oxfordshire accent 'roar[ing] out in rebellious opposition to the surrounding mellifluence' (*Picture Post*, 8 Mar. 1952). Alan Badel (1950) gave Don John a touch of the aristocrat in a performance 'poised between ... princely urbanity' and 'malicious scheming' (*Nottingham Guardian*, 8 June 1950).

In 1957 John Houseman and Jack Landau (ASF, Stratford, Connecticut) departed radically from the gracious Gielgud tradition with a production alternating between farce and romantic sentiment, set in mid-nineteenth-century Texas during the Spanish occupation (*SR*, NY, 24 Aug. 1957). Leonato's adobe ranch house had flamenco guitar music and Indian servants (*SC*, 18.250; Leiter, *Shakespeare*, 500); 'a Mexican desperado went shooting and shouting his way down the aisle to open the play' (*SQ* 8, 1957, 509); Don Pedro and his men returned from a skirmish 'clad in the silver and gold-trimmed, tight-fitting elegance of colonial hidalgos' (*CW*, Oct. 1957, 66); Dogberry was a 'muddled' western sheriff; and in the final act Don John was captured by the watch in 'a melodramatic chase across the piazza' (*SR*, NY, 24 Aug. 1957). In this hot-blooded Spanish–American atmosphere there was little scope for high-comic sophistication, but Don John's villainy, Claudio's impetuosity, the broken wedding and Beatrice's demand for a vendetta must have seemed more than usually plausible.

Douglas Seale, on the other hand, found the inspiration for his production (SMT 1958) in the nineteenth-century Italy of Verdi and Rossini (*DT*, 27 Aug. 1958). The production was described as 'Shakespeare with a musical comedy air' (*WA*, 29 Aug. 1958), its prevailing mood a light romantic gaiety with a touch of melodrama (*MG*, 29 Aug. 1958). Women with elegant crinolines and parasols consorted with cheroot-smoking men, 'dashing and debonair' in tightly tailored Italian military uniforms or light suits and straw hats (*NC*, 27 Aug. 1958; pr. photos). Tanya Moiseiwitsch's graceful settings evoked the picturesqueness of nineteenth-century theatre, the main set (see illustration 12) varied by eight pictorial backcloths. The Italian context provided a social milieu in which the Hero–Claudio–Don John story seemed more than usually believable (*NC*, 27 Aug. 1958; *SQ* 9, 1958, 528; *ST*, 31 Aug. 1958). However, the operetta atmosphere weakened the play's astringency, involving a 'loss of hard vigour' (*WA*, 29 Aug. 1958). Some thought the choice of period at odds with the Renaissance bawdy (Kitchin, *Mid-Century Drama*, 88; Gielgud, *Actor*, 136).

Michael Redgrave played Benedick with something of the casual, 'lightly lascivious mien' of a Manet dandy (*NC*, 27 Aug. 1958). Googie Withers was a gracious, warm-hearted, radiant Beatrice (*SQ* 9, 1958, 37; *CET*, 27 Aug. 1958), despite a quick wit and 'dangerously mocking glint in her eye' (*St*, 28 Aug. 1958). She and Redgrave tended to settle for 'charming playfulness' rather than sharp repartee (*Star*, 27 Aug. 1958). Love kindled quickly

12 Tanya Moiseiwitsch's picturesque set for 1.1, Shakespeare Memorial Theatre, Stratford-upon-Avon, 1958.

between them (Speaight, *Shakespeare*, 254), and the play ended on an unequivocal note of romantic harmony (*SCN*, 29 Aug. 1958).

As often in the twentieth century, the production discovered fresh possibilities in some of the other roles. Richard Johnson played Don John as 'a stiff-legged psychopath' with 'a perpetual sneer' and an 'air of Byronic fatalism' (*Sp*, 5 Sep. 1958; *CET*, 27 Aug. 1958; *Tablet*, 15 July 1961). Cyril Luckham made Leonato 'an amiable dodderer', though not without dignity (*PP*, Oct. 1958, 15). The self-importance of Patrick Wymark's imposing Dogberry was qualified at moments with a touching 'note of doubt which cre[pt] into his voice as he enumerate[d] his own glories', so that he seemed both 'vulnerable and inviolable' (*SH*, 29 Aug. 1958). However, the watch episodes seemed not quite compatible with the 'romantic fantasy' of the rest (*MG*, 29 Aug. 1958).

At the Festival Theatre in Stratford, Ontario, 1958, Michael Langham, too, offered a predominantly romantic version of the play set in the nineteenth century in a style suggestive of operetta (*NYT*, 26 June 1958). Eileen Herlie's Beatrice was sharper tongued than Wynyard and Ashcroft, but still recognisably in the tradition of warm-hearted, affectionate 'womanliness' (*NYT*, 26 June 1958). Christopher Plummer played a 'crisp, witty' Benedick, vain, ironic, 'lucid down to the last subtle flicker of mood' (*ibid.*). In the later scenes their relationship flowered with a 'sincerity of feeling' which heightened the romantic ending (*SQ* 10, 1959, 81).

In 1961 a much reshaped version of Langham's production was staged at Stratford-upon-Avon, England, with a new cast except for Plummer's Benedick. The elegant Regency costumes, the leafy trellised set and autumnal lighting suggested traditional values and an air of comfortable romanticism; but much in the production contested this impression. Actions and manners were modernised in line with Peter Hall's policy that the newly formed Royal Shakespeare Company should speak directly to the twentieth century (*DT*, 5 Apr. 1961; *G*, 6 Apr. 1961; *SS* 20, 1967, 133–4). Unlike Langham's graceful Canadian production (*NYT*, 26 June 1958), this was fast-paced and restless, with much comic business tending towards farce (*SH*, 7 Apr. 1961; *SQ* 12, 1961, 430; *Punch*, 12 Apr. 1961). Democratising tendencies replaced the aristocratic tradition of most previous productions (*TW*, May 1961, 27): Leonato was now played with some irreverence as a 'bumbling' country squire 'unused to grandeur' (*Punch*, 12 Apr. 1961), and Beatrice as a 'pert modern miss' (*Tatler*, 10 May 1961). The dominant patterns of *Much Ado* production in the 1950s were crumbling, and a period of radical change and experiment was about to emerge as part of the cultural and ideological upheaval of the late twentieth century.

New directions

The gender revolution of the late twentieth century has profoundly influenced the performance and reception of *Much Ado*, foregrounding the play's gender issues and bringing radical changes to the representation of Beatrice. The patriarchal ideologies and conventions of gender relations assumed in most productions from the nineteenth to the mid-twentieth centuries were now strongly contested. Whereas Peggy Ashcroft and Diana Wynyard had played Beatrice according to stereotypes of 'essential' womanhood associated with graciousness, warmth, gentleness and the softer emotions, these assumptions were now challenged by actresses playing the role in a much more aggressive and dominating manner. Barbara Jefford (Old Vic, 1956) interpreted the part in fiercely aggressive style, as a bold assertion of woman's power to master man (*SQ* 8, 1957, 468; *Star*, 24 Oct. 1956; *T*, 24 Oct. 1956). The reviews indicate how disturbing this performance was to critics' preconceptions of a 'womanly' Beatrice who should be attractive to men. Katharine Hepburn (Stratford, Conn., 1957) acted Beatrice with a hard surface and tart, biting wit (*NYT*, 8 and 18 Aug. 1957). Maggie Smith (NT 1965) challenged traditional gender stereotypes with a fiery, independent Beatrice who taunted Benedick mercilessly (DM, 17 Feb. 1965; *Sp*, 26 Feb. 1965; *PP*, July 1967, 43). Geraldine McEwan's performance (RST, 1961) was pert, waspish at times, and a little hoydenish (*Punch*, 12 Apr. 1961; *T*, 5 Apr. 1961). One male reviewer called her a 'hen-pecking Beatrice' (*O*, 9 Apr. 1961); others wished nostalgically for the 'tenderness' and 'depth of feeling' of more traditional interpretations (*DE*, 5 Apr. 1961; *MA*, 10 Apr. 1961). Janet Suzman (RST 1968) played Beatrice as a 'bespectacled intellectual', tough and defiant on the surface, though vulnerable beneath (*PP*, Sep. 1969, 55; Suzman in Cook, *Women in Shakespeare*, 33). She was described as an 'emancipated Beatrice' (*WES*, 15 Oct. 1968) and 'an aggressive governess' (*SunTel*, 20 Oct. 1968). Male critics who had found Beatrice likeable when acted by Wynyard and Ashcroft, now had difficulty coming to terms with performances which contested so vigorously the conventional stereotypes of femininity.

Not all late twentieth-century Beatrices were as sharply aggressive as those described above. Some contested patriarchal values more subtly, often disclosing a measure of sensibility beneath their wit. Yet most have shown tendencies to assertion and dominance, often establishing a decided superiority over the Benedicks. The Seattle Repertory company (1978) went further, placing 'signal emphasis' upon the way each male in the masquerade sequence 'was bested in wit combat by the woman' (*SQ* 30, 1979, 263). The frequency of powerful, assertive Beatrices in late twentieth-century productions is a manifestation of the broader cultural tendency for women to perceive themselves as no longer subordinate or submissive. Some actresses have played the part with a blurring of gender distinctions reminiscent of the gender ambiguities of the role in the Renaissance theatre. Jane Casson (Stratford, Ontario, 1971) wore severe spectacles and a 'mannish' black jacket (*SQ* 22, 1971, 369). Susan Fleetwood (RSC 1990) showed herself no mean hand with a rapier. Janet McTeer's 'Amazonian' and physically dominating Beatrice (Queen's, 1993) 'strode the stage in complete control', swinging Benedick across her back and rolling him about in the masquerade (*O*, 11 July 1993; *SS* 47, 1994, 193; *ES*, 7 July 1994). Maggie Steed (RSC 1988) was described as 'a mocking parody of the [stereotypical] feminine arts' (*T*, 14 Apr. 1988), 'threaten[ing]' within the play 'the status quo of a male-controlled world' (*RA*, 5 May 1988).

In contrast with the light-hearted, romantic, harmonising tendencies of *Much Ado* performances in the first half of the century, productions from the 1960s on have frequently represented the play as a more problematic piece than formerly. Numerous late twentieth-century revivals have placed particular emphasis on the dark elements in the play, such as the mistreatment of Hero, the malevolence of Don John, Claudio's behaviour, the male solidarity at the broken wedding, and the gender inequities of a patriarchal society. Some productions have drawn special attention to the masks, equivocations, postures and deceptions in *Much Ado*, or to the sinister potential of the power play within it. The postmodern theatre has been much more conscious than before of tensions, contrarieties and dissonances in the play, and of unresolved elements in its conclusion, especially the problematic ending of the Claudio-Hero story. The announcement of Don John's capture, often omitted in the nineteenth century, has been foregrounded in several late twentieth-century performances as a jarring interruption to the final festivities; and several productions have isolated Don Pedro as a sad or bitter figure at the end. A few directors, on the other hand, have presented the play mainly as broad farce.

The late twentieth century has seen extensive experimentation with different periods and settings for *Much Ado*. While non-traditional settings have sometimes been used mainly for the sake of novelty, in many productions they have given new vitality to the play, defamiliarising it to make available fresh perspectives and insights. Some of the most illuminating settings have been used to establish a social context in which cultural attitudes, codes, conventions and ideologies relevant to the play may be made explicit and comprehensible to the audience. Zeffirelli's Sicilian setting (1965) and Barton's Indian Raj (1976) presented male-dominated societies in which the patriarchal conventions of the play were made readily accessible: the male code of honour, the double standard, the assumption of male superiority, the mistreatment of women, the disregard for their feelings, the importance placed on virginity. The positioning of the play in relation to the cultural and ideological norms of particular societies contrasts with the apolitical, universalising tendencies of most productions in the earlier part of the century. Whereas most directors from Bridges-Adams to the 1950s aimed mainly at aesthetically pleasing performances representing the play as a delightful entertainment, late twentieth-century productions have often been more politically engaged, in many cases inviting a critical view of the society defined in performance. The aristocratic and patriarchal tendencies of earlier staging traditions have been subjected to particular challenge. Whatever the period represented in production, most late twentieth-century performers have tended to contemporise manners and speech intonations to some degree in the interest of audience appeal.

The period has produced a variety of interpretations of characters other than Beatrice and Benedick. Claudio has most frequently been represented as young, inexperienced, vulnerable and impetuous, deeply pained by Hero's supposed betrayal; but he has also been viewed, less sympathetically, as shallow, arrogant or heartless. Don Pedro has been presented variously as an urbane prince, a genial companion, or an authoritative presence. He has also been played as an ambiguous figure, jovial on the surface but remote or melancholic underneath. His manipulations of others have not always been seen as benevolent. Occasionally he has been shown as shallow or unfeeling. The late twentieth-century critique of patriarchy has often made Leonato a less venerable figure than formerly. In some productions the urbane host has been qualified by elements of the flustered or slightly ludicrous old man. Don John, traditionally acted as an aloof malcontent or Mephistophelian villain, has been played with greater depth as a jealous or melancholic psychopath, sometimes with a physical disability or a compulsive twitch or stammer. The late twentieth-century interest in power relations in the play has tended to give him fresh prominence. Dogberry, too, has sometimes been played from new perspectives: George Raistrick (RSC 1990) represented him not as the usual yokel, but as a *petit bourgeois*, 'florid and rotund but with aspirations to be fashionable', checking his appearance in Leonato's mirror and registering a 'wistful sense of achievement in his possession of two gowns' (*SQ* 42, 1991, 346). The minor roles have also at times been played with fresh insight.

From Zeffirelli to Barton (1965–1976)

Zeffirelli's production (NT 1965–7; BBC-TV, 1967) exploded with the hedonistic, liberated energies of the sixties. The dominant note was carnivalesque – exuberant, flamboyant, full of anarchic vitality. The production evoked the atmosphere of small-town Sicily about 1900, with its hot blood, passion and *joie de vivre* (*DT*, 17 Feb. 1965; *DM*, 19 Feb. 1965). The performance was a-dazzle with the verve of village fiesta (*TW*, Mar. 1965, 13), the stage, framed with festoon lights like a fun-fair, pulsating with colour (pr. photos; *YP*, 17 Feb. 1965). The costumes were designed after the gaudy sugar dolls of Sicilian folk art (programme). There were shawled women with thick black wigs and gigantic hats, Mafia-looking men with lacquered hair and curling moustaches, soldiers in crimson, blue and yellow, strutting 'with tight-fitting scorn and conceit' (*Sc*, 22 Feb. 1965), a town band, and frock-coated local dignitaries (*T*, 14, 17 Feb. 1965; *NEP*, 30 Mar. 1965; *L*, 4 Mar. 1965; *Tatler*, 10 Mar. 1965). The watch were portrayed as the local *carabinieri* (*Drama*, Summer 1965, 16). Farce and burlesque dominated the comic scenes (*FT*, 17 Feb. 1965; *SQ* 16, 1965, 314), colouring at times other episodes as well (*G*, 17 Feb. 1965). The darker moments called forth 'passion and intensity' (*Encore*, Mar.–Apr. 1965, 40), the Sicilian setting making immediate sense of the slur on Hero's virginity, the insulted male honours, and the demands for vengeance. However, there were elements of burlesque in the opening moments of the church scene (see commentary), where a comic tableau of St Sebastian full of arrows hung above the altar (*FT*, 22 Mar. 1967). The 'merry war' was fought with 'mercurial zest', Robert Stephens an extroverted Benedick and Maggie Smith a fiery Beatrice with 'a throw-away modern manner' (*LDP*, 17 Feb. 1965; *DM*, 17 Feb. 1965; *ILN*, 27 Feb. 1965). The small-town atmosphere shifted the characters down the social scale, the governor of Messina becoming a provincial mayor (*FT*, 22 Mar. 1967), and Don Pedro a strutting, cigar-puffing 'parody of a Latin American dictator' (*T*, 17 Feb. 1965; *Sc*, 22 Feb. 1965). Some players adopted Italian accents and the jerky, marionette-like movements of the popular Sicilian theatre (*Ind*, 28 Feb. 1965; *BP*, 27 Feb. 1965). 'Statues' became animate. The text was modernised in over three hundred places. The production sparked both enthusiasm and disapproval, fuelling a controversy in which the central issue was really how much creative freedom a society can tolerate in the performance of its cultural texts. If each production is to some extent a re-appropriation of the play, how radical a reworking will the public and the critics accept? The issue would be tested repeatedly in the late twentieth century.

Joseph Papp and A. J. Antoon's New York Shakespeare Festival production of *Much Ado* was also popular and contentious (Delacorte Theatre, Central Park, 1972; Winter Garden Theatre, 1972–3; CBS-TV, 1973). Antoon located the play in small-town America about 1910. The production style veered between farce and the sugary romantic, the darker passages passed over lightly (*NYP*, 13 Nov. 1972; *NYT*, 18 Aug. 1972; *DN*, NY, 13

Nov. 1972). Ming Cho Lee's double-balconied set featured a collage of period posters, photographs, and other Americana (Loney, *Staging Shakespeare*, slide 20). Aspects of the play were adapted to the period and setting: Beatrice and Benedick were sentimentalised as 'a confused young couple ... madly in love with each other' (*NYT*, 13 Nov. 1972), their interchanges spoken as 'Yankee sass' (*NR*, 9 Sep. 1972); Beatrice asserted her independence by sharing a cigarette with nervous girlfriends (Halio, *Shakespeare's Plays*, 26–7); the Messenger was transformed into a press reporter photographing the ladies with a sodium flare (*NYM*, 4 Sep. 1972); the men returned from campaigning in Rough Rider uniforms (*HR* 26, 1973, 337); the watch, played in the manner of Keystone Kops, arrived in a huffing veteran car (*NYT*, 27 Aug. 1972; *HR* 26, 1973, 337); Borachio and Conrade were dressed like Chicago gangsters (*NYT*, 18 Aug. 1972); in the finale the ladies entered on carousel horses (*NYM*, 4 Sep. 1972); and a six-piece band accompanied the action with period tunes (*NYT*, 18 Aug. 1972). Some critics acclaimed this version as a realisation of Papp's goal of making the classics accessible to a broad American public (e.g. *NYT*, 2 Feb. 1973; Halio, *Shakespeare's Plays*, 26). Others disagreed, arguing that the setting competed with the play rather than illuminating it, that the production style was inconsistent with the play's wit and verbal sophistication (especially the Renaissance sex jokes), and that setting and atmosphere were too comfortable to accommodate the play's darker elements (e.g. Coursen, *Shakespearean Performance*, 183, 185; *NYM*, 4 Sep. 1972; *NR*, 10 Feb. 1973; *NYT*, 14 Jan. 1973; *HR* 26, 1973, 337).

In contrast with these productions, Trevor Nunn's *Much Ado* (RSC 1968–9) projected a view of the play more complex, ambivalent and disturbing than most previous revivals. The production suggested to one reviewer an atmosphere of 'sombre and often sinister grandeur, a world of spies and peepers' (*Sp*, 25 Oct. 1968); another received the feeling that '*Much Ado* is an unpleasant play' (*L*, 31 Oct. 1968). Nunn took as his focal point the dark side of the Hero–Claudio–Don John story (*SH*, 17 Oct. 1968). Hero's suffering at the broken wedding was 'the penetrating point of the evening', 'the play's dark centre', towards which the production built (*ST*, 20 Oct. 1968; *Sp*, 25 Oct. 1968).

The acting area was enclosed in a severe rectangular box of translucent gauze screens dimly lit from behind to suggest interiors, moonlight, or the dappled green of an orchard, the vault-like effect darkening the mood of the play (*Sp*, 25 Oct. 1968; *O*, 20 Oct. 1968; *SH*, 17 Oct. 1968). Though the costumes included some bright colours, there were also shadowy olives and russets, and the dark mottled patterns resembling the camouflage on military uniforms reinforced the sombre stage ambience (*LSC*, 21 Oct. 1968; *CET*,

15 Oct. 1968; *GH*, 22 Oct. 1968), hinting at a harsh military world on the fringes of the action, and becoming a visual emblem of the dissembling and duplicity in the play. These effects were brought together in an ominous masquerade sequence 'in mottled scarlet, all dancing torches and leering silver visors' (*O*, 20 Oct. 1968), the sinister atmosphere intensified by a sword dance performed by sixteen weapon-clashing duellists in threatening masks with long, beak-like noses (pr. photo; *Punch*, 23 Oct. 1968).

Pervasive tensions and contrarieties made the production even more disturbing. In the dark ambience of this version, the youth of the central figures made them doubly vulnerable. Hero was portrayed as a shy young girl, perhaps fifteen, 'bursting with adolescent starry-eyed excitement' (*L*, 31 Oct. 1968; *FT*, 15 Oct. 1968; *LSC*, 21 Oct. 1968), an interpretation which made Don John's accusation seem more preposterous and malicious than ever (*BP*, 15 Oct. 1968). Despite the Elizabethan costumes, Janet Suzman and Alan Howard played Beatrice and Benedick as slightly eccentric young people of the 1960s, she emancipated, he with 'a fanciful touch of the zany' (*G*, 30 July 1969), their boisterous, energetic performances hinting mutual attraction even as the characters disparaged love with 'adolescent cynicism' (*SH*, 17 Oct. 1968; *ES*, 15 Oct. 1968; *SunTel*, 20 Oct. 1968). Sexuality was prominent, both in its positive energies and dark potential: Margaret was played 'with an erotic fire' which made it easy to imagine her nocturnal encounter with Borachio (*T*, 9 Aug. 1969). There were further ambiguities in the representation of Claudio and Don Pedro. Claudio was a 'pettish adolescent', 'lyrically idealistic', but also 'the calculating poseur' (*NS*, 25 Oct. 1968; *LSC*, 21 Oct. 1968; *EJ*, 16 Oct. 1968); Don Pedro 'grave, benevolent, attentive', with a disturbing 'undercurrent of malignity' (*Sp*, 25 Oct. 1968). In this production comedy and the sinister were continually in tension. Nunn's own attitude was ambivalent: in one interview he said, 'I have yet to see the play done with sufficient seriousness; "Kill Claudio" is for real' (Berry, *Directing Shakespeare*, 78); in another he spoke of the need to make contact with the audience 'through JOY, ENERGY and AFFIRMATION' (*DM*, 16 Oct. 1968). The comic energies managed in the end to push through the darkness, but only just, and were qualified even in the final moments as Don Pedro, isolated from the rest, drew on his gauntlets as if to return to armed conflict (Mason, *Much Ado*, 60).

Ronald Eyre's 1971 RSC production, on the other hand, was mainly sunny and light-hearted. The play was set in the early nineteenth century, the characters amusing themselves in aristocratic pastimes on a brightly lit stage framed at the rear within the curve of a pale-green conservatory dome. The play was rendered in a mode of game-like artifice, the darker elements lightly glossed over. Elizabeth Spriggs and Derek Godfrey played Beatrice and

Benedick as a couple inclining towards middle age, their banter good-humoured and mellow rather than sparkling. Spriggs was a cheerful, matronly Beatrice who had resigned herself to spinsterhood but unexpectedly discovered the happiness of love; Godfrey a smugly swaggering old campaigner with a knowing, man-of-the-world air. Claudio was played as a shallow, tempestuous adolescent, the companion of a prankish and rather frivolous Don Pedro.

James Edmondson's Oregon Shakespeare Festival production of 1976 used sumptuous Renaissance costumes and visual display to critique a society seen to place 'greater value on the manners, formalities and ceremonies of relationships than on their human essence' (*SQ* 28, 1977, 247).

The indictment of a flawed society was also central to John Barton's memorable RSC production of 1976–7. The play was set in late nineteenth-century imperial India, the stage enclosed with a double tier of timber balconies draped with awnings and muslin curtains to suggest a garrison town under the British Raj (pr. photos; *SQ* 28, 1977, 73). The social milieu created in this production realised the events and relationships in the play with surprising aptness. Here was a mingling of military and civilian worlds, an artificial society with amusements and intrigues appropriate to a comedy 'full of game-playing and disguises' (programme). In an atmosphere of 'colonial torpor', officers lounged in wicker chairs waited upon by turbaned servants, or amused themselves with charades and amateur theatricals, sports and practical jokes (*G*, 1 July 1977; pbk; pr. photos). For them 'everything [was] a game: cricket, shooting the wild life, framing an innocent girl' (*Ind*, 9 Apr. 1976) – all done with heartless irresponsibility (*FT*, 9 Apr. 1976).

The context focused the play's gender issues with particular clarity. In this society, with its male solidarity and code of honour, its Victorian morality, and patronising, often cynical attitudes to women, men were dominant, women marginalised to the household. The mistreatment of women was foregrounded starkly, Hero shown as a pawn in a male conspiracy, the plot against her hatched as Borachio 'goes in for his innings' (*T*, 1 July 1977). Claudio and Don Pedro were 'as coldly frivolous after the interrupted wedding as before it' (*FT*, 9 Apr. 1976). Judi Dench as Beatrice made a strong feminist point by taking as the key to her performance the allusion (2.1.209–13) to a previous encounter when Benedick had won her heart 'with false dice' (Dench, in Cook, *Women in Shakespeare*, 33). The pain of this experience showed in her hardness towards men, and became an emblem of the mistreatment of women generally.

Sinden played Benedick as 'an old soldier growing grisled in his bachelor-dom' (*DM*, 1 July 1977), an arrogant, choleric extrovert (*YP*, 10 Apr. 1976; *OT*, 16 Apr. 1976). 'To see [him] languidly stretched out in a wicker chair

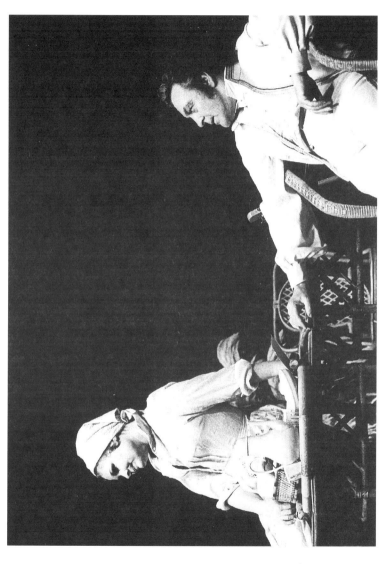

13 'Too wise to woo peaceably' (5.2): Judi Dench (Beatrice) and Donald Sinden (Benedick), Royal Shakespeare Theatre, Stratford-upon-Avon, 1976.

musing about the necessary virtues of a future wife [was] to see the high noon of male chauvinism' (*EN*, 9 Apr. 1976). Dench reacted to this egotism with 'abrasive distaste' (*ibid.*). Like Elizabeth Spriggs in 1971, she represented Beatrice as pushing towards middle age. With hair coiled old-maidishly on top, she had 'the mournful look of a lifelong spinster' (*DM*, 1 July 1977; pr. photos), her disdain stemming from a previously starved emotional life. At vulnerable moments she would turn a point of wit 'to expose, just for a second, a depth of sadness that ma[de] a theatre full of people hold their breath' (*Sunday Mercury*, 11 Apr. 1976). She and Sinden suggested from the start the history of 'a spiky, resentful relationship' (*PP*, June 1976, 21), swapping insults 'with a sort of desiccated desperation' (*DM*, 9 Apr. 1976), their witticisms both 'a self-defence and a cover-up' (*ST*, 3 July 1977). Yet beneath the front of cynicism was 'an undertow of reluctant affection' (*Sp*, 17 Apr. 1976). In the end Dench seized the opportunity for love 'with an awestruck rapture' (*NS*, 16 Apr. 1976), and Sinden developed a seriousness indicative of 'the huge moral gap between Benedick and his frivolous comrades' (*T*, 1 July 1977).

Dogberry was represented as an Indian sergeant proud of his accomplishments in English, but with less command of the language than he thinks (*O*, 11 Apr. 1976; *NS*, 16 Apr. 1976) – a conception which might not have passed muster a decade or so later. The watch were a ragged band of turbaned frontiersmen. Dogberry related to the British with a delightful blend of obsequiousness and mockery, his 'splay-fingered salute becom[ing] a snook when he turn[ed] his head' (*FT*, 9 Apr. 1976). The production succeeded in maintaining a satisfying balance between the serious and comic in *Much Ado*, and was noted for the subtlety, depth and complexity of its interpretation.

Variant settings

Directors in the late twentieth century have shown considerable ingenuity in devising variant settings for the play. Sicilian locations have been popular since Zeffirelli; Italian, Spanish or other Mediterranean settings have also been used. American directors have attempted to make the play more accessible to their audiences by settings in Spanish colonial America, Latin America or the United States. Latin American settings have also been used in some European productions (Prospect Theatre Company, UK, 1970; Nederlands Toneel Gent, Belgium, 1983). Since the late 1950s the play has been set in every century from the Renaissance on, the nineteenth being the most frequent choice, followed by the early twentieth. Since Barton's Indian Raj, at least two other directors have located the play in outposts of the British Empire (National SF, San Diego, 1981; Open Air Theatre, Regents

Park, London, 1981). It has also been set in the Netherlands of Vermeer (American Conservatory Theatre, San Francisco, 1980) and even in an exotic Arabian Nights context (Alabama SF, 1981). In 1985 the Folger Theatre, Washington, located the play on a Mediterranean cruise ship, the *SS Messina*, crewed by the watch; Don John, a Mafia-type villain, was arrested at the end by an 'unlisted' passenger who turned out to be an FBI agent (*SQ* 36, 1985, 465; Halio, *Shakespeare's Plays*, 27–8).

John Bell's production at the Nimrod Theatre, Sydney (1975, 1977) evoked the atmosphere of Sicilian carnival in a circus-ring setting which also foregrounded the pervasive theatricality in the play. The theme of equivocal appearance was highlighted by clowns in tragicomic masks who later transformed themselves, appropriately, into Dogberry and the watch (*SQ* 29, 1978, 288).

Terence Knapp's Tokyo production of 1979 demonstrated the successful adaptation of the play to another culture. The production, which included both western and Japanese elements, was set at a significant meeting point of the two cultures, the Meiji era of the late nineteenth century, when the emperor was encouraging western cultural influence in his country. Don Pedro was represented as having just quelled an insurrection of anti-Meiji traditionalists. The set was Japanese, based on Meiji woodblock prints, but the costumes were a cultural mix, with younger characters in western clothes and the older ones in kimonos. Period music with a blend of cultural styles was played on both Japanese and western instruments. The characters received Japanese names. Dogberry became a traditional Japanese comic figure. The Japanese sense of *bushido* or honour made Beatrice's 'Kill Claudio' entirely credible. The finale took the form of the *o-bon*, a national folk celebration, at the end of which Don Pedro was left alone on stage, a solitary and wistful figure (*SQ* 32, 1981, 365–7; Leiter, *Shakespeare*, 513–4).

The eighties and nineties

The RSC launched *Much Ado* into the eighties with a touring production by Howard Davies (1980) foregrounding the play's darker, problematic elements. The setting seemed like 'a hideaway for hill bandits', with riding gear, boots, ropes and guns completing an image of a brutal masculine world. Don John's malevolence, 'a palpable force' in this production, was partly motivated by the malice of his half-brother, represented as 'vain, authoritarian and spiteful'. A sardonic Benedick and a 'contemptuous and shrewish' Beatrice gained in 'dignity, purpose and self-respect', however, as they discovered love. Don Pedro was pointedly excluded from the closing reconciliations (*PP*, Feb. 1980, 21; Leiter, *Shakespeare*, 515).

Terry Hands's RSC production of 1982, on the other hand, was a stylish, visually dazzling performance of 'great lyric beauty', 'an unashamedly romantic version of the play' (*CL*, 13 May 1982) recalling in some ways the productions in the Bridges-Adams/Gielgud tradition, though more questioning and ambiguous, more theme-conscious, and more aware of contrariety. The set was a shimmering combination of black mirror floor and transparent perspex screens reflecting gold and bronze, backed by two delicately stylised images of leafless trees silhouetted against the cyclorama (pr. photos, pbk). Cavalier costumes suggested an aristocratic world of 'sophisticated courtliness' (*DT*, 21 Apr, 10 May 1982). The mounting emphasised the artifice of the play and of the society represented in it (*DM*, 22 Apr. 1982), suggesting 'a narcissistic world obsessed with surface appearances' (*SunTel*, 25 Apr. 1982), the characters repeatedly looking at themselves in the reflective surfaces (*SH*, 30 Apr. 1982). The multiple reflections highlighted the ambiguities, illusions and equivocations in a play where dissembling is pervasive. The visual effect also had 'a magical, other-worldly quality' (*ES*, 14 May 1983), an element of abstraction which tended, despite the period costumes, to deprive the action of the social specificity and detail evident in Barton's production (*TLS*, 7 May 1982; *G*, 21 Apr. 1982). The sexual polarities of the play were indicated well enough, 'the soldiers' masculine friendships ... set sharply against the very different emotions of the women' (*SQ* 34, 1983, 84); but the cruelties and injustices of a patriarchal society were less disturbingly confronted than in some other late twentieth-century performances (Leiter, *Shakespeare*, 499, 519).

Sinead Cusack's Beatrice showed ambiguities arising from a conflict of gender attitudes between the actress and her male director. 'When Terry Hands cast me as Beatrice', she reported, 'what he saw in me was femininity – that's what he cast, that's what he used in his direction of me. But ... I showed him other areas of the character. A Beatrice who is very angry. A woman who has been damaged by society' (Cusack, in Rutter, *Clamorous Voices*, xvi). Both perspectives were evident in her performance. On the one hand she was described as 'a more feminine Beatrice than most in recent years' (*Sp*, 28 May 1983), warm-hearted and inclined 'to simplify the part in the direction of emotional plangency' (*TLS*, 7 May 1982; *Sc*, 23 Apr. 1982). On the other hand she showed a 'frustration of spirit and inner agitation' as if she 'had once been hurt and was frightened of repeating the experience' (*ibid.*). After the broken wedding she unleashed her outrage against men in a torrent of passion (*DM*, 22 Apr. 1982). 'When she says ... "I'd eat his heart in the market place"', wrote Michael Billington, 'you'd better believe it' (*G*, 21 Apr. 1982). Yet she also seemed to be searching for love (*NS*, 7 May 1982), and showed a 'luminous softness' after discovering it (*CitL*, 20 May 1983).

14 Beatrice in formidable vein: Sinead Cusack (Beatrice) and Derek Jacobi (Benedick),
Royal Shakespeare Theatre, Stratford-upon-Avon, 1982.

Derek Jacobi acted Benedick initially as 'a skittish, larky, life-and-soul-of-
the-party bachelor', growing in depth as the play progressed (*G*, 21 Apr.
1982). Claudio (Robert O'Mahoney) was a romantic egotist, passionate and
impetuous (*ThJ*, May 1983, 260; *CE*, 22 Oct. 1982). Derek Godfrey made
Don Pedro a figure of authority, with a disturbing touch of cynicism. At first
he looked 'potentially more sinister' than his 'smooth-faced' brother (*TLS*, 7
May 1982); 'at the end, celibate and alone, he [was] as much an outcast as
Jacques or Malvolio' (*O*, 25 Apr. 1982; *Sc*, 23 Apr. 1982; *T*, 21 Apr. 1982).
The traditionally 'expected male–female couplings of the festive ending'
were further disrupted by 'combinations of men with men and women with
women' in the final dance, 'male–female couplings' proving 'only a minor
part of the spectrum' (Carlson, *Women and Comedy*, 64). However, the
closing moments were unambiguously romantic, Beatrice and Benedick
'dancing slowly together on a softly lit, petal-strewn stage', 'still miming
their animated talk', then holding a kiss as a 'huge orange sun' descended
behind the perspex screens (*ThJ*, May 1983, 261; *TLS*, 7 May 1982; *T*, 21
Apr. 1982), business which Emrys Jones thought too sweet and simple for the
preceding play (*TLS*, 7 May 1982).

The productions of John Neville (Stratford, Ontario, 1987) and Di Trevis

(RSC 1988) presented sharply angled ideological and social critiques with strong feminist perspectives. Neville's production, set in an English mansion in the late nineteenth century, censured the aristocratic and patriarchal values of the society represented. While Hero and Claudio were thoroughly conditioned by the social and gender norms about them, Beatrice was represented as 'an independent-minded, *fin-de-siècle* feminist, straining against the confines of her male-dominated society' (*SQ* 39, 1988, 226–7).

Trevis's production offered a scathing critique of modern affluence from a materialist–feminist perspective. The play opened with the characters sunbathing on a terrace of Leonato's mansion, which seemed 'a haven of privilege ... cocooned from the real world of struggle beyond its confines' (*SQ* 40, 1989, 84). Suddenly a helicopter was heard overhead, a wounded soldier was lowered to the stage, and Don Pedro and his soldiers entered in battle dress, exposing the leisured complacence of the civilians. The production, complete with fashion-plate fifties costumes and a grand society wedding, revealed the characters' way of life as shallow, ostentatious and selfish. Don John, marginalised in this society, was treated not unsympathetically.

The production's gender attitudes were boldly iconoclastic. Beatrice was represented as a brassy, domineering woman (*TES*, 29 Apr. 1988); Benedick was reduced to a balding, ineffective, slightly ridiculous little man (*SQ* 40, 1989, 85). The mistreatment of Hero was strongly emphasised. Claudio, played as 'a smug little sycophant', was more than usually unlikeable (*TES*, 29 Apr. 1988); and at the broken wedding Leonato turned violently on his speechless daughter. 'Here', wrote Nicholas Shrimpton, 'is the patriarchy, as a conspiracy of husbands and fathers, in full, unquestioning cry' (*ibid.*). The marriage festivities at the end were chillingly inauspicious, with Hero and Beatrice dressed in black, and black petals or confetti floating to the stage (*SQ* 40, 1989, 84). Trevis evidently shared the viewpoint of those feminist critics who have questioned whether marriage in Shakespearean comedy signifies a happy ending (e.g. Belsey, 'Disrupting sexual difference', 190).

Most critics anatomised the production, scandalised, one suspects, at the appropriation of the play with such polemical intent. Shrimpton argued that it was 'a very partial reading of the play' (*TES*, 29 Apr. 1988). 'With nearly all of the text there', commented Robert Smallwood, 'it is difficult to go on disliking the whole of Messina's high society as much as the production seems to want us to' (*SQ* 40, 1989, 84).

The Renaissance Theatre Company production of 1988, directed by Judi Dench, offered a simpler, less problematic interpretation of *Much Ado* than some late twentieth-century performances. In contrast with Trevis's production, which was not particularly interested in the psychological and emotional development of the characters, this revival was firmly centred in human values and relationships (*SS* 42, 1989, 134), though some thought it too blandly traditional (e.g. *FT*, 12 May 1989). The staging created a sense of sunshine, with actors in cream and white Regency costumes against a back-cloth of a white Italian loggia (*CitL*, 1 Sep. 1988; *G*, 27 Aug. 1988; *O*, 8 May 1988; *SS* 42, 1989, 131). The 'merry war' was 'conducted with the freshness and ... good humour of youth', with an underlying flirtatiousness close to the surface (*DT*, 27 Aug. 1988). Samantha Bond played a mischievous, spirited Beatrice, brimming with indignant wit (*What's On*, 7 Sep. 1988; *Ind*, 31 Aug. 1988; *O*, 8 May 1988), but betraying 'an inwardness of pain' at the line 'once before he won it of me with false dice' (*SS* 42, 1989, 131). Kenneth Branagh acted Benedick with an 'infectious flash and swagger' (*Ind*, 31 Aug. 1988), roguish, quick-tempered, and full of bluster (*CitL*, 1 Sep. 1988; *O*, 8 May 1988; *DE*, 28 Aug. 1988), making Benedick's conflict between love and friendship 'more than usually prominent' (*SS* 42, 1989, 133). The production, like Branagh's subsequent film of *Much Ado*, was praised for its 'extra-ordinary' success in turning Shakespeare into popular entertainment (*Ind*, 31 Aug. 1988).

Gerald Freedman (NYSF 1988) staged a broad, vigorous production focusing on the Beatrice–Benedick comedy at the expense of the rest (*Village Voice*, NY, 26 July 1988). In Central Park 'you've got to energise what you're doing to hold the audience', Freedman said (*NYT*, 10 July 1988). Kevin Kline played an ebullient Benedick, Blythe Danner a shrewish, spinsterish Beatrice with a 'hard edge of bitterness' (*NYr*, 1 Aug. 1988). The Regency costumes and picturebook village setting seemed out of character, however, with the production style (*NR*, 22 Aug. 1988).

Elijah Moshinsky (Strand, 1989) directed the play largely as contemporary farce, again with the main emphasis on the Beatrice–Benedick comedy. The play began with the actors eating spaghetti, surrounded by kitchen furniture in primary colours on a tilted floor against a bright blue cyclorama (*O*, 14 May 1989). Felicity Kendal played a 'sharp and schoolmarmish' Beatrice (*Punch*, 26 May 1989); Alan Bates's Benedick gave the impression of a middle-aged rake 'disillusioned with love' (*ES*, 12 May 1989). Their discovery of affection came as a surprise to both (*JC*, 19 May 1989).

Bill Alexander's production (RSC 1990–1) was more complex and exploratory, especially in its treatment of gender issues. Costumed in Elizabethan styles, the performance established a social milieu in which men regarded women as less important than male bonding and male-dominated social hierarchies (*SS* 44, 1991, 171). Yet in a striking reversal of traditional gender stereotypes, the production represented Beatrice as usurping aspects of masculine identity in a manner that seemed subversive in a male-oriented society. Susan Fleetwood as Beatrice entered at the beginning brandishing a rapier, engaged her uncle in a fencing bout and beat him comfortably, 'crowing with delight' as she lunged beneath his guard (*Ind*, 15 Apr. 1990; *SS* 44, 1991, 170). This business anticipated the verbal fencing in the play and established Beatrice as a woman not bound by conventional notions of femininity. It also gave ironic point to her mocking reference to Benedick as 'Signor Mountanto' (an upward thrust in fencing), a gibe at his masculinity with double reference to swordsmanship and sexual prowess. Fleetwood's representation of Beatrice affirmed a concept of womanhood altogether more complex and powerful than the traditional stereotypes of softness, gentleness and passivity. Her Beatrice was robust, competitive, formidable (*T*, 12 Apr. 1990). In her first interchange with Benedick she patrolled the stage flexing her rapier as she flashed sallies at him, flinging down her gauntlet in defiance as a prelude to the 'merry war'. In the game of wit this Beatrice was always dominant, with a much sharper intellect than Benedick (*Ind*, 15 Apr. 1990; *SQ* 42, 1991, 346). Yet unlike some of the fiercer Beatrices of the late twentieth century, she also showed a more than usual emotional depth (*SQ* 42, 1991, 347; *SH*, 20 Apr. 1990). Her interest in Benedick was never really in doubt (*DT*, 12 Apr. 1990); her anguish at the broken wedding intense, and 'her rage at her cousin's betrayal ... furious and frightening' (*FT*, 12 Apr. 1990). Yet her agonised 'Oh that I were a man!' was also a frustrated recognition of women's limitations in a patriarchal society, ironic after the fencing and challenge business in the opening acts. It was indicative of the broad shift in gender attitudes since the 1960s that whereas at that time male critics had mostly reacted unfavourably to the new wave of assertive and dominant Beatrices, Fleetwood's performance was now generally admired.

The social codes of a patriarchal society were otherwise well defined in the production, the men and women, for example, polarising into separate groups at the first Beatrice–Benedick interchange (pbk). An ambivalence in the representation of Hero underlined the inhibiting constraints conventionally placed on women: she was 'high-spirited' with her female attendants, but 'submissive and timorous ... in the public scenes' (*TLS*, 20 Apr. 1990).

Roger Allam represented Benedick at the beginning as a 'clubbable, raffish, vapid, eternal-bachelor stereotype' (*SQ* 42, 1991, 347); Don Pedro was played as 'an ageing Cavalier shrouded in solitude and hungry for emotional contact' (*G*, 12 Apr. 1990). Dogberry was represented as a Puritan to balance Don Pedro's Cavaliers (*PI*, June 1990). The ambiguities of the production were sustained to the end, Benedick's unabated hostility to Claudio cutting across the final reconciliations (*SS* 44, 1991, 171).

Subtlety of characterisation was also a feature of Michael Kahn's production at The Shakespeare Theatre, Washington, 1992. Kelly McGillis and

David Selby represented Beatrice and Benedick as 'sensitive and insecure characters hiding behind carefree facades'. Beatrice's 'witty high spirits' seemed to be covering 'some deeply rooted inner sadness'; Benedick's misogamy seemed 'largely a defence against the fear that no woman would ever wish to marry him'. Their sensitivity made the tenderness and depth of their ultimate affection believable and poignant. In a 'harrowing' broken wedding, Claudio's denunciation of Hero 'seemed to stem more from his deeply felt hurt than from self-righteousness' (*SQ* 43, 1992, 460–2).

The production directed by Matthew Warchus at the Queen's Theatre, London, 1993, balanced comedy with an emphasis on the themes of deception and false appearance (*G*, 8 July 1993). The marquee-like set drew attention to the artifice of the play and its pervasive theatricality. At the beginning eavesdroppers were silhouetted upstage and a blind Cupid presided over the action (*T*, 8 July 1993; *What's On*, 14 July 1993). Benedick arrived from the wars with head swathed in a blood-stained bandage, which he removed when the civilians were out of sight to reveal no trace of a wound (*G*, 8 July 1993). The surface impression of youthful exhilaration was undermined at various points by hints of the sinister, Don Pedro and Don John being linked as 'self-imprisoned egoists who get their kicks manipulating the relationships of others' (*Ind*, 11 July 1993). Much of the comedy came from the incongruities between Benedick and Beatrice. Mark Rylance portrayed Benedick as an awkward little Ulsterman 'hid[ing] his sensitivities behind the mask of a touchy curmudgeon', nervous, insecure, secretly petrified of women (*T*, 8 July 1993; *Ind*, 8 July 1993; *Mail on Sunday*, 11 July 1993; *What's On*, 14 July 1993). Janet McTeer's physically dominating Beatrice, on the other hand, 'strode the stage in complete control', spitting witticisms like a fury (*FT*, 9 July 1993; *O*, 11 July 1993; *SS* 47, 1994, 193; *DM*, 7 July 1993). At moments she signalled 'in little flashes of private anxiety' that she was less than comfortable with this image (*Ind*, 8 July 1993), however, an attitude which prepared the audience for her acceptance of love. The fact that most reviewers enjoyed her performance again indicated a shift in gender attitudes since the 1960s, when most critics had seemed nostalgic for the 'femininity' of an earlier tradition.

Film and television versions

The most successful Shakespearean films have typically involved a good deal of creative adaptation to bridge the differences between the conventions of Renaissance drama and the film medium. Apart from televised stage productions and documentaries featuring selected scenes, the film and television versions of *Much Ado* include a silent Hollywood adaptation (1926), two

Russian films (1956 and 1973), a 1958 American television production (Beatrice: Nina Foch; Benedick: Robert Norton), an East German film (1963), the 1984 BBC/Time–Life television production, and the 1993 Kenneth Branagh film (see Rothwell and Melzer, *Shakespeare on Screen*, 203–7). The two most recent of these versions are reviewed below.

The 1984 BBC/Time–Life production was constrained by the conservative expectations of its corporate sponsors. Their demand for 'authentic' Shakespeare meant Renaissance settings and costumes, unobtrusive camera work, minimal cuts, and little scope for creative interpretation. Such expectations, along with budgetary constraints allowing only a month's rehearsal and six days of filming, were a recipe for bland, unadventurous work. The dominant style of the production was formal and courtly, the palace settings and lavish costumes evoking an atmosphere of opulent grandeur. Heavy-looking sets and a series of slow-moving tableau-like sequences early in the production seemed inimical to comic vitality. Robert Lindsay's Benedick was inclined towards the caustic and severe. Cherie Lunghi played a quick-witted Beatrice, pleasant-spirited despite a hard edge of disdain, but scarcely merry. The broken wedding was played with conviction, and Michael Elphick's Dogberry brought a refreshing drollery to the watch scenes. But the camera work too often failed to resolve problems of overcrowding and restricted movement which were especially apparent on the small television screen.

Branagh's film, on the other hand, took full creative advantage of the visual possibilities of the medium. The film, shot on location at a villa in Tuscany, showed spectacular wide-angle panoramas of the house and surrounding countryside in various lights, including a dazzling evening thunderstorm. Branagh used the Italian setting to create a believable social context for the Hero–Claudio–Don John story and the hot-blooded emotions prominent in the film. Shooting on location supported a naturalistic approach to character and dialogue consistent with the dominant naturalism of cinematic convention, though somewhat at odds with the artifice of Shakespeare's play. However, the naturalism was balanced to some degree by camera work and editing which foregrounded the technical artifice of the film medium, including slow-motion footage of galloping horsemen, spectacular mood shots and overhead shots. Emotions were emphasised by frequent close-ups and by creative backlighting, dissolve and montage effects. Arresting cuts between sequences at times intensified contrasts and ironic juxtapositions.

The play's gender issues were foregrounded prominently. The song 'Sigh no more, ladies … / Men were deceivers ever' (2.3.53–68) became the keynote of the film, read wistfully at the beginning by Emma Thompson as

Beatrice, sung elegiacally in the garden, and repeated triumphantly at the finale. The 'fraud of men' (2.3.63) was underscored in the Hero–Claudio–Don John story; but the advice to 'sigh not so, but let them go' (2.3.57) was ironically countered by the film's powerful emphasis on the sexuality that impels women and men together. Emma Thompson as Beatrice seemed representative of twentieth-century feminism in its mature phase: not edgily assertive, like some Beatrices in the early years of the movement, but assured of her powers as a woman, and confident from the beginning of her ascendancy in the 'merry war' with Benedick. Branagh played a waggish, slightly smug, exclamatory Benedick. Both characters seemed romantics at heart beneath their defensive veneer, still fascinated with each other despite the hurt of a previous amorous encounter.

The film was much livelier than the BBC-TV version, with a strong emphasis on the physical: flying hoofs, men airborne in the saddle, sensuous women screaming with excitement at the soldiers' approach, naked bodies bathing and dressing, Conrade massaging Don John's back, Benedick splashing ecstatically in a fountain, Beatrice floating on a swing, Borachio and Margaret having sex at Hero's window, Claudio flinging Hero to the ground across a bench.

Branagh wanted an exciting, forthright production appealing to a broad popular audience (Branagh, ix). In pursuit of this aim he foregrounded plot and action, giving much stronger weight than usual to the passion, drama and intrigue of the Hero–Claudio–Don John story. However, the verbal artifice of the play was significantly depreciated. *Much Ado* is one of the most self-consciously verbal of all Shakespeare's plays, but in Branagh's version nearly five hundred lines of witty dialogue were deleted, including more than a hundred and eighty involving Beatrice and/or Benedick. The verbal abundance of Shakespearean drama is not entirely compatible with the predominantly visual mode of the cinema, and most successful Shakespearean films have pruned the text rather heavily, with extensive substitution of visual signifiers for verbal ones. Branagh cut over 40 per cent of *Much Ado*, bringing the dialogue closer to twentieth-century naturalism and to the terseness of most contemporary film scripts. The rearrangement of some of the events leading to Don John's deception of Claudio made for a stronger plot line. However, cuts to the dialogue of Claudio and Don Pedro, especially in the final act, made them appear more serious and sincere than in the play.

The film maintained a dynamic counterpoint between the 'blithe and bonny' and 'sounds of woe' (2.3.58–9), foregrounding the dark elements in the play strongly. Don John, Borachio and Conrade were sinister presences. The renunciation sequence and Beatrice's reaction to it were played with passion and intensity. Even the watchmen were gratuitously cruel to their prisoners, and were themselves terrified of a grim, psychopathic Dogberry (one missed the comedy in the watch scenes). At the end there was a chilling disruption to the festivities as the captured Don John was brought back and the two brothers eyed each other with hatred. But the final dance was joyous, at its climax even exultant, 'converting all your sounds of woe / Into hey nonny nonny' (2.3.67–8). The film has possibly been seen more widely than any other production of *Much Ado*, demonstrating the possibility of winning a broad popular audience with a Shakespeare play adapted to a contemporary medium.

Conclusion

In an interview in the late 1980s, the Shakespearean director Jonathan Miller said:

> It seems to me important to recognise that a play has an afterlife different from the life conceived for it by its author. There are all sorts of unforesee-able meanings which might attach to the play, simply by virtue of the fact that it has survived into a period with which the author was not acquainted, and is therefore able to strike chords in the imagination of a modern audi-ence which could not have been struck in an audience when it was first per-formed. (Holderness, *The Shakespeare Myth*, 195)

In every period, in each revival of the play, fresh meanings are generated, produced in the creative interaction between play text, directors, actors and audience. In each age the play's meanings are conditioned, as we have shown, by the cultural and ideological assumptions of the time. Changing theatrical conventions require the adjustment of the play to varying performance conditions. No single representation of a text can embody all its possible meanings, and so no production can ever be thought of as definitive. The meanings of the play keep on proliferating: there can be no closure.

The ideological and aesthetic assumptions of each period may be traced in the meanings which that period assigns to the play: performance history is thus a barometer of cultural change. We have shown, for instance, how the production history of *Much Ado* reveals the play as a site of contention for changing gender attitudes and concepts of womanhood. In the Renaissance theatre the ambiguities in the representation of Beatrice challenged patriar-chal ideologies and conventional notions of gender definition. The Restoration theatre adjusted Beatrice and Benedick towards the libertine spirit prominent in fashionable London society at the time. James Miller (1737) made the play's gender relations subserve a moral purpose. Audiences in the Garrick era enjoyed Beatrice for her aggressive wit. Most nineteenth-century critics, on the other hand, found her assertiveness an embarrassment. The nineteenth-century stage tended to soften and refine the role in an attempt to accommodate the character to contemporary notions of ideal womanhood. The gender revolution of the late twentieth century brought a radical reversal in the representation of Beatrice, actresses taking new pride in the character's independence and self-assertion, and using the role to contest traditional gender stereotypes.

Each age has attempted to appropriate *Much Ado* for its own times, refashioning the play to some degree in its own cultural image. Yet each period has also discovered in the text elements which are difficult to accommodate to its own culture, and which identify the play as the product of another age. The surrender of individuality implied in Beatrice's 'taming my wild heart to thy loving hand' (3.1.112) scarcely accords, for instance, with late twentieth-century feminist conceptions of gender relationships. The Beatrice who challenges male assumptions for much of the play is at the end subsumed, at least in outward forms, within the dominant patriarchal order. Despite the affinities which Beatrice shares with late twentieth-century constructions of womanhood, she is not, after all, wholly of our time. In all our attempts to reshape the play for our own culture, we are reminded that it is also a Renaissance text. The theatrical imperative to give the play contemporary relevance will always be in tension to some degree with its period quality.

LIST OF CHARACTERS

LEONATO, *Governor of Messina*
MESSENGER, *servant of Don Pedro*
BEATRICE, *niece of Leonato*
HERO, *daughter of Leonato*
DON PEDRO, *Prince of Arragon*
BENEDICK, *gentleman of Padua, in the court of Don Pedro*
DON JOHN, *bastard brother of Don Pedro, recently reconciled to him after a war*
CLAUDIO, *a count of Florence, in the court of Don Pedro*
ANTONIO, *old man, Leonato's brother*
CONRADE, *associate of Don John*
BORACHIO, *associate of Don John*
BALTHASAR, *musician in the service of Don Pedro*
MARGARET, *gentlewoman in Leonato's household*
URSULA, *gentlewoman in Leonato's household*
BOY, *servant to Benedick*
DOGBERRY, *Constable of Messina*
VERGES, *Headborough, Dogberry's partner in office*
GEORGE SEACOAL, *senior watchman*
WATCHMAN 1
WATCHMAN 2
FRIAR FRANCIS
SEXTON
SOLDIERS, COURTIERS, MUSICIANS, SINGERS, WATCHMEN *and other* ATTENDANTS

MUCH ADO ABOUT NOTHING

ACT I, SCENE I

The opening atmosphere has varied widely in performance. Macready, Charles Kean and Irving suggested the aristocratic splendour of Leonato's household. Tree created a meeting point of civilian and military life, with a banquet on the battlements interrupted by the rattle of a drawbridge and the entry of the Messenger in full armour (S69; costume design, UBTC). Others have suggested the civility of a noble household. In Sothern's 1904–5 production ladies made wreaths and garlands, entertained by a singer and mandolins (S59). In Bridges-Adams's 1933–4 productions Beatrice and Hero, discovered at a musical instrument, rose and curtsied as Leonato entered (S88). In Gielgud's productions they sat with lute and music book near a table set with elegant refreshments (S93–4, P-1952, pr. photo); in Eyre's production (1971) Beatrice sat painting near a table of fruit and flowers. A relaxed beginning has often highlighted the flurry at Don Pedro's arrival. Carey (1956) began with Leonato and Hero playing backgammon while Beatrice lay on a chaise-longue, her face covered by a straw hat (S95; *SQ* 8, 1957, 468). Langham (1961) commenced with bucolic languor, a gardener asleep on a bench and a woman shelling peas as villagers drifted on with the characters (S101). Zeffirelli, on the other hand, began with thunderous drums and storm music (pbk; *ILN*, 27 Feb. 65). Barton (1976) established a sharp distinction of gender roles with men attending to business, women to domestic functions, Leonato entering with a bundle of documents, Beatrice with a sewing-basket. Here was a society in which women served men: a maid helped Leonato out of his dressing-gown into a coat, Beatrice did up his buttons and adjusted his scarf, Hero passed him his band (pbk). Hands's production (1982) began romantically with a lone cellist playing melancholy music (*G*, 21 Apr. 1982). Freedman (NYSF 1988) set the keynote for a vigorous production with a cannon blast followed by a mock sword fight between Benedick and Claudio, during which Beatrice 'pointedly refused to look up from her book'. Kevin Kline, who played Benedick, said the intention was to highlight the battle motif, establish a sense of male bonding, and prefigure the 'merry war' (*NR*, 22 Aug. 1988, 26; *NYT*, 10 July 1988). In Branagh's 1993 film the opening was ambiguous, Beatrice reading 'Sigh no more, ladies' (2.3.53–68) against a background of happy picnickers. Fanny Davenport (1886) drew special attention to Beatrice by delaying her entry to line 18. Daly's initial stage direction (1896) included Leonato's wife Innogen, as in Q.

1.1 *Enter* LEONATO, *Governor of Messina*, HERO *his daughter and* BEATRICE *his niece, with a* MESSENGER

LEONATO I learn in this letter, that Don Pedro of Arragon comes this night to Messina.

MESSENGER He is very near by this, he was not three leagues off when I left him.

LEONATO How many gentlemen have you lost in this action? 5

MESSENGER But few of any sort, and none of name.

LEONATO A victory is twice itself, when the achiever brings home full numbers. I find here, that Don Pedro hath bestowed much honour on a young Florentine called Claudio.

MESSENGER Much deserved on his·part, and equally remembered by 10 Don Pedro. He hath borne himself beyond the promise of his age, doing in the figure of a lamb the feats of a lion. He hath indeed better bettered expectation than you must expect of me to tell you how.

LEONATO He hath an uncle here in Messina will be very much glad of it.

MESSENGER I have already delivered him letters, and there appears 15 much joy in him, even so much that joy could not show itself modest enough without a badge of bitterness.

LEONATO Did he break out into tears?

MESSENGER In great measure.

LEONATO A kind overflow of kindness: there are no faces truer than 20 those that are so washed. How much better is it to weep at joy, than to joy at weeping!

3ff. The Messenger's speeches were given to Balthasar by the Kembles, Vining, J. W. Wallack, Macready, C. Kean and W. Lacy.

7 In Hands's production (1982), where characters danced 'at the slightest provocation', Leonato danced a few delighted steps on hearing of Don Pedro's victory (*O*, 25 Apr. 1982).

9 In the BBC-TV production (1984) Hero's prior interest in Claudio was indicated by a dig in the ribs from Beatrice and significant looks between them. In Sothern's 1904–5 production Hero's interest at the mention of Claudio brought amusement from Ursula (s59); in Branagh's film, Margaret and Ursula 'oooed' mischievously.

12b–22 Often cut or abridged, reducing the sense of rhetorical artifice in the opening dialogue. Edwin Booth cut 6–22.

23 Kate Terry spoke this line with 'saucy mock contempt' (*T*, 26 July 1867), Ellen Terry 'with the very essence of good-humoured mischief beaming from each feature' (*DT*, 6 Jan. 1891). In Sothern's 1904–5 production the reference to Signor Mountanto brought enquiring looks from most on stage, Hero laughing to herself with recognition (s59). Kathleen Widdoes

BEATRICE I pray you, is Signor Mountanto returned from the wars or no?
MESSENGER I know none of that name, lady, there was none such in the
    army of any sort. 25
LEONATO What is he that you ask for, niece?
HERO My cousin means Signor Benedick of Padua.
MESSENGER O he's returned, and as pleasant as ever he was.
BEATRICE He set up his bills here in Messina, and challenged Cupid at
    the flight: and my uncle's fool, reading the challenge, subscribed for 30
    Cupid, and challenged him at the birdbolt. I pray you, how many hath
    he killed and eaten in these wars? But how many hath he killed? – for
    indeed I promised to eat all of his killing.
LEONATO Faith, niece, you tax Signor Benedick too much, but he'll be
    meet with you, I doubt it not. 35
MESSENGER He hath done good service, lady, in these wars.
BEATRICE You had musty victual, and he hath holp to eat it: he is a very
    valiant trencherman, he hath an excellent stomach.
MESSENGER And a good soldier too, lady.
BEATRICE And a good soldier to a lady, but what is he to a lord? 40

(1972) spelled out the pun on Mountanto by pronouncing the word 'Mount-on-to' (Halio, *Shakespeare's Plays*, 58). Emma Thompson (1993) asked the question with mischievous relish. Daly (1896) delayed Beatrice's entry and her dialogue with the Messenger until after the arrival sequence (118).

23–69 The adapted version of this dialogue in *The Universal Passion* (1737) made Liberia more severe and sarcastic than Beatrice in *Much Ado*, omitting Beatrice's waggish and sardonic anecdote about Benedick's challenge to Cupid (29–31), turning her jest about Benedick's excellent stomach (37–8) to sarcasm by adding 'at every thing, but fighting', deleting the passage (41–3) where she acknowledges Benedick's virtues (albeit with an ironic twist), and omitting Beatrice's ambiguous, not wholly uncomplimentary conclusion about the persistent effects of catching 'the Benedict' (64–5). On the other hand a note in Bell's acting edition (1773) suggests that in Garrick's productions 'Beatrice unfold[ed] her archness of character pleasantly, even at the outsetting'. Emma Thompson's gibes about Benedick were spoken playfully, amid laughter from the onlookers, as if she did not really dislike him.

27 Gielgud (1950) highlighted the reference to Benedick by laughter from the Messenger and Beatrice and by a pause at the end of the speech (s93).

29–31 Cut from Garrick to the first decade of the twentieth century, and often since, because of the assumed obscurity of the wit.

31b–2a Spoken teasingly by Susan Fleetwood (*FT*, 12 Apr. 1991).

40a Spoken slowly and knowingly by Emma Thompson (Branagh film).

MESSENGER A lord to a lord, a man to a man, stuffed with all honourable virtues.

BEATRICE It is so indeed, he is no less than a stuffed man, but for the stuffing – well, we are all mortal.

LEONATO You must not, sir, mistake my niece: there is a kind of merry war betwixt Signor Benedick and her: they never meet but there's a skirmish of wit between them.   45

BEATRICE Alas, he gets nothing by that. In our last conflict, four of his five wits went halting off, and now is the whole man governed with one: so that if he have wit enough to keep himself warm, let him bear it for a difference between himself and his horse, for it is all the wealth that he hath left to be known a reasonable creature. Who is his companion now? He hath every month a new sworn brother.   50

MESSENGER Is't possible?

BEATRICE Very easily possible: he wears his faith but as the fashion of his hat, it ever changes with the next block.   55

MESSENGER I see, lady, the gentleman is not in your books.

BEATRICE No, and he were, I would burn my study. But I pray you, who is his companion? Is there no young squarer now, that will make a voyage with him to the devil?   60

MESSENGER He is most in the company of the right noble Claudio.

BEATRICE O Lord, he will hang upon him like a disease: he is sooner caught than the pestilence, and the taker runs presently mad. God help the noble Claudio, if he hath caught the Benedict. It will cost

---

41–4   Cut in most productions from Garrick to the mid-nineteenth century. Edwin Booth cut 41–52a.

43   Davenant (*LL*, 274) altered this line to 'He is, indeed, no less than a stuft man'. Beatrice's ambiguous response in *Much Ado* is more generous. Ellen Terry smiled warmly as she spoke the line (s50).

44   Elizabeth Spriggs (1971) said 'Well, we are all mortal', 'rolling her eyes with the worldly-wise air of a woman who clearly knows it all' (*DT*, 16 Dec. 1971).

45–6   Gielgud drew attention to these lines, Leonato crossing upstage of the Messenger before speaking (s94).

48–9   Ellen Terry sounded puzzled that Benedick should want to continue the 'merry war' after his previous defeat (s50).

50–2   Often cut in Victorian productions and since the late 1940s. Tree cut 48b–56.

58   Cherie Lunghi (BBC-TV, 1984) gave her 'No' a dubious, tentative inflection, suggesting that her gibes about Benedick were not necessarily to be taken at face value.

59–60   Cut from Garrick to Craig, but not by Irving.

61   Hero's reaction in Barton's production indicated her prior interest in Claudio (*G*, 1 July 1977).

62   Julia Marlowe raised her hands in horror (s63).

him a thousand pound ere a be cured. 65
MESSENGER I will hold friends with you, lady.
BEATRICE Do, good friend.
LEONATO You will never run mad, niece.
BEATRICE No, not till a hot January.
MESSENGER Don Pedro is approached. 70

66–7 Cut in most productions from Garrick to Tree, but not by Irving, Craig and Poel. The lines are
significant for Beatrice's gracious response to the Messenger. Davenant (*LL*, 275) substituted
a harsh rejoinder: 'Y'ave the wit, Sir, to wish for your self.' Cherie Lunghi (1984) replied
kindly, with a sympathetic wink. Emma Thompson (1993) also replied warmly and
sympathetically. Maggie Smith (1965) tossed an apple to the Messenger as a token of truce
(pbk).

70 The excitement of Leonato's household at the army's arrival was strongly portrayed by
Irving, Tree, Zeffirelli, Alexander (1990) and Branagh (1993). In Gill's production (1981)
Beatrice and Hero rushed to each other and embraced (pbk). In Branagh's film the ladies
screamed with delight as Don Pedro and his men were seen galloping round a bend of the
road in the valley below. The picnickers then raced to the house to wash and dress for the
soldiers' arrival.

70 SD In the Renaissance theatre ceremonial entrances such as this were typically announced with
a flourish of trumpets or cornets (Hattaway, *Elizabethan Popular Theatre*, 61), a convention
regularly adopted for Don Pedro's arrival in productions from Garrick to Macready, and
often since. Edwin Booth, Irving and some other Victorian managers heralded the arrival by
march music. The major Victorian and Edwardian productions staged the arrival with
considerable spectacle. In Irving's productions Don Pedro and his officers, accompanied
by eight lords, twelve pages and a troop of soldiers, entered amid a clamour of greeting and
the waving of silken banners by members of Leonato's household at the portico. Don Pedro
(1891) drew attention to the spectacular set, interpolating 'What a beautiful place you have
here, Signor Leonato' (s50). During the welcoming formalities the crowd seemed to 'develop
from all quarters with kaleidoscopic variety in form and colour' (*GN*, 30 Aug. 1883; s46–7;
Howard, *Dramatic Notes, 1882*, 50). Tree gave the arrival a strongly martial flavour, the
soldiers, fully armed, banging down the butts of their spears as they halted (s69; costume
designs, UBTC). At the Old Vic, where economic considerations enforced simple production,
Harcourt Williams brought 'armies' on via the orchestra pit, their lances showing above the
edge of the stage with 'great effect' without the employment of a vast crowd (*Old Vic Annual
Report*, 1930–1, 11). Gielgud (1949) presented Don Pedro, Claudio and Benedick in armour,
but in subsequent revivals gave less emphasis to the martial element (pr. photos); in 1955
only the Messenger and captains were in armour (costume designs, tour wardrobe book,
SCL). In Houseman and Landau's American frontier production, the entry was noisy and
boisterous (*SQ* 8, 1957, 509). Zeffirelli staged the arrival as a gala event, the town band

Enter DON PEDRO, CLAUDIO, BENEDICK, BALTHASAR *and* JOHN *the bastard*

DON PEDRO Good Signor Leonato, are you come to meet your trouble? The fashion of the world is to avoid cost, and you encounter it.

LEONATO Never came trouble to my house in the likeness of your grace: for trouble being gone, comfort should remain: but when you depart from me, sorrow abides, and happiness takes his leave. 75

DON PEDRO You embrace your charge too willingly. I think this is your daughter?

LEONATO Her mother hath many times told me so.

BENEDICK Were you in doubt, sir, that you asked her?

LEONATO Signor Benedick, no, for then were you a child. 80

DON PEDRO You have it full, Benedick: we may guess by this, what you are, being a man. Truly, the lady fathers herself: be happy, lady, for you are like an honourable father.

BENEDICK If Signor Leonato be her father, she would not have his head on her shoulders for all Messina, as like him as she is. 85

parading as Don Pedro and his soldiers waved and shook hands with a crowd of frock-coated citizens (pbk; *T*, 17 Feb. 1965). Whereas most productions have used bright lighting to create an atmosphere of gaiety for the arrival, Nunn (1968) staged the entry by night with flaming torches (*O*, 20 Oct. 1968) in accord with the generally dark mood of his production. Eyre's arrival (1971) gave the impression 'that the splendid if overdressed' officers had been 'playing at war': immaculate in blue and scarlet with gold braid and white-plumed helmets, they entered 'in mock formation' and collapsed 'into schoolboy laughter' (*St*, 2 June 1971), setting the tone for a predominantly game-like production. In Barton's production (1976) the soldiers entered hot and sweaty as if from a campaign (pbk, pr. photos). Alexander (1990) and Branagh (1993) had the soldiers wash and change out of battle dress (*Pl*, June 1990, 35; *SH*, 20 Apr. 1990). Trevis (1988) presented the army's arrival less as a transition to civilian life than as a disruption of it (see introduction, p. 78).

71 Branagh's film represented Don Pedro as a figure of power, Leonato as a well-to-do farmer.
71–85 Tree foregrounded the transition to gracious civilian life as the officers were regaled with fruit and wine from a banqueting table (s69). Macready, Kean, Nunn, Barton and Hands highlighted formal courtesies and deference to rank in this sequence. Military habits jarred a little with civilian manners in Bridges-Adams's 1933–4 production: amid drinks and courtesies Benedick put his foot on a chair to dust his boots with his glove (s88).

During the welcoming sequence Ellen Terry cast glances towards Benedick suggesting she longed to renew their encounter, but Irving affected not to perceive her (*Std*, 13 Oct. 1882). Some Beatrices avoided Benedick: when Tree turned to Beatrice after kissing Hero's hand, he found she had disappeared into the house (s69). Kathleen Widdoes (1972), on the other hand, stood on a chair for a better view of Benedick (*NYM*, 4 Sep. 1972). Sinead Cusack

BEATRICE I wonder that you will still be talking, Signor Benedick, nobody marks you.

BENEDICK What, my dear Lady Disdain! Are you yet living?

BEATRICE Is it possible Disdain should die, while she hath such meet food to feed it, as Signor Benedick? Courtesy itself must convert to 90 Disdain, if you come in her presence.

(1982) was at first more interested in Benedick than he in her: when she 'plunged in to offer herself for Benedick's universal hand-kissing of the ladies', 'he deliberately ignored her' (Jacobi, in Cook, *Shakespeare's Players*, 31; Gay, *As She Likes It*, 168). Susan Fleetwood (1990) retreated behind a tree when Benedick entered, 'partly to steady her nerves, partly to savour the irritated discomfiture her delayed emergence [would] cause him'. The hidden, listening figure foreshadowed the multiple eavesdropping to come (*Ind*, 12 Apr. 1990). When she emerged, Benedick ignored her gaze with 'subtly provocative' disdain (*PI*, June 1990, 35). Hero and Claudio have often paired up during the welcoming formalities. In Sothern's 1904–5 production Claudio crossed to Hero at 83 and kissed her hand (s59); they exchanged occasional glances in Sothern's 1911 production (s63). In Branagh's film Hero eyed Claudio bashfully, he returning the gaze with unconcealed pleasure. In some productions Margaret has paired with Borachio (e.g. Sothern 1904–5, Payne 1936, Carey 1956). Don John and his companions have sometimes remained detached from the company until welcomed at line 114 (e.g. SMT 1933–4, 1936).

77 In Zeffirelli's production Hero knelt and presented a bouquet to Don Pedro, who took a rose and gave it to her (pbk).

80b–5 Poel cut the rakish innuendo at 80b–2, Bridges-Adams 81–2a. Tree cut the word-play on 'father' at 81b–5, Daly 84–5.

84–5 In Sothern's 1904–5 production and Branagh's film everyone stopped listening to Benedick (s59), giving point to Beatrice's gibe that 'nobody marks you'.

86ff. Though piqued by Benedick's self-assertion and professed contempt for women, Helena Faucit in this passage showed an attraction to him nevertheless (Faucit, 'Female characters', 210–11). Charles Kean parried Beatrice's jests with a 'half-hesitating humour' at first (*DT*, 22 Nov. 1858); as he warmed to the conflict, he returned her attacks with 'good-humoured relish', answering gibe for gibe with an 'arch twinkle of the eye', a 'glow of malicious satisfaction' lighting up his features (*Std*, 22 Nov. 1858). Louisa Herbert's words (1866) seemed a conscious pose to pique Benedick's vanity (*BWM*, 14 Apr. 1866). Ada Cavendish said 'nobody marks you' 'with an open ingenuous countenance' and 'a slight movement of the arms outwards', 'as though she were really convinced of the truth of it'; then 'clapp[ed] her hands and rippl[ed] over with laughter the moment that [Benedick's] face betrayed his discomfiture' (*E*, 1 May 1875). Ellen Terry spoke the words with an assumed contempt. Irving doffed his hat with an air of affected astonishment and kissed her hand, his reply less a retort than 'a humorous caress' (s45–7; *Std*, 13 Oct. 1882; *Letters of an Unsuccessful Actor*,

BENEDICK Then is Courtesy a turn-coat: but it is certain I am loved of all
ladies, only you excepted: and I would I could find in my heart that I
had not a hard heart, for truly I love none.

BEATRICE A dear happiness to women, they would else have been   95
troubled with a pernicious suitor. I thank God and my cold blood, I
am of your humour for that: I had rather hear my dog bark at a crow
than a man swear he loves me.

BENEDICK God keep your ladyship still in that mind, so some gentleman
or other shall scape a predestinate scratched face.   100

BEATRICE Scratching could not make it worse, and 'twere such a face as
yours were.

BENEDICK Well, you are a rare parrot-teacher.

BEATRICE A bird of my tongue is better than a beast of yours.

301). The ensuing repartee, though spirited, betrayed a subtle undercurrent of affection (*T*, 6
Jan. 1891; *O*, 15 Oct. 1882, 11 Jan. 1891). Commencing 'in the lightest possible way' (*Lloyd's*,
15 Oct. 1882), the interchange conveyed an 'infectious sense of enjoyment' (cutting, 15 Oct.
1882, TM); it seemed to have 'all the piquancy and zest of an impromptu attack', 'the flash
and animation' as of 'two alert minds brought into chance rivalry' (*Daily Inter-Ocean*,
Chicago, 16 Feb. 1884). Julia Marlowe (1892–3) 'flirted a rosebud' under Benedick's nose at
her opening sally (Shattuck, *Shakespeare on the American Stage*, II.256); in 1911 she waved
her fan at him (s63). Sothern bowed elaborately as he replied, throwing kisses to her (s59).
Her gibes at 101–2 and 104 were uttered with merry laughter (s63). Tree also responded
gallantly to Beatrice's first remark, bowing and kissing her hand (s69). Judi Dench (1976)
was not at all playful in this passage, but sharp and severe (*DT*, 9 Apr. 1976; *ES*, 9 Apr. 1976).
She seemed annoyed by Benedick, as if nursing a long-standing hurt, frustration and
repression (*NS*, 16 Apr. 1976; Dench, in Cook, *Women in Shakespeare*, 34). Daly (1896)
transposed this sequence to the end of 1.1 to climax the scene.

92a Louisa Nisbett (1843) laughed mockingly (s20).

92–4 Spoken by Irving as if venturing on 'something like a plea', a hint of a possible reconciliation
between himself and Beatrice (*PW*, 21 Oct. 1882, 219). At Burton's Theatre, NY (1857),
Beatrice laughed derisively at Benedick's claim to be 'loved of all ladies' (s21). Fanny
Davenport exclaimed 'Oh! Oh!' (P-1886); Julia Marlowe also protested (s59).

93b–4 Davenant's adaptation, 'I have a hard heart,/ And can love none' (*LL*, 276) was harsher and
more direct than the original text, where Benedick expresses a whimsical half wish that he
were not so hard-hearted. At 'I love none' Jacobi (1982) kissed the hands of Ursula and
another maid in mock gallantry (pbk).

96 **pernicious suitor** Jacobi poked Beatrice with his sword (pbk).

100 Allam's gibe (1990) brought a big reaction from his camp-mates at the wash-basin (pbk).
In Branagh's film the onlookers laughed at Benedick's gibes here and at 105, and 'oooed'
at Beatrice's riposte (101–2).

BENEDICK I would my horse had the speed of your tongue, and so good a 105
  continuer: but keep your way a God's name. I have done.
BEATRICE You always end with a jade's trick: I know you of old.
DON PEDRO That is the sum of all: Leonato, Signor Claudio and Signor
  Benedick, my dear friend Leonato, hath invited you all. I tell him we
  shall stay here at the least a month, and he heartily prays some 110
  occasion may detain us longer: I dare swear he is no hypocrite, but
  prays from his heart.
LEONATO If you swear, my lord, you shall not be forsworn. [*To Don John*]
  Let me bid you welcome, my lord, being reconciled to the prince your
  brother: I owe you all duty. 115
DON JOHN I thank you, I am not of many words, but I thank you.
LEONATO Please it your grace lead on?
DON PEDRO Your hand, Leonato, we will go together.
Exeunt all except Benedick and Claudio

105–6 In E. L Davenport's productions Beatrice flew at Benedick at 'so good a continuer' (s36).
  Here Fanny Davenport, Julia Marlowe and others made as if to reply, but were cut off by
  Benedick. Sothern backed away and held up his hands in defence (s25, s35, P-WHS, P-1886,
  s59, s63). At 'I have done' Rylance (1993), 'bested by Beatrice …, suddenly s[ank] down
  clutching his heavily bandaged head (hence her accusation of "a jade's trick")' (*SS* 47, 1994,
  192).

107 Julia Marlowe (1911) struck at Benedick with her fan and laughed (s63). Cherie Lunghi
  (BBC-TV, 1984) spoke 'I know you of old' with a deliberate sharp intent suggesting she had
  previously been jilted by Benedick. Emma Thompson (1993) spoke the first phrase with
  bitter gravity, the second with a knowing sadness. At the end of the interchange, the
  separation of male and female was emphasised in Alexander's production (1990) as
  Benedick rejoined his camp-mates at the wash-basin and Beatrice joined the women
  at the opposite side.

109b–10a This announcement brought general applause in Sothern's 1904–5 production (s59); in
  Tree's production Hero and Claudio exclaimed with delight (s69); in Alexander's 1990
  production and Branagh's film there were shrieks of delight from the women. In Gielgud's
  productions, by contrast, Benedick covered his face in mock dismay, and Beatrice made as if
  to cross herself, but turned the action into a curtsy (s93–4). Maggie Smith (1965) mopped
  her brow in vexation (pbk).

114 Poel drew special attention to Don John by delaying his arrival to this point. The contrast
  between Don John's entry with his 'army' and the earlier arrival of Don Pedro, Claudio and
  Benedick, accompanied only by two 'beefeaters' and two servants (s57), suggested open
  conflict between the two brothers and represented Don John as a dangerous subversive
  power.

116 Richard Johnson (SMT 1958) snarled this line with a twisted smile (*WI*, 31 Aug. 1958).

118 SD The Beatrice–Benedick business at the exit has often hinted a fascination beneath their

CLAUDIO Benedick, didst thou note the daughter of Signor Leonato?
BENEDICK I noted her not, but I looked on her.   120
CLAUDIO Is she not a modest young lady?
BENEDICK Do you question me as an honest man should do, for my
     simple true judgement? Or would you have me speak after my
     custom, as being a professed tyrant to their sex?
CLAUDIO No, I pray thee speak in sober judgement.   125
BENEDICK Why i'faith, methinks she's too low for a high praise, too
     brown for a fair praise, and too little for a great praise. Only this
     commendation I can afford her, that were she other than she is, she
     were unhandsome, and being no other, but as she is – I do not like
     her.   130
CLAUDIO Thou thinkest I am in sport. I pray thee, tell me truly how thou
     lik'st her?
BENEDICK Would you buy her, that you enquire after her?
CLAUDIO Can the world buy such a jewel?
BENEDICK Yea, and a case to put it into. But speak you this with a sad   135
     brow? Or do you play the flouting Jack, to tell us Cupid is a good hare-
     finder, and Vulcan a rare carpenter? Come, in what key shall a man
     take you, to go in the song?
CLAUDIO In mine eye, she is the sweetest lady that ever I looked on.
BENEDICK I can see yet without spectacles, and I see no such matter.   140
     There's her cousin, and she were not possessed with a fury, exceeds
     her as much in beauty as the first of May doth the last of December.

apparent antipathy. In the Kemble productions Benedick jestingly refused the offered hand
of Beatrice, but began to follow her as she ran off laughing (s6), business also adopted by
Dow (s25), Taylor (s35) and Irving (s47). Vining offered to lead Beatrice out, following her
when she declined (s12), business also adopted in Stephens's promptbook (P-WHS) and by
Fanny Davenport, who drew back with mock dignity (P-1886). Macready and Louisa Nisbett
merely turned from each other coldly (s19). Marie Drofnah (c.1900) coughed to attract
Benedick's attention, but went off laughing when he tried to kiss her hand (s56). When Tree
offered to escort Beatrice out she hurried away indignantly, he waving to acknowledge her
antipathy; as they retreated in opposite directions each turned simultaneously to look at the
other, Beatrice, embarrassed, going off quickly (s69). Julia Marlowe tossed a rose to
Benedick, then knocked it to the ground when he tried to return it; he kicked it downstage in
vexation (s59). Maggie Smith (1965) jestingly placed a glass in Benedick's hat as she went off
(pbk). Janet Suzman (1969) hinted interest in Benedick by returning to get a book when only
he and Claudio were left on stage (pbk). Susan Fleetwood (1990) threw down a glove to
Benedick as if challenging him to a duel; he picked it up as if accepting her challenge (pbk).

     Directors have often used this exit to highlight the Hero–Claudio relationship as well. In
Zeffirelli's production Hero dropped a rose for Claudio; in Barton's, Claudio escorted her off.

Some performances have indicated Don John as a potential threat to the Hero–Claudio relationship. In Fanny Davenport's production Hero glanced at Claudio as Don John offered her his hand. In Sothern's 1904–5 production Claudio, crossing to exit with Hero, was intercepted by Don John, who escorted Hero off, leaving a disappointed Claudio gazing after her. In Nunn's 1969 production Don John lingered briefly as a sinister presence as Claudio prepared to tell Benedick of his love for Hero. Poel (1904) and Hands (1982) hinted another possible threat to the Hero–Claudio relationship by having Margaret and Borachio exit together (pbks).

119ff.   Garrick gave extra prominence to Benedick with an interpolation in line 119:

> *Claud*. *Benedick*!
> *Bene*. What do you say, count?
> *Claud*. Didst thou note the daughter ... (Bell).

In the productions of Bridges-Adams (1933–4), Eyre (1971) and Barton (1976) Benedick took off helmet, sword or other armour, signifying a transition in the play from war to love (pbks). Benedick's carefree detachment from Claudio's anxiety about Hero has been suggested in numerous productions, Barnes (1886) playing with a feather while delivering his opinion of Hero, Sothern (1904–5) pouring himself a drink of wine, Tree (1905) sitting astride a cannon patting it, Michell (1956) stretched out on a chaise-longue, Redgrave (1958) lying on a sofa with his feet up on a chair, Stephens (1965) puffing at a cigar (pbks). In contrast, John Wyse as Claudio (SMT 1933–4) showed his diffidence about disclosing his feelings to Benedick by a fleeting inclination to follow the others offstage (s87–8). John McAndrew (RSC 1990) was so tense and insecure that he could not speak about Hero without kneading his hands (*T*, 14 Apr. 1990). Antoon (1972) suggested the camaraderie between Benedick and Claudio by staging this sequence as a bathtub scene (Halio, *Shakespeare's Plays*, 14).

119–215   In *UP* (pp.17–18) Protheus' responses in this sequence tended to be blunter and more sceptical than Benedick's. Miller excluded much of Benedick's qualifying pleasantry, as well as the hints (lines 122–4, 175–6) that his misogyny is partly a posture. Branagh conveyed in this dialogue Benedick's enjoyment at striking postures.

126–7   Hero must have been played originally by an actor of short stature (cf. 158).

132   Fanny Davenport (1886) stopped the music, drawing special attention to Benedick's reply (pbk).

134   Spoken rapturously at Burton's, NY, 1857 (s21).

135a   Spoken by Charles Kean in spirited mock-heroics, imitating the tone of Claudio's question (*Era*, 21 Nov. 1858). Similar business is recorded in s21, s25, P-WHS. Godfrey (1971) answered Claudio with a lengthened, derisive, low-pitched 'Ye--s'.

135b–8   Cut or abridged in most productions on account of the assumed obscurity of the allusions.

139   Prompted in Branagh's film by the sight of Hero gazing lovingly from an upper window.

141–2   Sothern looked off as if catching sight of Beatrice (s59, s63). Hayes (1933) and Holloway

But I hope you have no intent to turn husband, have you?

CLAUDIO I would scarce trust myself, though I had sworn the contrary, if
    Hero would be my wife.   145

BENEDICK Is't come to this? In faith, hath not the world one man, but he
    will wear his cap with suspicion? Shall I never see a bachelor of three
    score again? Go to, i'faith, and thou wilt needs thrust thy neck into a
    yoke, wear the print of it, and sigh away Sundays. Look, Don Pedro is
    returned to seek you.   150

Enter DON PEDRO

DON PEDRO What secret hath held you here, that you followed not to
    Leonato's?

BENEDICK I would your grace would constrain me to tell.

DON PEDRO I charge thee on thy allegiance.

BENEDICK You hear, Count Claudio, I can be secret as a dumb man – I   155

(1934) underscored Benedick's latent fascination with Beatrice by a significant pause
before the allusion to her good looks (s88). Gielgud drew attention to these lines, moving
thoughtfully to centre stage before speaking them (s94), in 1950 looking off after Beatrice
(s93). In Branagh's film the words were prompted by the sight of Beatrice, who had joined
Hero at an upper window.

143   Branagh's tone here and in the ensuing sequence expressed disgust and comic outrage
    that Claudio should have turned lover.

146–9   Sothern hit the table with his fist (146a); Jacobi (1982) and Branagh (1993) struck Claudio
    (147); Sothern and Tree took Claudio by the neck (148–9); Belton (Burton's, NY, 1857) and
    Jewett (1926) playfully pushed Claudio away (pbks). The allusion to cuckoldry (146b–7a)
    was cut by Kean, Irving, Craig, Tree, Bridges-Adams, Carey, Seale, Eyre, Barton and Branagh.

150 SD   In Q and F Don John entered at the same time as Don Pedro, and thus overheard, possibly
    from upstage or from behind a stage pillar, the dialogue in which Don Pedro agrees to win
    Claudio for Hero.

151ff.   In the 1958 SMT production Benedick lay on a sofa while Don Pedro stood, business which
    Laurence Kitchin (*O*, 31 Aug. 1958) thought inappropriate in view of the deference to rank
    expected in the nineteenth-century period chosen for the production. Muriel St Clare Byrne
    made a similar criticism of the 1956 Old Vic production, set in the Cavalier period (*SQ* 8,
    1957, 468). In the 1958 and 1968 Stratford productions Benedick, Claudio and Don Pedro
    established a sense of male bonding by taking drinks together. In the 1976 RSC production
    Claudio, preoccupied with his love for Hero, declined the drink (pbks).

153   In Davenport and Sothern's productions Claudio tried to restrain Benedick from telling
    (s36, s59).

154   Spoken with mock gravity in Sothern's 1904–5 production (s59).

155   Belton (NY, 1857) spoke mockingly (s21). In J. W. Wallack's productions Claudio put his

would have you think so. But on my allegiance (mark you this, on my
allegiance) he is in love. With who? Now that is your grace's part:
mark how short his answer is. With Hero, Leonato's short daughter.

CLAUDIO If this were so, so were it uttered.

BENEDICK Like the old tale, my lord: 'It is not so, nor 'twas not so, but   160
indeed, God forbid it should be so.'

CLAUDIO If my passion change not shortly, God forbid it should be
otherwise.

DON PEDRO Amen, if you love her, for the lady is very well worthy.

CLAUDIO You speak this to fetch me in, my lord.   165

DON PEDRO By my troth, I speak my thought.

CLAUDIO And in faith, my lord, I spoke mine.

BENEDICK And by my two faiths and troths, my lord, I spoke mine.

CLAUDIO That I love her, I feel.

DON PEDRO That she is worthy, I know.   170

BENEDICK That I neither feel how she should be loved, nor know how
she should be worthy, is the opinion that fire cannot melt out of me: I
will die in it at the stake.

DON PEDRO Thou wast ever an obstinate heretic in the despite of beauty.

CLAUDIO And never could maintain his part, but in the force of his   175
will.

BENEDICK That a woman conceived me, I thank her: that she brought

finger on his lip to urge Benedick to silence (s8).

158   'To hear Sinden's colonialist-prig Benedick [1976] describing Hero as "Leonato's *short
        daughter*" [was] to understand the disdain that once ruled an empire' (*Punch*, 21 Apr. 1976).
        In Sothern's 1911 production Don Pedro grinned at an embarrassed Claudio (s63).

160b–1   Chanted by Belton (s21).

173   Sothern struck the table with his fist (s59); Branagh also spoke most emphatically.

174   *UP* altered 'heretic' to 'foe' (p.17), suggesting greater hostility to love than Benedick implies
        in this passage in *Much Ado*.

175–6   These important lines in which Claudio recognises Benedick's anti-romantic stance as partly
        at least a self-conscious posture were cut by Tree, Carey, Eyre and Barton.

177   Belton (1857) raised his cap in mock respect (s21).

177–99   Davenant's adaptation of this passage (*LL*, 283) made Benedick's anti-romantic cynicism
        more extreme than in *Much Ado*. Davenant omitted Benedick's qualifying deference to
        women (177–8), commencing the passage 'How, marriage? it is a noose for Ninnies.'
        Garrick's raillery against marriage was spirited (Wilkes, *General View*, 260), and, if
        Gentleman's account of the play reflected stage performance, self-confident, though
        Gentleman also noted an element of posturing in Benedick's disdain (*DrC* 2, 1770, 307–8).
        Charles Kemble suggested this by an assumption of bravado (*MA*, 21 Jan. 1820). Macready's
        anti-romantic disdain, on the other hand, was no mere cavalier posture, but a 'fixed idea'

me up, I likewise give her most humble thanks: but that I will have a recheat winded in my forehead, or hang my bugle in an invisible baldrick, all women shall pardon me. Because I will not do them the   180
wrong to mistrust any, I will do myself the right to trust none: and the fine is (for the which I may go the finer) I will live a bachelor.

DON PEDRO I shall see thee, ere I die, look pale with love.

BENEDICK With anger, with sickness, or with hunger, my lord, not with love: prove that ever I lose more blood with love than I will get   185
again with drinking, pick out mine eyes with a ballad-maker's pen, and hang me up at the door of a brothel house for the sign of blind Cupid.

DON PEDRO Well, if ever thou dost fall from this faith, thou wilt prove a notable argument.   190

BENEDICK If I do, hang me in a bottle like a cat, and shoot at me, and he that hits me, let him be clapped on the shoulder, and called Adam.

DON PEDRO Well, as time shall try: 'In time the savage bull doth bear the yoke.'

(press cutting, BL), emphasised by heavy underscoring in his studybook for Benedick (S17: lines 161, 168, 171–3, 195–9). Irving's touches of exaggeration suggested a professed disdain which was not too deeply rooted (*CJ*, 14 Oct. 1882). Sinden's 'fretful, fidgety, overemphatic disclaimers' (RSC 1976) also indicated that he might not be as hostile to wedlock as he pretended (*NS*, 16 Apr. 1976).

178b–80a Often cut or abridged. The bawdy phrase 'or hang my bugle in an invisible baldrick' was regularly cut from Garrick to Daly.

181b–2 Spoken by Charles Kemble with an 'air of jovial triumph', 'the joyous freedom of a single life ... concentrated' in the word 'bachelor' (*JB*, 12 Apr. 1840). At the word 'finer', Redgrave (1958) made a long pause, during which he lay down on a sofa and lit a cheroot; then he said, with a finality that must have seemed absolute, 'I will live a bachelor' (S100).

183 In Branagh's film spoken seriously and with certainty.

185–6 Tree, who padded the text with stage business in a way that often gave little credit to the audience's imagination, quaffed a drink at the word 'drinking' (S69).

185–92 Directors have often cut sections of this passage considered obscure or indelicate. Belton (1857) and Daly altered 'brothel house' (187) to 'public house'.

188 Gielgud sat down firmly, giving an air of finality to his pronouncement against matrimony (S94). In Sothern's 1904–5 production Don Pedro and Claudio laughed at Benedick here and at several other points before his exit at 215 (S59).

191 In a bitter passage criticising Garrick for over-embroidering his dialogue with tricks of gesture and movement, Theophilus Cibber referred to his 'pantomimical acting every Word' at line 191. 'Methinks', wrote Cibber, 'this slight short Sentence requires not such a Variety of Action, as minutely to describe the Cat being clapp'd into the Bottle, then being hung up, and the farther painting of the Man shooting at it' (*Theophilus Cibber, to David Garrick*, 64).

BENEDICK The savage bull may, but if ever the sensible Benedick bear it, 195
pluck off the bull's horns, and set them in my forehead, and let me be
vilely painted, and in such great letters as they write, 'Here is good
horse to hire', let them signify under my sign, 'Here you may see
Benedick the married man.'
CLAUDIO If this should ever happen, thou wouldst be horn-mad. 200
DON PEDRO Nay, if Cupid have not spent all his quiver in Venice, thou
wilt quake for this shortly.
BENEDICK I look for an earthquake too then.
DON PEDRO Well, you will temporise with the hours. In the mean time,
good Signor Benedick, repair to Leonato's, commend me to him, and 205
tell him I will not fail him at supper, for indeed he hath made great
preparation.
BENEDICK I have almost matter enough in me for such an embassage,
and so I commit you –
CLAUDIO To the tuition of God: from my house if I had it – 210
DON PEDRO The sixth of July: your loving friend Benedick.
BENEDICK Nay, mock not, mock not: the body of your discourse is
sometime guarded with fragments, and the guards are but slightly
basted on, neither: ere you flout old ends any further, examine your
conscience: and so I leave you. *Exit* 215

200–4 Line 200, with its allusion to cuckoldry, was cut in most productions from Garrick to Bridges-
Adams, and in several productions since. In the twentieth century lines 201–4 have often
been cut or abridged on account of assumed obscurity.

208–11 Traditionally spoken in jest. In Taylor's Boston promptbook (s35) Benedick took off his hat
in mock solemnity at 'I commit you' (209); Sothern skipped lightly towards the house, then
turned and bowed elaborately (s63). In Sothern's 1904–5 production Claudio and Don
Pedro mimed writing at 210–11. The passage climaxed (211) in Macready's and Tree's
productions with laughter at Benedick's expense (pbks).

12b–14a Often cut in the twentieth century on account of assumed obscurity. Zeffirelli substituted:
'the body of your discourse is faced with bright patches of fancy, and they are none too
closely stitched on, neither'; 'old ends' (214) was altered to 'sober custom'. Daly cut 209–15a.

215 Charles Kemble's exit drew a mocking 'Ah!' from Claudio (s7). Vining, on the other hand,
sighed derisively at Claudio (s12), business adopted by C. Kean, Creswick, Irving, and others
(s26, s44, s47, s25, P-WHS). Sothern said 'Claudio! Claudio!', sighing and placing his hand on
his heart, and going off laughing (s59). Tree raised a laugh by clapping his helmet onto the
head of the page who was about to give him his armour (s69). Barton's production was
more attentive to military esprit, Sinden clicking his heels together in salute to the prince
(pbk). John Wyse as Claudio (SMT 1933–4) seemed half-inclined to follow Benedick out,
but turned, as if by an afterthought, to confide in Don Pedro (s88).

CLAUDIO My liege, your highness now may do me good.
DON PEDRO My love is thine to teach, teach it but how,
          And thou shalt see how apt it is to learn
          Any hard lesson that may do thee good.
CLAUDIO Hath Leonato any son, my lord?   220
DON PEDRO No child but Hero, she's his only heir:
          Dost thou affect her, Claudio?
CLAUDIO   O my lord,
          When you went onward on this ended action,
          I looked upon her with a soldier's eye,
          That liked, but had a rougher task in hand,   225
          Than to drive liking to the name of love;
          But now I am returned, and that war-thoughts
          Have left their places vacant, in their rooms
          Come thronging soft and delicate desires,
          All prompting me how fair young Hero is,   230
          Saying I liked her ere I went to wars.
DON PEDRO Thou wilt be like a lover presently,
          And tire the hearer with a book of words:
          If thou dost love fair Hero, cherish it,
          And I will break with her, and with her father,   235
          And thou shalt have her. Wast not to this end,
          That thou began'st to twist so fine a story?

216–54 During this sequence Kean (1858), Fanny Davenport (1886) and Daly (1896) showed the
        evening gradually darkening into night (s26; p-1886; Daly). In Kean's production the moon
        slowly rose over the bay (*Era*, 21 Nov. 1858), providing a romantic atmosphere for Claudio's
        confession of love. In Fanny Davenport's production lights were shining brightly from
        Leonato's house by the end of the scene. Borachio eavesdropped during the sequence in
        productions by Macready, Irving, Sothern, Poel, O'Riordan, Jewett, Bridges-Adams, Payne
        (SMT), Branagh and Bell (pbks; *SS* 8, 1955, 78), overhearing the plans for the wooing of
        Hero. Antonio as well as Borachio eavesdropped in Bridges-Adams's productions in the
        1920s (s86). In Hands's production (1982) the eavesdropper was Antonio's servant (pbk),
        an arrangement which prepared for the dialogue in 1.2.

216   John McAndrew as Claudio (RSC 1990) knelt and kissed Don Pedro's hand (pbk).

217   Don Pedro took Claudio's hand in Fanny Davenport's production, and in Sothern's placed
        his hand on Claudio's shoulder (pbks).

232ff. Don Pedro 'caressed Claudio's cheek as if bidding farewell to a lover' in Hands's 1985
        American tour (*SQ* 36, 1985, 466). John Carlisle's Don Pedro (RSC 1990), a lonely figure
        'hungry for emotional contact', 'enter[ed] into the proxy wooing of Hero with suspicious
        enthusiasm' (*G*, 12 Apr. 1990). *UP* omitted the episodes relating to the proxy wooing of Hero.
        Lines 232–45 have often been abridged.

246   In the Bell Shakespeare Company's 1996 production at the Sydney Opera House, Antonio

CLAUDIO How sweetly you do minister to love,
        That know love's grief by his complexion!
        But lest my liking might too sudden seem,   240
        I would have salved it with a longer treatise.
DON PEDRO What need the bridge much broader than the flood?
        The fairest grant is the necessity.
        Look what will serve is fit: 'tis once, thou lovest,
        And I will fit thee with the remedy.   245
        I know we shall have revelling tonight,
        I will assume thy part in some disguise,
        And tell fair Hero I am Claudio,
        And in her bosom I'll unclasp my heart,
        And take her hearing prisoner with the force   250
        And strong encounter of my amorous tale:
        Then after, to her father will I break,
        And the conclusion is, she shall be thine:
        In practice let us put it presently.

Exeunt

and Borachio appeared at separate upstage entrances to eavesdrop, Antonio hearing only
enough to assume that the prince intended to woo Hero for himself, Borachio remaining for
Don Pedro's concluding assurance, 'she shall be thine' (253). This arrangement explained
the discrepant reports of the conversation given by Antonio (1.2) and Borachio (1.3). It also
gave comic irony in 1.2 to Antonio's references to the eavesdropper as 'a man of mine', and
'a good sharp fellow' (1.2.8–9, 14).

254   As darkness gathered in Kean's 1858 production lights appeared in windows and in the
lighthouse on the mole (S26); in Daly's production servants lit lamps in Leonato's garden in
preparation for the coming festivities (Daly). The gathering darkness provided a gloomy
atmosphere for the Don John sequence (1.3), which in nineteenth-century productions
followed immediately. In Hands's production (1982) the Claudio–Don Pedro sequence
ended with a lingering handclasp sealing their friendship, both 'obviously reluctant to part'
(*SQ* 34, 1983, 83). In Macready's production the sequence ended less auspiciously, Borachio
dogging Claudio and Don Pedro as they went off (S15). In the productions of Fanny
Davenport (1886) and Sothern (1904–5) the mood darkened as Don Pedro and Claudio,
making their exit, met Don John and Conrade on the steps of the house (P-1886, S59). As
Don John crossed to a garden bench in Sothern's production he glowered back at Don
Pedro and Claudio, then shrugged his shoulders. The sinister atmosphere was intensified
by the furtive actions of Borachio, who emerged from the bushes and went off unseen by
Don John, placing a finger to his lips as a look of intelligence passed between himself and
Conrade (S59). Branagh's film cut to Borachio eavesdropping from a window, then dissolved
to Don John's room, placing the 'practice' proposed by the prince (254) in ironic
relationship with the deceptive practices of his brother and Borachio.

ACT I, SCENE 2

Enter LEONATO *and an old man* [ANTONIO,] *brother to Leonato*

This scene was omitted by Warren and Wood (1804), Bunn (Birmingham, 1819), Wood (Baltimore, 1829), Creswick (1874), Saker, Edwin Booth, Daly, Hanford (c.1900), Tree, Hunt and Branagh. From Garrick to Sothern, managers retaining the scene regularly transposed it in altered form to the beginning of 2.1, an arrangement also adopted by Jewett (1926) and Nunn (1969). In Garrick's altered version of 1.2 Antonio gave a more accurate account of Don Pedro's plan to woo Hero than in the full text, an arrangement eliminating one instance of misprision from the play:

> *Leonato*. How came you to this?
> *Ant*. I tell you, the prince, and Count *Claudio*,
> Walking before supper in the thick pleach'd
> Alley of the orchard, were overheard by a
> Man of mine. It was agreed upon, that the prince
> should in a dance, woo *Hero*, as for himself; and
> having obtain'd her, give her to Count *Claudio*. (Bell)

This was followed by a slightly altered version of lines 13–18. Garrick's adaptation of 1.2 was adopted by the Kembles, and thence by Vining, J. W. Wallack, W. Lacy, E. L. Davenport, J. B. Booth Jr, and at Burton's, NY (1857). Macready played a slightly altered version of lines 3a–21, Charles Kean a slight alteration of 3a–18. Most late Victorian and Edwardian managers who retained the scene played a version close to Kean's. Cuts and minor alterations to 1.2 have been frequent in the twentieth century. Hands commenced the scene with a dumb show in which the servant reported to Antonio what he had heard (see commentary on 1.1.216–54).

0 SD   In Trevis's production (1988) a curtain was withdrawn from an alcove upstage to reveal a piano, a drum kit and music stands ready for the masquerade (pbk, pr. photo).

LEONATO How now, brother, where is my cousin your son? Hath he
  provided this music?

ANTONIO He is very busy about it: but, brother, I can tell you strange
  news that you yet dreamed not of.

LEONATO Are they good? 5

ANTONIO As the events stamps them, but they have a good cover: they
  show well outward. The prince and Count Claudio walking in a
  thick-pleached alley in mine orchard, were thus much overheard by a
  man of mine: the prince discovered to Claudio that he loved my niece
  your daughter, and meant to acknowledge it this night in a dance, and 10
  if he found her accordant, he meant to take the present time by the
  top, and instantly break with you of it.

LEONATO Hath the fellow any wit that told you this?

ANTONIO A good sharp fellow, I will send for him, and question him
  yourself. 15

LEONATO No, no, we will hold it as a dream till it appear itself: but I will
  acquaint my daughter withal, that she may be the better prepared for
  an answer, if peradventure this be true: go you, and tell her of it.
  [*Several persons cross the stage*]
  Cousins, you know what you have to do. O I cry you mercy, friend, go
  you with me and I will use your skill: good cousin, have a care this 20
  busy time.

Exeunt

1–18 Performances have often shown a flustered Leonato amid hurried preparations for the
  masquerade. In Zeffirelli's production the musicians were heard tuning up; Ursula fussed
  around Antonio; Margaret entered with a tray of apples; women crossed with sheets, a jelly
  and a vase of flowers; Balthasar entered, dropped his sheet music and scrabbled for it on
  the floor; two men struggled on with a statue (18), Leonato rushing to help them while
  Margaret whisked the statue with a feather duster; then Margaret, making to exit, caught
  sight of Don John, screamed, and rushed off in another direction (pbk).

19–20 In Macready's production 19a was addressed to six gentlemen, 19b to one of four servants
  with lutes. At 'skill', the attendants in the 1981 NT production collided, spilling chairs and
  goblets across the stage (pbks).

ACT I, SCENE 3

Enter DON JOHN *the bastard and* CONRADE *his companion*

CONRADE What the good year, my lord, why are you thus out of measure
    sad?

DON JOHN There is no measure in the occasion that breeds, therefore the
    sadness is without limit.

CONRADE You should hear reason.   5

In Victorian and Edwardian productions 1.3 was often staged before front curtains or a painted front cloth. Some managers provided impressive settings: Kean (1858) a terrace with lofty classical columns (scene design, V&A), Edwin Booth and Sothern a stately hall (s41, s63), Alexander (1898) a chamber opening onto a colonnaded balcony with elaborately wrought Gothic stonework (photo, UBTC). Sombre settings have often been used to evoke a sinister atmosphere: in Tree's production a dark armoury, with Conrade at a workbench polishing his armour by candlelight (s69; property plot, UBTC); in Seale's (1958) a night view of a fort backed by a rough sea (pr. photo). In Warchus's production (1993), Don John was immured as if in a dark interior behind huge black shutters, a caged and isolated man (*SS* 47, 1994, 192; *What's On*, 14 July 1993).

    In the Renaissance theatre Don John probably wore the black of melancholy and evil (see Gurr, *Shakespearean Stage*, 198), a convention often used since. Some productions have used ominous theme music for the Don John sequences (e.g. Old Vic 1934, SMT 1958, NT 1965).

0 SD   Bridges-Adams (SMT 1933–4) contrasted the civility of Leonato's household with the evil entering it, Don John seating himself at the musical instrument where Beatrice and Hero had sat a few minutes before (s88). Ian McDiarmid (RSC 1976) showed Don John's moodiness and resentment by entering slowly with a book, beginning to read, then slamming the book shut with a sigh (pbk).

1–29   The dialogue with Conrade was often abridged in Victorian productions, the most common cuts being 3–4, 8–15a, 22b–4a. Saker cut 1–29.

DON JOHN And when I have heard it, what blessing brings it?

CONRADE If not a present remedy, at least a patient sufferance.

DON JOHN I wonder that thou (being as thou sayest thou art, born under
Saturn) goest about to apply a moral medicine to a mortifying
mischief. I cannot hide what I am: I must be sad when I have cause,   10
and smile at no man's jests: eat when I have stomach, and wait for no
man's leisure: sleep when I am drowsy, and tend on no man's
business: laugh when I am merry, and claw no man in his humour.

CONRADE Yea, but you must not make the full show of this till you may do
it without controlment. You have of late stood out against your   15
brother, and he hath ta'en you newly into his grace, where it is
impossible you should take true root, but by the fair weather that you
make yourself: it is needful that you frame the season for your own
harvest.

DON JOHN I had rather be a canker in a hedge, than a rose in his grace,   20
and it better fits my blood to be disdained of all, than to fashion a
carriage to rob love from any. In this (though I cannot be said to be a
flattering honest man) it must not be denied but I am a plain-dealing
villain. I am trusted with a muzzle, and enfranchised with a clog,
therefore I have decreed not to sing in my cage. If I had my mouth, I   25
would bite: if I had my liberty, I would do my liking. In the mean time,
let me be that I am, and seek not to alter me.

CONRADE Can you make no use of your discontent?

DON JOHN I make all use of it, for I use it only. Who comes here?

Enter BORACHIO

What news, Borachio?   30

BORACHIO I came yonder from a great supper, the prince your brother is

---

1–55 Some directors have created an ironic counterpoint between the Don John scene and the
festivities in Leonato's house: in Fanny Davenport and Jewett's productions laughter and
merrymaking were heard offstage, in Barton's intermittent piano music (pbks). At the
Shakespeare Theatre, Washington, 1992, the villains plotted on the terrace while the rest
of the company were visible within laughing and talking at dinner (*SQ* 43, 1992, 460).

1 Conrade has often been played as a hard-bitten soldier; in Langham's 1961 production
he had the look of 'a rugged and decayed campaigner' (*TW*, May 1961, 27).

2ff. In Zeffirelli's production Don John played the scene in great agitation, pacing about the
stage, grabbing Conrade and later Borachio by the lapels, and slapping Conrade's hand
(pbk).

5 In Branagh's film Don John sprang up menacingly.

27 Spoken in Branagh's film with great menace, Don John grasping Conrade by the cheeks. At
once a hideously masked face burst into the room with a roar modulating to a sinister laugh
as Borachio revealed himself.

royally entertained by Leonato, and I can give you intelligence of an intended marriage.

DON JOHN Will it serve for any model to build mischief on? What is he for a fool that betroths himself to unquietness?   35

BORACHIO Marry, it is your brother's right hand.

DON JOHN Who, the most exquisite Claudio?

BORACHIO Even he.

DON JOHN A proper squire! And who, and who, which way looks he?

BORACHIO Marry, on Hero, the daughter and heir of Leonato.   40

DON JOHN A very forward March-chick. How came you to this?

BORACHIO Being entertained for a perfumer, as I was smoking a musty room, comes me the prince and Claudio, hand in hand, in sad conference: I whipped me behind the arras, and there heard it agreed upon, that the prince should woo Hero for himself, and having   45 obtained her, give her to Count Claudio.

DON JOHN Come, come, let us thither, this may prove food to my displeasure, that young start-up hath all the glory of my overthrow: if I can cross him any way, I bless myself every way. You are both sure, and will assist me?   50

CONRADE To the death, my lord.

DON JOHN Let us to the great supper, their cheer is the greater that I am subdued. Would the cook were a my mind: shall we go prove what's to be done?

BORACHIO We'll wait upon your lordship.   55

Exeunt

---

29 SD In Carey's production (1956) Borachio entered eating grapes, as if from the 'great supper'; in Zeffirelli's Don John said with an Italian accent: 'Ah! God, Borachio. How now, Borachio' (pbks).

33 Patrick Stewart as Borachio (RSC 1969) indicated his churlishness by taking and eating an apple which Conrade had been enjoying (pbk).

41 Richard Pasco's reference to Hero as 'a very forward March-chick' (RSC 1971) 'revealed enough spite and envy to fuel a hundred such plots' (*SS* 25, 1972, 166).

41b–6 Cut by Garrick, the Kembles, Vining, J. W. Wallack, Davenport, W. Lacy and E. Booth. Macready altered 42–4 to: 'The prince and Claudio were here e'en now in sad conference: I whipt me behind the column, and there heard it agreed ...' From C. Kean to Bridges-Adams most productions began the speech: 'I heard it agreed ...'

47b–9a Spoken confidentially in Sothern's 1911 production (s63).

49b–52a In Sothern's 1904–5 production Don John extended both hands to Conrade and Borachio at 49b, but at 52a eyed them suspiciously. At 49b Ian Richardson as Don John (RSC 1961) offered them money for their complicity. In Fanny Davenport's production the stopping of the music at the end of line 50 heightened the sinister effect of their reply (pbks).

52b–3a **their ... subdued** Craig added: 'I'm d–d if I am subdued' (P-1903a). Clifford Rose (RSC 1969) drew attention to these resentful words by a false exit immediately before them (pbk).

53 **Would ... mind** The scene ended with these words in most productions from Garrick to Tree (Macready, Kean and Poel excepted). In Fanny Davenport and Sothern's productions laughter and music burst from the house in ironic contrast with Don John's vindictiveness. The transition to the masquerade was made in Fanny Davenport's production as a bevy of girls ran down the steps in boisterous revelry, one blindfolded, another falling and caught by her companion (pbks).

55 In Barton's production Don John, making his exit, nearly bumped into Ursula entering with a punch-bowl for the masquerade. Alexander (1990) underlined the sinister potential of masquerading, Don John, Borachio and Conrade donning masks as Leonato and Antonio entered disguised (pbk).

ACT 2, SCENE I

Enter LEONATO, *his brother* [ANTONIO], HERO *his daughter and* BEATRICE *his niece*

LEONATO Was not Count John here at supper?
ANTONIO I saw him not.
BEATRICE How tartly that gentleman looks, I never can see him but I am
    heart-burned an hour after.
HERO He is of a very melancholy disposition.   5
BEATRICE He were an excellent man that were made just in the mid-way
    between him and Benedick: the one is too like an image and says
    nothing, and the other too like my lady's eldest son, evermore tattling.
LEONATO Then half Signor Benedick's tongue in Count John's mouth,

From Garrick to Sothern, Act 2 often commenced with dialogue transposed from 1.2, an arrangement also adopted by Jewett (1926) and Nunn (1969). This saved a scene change, but effaced the connection between Don John's exit in 1.3 and the discussion of him at 2.1.1–5. 2.1 has generally been staged as a night scene, usually within Leonato's house, sometimes outdoors (Tree, Seale, Alexander 1990). In some performances the opening dialogue (1–60) has been relaxed and intimate, the characters in Gielgud's production eating sweets near a table of fruit and wine (pr. photo), in Zeffirelli's chatting over coffee (pbk). Other directors have suggested a festive atmosphere from the start: Irving had servants cross with lights, food and dishes, one with a peacock on a golden charger (s47; *GN*, 30 Aug. 1883); Sothern showed people dressing for the masquerade. Tree staged a serenade to the ladies with an interpolated song, 'Take all my loves', after which a reveller chased the singer offstage as a clown, harlequin and pantaloon appeared. Jewett showed dancers making the final bow of a minuet amid general laughter and chatter; Alexander (1990) began with women rushing into the garden and Hero pushing Beatrice on a swing (pbks).

3–4 In Edwin Booth, Daly and Hanford's productions Beatrice spoke these words with her eye on Don John as he retreated after 1.3; lines 1–2 were cut in these productions (s41; Daly; s56). In Sothern's 1911 production Leonato had drawn Antonio aside, Beatrice's speech interrupting their private conversation (s63). In Branagh's film Don John grabbed Hero's hand and kissed it as she and her family were on their way to the masquerade; her discomfort at his action fuelled their disparaging remarks about him (3–5).

and half Count John's melancholy in Signor Benedick's face –   10

BEATRICE With a good leg and a good foot, uncle, and money enough in his purse, such a man would win any woman in the world if a could get her good will.

LEONATO By my troth, niece, thou wilt never get thee a husband, if thou be so shrewd of thy tongue.   15

ANTONIO In faith, she's too curst.

BEATRICE Too curst is more than curst, I shall lessen God's sending that way: for it is said, God sends a curst cow short horns, but to a cow too curst, he sends none.

LEONATO So, by being too curst, God will send you no horns.   20

BEATRICE Just, if he send me no husband, for the which blessing I am at him upon my knees every morning and evening: Lord, I could not endure a husband with a beard on his face, I had rather lie in the woollen!

LEONATO You may light on a husband that hath no beard.   25

BEATRICE What should I do with him – dress him in my apparel and make him my waiting gentlewoman? He that hath a beard is more than a youth: and he that hath no beard is less than a man: and he that is more than a youth, is not for me, and he that is less than a man, I am not for him: therefore I will even take sixpence in earnest of the   30 bearward, and lead his apes into hell.

LEONATO Well then, go you into hell.

BEATRICE No, but to the gate, and there will the devil meet me like an old cuckold with horns on his head, and say, get you to heaven, Beatrice, get you to heaven, here's no place for you maids. So deliver I up my   35 apes, and away to Saint Peter: for the heavens, he shows me where the

---

12   **win ... world** In Sothern's 1904–5 production Hero demurred with an 'Oh' (s59).

13   In the Kembles' productions Antonio drew Hero aside to inform her of Don Pedro's plan to woo her for Claudio (Kemble 1810).

14–15   *UP*'s alteration ('thou will't never get a Man to venture upon thee with that persecuting Wit of thine') effaced the ambiguity of 'shrewd' (sharp-tongued/sharp-witted) in *Much Ado*. Penelope Wilton (1981) countered Leonato's statement with a kiss exhibiting her capacity for affection (pbk).

16–21a   Cut from Garrick to Bridges-Adams, and sometimes since, on account of the obscurity and indelicacy of the word play.

21ff.   Ellen Terry scoffed at men and marriage with a merriment signifying that her antipathy was 'only skin deep' (*Th*, 1 Nov. 1882, 299; 1 Oct. 1880, 218).

30–7   From the Kembles to Tree these jests were cut or abridged as too irreverent for the stage.

33   Geraldine McEwan (1961), watching Margaret and Ursula select masks for the guests, held up a horned devil mask (pbk, pr. photo).

bachelors sit, and there live we, as merry as the day is long.
ANTONIO Well, niece, I trust you will be ruled by your father.
BEATRICE Yes faith, it is my cousin's duty to make curtsy, and say, father,
as it please you: but yet for all that, cousin, let him be a handsome   40
fellow, or else make another curtsy, and say, father, as it please me.
LEONATO Well, niece, I hope to see you one day fitted with a husband.
BEATRICE Not till God make men of some other metal than earth: would
it not grieve a woman to be overmastered with a piece of valiant dust?
to make an account of her life to a clod of wayward marl? No, uncle,   45
I'll none: Adam's sons are my brethren, and truly I hold it a sin to
match in my kindred.
LEONATO Daughter, remember what I told you: if the prince do solicit
you in that kind, you know your answer.
BEATRICE The fault will be in the music, cousin, if you be not wooed in   50
good time: if the prince be too important, tell him there is measure in
everything, and so dance out the answer. For hear me, Hero, wooing,
wedding, and repenting, is as a Scotch jig, a measure and a
cinquepace: the first suit is hot and hasty like a Scotch jig (and full as
fantastical), the wedding mannerly modest (as a measure) full of state   55
and ancientry, and then comes Repentance, and with his bad legs falls
into the cinquepace faster and faster, till he sink into his grave.
LEONATO Cousin, you apprehend passing shrewdly.
BEATRICE I have a good eye, uncle, I can see a church by daylight.
LEONATO The revellers are entering, brother, make good room.   60

[*Exit Antonio*]

Enter DON PEDRO, CLAUDIO, BENEDICK *and* BALTHASAR, *Maskers with
a drum;* [*re-enter* ANTONIO, *masked, followed by*] DON JOHN [*and*
BORACHIO *and others including* MARGARET *and* URSULA. *The dance begins*]

DON PEDRO Lady, will you walk a bout with your friend?

37 **bachelors** Peggy Ashcroft took the arm of Antonio, who laughed at the idea of living merrily
with Beatrice (s93). Judi Dench hinted a 'gentle regret' at being placed with the bachelors
(David, *Shakespeare*, 219).

42 In Langham's 1961 production Leonato kissed Beatrice, suggesting a warmth of affection
between them; she hugged him at 241 (pbk).

44 **piece … dust** Sinead Cusack (1982) shook Antonio (pbk).

46–7 Spoken 'puritanically' at Burton's, NY, 1857 (s21).

50–7 Julia Marlowe lifted her skirt daintily, pointing her toe as in a dance measure (s63). Judi
Dench (1976) instructed Hero as if from sad experience (pr. photo). *UP* and Langham (1961)
omitted 52b–7, Edwin Booth 48–57.

59 Julia Marlowe ran off laughing (s63).

60 Susan Fleetwood (1990) spun with delight on her swing (pbk). Branagh's film introduced the
revelry with a burst of flame from a fire-blower.

61–114   In Renaissance performances the masquerade may have conveyed something of the ambiguity of carnival, servants and nobility becoming for the moment equals in disguise, and licence of speech and behaviour sanctioned temporarily within a containing social order (see Bristol, *Carnival and Theatre*, 1985). The sequence was probably staged with some spectacle (see the references to sumptuous entertainments at 1.1.206–7; 1.3.31–2; 2.1.127). The male characters wore visors (69–70a, 116b–17) and may have been further disguised (1.1.246–7; 2.1.67–8, 82–91, 94–5). Elizabethan masquerade costumes are known to have included motifs from mythology, folk tale, biblical themes, pageantry, clownage, and primitivism (Hattaway, *Elizabethan Popular Theatre*, 137). The Folio stage directions indicate 'Maskers with a drum' (60), and music and dancing (114).

     UP omitted the masquerade, except for a passing allusion (p.18). Garrick advertised it as a special entertainment with professional dancers (playbills), *The Macaroni and Theatrical Magazine* (Oct. 1773) listing his masquerade as one of the most impressive theatrical spectacles of the period. Timings recorded by Haymarket prompter J. R. Brownsmith suggest that Garrick's masquerade dances may have occupied seven or eight minutes: his Act 2 (thirty-two minutes) took double the performance time of Act 1 with a text only one-and-a-half times as long (*Time-Piece*, 68). The major Victorian and Edwardian productions made the masquerade a grand spectacle (see introduction). Craig gave the revelry thematic significance with a masque (line 60) illustrating the alternation of peace and war and the inconstancy of men's love for women. The god of war appeared amid flaming torches and a roll of drums; then the god and goddess of love tripped through a bower and ladies were wooed by advancing lovers. This was interrupted by a call to war, and as Don Pedro began his dialogue with Hero there was a prophetic spectacle of weeping ladies forsaken by their lovers (P-1903b). The masquerade included a dance with soldiers in red and black and thirty masked revellers fantastically dressed in gold and green with diadems of mistletoe on their heads, bearing lighted candles and waving great hoops of green leaves (P-1903b; Craig's production notes; *Lloyd's*, 24 May 1903; *St*, 28 May 1903; *SR*, 30 May 1903; Byam Shaw woodcut, souvenir programme, BL; photo, *ILN*, 16 June 1903, 894). In Langham's 1958 production (Stratford, Ontario) 'the masked ball was a Straussian entertainment … on an open stage decorated with Chinese lanterns' (*SQ* 9, 1958, 537). Seale (1958) included a colourful dance of lancers with pennants (*LDP*, 27 Aug. 1958). Zeffirelli's masquerade was flamboyant, with five elaborate dance sequences and bizarre costumes: Hero wore a huge headdress petalled like a sunflower, Claudio a visored helmet with enormous plumes (pbk; pr. photos). The 1968 and 1982 RSC productions included a sinister martial element, with displays of swordsmanship by troupes of masked swordfighters (*Punch*, 23 Oct. 1968; *SH*, 30 Apr. 1982; P-1982; pr. photos). The masquerade in Barton's production included a dumb show suggesting behind the civilised face of the British Raj a colonialist world of violence, obsessive imperialism (repeated saluting of the flag) and precarious rule. The dumb show also shadowed the male rivalry and power play of *Much Ado*. Claudio entered through a makeshift proscenium stretched between bamboo poles. Hearing galloping horses, he

HERO So you walk softly, and look sweetly, and say nothing, I am yours for
    the walk, and especially when I walk away.
DON PEDRO With me in your company.
HERO I may say so when I please.   65
DON PEDRO And when please you to say so?
HERO When I like your favour, for God defend the lute should be like the
    case.
DON PEDRO My visor is Philemon's roof, within the house is Jove.
HERO Why then your visor should be thatched.
DON PEDRO   Speak low if you speak love.   70
                    [*They move on in the dance*]
[BALTHASAR] Well, I would you did like me.

searched about with his telescope, exclaiming 'Oh my God' as he sighted the 'enemy'. Don
Pedro, disguised as a local chieftain, entered and killed Claudio. In a second dumb show the
flag was lowered to the sound of the last post; Don Pedro 'slit' Claudio's throat, ran round
the stage triumphantly with the flag, and claimed Hero as his prize (pbk; pr. photos). This
business gave an ominous undertone to the ensuing Don Pedro–Hero dialogue (61–70). At
the Seattle Repertory Theatre, 1978, the dark potential of the masquerade was suggested by
eerie music, sombre lighting and visors made of shining reflective squares foregrounding
the idea of illusion (*SQ* 30, 1979, 263). Warchus's masquerade (1993), a lively Western
hoedown in costumes of the late 1920s, gave an impression of 'youthful exhilaration and
gaiety' qualified by equivocal appearance (*Sp*, 17 July 1993). The carnivalesque revelry in
Branagh's film was qualified by cuts from figure to figure showing a lion face and masks with
long beaks, sinister and threatening. In most productions the players have used hand-held
masks, sometimes more elaborate disguises. There are often dances between (occasionally
during) the dialogues.

From the Kembles to the first decade of the twentieth century it was traditional for
Benedick to evade a pursuing Beatrice during the masquerade. When she finally caught up
with him in Alexander's 1898 production, he showed 'his recalcitrance by stamping his foot
in the middle of the minuet' (Grein, *Dramatic Criticism*, I.46).

61–70 In the promptbooks of the Kembles, Dow (Philadelphia, 1854), Taylor (Boston, c.1860) and
    Irving, Claudio watched Don Pedro and Hero closely while Don John and Borachio observed
    all three (s5–6, s25, s35, s46), Don John in Irving's production smiling behind his mask in
    anticipation of his plot (*Time*, Nov. 1882, 958). Tree, Carey, Seale and Branagh (1993)
    abridged the Don Pedro–Hero dialogue, Branagh using only the first line.

71–81 Macready gave the first three speeches in this sequence to Benedick, as in Q. Several
    directors highlighted the relationship between Borachio and Margaret by giving the male
    speeches in this sequence to Borachio (Bridges-Adams 1933–4, Gielgud, Seale, Langham,
    Barton, Gill and Branagh). George Foss (Old Vic, 1918) had Margaret evade Balthasar at 81
    and run off with Borachio (Foss, *What the Author Meant*, 116); Zeffirelli and Hands also

MARGARET So would not I for your own sake, for I have many ill
qualities.

[BALTHASAR] Which is one?

MARGARET I say my prayers aloud. 75

[BALTHASAR] I love you the better, the hearers may cry amen.

MARGARET God match me with a good dancer.

BALTHASAR Amen.

MARGARET And God keep him out of my sight when the dance is done:
answer, clerk. 80

BALTHASAR No more words, the clerk is answered.

[*They move on in the dance*]

URSULA I know you well enough, you are Signor Antonio.

ANTONIO At a word, I am not.

URSULA I know you by the waggling of your head.

ANTONIO To tell you true, I counterfeit him. 85

URSULA You could never do him so ill-well, unless you were the very
man: here's his dry hand up and down, you are he, you are he.

ANTONIO At a word, I am not.

URSULA Come, come, do you think I do not know you by your excellent
wit? Can virtue hide itself? Go to, mum, you are he, graces will 90
appear, and there's an end.

[*They move on in the dance*]

BEATRICE Will you not tell me who told you so?

paired them at this point. Most managers from the Kembles to Tree cut 71–81, but not
Macready, J. W. Wallack, Saker or Poel. Nunn (1969) transposed the sequence to 114;
Branagh transposed a shortened version to 91.

82–91 In Sothern's productions Antonio tried to disguise his voice, but was recognised by the
wagging of his head. He showed pleasure at Ursula's reference to his 'excellent wit', failing
to detect the irony (S59, S63). The Ursula–Antonio dialogue was cut in most productions
from Garrick to the 1870s, and by Tree. Nunn transposed it to 138. In eighteenth- and
nineteenth-century productions the omission of one or both the dialogues at 71–91 gave
added prominence to the Beatrice–Benedick interchange (92–114).

91 SD Fanny Davenport introduced a boisterous sequence in which a youth chased a girl through
the crowd, bringing her down with a kiss and binding her in a scarf (P-1886). Edwin Booth
and Hanford cleared the stage to give special prominence to the Beatrice–Benedick dialogue
(S41, S56).

92 Spoken by Helena Faucit 'with a plaintive, ill-used air' (Faucit, 'Female characters', 215).

92–114 In several productions from the Kembles on, Beatrice asserted her superiority over Benedick
by pursuing him about the stage in this sequence (S5–6, Dolby, S21, S25, S35, S59, S92; *E*, 1
May 1875). Macready disguised his voice in a hoarse whisper (Pollock, *Macready*, 132),
Irving, Sothern and Holloway in a falsetto (*NY Mirror*, 5 Apr. 1884; S59, S63, S88), Branagh
(1993) in a foreign accent. Holloway (1934) also pretended to be a lame old man (S88).

BENEDICK No, you shall pardon me.

BEATRICE Nor will you not tell me who you are?

BENEDICK Not now.   95

BEATRICE That I was disdainful, and that I had my good wit out of *The Hundred Merry Tales*: well, this was Signor Benedick that said so.

BENEDICK What's he?

BEATRICE I am sure you know him well enough.

BENEDICK Not I, believe me.   100

BEATRICE Did he never make you laugh?

BENEDICK I pray you, what is he?

BEATRICE Why he is the prince's jester, a very dull fool, only his gift is, in devising impossible slanders: none but libertines delight in him, and the commendation is not in his wit, but in his villainy, for he both   105 pleases men and angers them, and then they laugh at him, and beat him: I am sure he is in the fleet, I would he had boarded me.

Branagh (1993) approached Beatrice giggling in a grinning clown mask, giving point to her gibe about 'the prince's jester, a very dull fool'.

In a comment indicative of Victorian perceptions of womanhood, Edward Russell observed that Helena Faucit was 'too full of mischief and gaiety to spare her butt a single arrow, but too bewitching and too truly a lady ever to seem too bold or too reckless an archer' (*LDP*, 16 Dec. 1870). Ellen Terry made the interchange essentially sportive: it was 'all done in pure *diablerie*', in 'simple mischief, inspired by keen delight at finding her butt so agreeably vulnerable' (*Th*, 1 Oct. 1880, 218); 'only he who was blind would fail to perceive the half-veiled presence of her love' (*PhI*, 19 Mar. 1884). Yet her taunts were telling enough to force Benedick to 'seek an ignominious shelter' among the crowd of guests (*Time*, Nov. 1882, 958). He finally hid in a curtain, where to his great vexation she caught him without his mask (*MN*, Chicago, 16 Jan. 1885).

96–7 Sothern nodded assent at 'disdainful', and nodded vigorously at the idea that Beatrice's wit was borrowed from *The Hundred Merry Tales*.

103 **the prince's jester** In this sequence John Bell as Benedick (1996) was disguised in a parti-coloured jester's costume.

103–7 John and Charles Kemble walked about 'much vexed' (s5), business also adopted in Taylor's Boston promptbook (s35). Irving, wincing under Beatrice's attack, assumed a false bravado and tried to carry off his defeat 'as a victory yielded out of consideration for an inferior opponent' (*O*, 11 Jan. 1891). Sothern started angrily at 'prince's jester' and looked uneasy when called a 'very dull fool' (s59, s63). Peggy Ashcroft laughed and dropped a curtsy at these words; McBean's photographs (SCL) show her with a whimsical expression directing her taunts at the long nose of Gielgud's mask, while behind it he listens startled and wide-eyed. The indelicate 'I would he had boarded me' (107) was cut in most Victorian and

BENEDICK When I know the gentleman, I'll tell him what you say.

BEATRICE Do, do, he'll but break a comparison or two on me, which peradventure (not marked, or not laughed at) strikes him into   110 melancholy, and then there's a partridge wing saved, for the fool will eat no supper that night. We must follow the leaders.

BENEDICK In every good thing.

BEATRICE Nay, if they lead to any ill, I will leave them at the next turning.

    Music for the Dance. [They Dance.] Exeunt [all but Don John,
           Borachio and Claudio]

DON JOHN Sure my brother is amorous on Hero, and hath withdrawn her   115 father to break with him about it: the ladies follow her, and but one visor remains.

BORACHIO And that is Claudio, I know him by his bearing.

DON JOHN Are not you Signor Benedick?

CLAUDIO You know me well, I am he.   120

Edwardian productions, and sometimes since. Emma Thompson (1993) gave these words an inflection of desire.

108   Spoken as a threat by Macready (Pollock, *Macready*, 132). Sothern, nettled, momentarily forgot his falsetto; in 1911 he stamped his foot (s59, s63).

113–14   Cut in most nineteenth-century productions.

114 SD   Many productions have staged a dance as in Q and F. In the Kemble productions Benedick ran off pursued by Beatrice (s2, s5), business adopted in several American promptbooks (s21, s25, s35, P-WHS, s81). During the dance Julia Marlowe (1904–5) abandoned Benedick, who seized a small child for a partner (s59). In 1911 she refused to take his hand in the dance, striking him with her fan (s63). Susan Fleetwood (1990) also slapped Benedick's hand and ran off (pbk). Fanny Davenport and Tree made an effective transition to the ensuing dialogue by having Don Pedro exit with Hero, closely observed by Claudio, Don John and Borachio; in Tree's production Don Pedro also kissed her hand (pbks). In Irving's production Borachio made a hurried assignation with Margaret at the exit (cutting, Fitzgerald's Irving scrapbooks, VIII.29). Poel (s57) left Margaret on stage with Borachio during the ensuing dialogue (115–27).

115–18   The social harmony normally signified by dancing in the Renaissance period (Thomson, *Shakespeare's Theatre*, 100) was here undercut as Don John began to subvert the planned match between Hero and Claudio. In the Kemble productions Don John, signalling to Borachio that he was about to dissemble, spoke with 'affected loudness and emotion, in order to be observed by Claudio' (Oxberry); Borachio's reply was whispered (s6). Garrick, less subtly, prefaced Don John's speech with an aside: 'Now then for a trick of contrivance' (Bell). In Sothern and Jewett's productions Don John spoke so as not to be heard by Claudio (s59, s81). In Gill's production (1981) secrecy and entrapment were suggested as Borachio moved to close the upstage doors (118) before the dialogue with Claudio (pbk).

DON JOHN Signor, you are very near my brother in his love, he is
    enamoured on Hero, I pray you dissuade him from her, she is no
    equal for his birth: you may do the part of an honest man in it.
CLAUDIO How know you he loves her?
DON JOHN I heard him swear his affection. 125
BORACHIO So did I too, and he swore he would marry her tonight.
DON JOHN Come, let us to the banquet.

                              Exeunt Don John and Borachio

CLAUDIO Thus answer I in name of Benedick,
      But hear these ill news with the ears of Claudio:
      'Tis certain so, the prince woos for himself, 130
      Friendship is constant in all other things,
      Save in the office and affairs of love:
      Therefore all hearts in love use their own tongues.
      Let every eye negotiate for itself,
      And trust no agent: for beauty is a witch, 135
      Against whose charms faith melteth into blood:
      This is an accident of hourly proof,
      Which I mistrusted not: farewell therefore, Hero.

                  Enter BENEDICK

BENEDICK Count Claudio.
CLAUDIO Yea, the same. 140

121–6   Angus McBean's photograph of this sequence in Gielgud's 1950 production shows Don John
       and Borachio standing behind Claudio's shoulders like tempters, Don John looking slightly
       cynical, Borachio superior and self-satisfied, Claudio jealously brooding and a little alarmed
       (SCL). In Branagh's film Claudio watched Hero embrace Don Pedro, who then kissed her
       hands tenderly.

125   Claudio gave a start in Sothern's 1904–5 production (s59).

128–38   Claudio tore off his mask in Sothern's 1911 production; in the 1904–5 production he sank into
       a chair, his desolation contrasting with the gaiety of three couples who entered chatting and
       laughing (s59, s63). In Branagh's film Claudio spoke in agonised bitterness, uttering
       'farewell therefore, Hero' with a jealous spite foreshadowing the renunciation sequence.

139–53   In Macready's production Claudio signified his agitation and reluctance to talk by repeated
       stage crossings (s15–16); in Sothern's production he sighed and buried his face in his arm
       on the table, Benedick assuming a tone of mock sympathy (s59). In Gielgud's 1949–50
       productions Benedick needled Claudio by tapping him on the shoulder, prodding him with
       his mask, sitting beside him and taking his hand; Claudio threw him off petulantly at 150
       (s92–3). At the Seattle Repertory Theatre, 1978, Benedick's rudeness to Claudio was
       'motivated by genuine annoyance, if not anger, at Beatrice's dancing barbs' (*SQ* 30, 1979,
       262). In a production which highlighted the pervasive eavesdropping in the play, Hands
       (1982) introduced a piece of double eavesdropping, Beatrice observing Benedick and

BENEDICK Come, will you go with me?

CLAUDIO Whither?

BENEDICK Even to the next willow, about your own business, county:
what fashion will you wear the garland of? About your neck, like an
usurer's chain? Or under your arm, like a lieutenant's scarf? You   145
must wear it one way, for the prince hath got your Hero.

CLAUDIO I wish him joy of her.

BENEDICK Why that's spoken like an honest drovier, so they sell bull-
ocks: but did you think the prince would have served you thus?

CLAUDIO I pray you leave me.   150

BENEDICK Ho now you strike like the blind man, 'twas the boy that stole
your meat, and you'll beat the post.

CLAUDIO If it will not be, I'll leave you.   *Exit*

BENEDICK Alas poor hurt fowl, now will he creep into sedges: but that my
Lady Beatrice should know me, and not know me: the prince's fool!   155
Hah, it may be I go under that title because I am merry: yea but so I
am apt to do myself wrong: I am not so reputed, it is the base (though
bitter) disposition of Beatrice, that puts the world into her person,
and so gives me out: well, I'll be revenged as I may.

Enter DON PEDRO

DON PEDRO Now, signor, where's the count, did you see him?   160

BENEDICK Troth, my lord, I have played the part of Lady Fame, I found
him here as melancholy as a lodge in a warren; I told him, and I think I
told him true, that your grace had got the good will of this young lady,
and I offered him my company to a willow tree, either to make him a
garland, as being forsaken, or to bind him up a rod, as being worthy to 165
be whipped.

DON PEDRO To be whipped: what's his fault?

BENEDICK The flat transgression of a schoolboy, who being overjoyed

---

Claudio while all three were observed by Borachio and Margaret (pbk).

143–6 Spoken teasingly by Sothern (s59). Robert Lindsay (BBC-TV, 1984) spoke this and the next
two speeches in a hard, derisive tone.

147 Spoken spitefully at Burton's, NY, 1857 (s21), angrily in Sothern's 1904–5 production (s59).

153 Spoken pettishly at Burton's, NY. As Claudio went off Sothern put his hand on his heart and
laughed mockingly (s59).

155 **prince's fool** Macready glared with indignation, jabbing out the words of this and the
following speeches with fierce emphasis (s17).

156 Irving repeated 'merry' with a 'hard, dry and blockish' contempt (s47).

160ff. Poel highlighted the misprision and false appearance in this sequence by the symbolic
presence upstage of servants with cloak and mask (s57). In some productions Don Pedro
brought Hero on with him to give to Claudio (NT 1965, 1981; Branagh film).

168–9 Allam (1990), assuming that Don Pedro had wronged Claudio, spoke with a resentment

with finding a bird's nest, shows it his companion, and he steals it.

DON PEDRO Wilt thou make a trust a transgression? The transgression is   170
in the stealer.

BENEDICK Yet it had not been amiss the rod had been made, and the
garland too, for the garland he might have worn himself, and the rod
he might have bestowed on you, who (as I take it) have stolen his
bird's nest.   175

DON PEDRO I will but teach them to sing, and restore them to the owner.

BENEDICK If their singing answer your saying, by my faith, you say
honestly.

DON PEDRO The Lady Beatrice hath a quarrel to you, the gentleman that
danced with her told her she is much wronged by you.   180

BENEDICK Oh she misused me past the endurance of a block: an oak but
with one green leaf on it, would have answered her: my very visor
began to assume life, and scold with her: she told me, not thinking I
had been myself, that I was the prince's jester, that I was duller than a
great thaw, huddling jest upon jest, with such impossible conveyance   185
upon me, that I stood like a man at a mark, with a whole army shooting
at me: she speaks poniards, and every word stabs: if her breath were
as terrible as her terminations, there were no living near her, she
would infect to the north star: I would not marry her, though she were
endowed with all that Adam had left him before he transgressed: she   190

foreshadowing his later willingness to take up the cause of the wronged Hero (*FT*, 12 Apr.
1990). The elaborate exchange about the stolen bird's nest (167–78) was cut or abridged by
Saker, Daly, Tree, Sothern (1911) and Eyre.

179–80   In Sothern's 1904–5 production spoken in response to offstage laughter by Beatrice (S59). In
the BBC-TV production (1984) Don Pedro goaded Benedick with some cruelty; in Branagh's
film he spoke as if confronting Benedick for a breach of chivalry.

181–97   Spoken with caustic bitterness by Lindsay (BBC-TV, 1984). Branagh (1993) became
increasingly exasperated, to the amusement of Hero and Don Pedro. Several Benedicks
from C. Kemble to Sothern interpolated 'Wronged! She wronged!' before this speech
(Dolby, S3, S36, S41, S46, Daly, S59), Irving voicing the words in a puzzled, questioning tone,
then bursting forth indignantly, 'Oh! ah! she misused me ...' (S46; *Lloyd's*, 15 Oct. 1882).

187   **stabs** In several nineteenth-century American productions Don Pedro interjected, 'Marry
her Benedick.'

187b–9a   Cut in most productions from the Kembles to Bridges-Adams.

189b–90   'I would not marry *her*', said Charles Kemble, his emphasis signalling a crack in Benedick's
asserted misogamy (*JB*, 12 Apr. 1840). Irving spoke the sentence with 'infinite cynicism' (*Th*, 1
Nov. 1882, 302). Sinead Cusack (1982) added a comic touch by an upstage entry to overhear
Benedick's assertion (pbk).

190b–3a   Often cut or abridged.

would have made Hercules have turned spit, yea, and have cleft his
club to make the fire too: come, talk not of her, you shall find her the
infernal Ate in good apparel. I would to God some scholar would
conjure her, for certainly, while she is here, a man may live as quiet in
hell, as in a sanctuary, and people sin upon purpose, because they   195
would go thither, so indeed all disquiet, horror and perturbation
follows her.

> *Enter* CLAUDIO *and* BEATRICE, LEONATO [*and*] HERO

DON PEDRO Look, here she comes.
BENEDICK Will your grace command me any service to the world's end? I
will go on the slightest errand now to the Antipodes that you can   200
devise to send me on: I will fetch you a tooth-picker now from the
furthest inch of Asia: bring you the length of Prester John's foot: fetch
you a hair off the Great Cham's beard: do you any embassage to the
Pygmies, rather than hold three words conference with this Harpy:
you have no employment for me?   205
DON PEDRO None, but to desire your good company.
BENEDICK Oh God, sir, here's a dish I love not, I cannot endure my Lady
Tongue.   *Exit*

197 SD   In nineteenth- and early twentieth-century productions Beatrice's approach was frequently
signalled by offstage laughter. Ellen Kean's joyous laugh seemed to refute Benedick's
complaint about her fierceness (*Appleton's Journal*, Oct. 1880).

198   Belton (Burton's, NY, 1857) started in perturbation (S21).

199–205   C. Kemble pleaded to be sent 'to the world's end' with particular eagerness (*MP*, 14 Jan.
1811). Don Pedro replied in Sothern's 1911 production with a laugh and shake of the head
(S63). Irving began the speech slowly and quietly, modulating through laughter and
resolution to terror (S45). Benedick's description of Beatrice as a 'Harpy' (204) was
countered in Fanny Davenport's production by a laugh from Don Pedro, in Branagh's film
by a cut to Beatrice, looking troubled but by no means harpyish. In several productions
Benedick struggled to exit during the speech, but was held back by Don Pedro (Macready,
Irving, Sothern, Tree, Bridges-Adams, Zeffirelli). Some American productions delayed
Beatrice's entry to 208, her offstage laughter during Benedick's speech heightening his
agitation (S21, S25, P-WHS, S35, S59, S81).

207b–8   **I ... Tongue** Spoken by Gielgud with an ironic bow to Beatrice, who returned a curtsy
(S93–4). Godfrey (1971) struck a note of extravagant posturing. Branagh (1993) shouted
in exasperation and stalked off, drawing an explosive laugh from Don Pedro. The words
brought Sinead Cusack to the brink of tears (*T*, 21 Apr. 1982). In the Breach of the Piece
production, Edinburgh Festival, 1993, Beatrice, hurt to tears, began 'flirting with Don Pedro
out of a frantic need to regain her self-esteem' (*SQ* 45, 1994, 349).

208 SD   Gentleman referred to the comic effect of Benedick's 'hasty' exit, 'as if terrified' by the

DON PEDRO Come, lady, come, you have lost the heart of Signor
   Benedick.   210
BEATRICE Indeed, my lord, he lent it me a while, and I gave him use for it,
   a double heart for his single one: marry once before he won it of me,
   with false dice, therefore your grace may well say I have lost it.
DON PEDRO You have put him down, lady, you have put him down.
BEATRICE So I would not he should do me, my lord, lest I should prove   215
   the mother of fools: I have brought Count Claudio, whom you sent
   me to seek.
DON PEDRO Why how now, count, wherefore are you sad?
CLAUDIO Not sad, my lord.
DON PEDRO How then? Sick?   220
CLAUDIO Neither, my lord.
BEATRICE The count is neither sad, nor sick, nor merry, nor well: but
   civil, count, civil as an orange, and something of that jealous
   complexion.

approach of Beatrice (Bell; *DrC* 2, 1770, 310). In his panic to escape, Sothern collided with
a page carrying a pitcher on a tray, Don Pedro convulsing with laughter (s59). Penelope
Wilton (1981) tried to hit Benedick (Michael Gambon) as he went out through a door; he
opened it slightly and made a face at her, then as she launched herself at him, slammed
it in her face (pbk). Allam (1990) cast at Beatrice the glove she had thrown down in
challenge at 1.1.118 (pbk; *SS* 44, 1991, 171).

211–13 The feminist revolution of the late twentieth century has given special prominence to these
lines. Judi Dench (1976) made them central to her representation of Beatrice, speaking with
a 'flicker of pain' in her eyes suggesting 'a whole history of a growing love that somehow
came to nothing' (*CL*, 5 May 1988; David, *Shakespeare*, 219). 'You fe[lt] her wit [was] a
defence against further breakages' (*G*, 1 July 1977). Samantha Bond (1988) also 'suggested
an inwardness of pain' (*SS* 42, 1989, 132). Sinead Cusack was 'visibly upset by the memory'
(Gay, *As She Likes It*, 168). Emma Thompson spoke the lines ruefully, with a slow, meditative
intensity. They were cut in most productions from Garrick to Craig, and by Hunt, Carey and
Langham; Bridges-Adams and Seale abridged them. Furness (1899), however, recognised
their significance: 'It is strange,' he wrote, 'that into no discussion (that I can recall) is any
weight given, or indeed any reference made, to this speech. Enough is here told to explain
Benedick's first greeting to Beatrice as "Lady Disdain". Between the lines, there can be
almost discerned the plot of another play' (New Variorum edition, 88).

214–16a The bawdy jest was cut by Warren and Wood (1804), and in numerous productions from
Macready to Bridges-Adams.

222–4 Spoken mockingly by Julia Marlowe. She uttered 'sick' with a very long face; 'nor well' in a
'lugubrious tone'. Claudio turned away dejectedly, struggling to control his chagrin as the
others laughed at his expense (s63).

DON PEDRO I'faith, lady, I think your blazon to be true, though I'll be 225
sworn, if he be so, his conceit is false: here, Claudio, I have wooed in
thy name, and fair Hero is won: I have broke with her father, and his
good will obtained: name the day of marriage, and God give thee joy.

LEONATO Count, take of me my daughter, and with her my fortunes: his
grace hath made the match, and all grace say amen to it. 230

BEATRICE Speak, count, 'tis your cue.

CLAUDIO Silence is the perfectest herald of joy, I were but little happy if I
could say, how much! Lady, as you are mine, I am yours: I give away
myself for you, and dote upon the exchange.

BEATRICE Speak, cousin, or (if you cannot) stop his mouth with a kiss, 235
and let not him speak neither.

DON PEDRO In faith, lady, you have a merry heart.

BEATRICE Yea, my lord, I thank it, poor fool it keeps on the windy side of
care: my cousin tells him in his ear that he is in her heart.

CLAUDIO And so she doth, cousin. 240

BEATRICE Good Lord for alliance: thus goes every one to the world but I,

226–34 In C. Kemble's performances Claudio's confession of love drew a comic sigh from Beatrice
(Dolby, Cumberland). Gielgud staged the betrothal with grace and finesse. Don Pedro
brought Hero downstage for Leonato to present to Claudio and then stepped back as the
young lovers faced each other, speechless. With a gentle touch of her fan Beatrice reminded
Claudio of his cue, at which he knelt beside Hero, clasped her hand in his, and kissed it
(s93–4). In Nunn's production 'the incredulous conceit of this beaming pair, and their
desperate awkwardness, as they [stood] tongue-tied surrounded by a ring of curious
spectators, [was] most delicately taken' (*Sp*, 25 Oct. 1968). In the military society of Barton's
production, Claudio 'stroll[ed] about shaking hands as at a governor-general's garden party'
(*NS*, 16 Apr. 1976). The betrothal was clearly an arrangement negotiated by males, Leonato
and Don Pedro shaking hands as if congratulating one another on the closure of a business
deal (pbk). Some directors added a touch of foreboding, Don John here eavesdropping from
a balcony in Bridges-Adams's 1933–4 production, and flitting across the back of the stage in
Alexander's, 1990 (*SS* 44, 1991, 170).

231–2 In the Renaissance theatre, where speech was almost continuous, stage silences were
infrequent and significant (Gurr, *Shakespearean Stage*, 178); Claudio is here speechless
with emotion. As Claudio paused at the word 'silence' in the 1990 RSC production, Hero
started, thinking he was refusing any response to their betrothal (pbk).

237ff. Hero and Claudio traditionally whisper to each other apart from the rest of the group.

241–3 Helena Faucit gave a fleeting look as if half inclined to cry (*MET*, 2 Nov. 1869). Ellen Terry's
delight mingled with a touch of pathos; there were tears in her eyes and voice (*LDP*, 27 Sep.
1883; *MN*, Chicago, 16 Jan. 1885). Julia Marlowe and Susan Fleetwood sank to a seat in
momentary sadness (pbks), Elizabeth Spriggs (1971) to the ground with a longing sigh

and I am sunburnt, I may sit in a corner and cry, 'Heigh ho for a
husband.'
DON PEDRO Lady Beatrice, I will get you one.
BEATRICE I would rather have one of your father's getting: hath your   245
grace ne'er a brother like you? Your father got excellent husbands, if a
maid could come by them.
DON PEDRO Will you have me, lady?
BEATRICE No, my lord, unless I might have another for working-days,
your grace is too costly to wear every day: but I beseech your grace   250
pardon me, I was born to speak all mirth, and no matter.
DON PEDRO Your silence most offends me, and to be merry, best
becomes you, for out a question, you were born in a merry hour.
BEATRICE No sure, my lord, my mother cried, but then there was a star
danced, and under that was I born: cousins, God give you joy.   255

suggesting she would love to be married. Judi Dench restrained her tears with difficulty
(*G*, 1 July 1977), speaking the lines as a 'melancholy, sentient' woman 'hungry for something
she'[d] long stopped expecting to find' (*NS*, 16 Apr. 1976). Emma Thompson (1993) spoke
with regret and resignation.

244–8   Until the late twentieth century Don Pedro's proposal was typically offered as 'pleasant
raillery': 'the man is paying a compliment, no more' (*NYT*, 27 Aug. 1972). Bridges-Adams
(1933–4) staged the moment as an intimate *tête-à-tête*, Beatrice seated at a musical
instrument, Don Pedro leaning over it (s87–8). Anthony Nicholls (SMT 1958) proposed with
a show of gallantry, kissing Beatrice's hand (pbk). Douglass Watson (NYSF 1972) made a
thoughtful pause and proposed 'in dead earnest', gracefully accepting Beatrice's 'polite
rejection' (*NYT*, 27 Aug. 1972). The proposal has been seriously intended in several other
late twentieth-century productions (Champlain SF, 1975; Oregon SF, 1976; RSC 1990;
Shakespeare Theatre, Washington, 1992; Branagh's film: *SQ* 27, 1976, 41; 28, 1977, 247; 43,
1992, 460; *G*, 12 Apr. 1990). John Carlisle (RSC 1990) proposed 'with direct urgency' (*G*, 12
Apr. 1990); Derek Godfrey (RSC 1982) seemed 'half-in-earnest' (*G*, 14 May 1983). Lines
244–7 were often cut in nineteenth-century and Edwardian productions.

249–51   Ellen Terry gracefully turned aside Don Pedro's proposal with a curtsy (s47), a sparkle of
mischief mingling with a delicate nuance of deference (*Th*, 1 Oct. 1880, 1 Nov. 1882; *SR*, 18
June 1887, 875; Bancroft, *Stage and Bar*, 72). Julia Marlowe laughed at 'unless … days';
Leonato held up a warning finger; then, as she begged pardon, she gave a low curtsy and
crossed away laughing (s59, s63). Diana Wynyard's Beatrice could not resist the initial
retort; 'then, feeling she ha[d] let her tongue run away with her just a little too far this time,
she excuse[d] herself with delicate grace' (*DT*, 12 Jan. 1952). Joan Plowright apologised 'with
a wonderful blending of innocence, wisdom and sheer poetic truth' (*St*, 30 Mar. 1967).
Kathleen Widdoes' sudden shy embarrassment at the proposal suggested a hidden
vulnerability (*NYT*, 27 Aug. 1972). At the Champlain Shakespeare Festival, 1975, Don Pedro's

'sincere hesitant query' took Beatrice (Rita Litton) 'completely by surprise'; 'this time a joke would not smooth things over', and she excused herself 'with great tenderness and humility' (*SQ* 27, 1976, 41). Samantha Bond's 'gently turned refusal' was 'delicately underscored' (*DM*, 26 Aug. 1988), 'a discreet softening of tone' signalling 'that for once a compliment [was] not only well-turned but heartfelt' (*FT*, 26 Aug. 1988). 'It is at this moment, one feels, that she suddenly realises her love for Benedick' (*DT*, 27 Aug. 1988). There was 'a wonderful suppressed pain' about Felicity Kendal's refusal, 'as if these [were] matters too serious to be trifled with' (*G*, 13 May 1989). In an American production directed by David Richman, Beatrice momentarily dropped her façade, 'revealing uncertainty and sadness' and 'unease beneath the wit'; her 'tongue stumbled over suddenly difficult words, and her face crumpled' (Richman, *SC* 18.266). Susan Fleetwood's refusal was 'not a graceful evasion but a direct snub that reduce[d Don Pedro] to hurt silence', his feelings and his status ridiculed (*Ind*, 15 Apr. 1990; *SS* 44, 1991, 171). In Warchus's production (1993), Don Pedro was also hurt and belittled by Beatrice's rejection, his resultant anger fuelling his plot to match her with Benedick as an act of revenge (*SS* 47, 1994, 192–3). Kelly McGillis (Shakespeare Theatre, Washington, 1992) 'struggled for the right response, and winced in dismay at the inappropriate witticisms that she could not help herself from making' (*SQ* 43, 1992, 460). Emma Thompson (1993) pondered seriously for a few moments before declining with a sincere and regretful apology. Anna Volska (1996) declined at once, on impulse; then, in a long silence charged with glimpses of unsuspected feeling, it dawned on her that the proposal may have been more serious than she took it for. She seemed to waver in uncertainty how she might have responded had she realised, then tried to mask these responses with an awkward, hesitant jest ('unless I might have another ...'), the inappropriateness of which left her deeply embarrassed.

252–3   In Branagh's film spoken quietly and romantically, with deep feeling.

254–5   Helena Faucit and Diana Wynyard gave the lines a slight inflection of pathos (Faucit, 'Female characters', 217; *MG*, 21 Apr. 1949). Ellen Terry had tears in her eyes at 'my mother cried', then modulated to joyous merriment at 'a star danced' (Bancroft, *Stage and Bar*, 72). At these words 'there was a tip-toe elevation of gladness in her look, a jubilant ring in her voice, and happiness itself in the soft ripple of laughter ... accompanied by a gesture so exultant ... as to command unbounded admiration' (*Phl*, 19 Mar. 1884). 'With her right hand she made a sudden vertical dart upward, and with pointed forefinger gave a swift little flourish as if she would shake rays of light from its tip' (*BDA*, 28 Feb. 1884). Dorothy Green spoke seriously, with 'slow intensity' rather than a 'sudden flash' (Crosse, 'Performances', XII.135; *L*, 26 Mar. 1931). Peggy Ashcroft's words 'bubble[d] up naturally, glint[ed] on the stream' (*BP*, 22 July 1955). Judi Dench spoke wistfully (David, *Shakespeare*, 219), she and Penelope Wilton lingering more deliberately than most on 'my mother cried' (*NS*, 16 Apr. 1976; *FT*, in *LTR*, 13–26 Aug. 1981). Susan Fleetwood's 'star danced' suggested a gaiety more willed than spontaneous (*Ind*, 12 Apr. 1990). Kelly McGillis (1992) 'choked back tears' and 'quickly fled the scene', Hero 'gaz[ing] at her cousin in consternation' (*SQ* 43, 1992, 460).

LEONATO Niece, will you look to those things I told you of?

BEATRICE I cry you mercy, uncle: by your grace's pardon.   *Exit*

DON PEDRO By my troth a pleasant spirited lady.

LEONATO There's little of the melancholy element in her, my lord, she is
    never sad, but when she sleeps, and not ever sad then: for I have   260
    heard my daughter say, she hath often dreamed of unhappiness, and
    waked herself with laughing.

DON PEDRO She cannot endure to hear tell of a husband.

LEONATO Oh by no means, she mocks all her wooers out of suit.

DON PEDRO She were an excellent wife for Benedick.   265

LEONATO Oh Lord, my lord, if they were but a week married, they would
    talk themselves mad.

DON PEDRO County Claudio, when mean you to go to church?

CLAUDIO Tomorrow, my lord: time goes on crutches, till love have all his
    rites.   270

Emma Thompson spoke the lines wistfully. One of the unhappiest alterations in *UP* was the amendment of Beatrice's dancing star to a 'merry little Twinkler'.

255   **cousins ... joy** Louisa Nisbett (1843), less refined than some of the leading Beatrices of the nineteenth century, knocked Hero and Claudio's heads together with a loud laugh (S20). Julia Marlowe spoke teasingly (S63), pushing their heads together and running off laughing (S59). Ellen Kean moved graciously to the ottoman where Hero was whispering to Claudio and took their hands in hers (S26). In Bridges-Adams's productions Beatrice kissed Hero, as did Peggy Ashcroft and Sinead Cusack (S86, S88, S94, P-1982).

257   Beatrice has sometimes curtsied to Don Pedro at her exit (S19, S35, S46, S63, S88, S92–4). Robert Swann as Don Pedro (NT 1981) looked wistfully after her (pbk). Julia Marlowe glanced back at Hero and Claudio, a sigh mingling with her merriment (S59).

258   In Branagh's film spoken straight at the camera with deep conviction.

259–67   Cut from Garrick to the 1870s. The deletion of this light-hearted passage gave a more sober air than in the full text to the discussion of the plot to match Beatrice and Benedick, the omission of 265 making the idea seem less a sudden impulse of Don Pedro's than a deliberate plan. Craig, Sothern and Nunn (1969) cut 259–62.

265   Spoken as a sudden inspiration in Sothern's 1904–5 production, Don Pedro slapping his knees (S59). Eric Maxon's Don Pedro (SMT 1933–4) opened a music book, reflecting wistfully on Beatrice, then with a sudden change of mood snapped the book shut and proposed the match between her and Benedick (S87–8). Most nineteenth- and early twentieth-century productions represented Don Pedro's plan as a benevolent inspiration arising from shrewd observation of Beatrice and Benedick. The 1973 Young Vic production, on the other hand, conceived it as manipulative interference (Coffey, intro. to Folio Society edition of *Much Ado*, 7–9), Warchus's 1993 production as an act of recrimination (see commentary on 249–51).

LEONATO Not till Monday, my dear son, which is hence a just seven-
night, and a time too brief too, to have all things answer my mind.

DON PEDRO Come, you shake the head at so long a breathing, but I
warrant thee, Claudio, the time shall not go dully by us. I will in the
interim undertake one of Hercules' labours, which is, to bring Signor   275
Benedick and the Lady Beatrice into a mountain of affection, th'one
with th'other: I would fain have it a match, and I doubt not but to
fashion it, if you three will but minister such assistance as I shall give
you direction.

LEONATO My lord, I am for you, though it cost me ten nights' watchings.   280

CLAUDIO And I, my lord.

DON PEDRO And you too, gentle Hero?

HERO I will do any modest office, my lord, to help my cousin to a good
husband.

DON PEDRO And Benedick is not the unhopefullest husband that I know: 285
thus far can I praise him, he is of a noble strain, of approved valour,
and confirmed honesty. I will teach you how to humour your cousin,
that she shall fall in love with Benedick, and I, with your two helps,
will so practise on Benedick, that in despite of his quick wit, and his
queasy stomach, he shall fall in love with Beatrice: if we can do this,   290
Cupid is no longer an archer, his glory shall be ours, for we are the
only love-gods. Go in with me, and I will tell you my drift.

Exeunt

286   Anthony Ireland's Don Pedro (SMT 1955) nudged the star-struck Hero to pay attention to his
plot to bring Beatrice and Benedick together (s94).

37b–90   In Sothern's 1904–5 production Don Pedro lowered his voice and looked about cautiously,
speaking with suppressed laughter (s59).

290   Robin Ellis's Don Pedro (RSC 1976) yawned (pbk), his proposed match between Beatrice and
Benedick motivated as much by boredom as the other amusements of Barton's Indian Raj
society.

292   Fanny Davenport brought all the masked revellers on stage to celebrate the betrothal of
Hero and Claudio; the couple were surrounded by children throwing flowers and apples to
companions on a gallery above (pbk). Daly ended the scene with a serenade to Hero and
Claudio, Saker and Tree with joyous dancing (Daly, Saker, s69). In the 1981 NT production,
on the other hand, an emotionally starved Don Pedro grabbed Hero's arm and rushed off
with her (pbk). Langham (Stratford, Ontario, 1958) ended the scene with a thunder-shower,
during which servants with umbrellas removed tables and other props as the cast scurried
for cover (*SQ* 9, 1958, 537; Babula, *Shakespeare*, 496; Leiter, *Shakespeare*, 506). In
Warchus's production (1993) a huge window dropped in front of Hero and Claudio, through
which they were seen, 'looking sadly vulnerable now, from the prying perspective of Don
John' (*Ind*, 8 July 1993). Branagh's film cut to a fierce red face mask, eagle-beaked, from
beneath which Don John emerged to ominous music.

ACT 2, SCENE 2

Enter [DON] JOHN *and* BORACHIO

DON JOHN It is so, the Count Claudio shall marry the daughter of
Leonato.

BORACHIO Yea, my lord, but I can cross it.

DON JOHN Any bar, any cross, any impediment, will be medicinable to
me, I am sick in displeasure to him, and whatsoever comes athwart his   5
affection, ranges evenly with mine. How canst thou cross this
marriage?

BORACHIO Not honestly, my lord, but so covertly, that no dishonesty
shall appear in me.

DON JOHN Show me briefly how.   10

BORACHIO I think I told your lordship a year since, how much I am in the
favour of Margaret, the waiting gentlewoman to Hero.

Warren and Wood (1804) and Fanny Davenport (1886) transposed this scene to follow 2.3;
Branagh's film transposed it, much abbreviated, to 3.3.77. Edwin Booth cut about one-third
of the scene (16–25a, 27–30a), Fanny Davenport nearly three-quarters (4–9, 11–17, 19b–20a,
21–4, 27–30a, 38), Tree about 40 per cent (4–11a, 13, 17a, 19b–20a, 27–30a, 40–2). Sothern
set up an ironic counterpoint between the sinister dialogue of the scene and intermittent
offstage laughter from Claudio, Don Pedro and Leonato (pbk).

0 SD   Margaret entered with Borachio in Hunt's 1947 production (pbk).

1–2   In Bridges-Adams's 1933–4 production Don John's certainty stemmed from his having just
witnessed the betrothal of Hero and Claudio from the balcony where he was now speaking
(s87–8). In Gielgud's productions he and Borachio entered as Hero and Claudio were
shaping their parting kiss (s93–4). In the nineteenth century, where scene breaks masked
such connections, managers often tried to improve the sense of Don John's opening words
by altering them to a question ('Is it so …?').

3   Claudio and Hero ironically crossed the stage at this line in Barton's production, Claudio and
Don John bowing to each other, and Borachio conversing briefly with the couple (pbk).

11   Borachio spoke confidentially in Sothern's productions, after checking that no-one else was

DON JOHN I remember.

BORACHIO I can at any unseasonable instant of the night, appoint her to
look out at her lady's chamber window. 15

DON JOHN What life is in that to be the death of this marriage?

BORACHIO The poison of that lies in you to temper; go you to the prince
your brother, spare not to tell him, that he hath wronged his honour in
marrying the renowned Claudio, whose estimation do you mightily
hold up, to a contaminated stale, such a one as Hero. 20

DON JOHN What proof shall I make of that?

BORACHIO Proof enough, to misuse the prince, to vex Claudio, to undo
Hero, and kill Leonato; look you for any other issue?

DON JOHN Only to despite them I will endeavour anything.

BORACHIO Go then, find me a meet hour to draw Don Pedro and the 25
Count Claudio alone, tell them that you know that Hero loves me,
intend a kind of zeal both to the prince and Claudio (as in love of your
brother's honour who hath made this match, and his friend's reputation, who is thus like to be cozened with the semblance of a maid)
that you have discovered thus: they will scarcely believe this without 30
trial: offer them instances which shall bear no less likelihood, than to
see me at her chamber window, hear me call Margaret Hero, hear
Margaret term me Claudio, and bring them to see this the very night
before the intended wedding, for in the mean time, I will so fashion
the matter, that Hero shall be absent, and there shall appear such 35
seeming truth of Hero's disloyalty, that jealousy shall be called
assurance, and all the preparation overthrown.

DON JOHN Grow this to what adverse issue it can, I will put it in practice:
be cunning in the working this, and thy fee is a thousand ducats.

BORACHIO Be you constant in the accusation, and my cunning shall not 40
shame me.

DON JOHN I will presently go learn their day of marriage.

Exeunt

listening (s59, s63). In Gielgud's 1950 production he sniffed the posy that he had received
from Margaret in the masquerade (s93).

22–3 Spoken in a low voice in Sothern's 1904–5 production; Don John sighed with satisfaction and
shook Borachio's hand warmly (s59).

27–9 Cut by Macready, in most productions from the 1870s to Tree, and occasionally since.

32–3 **hear Margaret term me Claudio** Most managers from Garrick to Tree altered 'Claudio' to
'Borachio'. Zeffirelli substituted 'whatever she will, save Claudio'. Saker, Bridges-Adams,
Hunt, Gielgud, Barton and Trevis cut the phrase as implausible.

42 Tree staged a five-minute 'intermezzo' as a transition to 2.3 (see introduction, p. 45).
Warchus (1993) left Borachio alone on stage 'silently imagin[ing], with the help of projected
photographs, his encounter with Margaret' (*SS* 47, 1994, 192).

ACT 2, SCENE 3

Enter BENEDICK *alone*

BENEDICK Boy.
BOY [*within*] Signor.

[*Enter* BOY]

BENEDICK In my chamber window lies a book, bring it hither to me in
the orchard.
BOY I am here already, sir.
BENEDICK I know that, but I would have thee hence and here again.   5

Exit [*Boy*]

I do much wonder, that one man seeing how much another man is a
fool, when he dedicates his behaviours to love, will after he hath

Usually set in a garden or orchard. The scene has often been heavily cut, with the effect of
foregrounding Benedick. Branagh linked the gulling of Benedick and Beatrice (2.3, 3.1) as a
continuous sequence, cutting over half the text in the two episodes.

1-6   Cut in most productions from Garrick to the late nineteenth century, and by Poel; Irving
and Fanny Davenport retained the passage. At Burton's, NY (1857) the scene opened with
Benedick sprawled on a marble couch under a grapevine plucking and eating fruit (s21).
Fanny Davenport commenced with a page-boy singing to Benedick (pbk). Tree entered with
the boy, fresh from hawking (s69). Waterston (1972) came in paddling a canoe on the stage
revolve (*NR*, 9 Sep. 1972); Merrison (RSC 1988) emerged with 'white, stick-insect legs', to
sunbathe (*CL*, 5 May 1988). In Barton's production a studious, bespectacled Benedick busied
himself with pen and books at a table (pbk, pr. photo), business which made sense of his
request to the boy and suggested a depth of mind that set him apart from his companions.
The 'boy' was 'an impassive Indian servant' who 'produced a book from the folds of his
garment' (line 6) and 'laid it on the table before moving quietly away'. As Benedick realised
'with astonishment' that this was the very book he had called for, 'there was a comical sense
that the mystery of the East had asserted itself once again' (Wells, 'Editorial treatment', 15).

7-28   Garrick seemed confident of his immunity to love (*DrC* 2, 1770, 311). Macready, who spoke
the soliloquy 'walking up and down and eating cherries' (*JB*, 4 Mar. 1843), was nonplussed

laughed at such shallow follies in others, become the argument of
his own scorn, by falling in love: and such a man is Claudio. I have   10
known when there was no music with him but the drum and the fife,
and now had he rather hear the tabor and the pipe: I have known
when he would have walked ten mile afoot, to see a good armour,
and now will he lie ten nights awake carving the fashion of a new
doublet: he was wont to speak plain and to the purpose (like an   15
honest man and a soldier) and now is he turned orthography, his
words are a very fantastical banquet, just so many strange dishes:
may I be so converted and see with these eyes? I cannot tell, I think
not: I will not be sworn but love may transform me to an oyster, but
I'll take my oath on it, till he have made an oyster of me, he shall   20
never make me such a fool: one woman is fair, yet I am well: another
is wise, yet I am well: another virtuous, yet I am well: but till all
graces be in one woman, one woman shall not come in my grace:
rich she shall be, that's certain: wise, or I'll none: virtuous, or I'll
never cheapen her: fair, or I'll never look on her: mild, or come not   25

at Claudio's transformation to a lover (emphasis marks, s17), bursting with amusement ('Ha!
Ha! Ha! Oh, oh my God') at his companion's strange behaviour. Macready's confidence of
his own immunity was indicated by heavy emphases (s17: 22ff.). Irving spoke with a 'sly
humour' (*Th*, 1 Nov. 1882, 302), his speech emphases and a derisive groping stagger (18a)
expressing contempt for Claudio's transformation. In his vision of the ideal woman the
emphasis on 'mild' and 'good discourse' seemed to exclude Beatrice, yet his own capacity
for romance was hinted in his ardent repetition, 'her hair! Oh, her hair ...' (s45–7; *Pittsburgh
Dispatch*, 27 Dec. 1884). Tree's soliloquy was triggered by the image of the love-lorn Claudio
composing a sonnet to Hero, Plummer's (1961) by the sight of Claudio and Hero on a
balcony (pbks). Gielgud made it plain in every word that he himself was 'ripe to fall' (*NYHT*,
27 Sep. 1959). Godfrey's uncertain tone at 'May I be converted?' (1971) suggested conversion
as a distinct possibility.

10   In Daly and Jewett's productions the boy returned with the book requested by Benedick
     (Daly, s81).

23   In Zeffirelli's production the mermaids in the fountain tittered, to Benedick's astonishment
     (pbk).

24–7 'As [Benedick] begins to catalogue all these virtues it gradually begins to dawn on him that
     he is describing someone he knows and ... when he gets to the colour of her hair he realises
     it is Beatrice' (Jacobi on his 1982 Benedick, in Cook, *Shakespeare's Players*, 31). Branagh
     placed particular emphasis on 'mild, or come not near me'.

27b–8a The frontispiece to Wenman's acting edition shows Garrick in one of his characteristic and
     slightly exaggerated starts as he utters these words (see illustration 1).

28b Whether a property arbour was used in Renaissance productions of *Much Ado* is open to

near me: noble, or not I for an angel: of good discourse, an excellent
musician – and her hair shall be of what colour it please God. Hah!
the prince and Monsieur Love, I will hide me in the arbour.

Enter DON PEDRO, LEONATO, CLAUDIO [*and* BALTHASAR *with*] *music*

DON PEDRO Come, shall we hear this music?
CLAUDIO Yea, my good lord: how still the evening is,   30
    As hushed on purpose to grace harmony!
DON PEDRO See you where Benedick hath hid himself?
CLAUDIO Oh very well, my lord: the music ended,
    We'll fit the kid-fox with a pennyworth.
DON PEDRO Come, Balthasar, we'll hear that song again.   35
BALTHASAR Oh, good my lord, tax not so bad a voice,

conjecture. An illustration on the title page of the 1615 edition of Kyd's *The Spanish Tragedie*
shows a property arbour in use in a performance of that play. A property arbour is also
indicated in a stage direction in *A Looking Glass for London and England* (1590), performed
at the Rose Theatre (Hattaway, *Elizabethan Popular Theatre*, 37). However, in the
Renaissance theatre audiences frequently imagined locations indicated in the text without
the help of stage properties (see Dessen, *Elizabethan Stage Conventions*, 1984). Benedick
may simply have hidden behind one of the stage pillars or have retreated upstage, where he
could be imagined as concealed from his friends. In most productions from Garrick to the
late nineteenth century Benedick hid in a property arbour or, like Irving, behind cut-out
shrubbery (s46–7). Richman (1896) hid behind a fountain (Daly); Tree (1905) and Allam
(1990) climbed a tree (s69, pr. photo). In some twentieth-century productions Benedick has
simply retreated upstage or behind a pillar, or crouched on steps to the pit. Bridges-Adams
placed Benedick in a dimly lit arbour upstage (*SR*, 6 Feb. 1926; *SH*, 15 July 1927); Gielgud, on
the other hand, stood downstage behind a lattice at the proscenium arch, visible to plotters
and audience (pr. photos). 'I was glad ...', wrote Gielgud, 'to be able to prove one of my
favourite theories; that, in the over-hearing scenes in Shakespeare, the character at whom
the scene is aimed should be closest to the audience' (*Stage Directions*, 41). Redgrave hid
behind a red umbrella (pr. photos; *DT*, 27 Aug. 1958), Godfrey (1971) behind a screen used
as a bird-watching hide, Waterston (NY, 1972) behind his upturned canoe (*NYT*, 18 Aug.
1972). Gambon (NT 1981) ran around with a stepladder, climbing it periodically to peer over
a wall at his companions (pbk).

28 SD F's stage direction names the singer as Iacke Wilson. Four seventeenth-century musicians
of that name have been identified (see Mares, New Cambridge Shakespeare, 146).

29–31 Gielgud yawned as Claudio poeticised on the stillness of the evening (s94).

33–4 Cut in most productions from Garrick to Tree.

36–52 Acted in Drake's production (1946) with a tinge of melancholy, intensified by a plaintive
musical setting for 'Sigh no more' (*St*, 26 Sep. 1946). Lines 36–52 were cut or abridged from

> To slander music any more than once.
>
> DON PEDRO It is the witness still of excellency,
>> To put a strange face on his own perfection:
>> I pray thee sing, and let me woo no more.   40
>
> BALTHASAR Because you talk of wooing I will sing,
>> Since many a wooer doth commence his suit,
>> To her he thinks not worthy, yet he woos,
>> Yet will he swear he loves.
>
> DON PEDRO   Nay, pray thee come,
>> Or if thou wilt hold longer argument,   45
>> Do it in notes.
>
> BALTHASAR   Note this before my notes,
>> There's not a note of mine that's worth the noting.
>
> DON PEDRO Why these are very crotchets that he speaks,
>> Note notes forsooth, and nothing.
>
>>   [*Music*]
>
> BENEDICK Now divine air, now is his soul ravished: is it not strange that   50
> sheep's guts should hale souls out of men's bodies? Well, a horn for
> my money when all's done.
>
>>   *The Song*
>
> [BALTHASAR] Sigh no more, ladies, sigh no more,

Garrick to Tree, and by Hunt, Carey and Eyre. J. B. Booth Jr (s42) omitted the entire Balthasar sequence (29–80), Edwin Booth most of it. The omission of the passages about love's deceptions and about 'noting' weakened the play on equivocal appearance and diminished the contemplative tone which in the full text balances the comedy of the gulling trick. The deletion of Benedick's sceptical response to music (50–2) softened the irony of his imminent romantic 'conversion'.

42–4 In Gielgud's 1955 production Balthasar directed his lines about love's deceptions pointedly at Claudio, who reacted with bad grace (s94).

53–68 Transposed in *UP* to the scene corresponding to the gulling of Beatrice. Sung in Garrick's productions as a tenor solo to the music of Thomas Arne (*Six Cantatas*, c.1749). Garrick altered 'bonny' (58) to 'merry', 'nonny nonny' (60) to 'down derry', and lines 66–8 to

> Nor be you dull or whining;
> Men have been false, and will be so,
> While love-sick maids are pining. (Bell)

The Kembles, Macready, Kean, Davenport and others (s21, s25, s35) used R. J. S. Stevens' glee for several voices (playbills, pbks). In other productions 'Sigh no more' has most commonly been sung as a solo with instrumental accompaniment. In Zeffirelli's production it was sung by a 'lachrymose tenor' in mock-Rossini style, with hedges and fountain swinging to the music (*FT*, 17 Feb. 1965; *MCT*, 26 Feb. 1965; pbk); the song caught on as the

Men were deceivers ever,
One foot in sea, and one on shore,   55
To one thing constant never.
Then sigh not so, but let them go,
And be you blithe and bonny,
Converting all your sounds of woe,
Into hey nonny nonny.   60

Sing no more ditties, sing no mo,
Of dumps so dull and heavy,
The fraud of men was ever so,
Since summer first was leavy.
Then sigh not so, but let them go,   65
And be you blithe and bonny,
Converting all your sounds of woe,
Into hey nonny nonny.

DON PEDRO By my troth a good song.
BALTHASAR And an ill singer, my lord.   70
DON PEDRO Ha, no no faith, thou sing'st well enough for a shift.
BENEDICK And he had been a dog that should have howled thus, they
would have hanged him: and I pray God his bad voice bode no
mischief, I had as lief have heard the night-raven, come what plague
could have come after it.   75
DON PEDRO Yea marry, dost thou hear, Balthasar? I pray thee get us
some excellent music: for tomorrow night we would have it at the
Lady Hero's chamber window.

theme tune of the evening, hummed at random by various characters (*MCT*, 26 Feb. 1965).
In Eyre's production (1971) it was guyed as a close harmony quartet sung by Balthasar and
the conspirators. In Antoon's production (1972) it was given a lilting music-hall setting with
trombone and banjo accompaniment, burlesqued at the end by the pop of a champagne
cork (*NR*, 9 Sep. 1972; Coursen, *Shakespearean Performance*, 183; *NYT*, 14 Jan. 1973).
Barton underlined the thematic significance of 'men were deceivers ever' by the presence
on stage of Don John, Borachio, Margaret and Hero (pbk). Branagh made the song the
keynote of his film (see introduction, p.82). Sothern as Benedick showed his impatience
with the song, putting his hands over his ears at line 56. A bored Howard (1969) climbed
a ladder and started to clip the hedge (61), to sounds of 'Shhh' from the others (pbks).

69–76a The discussion of Balthasar's singing was cut in most productions from the Kembles to the
1870s, and substantially abridged by Daly and Tree. Lines 73–5 have often been cut or
abridged since Irving.

78 Robin Ellis as Don Pedro (RSC 1976) ironically put his arm around Don John at the reference
to Hero's chamber window (pbk).

BALTHASAR The best I can, my lord.
DON PEDRO Do so, farewell.   80
                                                            Exit Balthasar
   Come hither, Leonato, what was it you told me of today, that your
   niece Beatrice was in love with Signor Benedick?
CLAUDIO Oh aye, stalk on, stalk on, the fowl sits. I did never think that
   lady would have loved any man.
LEONATO No nor I neither, but most wonderful, that she should so dote   85
   on Signor Benedick, whom she hath in all outward behaviours
   seemed ever to abhor.
BENEDICK Is't possible? Sits the wind in that corner?
LEONATO By my troth, my lord, I cannot tell what to think of it, but that
   she loves him with an enraged affection, it is past the infinite of   90
   thought.

81ff.   In the late eighteenth and early nineteenth centuries Don Pedro, Claudio and Leonato
        traditionally played the gulling sequence rather soberly, the comedy being expressed mainly
        through Benedick's reactions (*UM* 9, 1808, 45). By the late nineteenth century a tendency
        was emerging for the conspirators to play for broad comedy, despite Benedick's remark that
        'the conference was sadly [seriously] borne' (181). While in some of Irving's performances
        the plotters acted with 'a gravity just tinged with a trace of ... inward amusement' (*BDA*, 9
        Feb. 1885; *Std*, 13 Oct. 1882), they did not always resist the temptation to play for easy laughs
        (*BDA*, 28 Feb. 1884; *Tribune*, Chicago, 16 Jan. 1885; Fitzgerald, *Shakespearean
        Representation*, 65). Craig's 1891 studybook (S50) bears a warning note, 'Easy!! Easy!'
        Twentieth-century productions have often staged the sequence with a good deal of comic
        exaggeration.

82ff.   Audience interest in the gulling sequence has focused strongly on Benedick's reactions.
        Wilkes found 'the eager solicitude' of Garrick's looks 'perfectly comic' (*General View*,
        259–60). Thomas Cooper was praised for his gradations of feeling (*Southern Patriot*,
        Charleston, 5 Jan. 1838). Macready listened 'with a mixture of reluctance and gratification'
        (Pollock, *Macready*, 133). A gradual seriousness stole over Kean's features as he moved
        from surprise to doubt to eager interest (*DT*, 22 Nov. 1858; *Std*, 22 Jan. 1858). Irving moved
        from amazement and half-pleasure through suspicion to gradual conviction (*Std*, 13 Oct.
        1882). Gielgud's astonishment gave way to alternate hope and apprehension (*SQ* 2, 1951, 75;
        Drama 25, Summer 1952, 14; *T*, 12 Jan. 1952). Many players have been less subtle. At line 82
        Garrick exclaimed, 'How's this?' (Bell). Sothern dropped his book, and later knelt on the seat
        in the arbour drinking every word (S59). Waterston almost dropped the canoe behind which
        he was hiding (*HR* 26, 1973, 338), 'flash[ing] looks of unconcealed pleasure' as he heard
        more (*NYT*, 18 Aug. 1972). Howard (1969), clipping the hedge, dropped his shears in
        astonishment (pbk). Sinden 'explod[ed] into apoplectic amazement' (*T*, 2 July 1977). Godfrey
        (1971) exclaimed with unconcealed delight, 'Is't possible?' Kline almost fell from the tree

DON PEDRO May be she doth but counterfeit.

CLAUDIO Faith like enough.

LEONATO Oh God! Counterfeit? There was never counterfeit of passion, came so near the life of passion as she discovers it. 95

DON PEDRO Why what effects of passion shows she?

CLAUDIO Bait the hook well, this fish will bite.

LEONATO What effects, my lord? She will sit you – you heard my daughter tell you how.

CLAUDIO She did indeed. 100

DON PEDRO How, how, I pray you! You amaze me, I would have thought her spirit had been invincible against all assaults of affection.

LEONATO I would have sworn it had, my lord, especially against Benedick. 105

BENEDICK I should think this a gull, but that the white-bearded fellow speaks it: knavery cannot sure hide himself in such reverence.

CLAUDIO He hath ta'en th'infection, hold it up.

DON PEDRO Hath she made her affection known to Benedick?

LEONATO No, and swears she never will, that's her torment. 110

---

where he had been drinking a bottle of wine (*NR*, 22 Aug. 1988). Allam, also listening from a tree, coughed up lungfuls of cigar-smoke like distress signals every time his name was linked to Beatrice, and at 128 fell out of the tree in astonishment (*G*, 12 Apr. 1990; pbk). Merrison (1988) and Branagh (1993) flopped into a deck-chair which collapsed under them (*TES*, 29 Apr. 1988). In several productions the comedy has been heightened by the appearance at inopportune moments of the boy with the book Benedick had requested (Lyceum, 1882; SMT 1949–50; RSC 1968–9, 1982, 1990; Bell Shakespeare Company, 1996).

92 In Barton's production Don Pedro drew attention to the thematically significant word 'counterfeit' by swinging his cricket bat (pbk).

98 In Sothern's 1911 production Leonato motioned Don Pedro and Claudio close to him and whispered, Benedick making frantic efforts to hear (s63).

101 When Leonato's invention dried up at Don Pedro's question 'How, how, I pray you!', the prince in the 1971 and 1990 RSC productions exclaimed 'You amaze me', as if Leonato had actually communicated something in the intervening silence (editor's observation; *SS* 44, 1991, 171). In Branagh's film Leonato covered his lack of invention by whispering in Don Pedro's ear.

108 Tree's business here was typical of the comic by-play padding his production. The boy returned looking for Benedick, took off his hat 'as if to salute the prince', then dropped it on a fallen orange. Picking up the orange in his hat, he turned his back to the audience and held the hat behind him to exhibit his prize (s69).

110 Benedick interpolated 'So, so' in most productions from Garrick to the late nineteenth century.

CLAUDIO 'Tis true indeed, so your daughter says: shall I, says she, that have so oft encountered him with scorn, write to him that I love him?

LEONATO This says she now when she is beginning to write to him, for she'll be up twenty times a night, and there will she sit in her smock, till she have writ a sheet of paper: my daughter tells us all. 115

CLAUDIO Now you talk of a sheet of paper, I remember a pretty jest your daughter told us of.

LEONATO Oh when she had writ it, and was reading it over, she found Benedick and Beatrice between the sheet. 120

CLAUDIO That.

LEONATO Oh she tore the letter into a thousand halfpence, railed at herself, that she should be so immodest to write to one that she knew would flout her: I measure him, says she, by my own spirit, for I should flout him, if he writ to me, yea, though I love him I should. 125

CLAUDIO Then down upon her knees she falls, weeps, sobs, beats her heart, tears her hair, prays, curses, Oh sweet Benedick, God give me patience.

LEONATO She doth indeed, my daughter says so, and the ecstasy hath so much overborn her, that my daughter is sometime afeared she will do a desperate outrage to herself, it is very true. 130

DON PEDRO It were good that Benedick knew of it by some other, if she will not discover it.

CLAUDIO To what end? He would make but a sport of it, and torment the poor lady worse. 135

DON PEDRO And he should, it were an alms to hang him: she's an excellent sweet lady, and (out of all suspicion) she is virtuous.

CLAUDIO And she is exceeding wise.

DON PEDRO In everything but in loving Benedick.

LEONATO Oh my lord, wisdom and blood combating in so tender a body, we have ten proofs to one, that blood hath the victory: I am sorry for her, as I have just cause, being her uncle, and her guardian. 140

DON PEDRO I would she had bestowed this dotage on me, I would have

---

111–28 Cut in most productions from Garrick to Craig; abridged by Fanny Davenport, Sothern, Poel, Tree, Bridges-Adams and Barton.

120 To the conspirators' delight, Gielgud could not help laughing at this jest (592–4).

131 Benedick responded, 'Poor thing! Poor thing!' in numerous Victorian productions. Sothern gave a short sigh (559).

134–72 Heavily cut in the eighteenth and nineteenth centuries and in some twentieth-century productions. Saker cut 134–67.

135 Sothern started indignantly (563).

daffed all other respects, and made her half myself: I pray you tell 145
Benedick of it, and hear what a will say.

LEONATO Were it good, think you?

CLAUDIO Hero thinks surely she will die, for she says she will die, if he
love her not, and she will die ere she make her love known, and she
will die if he woo her, rather than she will bate one breath of her 150
accustomed crossness.

DON PEDRO She doth well: if she should make tender of her love, 'tis
very possible he'll scorn it, for the man (as you know all) hath a
contemptible spirit.

CLAUDIO He is a very proper man. 155

DON PEDRO He hath indeed a good outward happiness.

CLAUDIO Before God, and in my mind, very wise.

DON PEDRO He doth indeed show some sparks that are like wit.

LEONATO And I take him to be valiant.

DON PEDRO As Hector, I assure you, and in the managing of quarrels 160
you may say he is wise, for either he avoids them with great discre-
tion, or undertakes them with a most christianlike fear.

LEONATO If he do fear God, a must necessarily keep peace: if he break
the peace, he ought to enter into a quarrel with fear and trembling.

DON PEDRO And so will he do, for the man doth fear God, howsoever it 165
seems not in him, by some large jests he will make: well, I am sorry
for your niece: shall we go seek Benedick, and tell him of her love?

CLAUDIO Never tell him, my lord, let her wear it out with good counsel.

LEONATO Nay that's impossible, she may wear her heart out first.

DON PEDRO Well, we will hear further of it by your daughter, let it cool 170
the while: I love Benedick well, and I could wish he would modestly
examine himself, to see how much he is unworthy so good a lady.

LEONATO My lord, will you walk? Dinner is ready.

CLAUDIO If he do not dote on her upon this, I will never trust my
expectation. 175

DON PEDRO Let there be the same net spread for her, and that must
your daughter and her gentlewomen carry: the sport will be, when
they hold one an opinion of another's dotage, and no such matter:

---

154 Benedicks from Garrick to Irving often responded 'Very well!' Sothern shook his fist at the
conspirators (s59) or mimed indignant words (s63). Tree showered them with oranges from
the tree he had climbed (s69). Branagh yelled a protesting 'Ah!', then tried to cover himself
by a series of similar cries mimicking a bird-call.

158 Jacobi (1982) rolled up his sleeves and moved as if to punch Don Pedro, but was stopped in
his tracks by the prince's next words (pbk).

173 A bell announced dinner in most nineteenth-century productions.

that's the scene that I would see, which will be merely a dumb show:
let us send her to call him in to dinner.   180

[Exeunt all but Benedick]

BENEDICK This can be no trick, the conference was sadly borne, they
have the truth of this from Hero, they seem to pity the lady: it seems
her affections have their full bent: love me? Why, it must be
requited: I hear how I am censured, they say I will bear myself
proudly, if I perceive the love come from her: they say too, that she   185
will rather die than give any sign of affection: I did never think to
marry, I must not seem proud, happy are they that hear their detrac-
tions, and can put them to mending: they say the lady is fair, 'tis a

176–9   Cut or abridged by Warren and Wood (1804), F. Davenport, Tree, Bridges-Adams, Eyre and
Barton.

180 SD   Macready looked after the retreating conspirators 'with a very vague expression' (S19),
dragged a chair to the front and sank into it 'with an air of rapt abstraction' (Pollock,
Macready, 133), crossing and recrossing his legs in 'puzzled contemplation' for half a minute
before he spoke (S19–20; *E*, 4 Mar. 1843). The variations in his looks expressed a conflict
between 'grave bewilderment' (*E*, 4 Mar. 1843), scepticism (*CJ*, 4 Mar. 1843), amazement at
his sudden 'unaccountable conversion' (Marston, *Recent Actors*, I.88), 'distress ... on finding
the theory of a whole life knocked down by one slight blow' (*T*, 24 Jan. 1851), and a dawning
sense of gratification (Marston, *Recent Actors*, I.87). Kean looked puzzled, in a fog of
wonder (*T*, 22 Nov. 1858, 30 Jan. 1861). Irving paused in pleased bewilderment (*North British
Daily Mail*, 28 Aug. 1883), sighing before he spoke (S47). In Sothern's 1904–5 production the
conspirators made their exit doubled up with laughter; Sothern stood reflecting, twirled his
moustache, smiled confidently, then drew himself up for his soliloquy (S59). Tree's
conspirators added:

   Leonato: Poor Benedick.
   Don Pedro and Claudio: No no, poor Beatrice.
   All: Yes, poor Beatrice.

They then gave a big sigh and went off laughing. Tree came forward saying 'Poor Beatrice',
pondered, tried in vain to speak, and at last began his soliloquy (S69). Sinden (1976)
'emerged with a rush' and spoke directly to the audience, his speech 'at first almost
inarticulate with horrified surprise' (David, *Shakespeare*, 220).

81–200   This soliloquy has been considered one of the principal tests of the actor of Benedick.
Garrick, who delivered it with comic gravity, made it one of his masterpieces (Wilkes,
General View, 259–60; *LC*, 19–22 Mar. 1757; *Lloyd's Evening Post*, 6–8 Nov. 1775), as did
Charles Kemble. Macready's newly discovered inclination for Beatrice was a bewildering
reversal of his previous anti-romantic fixation (*T*, 24 Jan. 1851). He set forth 'with ludicrous
minuteness the psychological state of a man who suddenly finds himself in a false position,

and then, perceiving he cannot get out of it, recklessly resolves to brave all consequences' (*Sp*, 25 Jan. 1851). Irving's new attitude to Beatrice, on the other hand, was 'only the bursting forth of a flame that ha[d] all along been smouldering' (*DN*, 12 Oct. 1882). He delivered the soliloquy more quietly than most Victorian actors, with a 'quaint commingling of gravity and humor' (*BH*, 28 Feb. 1884), replacing the traditional starts and raisings of the voice with a sense of inwardness and self-communing (*DC*, 12 Oct. 1882). Tree gave the impression less of a man communing with himself than of one playing up to his audience (*Referee*, 29 Jan. 1905). Gielgud spoke with comic gravity (*T&B*, 23 Jan. 1952), conveying 'conscious enjoyment of the ironies while maintaining the illusion that Benedick has been taken in' (Kitchin, *Mid-Century Drama*, 55). Branagh's logic and wit (RTC 1988) only barely concealed his delight at the conspirators' revelation (*What's On*, 7 Sep. 1988).

181–3a   Charles Kemble spoke the opening lines with hesitant deliberation (*MP*, 21 Jan. 1820). Macready and Kean pronounced 'This can be no trick' with mystified suspicion (s17; *T*, 30 Jan. 1861). Gielgud's 'prim and self-satisfied' utterance of the phrase was 'gloriously' and self-consciously 'fatuous' (*NYHT*, 27 Sep. 1959). Gambon spoke it as if completely taken in (*FT*, in *LTR*, 13–26 Aug. 1981), Branagh (1988) seriously, as if 'shaken to hear something he already half knew' (*SS* 42, 1989, 133).

183b–4a   **love ... requited** Macready sought to rationalise his changing attitude 'rather upon the ground of pity and courtesy than of his own strong inclining' (Marston, *Recent Actors*, I.87–8). Irving spoke in a half humorous, half pitying tone (*PhI*, 19 Mar. 1884), condescending to the lady with an 'air of patronage' (*SR*, 18 June 1887); he said 'requited' with a dash of resolution followed by an interpolated 'Ay', uttered with a smile of triumphant satisfaction (s45–6; *T*, 24 Oct. 1882). At 'love me' Gielgud's eyes 'wrinkle[d] up in modest pleasure. His lips purse[d] patronisingly, half of a mind to dismiss the thought that anyone could be so crazy about him, half already wreathed in a vast contented smile. He tosse[d] his head back. After all, why not?' (*NYHT*, 18 Sep. 1959). Rylance (1993) reacted with 'stunned bewilderment': 'Love me? Why?' (*Ind*, 11 July 1993). Branagh (1993 film) cried 'Love me!' in astonished ecstasy, flinging his arms in the air; his expansive 'Why' followed half joyfully, half questioningly, with a touch of disbelief.

184ff.   As 'sufficient reasons in favour of marriage beg[an] to dawn upon him', Charles Kemble seemed to smile inwardly at his own recantation (*E*, 20 Dec. 1829); Macready changed to a tone of chuckling self-satisfaction (s19; *T*, 25 Feb. 1843); Kean's face lit up 'with luxurious self-complacency' (*T*, 30 Jan. 1861), a smile of 'tickled vanity' (*GI*, 22 Nov. 1858). Irving spoke 184–8a with earnest self-scrutiny, ruefully recollecting that he had never thought to marry (*T*, 24 Oct. 1882). For a moment he stood, breathing hard from mental effort, fanning himself with his hat; then, folding his arms, he began to ponder the lady's virtues with gallantry and ironic humour (s46–7; Crosse, 'Performances', 60). James Dale became engagingly informal and intimate, appealing to the audience to witness the soundness of his argument (*Queen*, 7 May 1936; *BP*, 24 Apr. 1936). Henry Ainley's initial puzzlement changed to a coy smile, then to flattered vanity (*TT*, 5 Mar. 1926). Kline said 'I did never think to

truth, I can bear them witness: and virtuous, 'tis so, I cannot reprove
it: and wise, but for loving me: by my troth it is no addition to her   190
wit, nor no great argument of her folly, for I will be horribly in love
with her: I may chance have some odd quirks and remnants of wit
broken on me, because I have railed so long against marriage: but
doth not the appetite alter? A man loves the meat in his youth, that
he cannot endure in his age. Shall quips and sentences, and these   195
paper bullets of the brain awe a man from the career of his humour?
No, the world must be peopled. When I said I would die a bachelor,

marry' on a wistful sigh (*Drama* 4, 1988, 41).

191b–2a **I will be horribly in love** Charles Kemble spoke these words more as 'a relief than a new
resolution' (*E*, 25 Dec. 1836). Macready rose with joy and walked to one side of the stage,
amazed at his decision (Marston, *Recent Actors*, I.187), then paused and returned, struggling
with the fear of ridicule (Pollock, *Macready*, 133; S19). Kean spoke the words with a 'rush' of
'joyous resolution' (*ST*, 28 Jan. 1858). Irving stabbed at decision, then scratched his head
uneasily (S46). Sothern slapped his thigh with glee (S63). Gielgud spoke the phrase with 'a
resolute jut of the chin' (*Sk*, 30 Jan. 1952). Godfrey uttered 'horribly' with a 'salacious growl'
(*NS*, 4 June 1971), Sinden with growling relish (*YP*, 10 Apr. 1976). Branagh (1993 film)
stabbed each word slowly, emphatically, flinging his arms wide in ecstasy.

194–6 Irving rationalised rapidly through this passage (S45). At 195a Macready pushed his chair
away with a sudden resolution of defiance to all scoffers (S19; Marston, *Recent Actors*, I.88).
Sinden (1976) was 'indignantly argumentative as if rebutting an accusation that the audience
had made' (David, *Shakespeare*, 220).

197 **the world ... peopled** Charles Kemble uttered this 'grand final reason for marrying ... with
his hands linked behind him, a general elevation of aspect, and a sort of look at the whole
universe before him, as if he saw all the future generations that might depend on his verdict'
(*Tatler*, 18 Feb. 1831). Critics admired the carefully conceived progression by which he
approached this conclusion: 'the doubts, the clearings up, the arguing with self as with an
adversary, the hesitations', 'the countenance lighting up with each thought as it chased
through the busy brain', till the whole 'merged in one burst of resolution, "The world must
be peopled"' (*T*, 8 Apr. 1840; *JB*, 12 Apr. 1840). Charles Kean seized upon this concept as if it
were a new discovery, with the satisfaction of a man who has suddenly hit upon a plausible
reason for an inconsistent act (*ST*, 28 Nov. 1858), his 'eager, self-deceiving philosophic
unction' putting the house in a roar (*DT*, 22 Nov. 1858). Irving made the point with sly,
impish humour, without the loud tones and emphatic stride across the stage affected by
some Victorian actors (*T*, 24 Oct. 1882; Williams, in Saintsbury and Palmer, *We Saw Him
Act*, 236). Ainley (1926) spoke the words with comical mock grandeur (Dent, broadcast
typescript, 24 Apr. 1949, 10), Walter 'with all the implied relief of a man ... who at last sees
the straw to save him' (*SH*, 2 May 1930). Redgrave spoke the line with 'cheerful defiance'
(*SH*, 29 Aug. 1958). Howard shouted it exultantly, smashing his gardener's hat between his

> I did not think I should live till I were married – here comes
> Beatrice: by this day, she's a fair lady, I do spy some marks of love in
> her. 200

Enter BEATRICE

BEATRICE Against my will I am sent to bid you come in to dinner.
BENEDICK Fair Beatrice, I thank you for your pains.
BEATRICE I took no more pains for those thanks, than you took pains to

fists (*T*, 30 July 1969). Jacobi drew himself up into 'a grandiloquent posture' which was really 'a resilient gesture of self-defence' (*FT*, 21 Apr. 1982). Rylance (1993) made the line 'a drily matter-of-fact, duty-calls confidence to the audience' (*JC*, 9 July 1993). Branagh (1993) shouted it with aggressive emphasis.

197b–8 Charles Kemble and J. W. Wallack paused and walked about agitated before delivering this final rationalisation (Dolby, s9). Macready spoke it in a self-satisfied tone (*MP*, 24 Jan. 1851), Irving with comic solemnity (Williams, in Saintsbury and Palmer, *We Saw Him Act*, 236), Gielgud with a 'self-congratulatory smirk' (*NYHT*, 18 Aug. 1959). In Sothern's 1904–5 production, mandolins offstage began to play 'Sigh no more' very softly at the word 'married' (s59).

198b–200 Charles Kemble, J. W. Wallack, Vezin, Richman, Sothern and Jewett quickly spruced themselves up as Beatrice approached (Dolby; Cumberland; s8; *DT*, 27 Apr. 1875; Daly; s59, s81).

200 SD–201 Louisa Nisbett entered 'working on a bit of gold embroidery', turning her back on Benedick as she called him to dinner. Macready walked round her, trying to catch sight of her face, but she kept turning until both were in their original positions (s19, s21). Helena Modjeska stretched and yawned elaborately at her entry (Towse, *Sixty Years*, 272). Julia Marlowe languidly hummed 'Sigh no more', Sothern making a sweeping bow to her (s59). Judi Dench entered 'with studied contempt', carrying 'a gong which she sporadically bashe[d], as if [Benedick] were some spectacularly imbecilic child' (*NS*, 16 Apr. 1976): 'Against my will (*pause*) I am sent (*pause; glower; then very emphatically*) to bid you (*then very fast, very loud*) come in to dinner!' (*SS* 30, 1977, 172). Janet McTeer (1993) 'str[ode] on with a knife and a brutalised banana, threatening to emasculate [Benedick], and anyone else, without a word uttered' (*O*, 11 July 1993).

202–5 One of John Kemble's finest 'points' was his stare and smile at Beatrice's entry (*W*, 28 Nov. 1789). Macready gave himself to lovemaking in the manner of an 'unbeliever turned fanatic', 'distressfully endeavouring to make himself heard as he followed the angered Beatrice about' (*T*, 24 Jan. 1851). Irving scanned her face earnestly for the expected signs of love, then bowed, and replied (s47; *Std*, 13 Oct. 1882). In Bridges-Adams's 1933–4 productions Benedick smiled foolishly at 202, and at 205 giggled and twisted his foot at the thought of her taking pleasure in the message (s87).

203–7 Ellen Terry replied coquettishly (203–4), with a curtsy and a little smothered yawn, then, thank me, if it had been painful I would not have come.

BENEDICK You take pleasure then in the message.   205

BEATRICE Yea, just so much as you may take upon a knife's point, and choke a daw withal: you have no stomach, signor, fare you well. *Exit*

BENEDICK Ha, against my will I am sent to bid you come in to dinner: there's a double meaning in that: I took no more pains for those thanks than you took pains to thank me: that's as much as to say, any   210 pains that I take for you is as easy as thanks: if I do not take pity of her I am a villain, if I do not love her I am a Jew, I will go get her picture.   *Exit*

humming a tune (207), tripped off with a lapwing movement and 'delicious disdain' (s47; *Evening Express*, Liverpool, 27 Sep. 1883; *BDA*, 28 Feb. 1884; *MN*, Chicago, 16 Jan. 1885; Scott, *Terry*, 15–16). Peggy Ashcroft showed some embarrassment at finding Benedick so strangely amenable, retreating behind a garden bench as he advanced with broadening grin to thank her for her pains; as he motioned her to sit beside him she broke away upstage (s93; Sykes, 'Journal Notes', 1955). Sinead Cusack (1982) gave Benedick the finger during this sequence (pr. photo).

206 Sothern, interpreting Beatrice's 'Yea' as a sign of affection, approached her eagerly (s59).

207 At 'choke ... withal' Julia Marlowe snapped her fan at Benedick (s63). As Marie Drofnah moved away, yawning, she turned and saw Benedick bowing very low, and went out laughing (s56). In Zeffirelli's production the 'mermaids' supporting the fountain tittered as Beatrice went off (pbk).

208–13 Garrick's 'self-flattering' air was highly comic (Wilkes, *General View*, 259–60). Lewis's 'sudden passion for Beatrice ... appeared less like a new light breaking in upon him, than a joyful ebullition that he had at last found an excuse for doing what he had long had an inclination to do' (intro. to Cumberland, 6). Belton (Burton's, NY, 1857) sounded thoughtful and disappointed at 208, then at 209a ('there's a double meaning ...') slapped his hat on his head 'as if struck with a pleasant idea' (s21). 'The balance between [Gielgud's] logical caution and his illogical passion teeter[ed] hilariously' in this speech (*SR*, NY, 3 Oct. 1959). After Judi Dench's unappetising invitation to dinner, 'Sinden's triumphant "There's a double meaning in that" justly brought the house down' (*SS* 30, 1977, 172). Zeffirelli, with a view to political correctness, deleted the reference to 'Jew' (212); Barton altered it to 'villain', Hands to 'fool'.

213 SD Hanford (c.1900) slammed his hat on with comic resolution; Stephens (1965) shook hands with the 'triton' in the fountain; Howard (1969) threw his hat ecstatically in the air (pbks). In Hands's production (1982) the boy tried one last time to give the book to Benedick; ignored yet again, he hurled the book after his retreating master and ran off (pbk; *T*, 21 Apr. 1982). After Benedick's exit, Gielgud (1955), Nunn (1969) and Hands (1982) showed Borachio and Margaret arranging their midnight assignation (pbks).

ACT 3, SCENE I

Enter HERO *and two gentlewomen,* MARGARET *and* URSULA

HERO Good Margaret, run thee to the parlour,
      There shalt thou find my cousin Beatrice,
      Proposing with the prince and Claudio,
      Whisper her ear and tell her I and Ursley
      Walk in the orchard, and our whole discourse   5
      Is all of her, say that thou overheard'st us,
      And bid her steal into the pleachèd bower,
      Where honeysuckles ripened by the sun,
      Forbid the sun to enter: like favourites,
      Made proud by princes, that advance their pride,   10
      Against that power that bred it: there will she hide her,
      To listen our propose: this is thy office,
      Bear thee well in it, and leave us alone.
MARGARET I'll make her come I warrant you, presently.   *Exit*
HERO Now, Ursula, when Beatrice doth come,   15
      As we do trace this alley up and down,
      Our talk must only be of Benedick:
      When I do name him, let it be thy part,
      To praise him more than ever man did merit:
      My talk to thee must be how Benedick   20

The difficulty of sustaining interest through two consecutive gulling scenes has often led directors to cut 3.1 extensively and to load the scene with comic business. Garrick, the Kembles and others cut over 20 per cent of the scene; Victorian managers often cut well over 30 per cent, the most common cuts being 3, 8–11, 16, 27–33, 39, 44–8, 59–73, 80, 92–7, 100–3. Most productions used the same set as for 2.3, sometimes with a change of lighting; Fanny Davenport and Hands, for instance, staged the scene by moonlight (pbks). In Irving's production an offstage chorus sang 'Sigh no more, ladies' between 2.3 and 3.1 (S47).

1ff. In contrast with the gentleness of most performances of Hero in the nineteenth and early twentieth centuries, Miss Taylor (1831) played this scene mischievously (*O*, 20 Feb. 1831), Viola Tree with 'roguish animation' (*PMG*, 11 Feb. 1905).

> Is sick in love with Beatrice: of this matter
> Is little Cupid's crafty arrow made,
> That only wounds by hearsay: now begin,

Enter BEATRICE

> For look where Beatrice like a lapwing runs
> Close by the ground, to hear our conference.   25
> URSULA The pleasant'st angling is to see the fish
> Cut with her golden oars the silver stream,
> And greedily devour the treacherous bait:
> So angle we for Beatrice, who even now,
> Is couchèd in the woodbine coverture: 30
> Fear you not my part of the dialogue.

23 SD   The grace and lightness of Ellen Terry's 'lapwing' entry became proverbial: 'Who ... can forget that figure passing behind the pleached hedge, the gliding step, the long dress just lifted, without showing her feet, the limbs in such perfect control, the eager face and, with it all, restraint and the grand manner!' (Gielgud, *Kate Terry Gielgud*, 92). Peggy Ashcroft also 'move[d] beautifully in a fluttering bird-like way' (*NS*, 17 June 1950, 683). On the other hand, Sybil Thorndike, whose forte was tragedy, 'crept slowly into the arbour like Lady Macbeth going to Duncan's chamber' (Crosse, *Playgoing*, 52). Janet Suzman (1969) entered as if playing hide and seek, whispering 'Where's Hero?' to the gardener. Susan Fleetwood (1990) popped her head over a hedge (pbks).

30ff.   Whether a property arbour was used in Renaissance productions is open to conjecture (see commentary on 2.3.28). An upstage arbour was traditional in 3.1 from the Kembles to the early twentieth century. Bridges-Adams (1933–4) placed Beatrice downstage on a garden seat and Ursula and Hero, winding wool, in a recess in a vine-clad wall upstage (s87–8; *SP*, July 1933, 109). Seale and Eyre sat Hero and Ursula in front of a large open umbrella (1958 pr. photo; *SQ* 22, 1971, 359); Antoon had them picnicking (*NYT*, 27 Aug. 1972). Katharine Hepburn's Beatrice (ASF 1957) hid under a table which she moved about to hear the gossips (*CW*, Oct. 1957, 66). Maggie Smith (1965) concealed herself behind a clothes-line full of washing which Hero and Ursula were pegging out; as she listened they piled sheet after sheet on her head, so that she emerged for her soliloquy (107–16) absent-mindedly clutching a heap of linen (pbk, pr. photos, *Sp*, 26 Feb. 1965, 266). Judi Dench stood behind an Indian blind (*DT*, 1 July 1977), four housemaids leaning over the balcony above trying to detect her reactions (P-1976, pr. photo). Sinead Cusack appeared 'almost transparent' upstage through 'misty' perspex screens (*FT*, 21 Apr. 1982). Maggie Steed (1988) splashed about in a fish pond (*SQ* 40, 1989, 85). Blythe Danner swung on a trellis door, throwing lemons at Hero and Ursula (*NR*, 22 Aug. 1988). Felicity Kendal (1989) stood silhouetted behind a beige traverse curtain (*Ind*, 13 May 1989; *FT*, 15 May 1989), Susan Fleetwood (1990) against the proscenium arch in view of the conspirators (*SS* 44, 1991, 170; *FT*, 12 Apr. 1990).

HERO Then go we near her, that her ear lose nothing
         Of the false sweet bait that we lay for it:
         No truly, Ursula, she is too disdainful,
         I know her spirits are as coy and wild,   35
         As haggards of the rock.
URSULA   But are you sure,
         That Benedick loves Beatrice so entirely?
HERO So says the prince, and my new trothèd lord.
URSULA And did they bid you tell her of it, madam?
HERO They did entreat me to acquaint her of it,
         But I persuaded them, if they loved Benedick,   40
         To wish him wrestle with affection,
         And never to let Beatrice know of it.
URSULA Why did you so? Doth not the gentleman
         Deserve as full as fortunate a bed,   45
         As ever Beatrice shall couch upon?
HERO Oh God of love! I know he doth deserve,
         As much as may be yielded to a man:
         But nature never framed a woman's heart
         Of prouder stuff than that of Beatrice: 50
         Disdain and scorn ride sparkling in her eyes,
         Misprising what they look on, and her wit
         Values itself so highly, that to her
         All matter else seems weak: she cannot love,
         Nor take no shape nor project of affection,   55
         She is so self-endeared.

34ff.   In the 1901 OUDS production Hero and Ursula spoke solemnly until Hero started to giggle. Ursula, alarmed, tried to rouse Beatrice to jealousy by kissing a locket in pretence of loving Benedick herself (Foss, *What the Author Meant*, 119).

36bff.   Helena Faucit was at first blankly incredulous at the account of Benedick's love (Martin, *Faucit*, 219; *LDP*, 16 Dec. 1870), but as Hero and Ursula censured her disdain, she 'presented a pained appearance' of deepening self-reproach (*MG*, 11 Apr. 1866; Martin, *Faucit*, 219). At line 37 Julia Marlowe exclaimed 'Why!' in astonishment, clapping both hands over her mouth to smother the ejaculation (s59, s63). Sybil Thorndike 'sat still and tense, showing her emotion by her face only' (Crosse, 'Performances', XI.32). A 'sudden and … beautiful gravity' (Hobson, *Theatre Now*, 135) stole over Diana Wynyard's features as she listened 'with a superb confusion of disbelief and delight' (*DM*, 12 Jan. 1952). At line 37 Peggy Ashcroft, who earlier had darted from her hiding place in a grotto to slip behind a statue in an alcove, popped out of the alcove in astonishment, bearing off the statue to the grotto (s94; *BP*, 22 July 1955). Sinead Cusack was 'lost in wonderment' (*G*, 21 Apr. 1982).

43   Julia Marlowe mimed 'Oh' in disapproval (s63).

49–56a   Penelope Wilton (1981) clawed at her detractors and beat her head against the orchard wall

URSULA   Sure I think so,
      And therefore certainly it were not good,
      She knew his love, lest she'll make sport at it.
HERO Why you speak truth, I never yet saw man,
      How wise, how noble, young, how rarely featured,   60
      But she would spell him backward: if fair-faced,
      She would swear the gentleman should be her sister:
      If black, why Nature drawing of an antic,
      Made a foul blot: if tall, a lance ill-headed:
      If low, an agate very vilely cut: 65
      If speaking, why a vane blown with all winds:
      If silent, why a block moved with none:
      So turns she every man the wrong side out,
      And never gives to truth and virtue, that
      Which simpleness and merit purchaseth.   70
URSULA Sure, sure, such carping is not commendable.
HERO No, not to be so odd, and from all fashions,
      As Beatrice is, cannot be commendable:
      But who dare tell her so? If I should speak,
      She would mock me into air, oh she would laugh me   75
      Out of myself, press me to death with wit:
      Therefore let Benedick like covered fire,
      Consume away in sighs, waste inwardly:
      It were a better death, than die with mocks,
      Which is as bad as die with tickling.   80
URSULA Yet tell her of it, hear what she will say.
HERO No rather I will go to Benedick,
      And counsel him to fight against his passion,
      And truly I'll devise some honest slanders,
      To stain my cousin with, one doth not know   85
      How much an ill word may empoison liking.
URSULA Oh do not do your cousin such a wrong,
      She cannot be so much without true judgement,
      Having so swift and excellent a wit,
      As she is prized to have, as to refuse   90
      So rare a gentleman as Signor Benedick.

(*G*, in *LTR*, 13–26 Aug. 1981). Sinead Cusack (1982) stood immobile, taking the criticisms to heart (*SQ* 34, 1983, 84). Susan Fleetwood showed concern and remorse, a shadow passing across her face at 'she cannot love' (54b) (*FT*, 12 Apr. 1990; *T*, 12 Apr. 1991). Samantha Bond appeared 'genuinely worried' at these words, 'fearing that she [might] be left out of the game of marriage' (*What's On*, 7 Sep. 1988). Emma Thompson looked shocked and offended. At 56a Julia Marlowe shook her head with an 'Oh' of disapproval (s63).

86   Julia Marlowe gave a big start, restraining herself with difficulty (s63).

HERO He is the only man of Italy,
        Always excepted my dear Claudio.
URSULA I pray you be not angry with me, madam,
        Speaking my fancy: Signor Benedick,   95
        For shape, for bearing, argument and valour,
        Goes foremost in report through Italy.
HERO Indeed he hath an excellent good name.
URSULA His excellence did earn it, ere he had it:
        When are you married, madam?   100
HERO Why every day tomorrow: come go in,
        I'll show thee some attires, and have thy counsel,
        Which is the best to furnish me tomorrow.
URSULA She's limed I warrant you, we have caught her, madam.
HERO If it prove so, then loving goes by haps,   105
        Some Cupid kills with arrows, some with traps.

                                         Exeunt Hero and Ursula
BEATRICE What fire is in mine ears? Can this be true?
        Stand I condemned for pride and scorn so much?
        Contempt, farewell, and maiden pride, adieu,
        No glory lives behind the back of such.   110
        And Benedick, love on, I will requite thee,
        Taming my wild heart to thy loving hand:
        If thou dost love, my kindness shall incite thee
        To bind our loves up in a holy band,
        For others say thou dost deserve, and I   115
        Believe it better than reportingly.   *Exit*

---

106 SD   In Fanny Davenport's production Hero and Ursula went off laughing, looking back at Beatrice. Beatrice advanced cautiously after their exit in the productions of Charles Kemble, Wood (1829) and Edwin Booth (Cumberland, s9, s41).

107–16   The adaptation of Beatrice's soliloquy in *UP* was vulgarised and garrulous. Garrick cut the last three lines, substituting: 'Love as thou wilt, *Beatrice* shall requite thee', Francis Gentleman commenting that 'after Benedick's first excellent soliloquy ... it was very judicious to limit Beatrice's reflections here; she could have uttered nothing so pleasing and pertinent, without being merely a repetition' (Bell). In 1775 Frances Abington hurried over the speech flippantly (*MP*, 7 Nov. 1775). From the Garrick era to the first two decades of the nineteenth century the soliloquy appears to have been given a comic flavour, *The Morning Herald* (28 Jan. 1824) criticising Eliza Chester for speaking it too seriously, claiming that her reflections should have been like Benedick's 'after he has been practised on the same way – of a ludicrous or serio-comic cast'. The Victorians placed great importance on the soliloquy for its revelation of the serious and tender aspects of Beatrice. 'This is the point in the play in which the underlying nobleness and generosity of Beatrice leap into view', wrote Helena

Faucit. She is 'dazed, astounded at what she has overheard', and as wonder mingles with self-reproach, a 'marked change' comes over her life (Faucit, 'Female characters', 220–1). Ellen Kean's glow of feeling and reproach of her former disdain demonstrated, according to *The Sunday Times* (28 Nov. 1858), that the high-spirited Beatrice of the earlier scenes was indeed 'a true woman at heart'. Amy Sedgwick and Louisa Herbert suggested that Beatrice's 'heart had not been filled with a new thought, but only opened' (*E*, 27 Feb. 1858; *T*, 6 Apr. 1866; *BWM*, 14 Apr. 1866). Kate Terry revealed a heart 'as tender as … may be' (*ST*, 28 July 1867). Ada Cavendish resolved to love Benedick (111) with 'impassioned earnestness' (*Lloyd's*, 2 May 1875). Ellen Terry sank onto a garden seat (*Th*, 1 Oct. 1880, 219), speaking with 'great feeling' and 'exquisite womanly tenderness' (Crosse, 'Performances', 60; *Sc*, 11 Sep. 1883), her face radiant and her tones 'sweetly compassionate' (*Std*, 13 Oct. 1882; *T*, 24 Oct. 1882). Julia Marlowe spoke 108 with a 'dreamy self-questioning attitude' conveying puzzlement and 'a delicate prophecy of relenting'; she uttered 'Benedick, love on', 'wildly, almost hysterically', followed by a peal of joyful laughter (*RHC*, 28 Sep. 1904; s59). Charles Hanford's production (c.1900) took a less momentous view of the speech, undercutting the final line with a burst of offstage laughter (s56). The view of womanhood implied in most Victorian accounts of the soliloquy continued in many reviews until at least the mid-twentieth century, *The Sketch* (30 Jan. 1952) observing, for example, that Diana Wynyard here showed a woman's heart to balance the flashing mind. In the late twentieth century the lines have often been spoken quietly and thoughtfully, as in Geraldine McEwan's interpretation (*BP*, 5 Apr. 1961). Elizabeth Spriggs showed no excitement at the news she had heard – 'only a splendid gravity, the thoughtfulness of a woman who has always longed to be loved … and is now timidly, doubtfully visited by the wonder that perhaps what she has ardently and secretly wanted may at last become hers' (*ST*, 30 Apr. 1971). Judi Dench very slowly lifted from its bottom edge the blind behind which she had been hiding (*PP*, June 1976, 21), speaking the soliloquy as 'a quietly rapt and entirely serious response' (*T*, 2 July 1977). Sinead Cusack, on the other hand, twirled about with elation (P-1982; *CL*, 13 May 1982), delivering the speech 'in a molten lather of confusion and incipient passion' (*FT*, 21 Apr. 1982). Samantha Bond (1988) spoke it as 'the revelation of a newly acquired self-knowledge' (*SS* 42, 1989, 132). Maggie Steed, dripping wet from the pool, had to struggle against the audience's laughter (*SQ* 40, 1989, 85). Emma Thompson (1993), sun backlighting her hair radiantly, spoke with a thoughtful intensity rising at the end to ecstasy.

116 SD   Sothern (1904–5) ended the scene with 'Sigh no more' sung offstage to a mandolin accompaniment, Julia Marlowe running back into the arbour to spy on Benedick as he entered in foppish costume for 3.2 (s59). Tree's production sentimentalised Beatrice's exit: Winifred Emery picked up a pair of gloves dropped by Benedick, whispered his name and kissed them; then as Hero and Claudio crossed the stage, deeply in love, she gave a long sigh and went off, still kissing the gloves (s69). Zeffirelli ended the scene on a farcical note: a plaster Cupid attached to the clothes-line was drawn swiftly offstage past Beatrice, who waved to it as it sailed by (pbk; *FT*, 17 Feb. 1965). Branagh's film climaxed the scene with

a big orchestral crescendo and a montage of alternate dissolve shots showing Benedick splashing about ecstatically in the fountain and Beatrice in rapturous motion on a swing, a conception which brought the two into emotional accord much sooner than in most productions (*Ind*, 27 Aug. 1993).

ACT 3, SCENE 2

Enter DON PEDRO, CLAUDIO, BENEDICK *and* LEONATO

In Branagh's film 3.2 was transposed, much abbreviated, to 3.3.77, where it followed a transposed version of 2.2. The sequence in which Benedick's friends mock his transformation to a lover was in *UP* adapted and transposed to the final scene of the play. In nineteenth-century and Edwardian productions 3.2 was often set within Leonato's house or in a garden or orchard. Gielgud used a two-level balcony set slid on from each side (pbks, pr. photo). Antoon introduced a barber's shop sequence suggested by line 34 (Halio, *Shakespeare's Plays*, 14).

0 SD Benedick's transformation to a lover has commonly been signified by extravagant costume and a mournful demeanour. Melancholy was a conventional sign of the Renaissance lover (e.g. *AYL*, 2.7.147–9). Elizabethan gallants characteristically wore ostentatious finery, often with high hat (see line 32) and long plume. Yellow was also a sign of a lover; e.g. Malvolio in *TN* (Gurr, *Shakespearean Stage*, 197–9). Sothern (1904–5) entered with plumed hat and lace handkerchief, sighing profusely, the page-girl who carried his writing materials rushing off bursting with laughter. He sat down and tried to write verses, twice crunching up his attempts, Don Pedro, Leonato and Claudio watching silently until they began to shake with laughter (S59). Allam (1990) appeared as a 'Restoration popinjay' in 'green and pink frills', 'tottering about in high heels' (*G*, 12 Apr. 1990; *T*, 12 Apr. 1990). Benedick has often worn a bandage or scarf to hide his new-shaven face and to suggest toothache. Gielgud was discovered shaving in undergarments on an upper level, a gorget round his neck to catch the soap, a servant holding towel, bowl and mirror (S93–4; pr. photos). His friends, entering at stage level, noticed him only when he cried out on cutting himself (S93). Plummer (1961) also entered with his barber; Godfrey (1971) and Sinden (1976) as if from shaving (pbks). Stephens (1965) masked his shaven chin with his hat, watched by two 'inanimates' peering through the back of a sofa (pbk, pr. photo). Merrison (1988) sat dabbing his face with after-shave, placing his hat over the bottle as his friends entered (pbk). In Branagh's film the friends surprised him dressing in his bedroom. Some productions contrasted Benedick's discomfort with the holiday mood of his companions. Nunn, contextualising the reference to tennis balls (35), showed Don Pedro and Claudio on a court preparing to play tennis (pbk; *ILN*, 9 Aug. 1969). In Eyre's production Don Pedro, immaculate in cream striped trousers, cream coat and hat, entered swinging a butterfly net; in Barton's Don Pedro and Claudio

DON PEDRO I do but stay till your marriage be consummate, and then
     go I toward Arragon.

CLAUDIO I'll bring you thither, my lord, if you'll vouchsafe me.

DON PEDRO Nay that would be as great a soil in the new gloss of your
     marriage, as to show a child his new coat and forbid him to wear it: I   5
     will only be bold with Benedick for his company, for from the crown
     of his head, to the sole of his foot, he is all mirth: he hath twice or
     thrice cut Cupid's bow-string, and the little hangman dare not shoot
     at him: he hath a heart as sound as a bell, and his tongue is the
     clapper, for what his heart thinks, his tongue speaks.   10

BENEDICK Gallants, I am not as I have been.

LEONATO So say I, methinks you are sadder.

CLAUDIO I hope he be in love.

DON PEDRO Hang him, truant, there's no true drop of blood in him to
     be truly touched with love: if he be sad, he wants money.   15

BENEDICK I have the tooth-ache.

DON PEDRO Draw it.

BENEDICK Hang it.

CLAUDIO You must hang it first, and draw it afterwards.

DON PEDRO What, sigh for the tooth-ache?   20

     entered as if from hunting, with servants carrying birds strung from a pole. In Trevis's
production Benedick, stiffly uniformed and with a scarf around his face, looked ridiculous
beside his companions on the sun-deck in dressing-gowns and casual gear; in Alexander's
production (1990) Benedick's friends played quoits (pbks; pr. photos). In Warchus's
production (1993) Beatrice was still on stage as Benedick entered 'trying to sing "Sigh no
more" in a cracked voice'. The two sat awkwardly, 'not knowing ... how to begin to express
what they felt'; as Benedick's companions arrived, Beatrice ran off and Benedick stuffed the
words of the song into his mouth, passing off the lump in his cheek as toothache (*SS* 47,
1994, 193; *What's On*, 14 July 1993).

4–10   Often abridged.

6ff.   Benedick's companions have traditionally mocked his transformation to a lover with
laughter, taunts and comic by-play. The frequent abridgement of their jests in the theatre
has often made Don Pedro and Claudio, however, seem less frivolous than in the full text. In
UP Protheus was at first dismayed by his friends' taunts. Garrick played up to their ridicule,
cutting 'a very laughable figure' (Bell). *The Times* (18 Feb. 1831) thought Charles Kemble's
embarrassment a little too sheepish. Macready chafed with vexation (s15). Sothern, sighing
repeatedly, glared at his friends and (16) stamped his foot at their mockery (s63). Ainley
retained his dignity (*SR*, 6 Feb. 1926). Gielgud was somewhat crestfallen, but by no means
cowed (pr. photo, 1950). Vining, Macready, Kean and Belton (Burton's, NY, 1857) looked
particularly glum at the word 'mirth' (pbks).

11   Spoken by Irving with a rueful, half-comic expression (Fitzgerald, *Irving*, 196); by Richman
(1896) and Sothern with a mournful sigh (Daly, s63).

LEONATO Where is but a humour or a worm.

BENEDICK Well, everyone cannot master a grief, but he that has it.

CLAUDIO Yet say I, he is in love.

DON PEDRO There is no appearance of fancy in him, unless it be a fancy
　　that he hath to strange disguises, as to be a Dutchman today, a　25
　　Frenchman tomorrow, or in the shape of two countries at once, as a
　　German from the waist downward, all slops, and a Spaniard from
　　the hip upward, no doublet: unless he have a fancy to this foolery, as
　　it appears he hath, he is no fool for fancy, as you would have it
　　appear he is.　　30

CLAUDIO If he be not in love with some woman, there is no believing
　　old signs: a brushes his hat a-mornings, what should that bode?

DON PEDRO Hath any man seen him at the barber's?

CLAUDIO No, but the barber's man hath been seen with him, and the
　　old ornament of his cheek hath already stuffed tennis balls.　　35

LEONATO Indeed he looks younger than he did, by the loss of a beard.

DON PEDRO Nay, a rubs himself with civet, can you smell him out by
　　that?

24–30　The jests about foreign dress styles were cut in most productions from Garrick to the late
　　nineteenth century, and have often been abridged since. The omission from F of the jest on
　　German and Spanish fashions ('or ... doublet', 26–8) may have reflected an early stage cut,
　　perhaps made in deference to Prince Frederick, the Elector Palatine, when the play was
　　performed at court in the winter of 1612–13 during the festivities for his marriage to Princess
　　Elizabeth (Chambers, *Shakespeare*, I.238–241). At 'strange disguises' (25) Gielgud's valet,
　　dressing him in gallant's finery, took his coat from a hook and brushed it (S93).

　32　Spoken as Sothern flicked his hat with his handkerchief and blew away the last flecks of dust
　　(S63). Macready's companions snatched the freshly brushed hat which he had tried to
　　conceal in front of him and tossed it from one to the other (S16, S19). The hat-throwing
　　business has featured in many productions since. In Trevis's production Claudio picked up
　　Benedick's hat, disclosing the after-shave bottle beneath; as Benedick dived for the hat his
　　scarf dropped from his face revealing his loss of a beard (pbk).

33–6　These lines about Benedick's shaven beard were cut from Garrick to Davenport and by
　　Edwin Booth. In other productions Benedick's companions have traditionally pulled away
　　the handkerchief, scarf or towel hiding his shaven face. At line 36 Gielgud, who had
　　retreated in exasperation to one of the window frames on the upper level, drew a curtain
　　to finish dressing in private. He descended to the stage at line 45 (S93–4). Jacobi took as a
　　compliment the reference (36) to his youth (P-1982).

　37　Benedick's companions have traditionally snatched his handkerchief, scarf or towel, smelled
　　it, and tossed it from one to another, Benedick trying to recover it (pbks). In Eyre's
　　production his underpants were thrown about (*T*, 28 May 1971). At 'civet', David Lyon's Don
　　Pedro (RSC 1988) smelled Benedick's after-shave bottle and passed it to Claudio (pbk).

CLAUDIO That's as much as to say, the sweet youth's in love.

DON PEDRO The greatest note of it is his melancholy. 40

CLAUDIO And when was he wont to wash his face?

DON PEDRO Yea, or to paint himself? For the which I hear what they say of him.

CLAUDIO Nay but his jesting spirit, which is now crept into a lute-string, and now governed by stops. 45

DON PEDRO Indeed that tells a heavy tale for him: conclude, conclude, he is in love.

CLAUDIO Nay but I know who loves him.

DON PEDRO That would I know too, I warrant one that knows him not.

CLAUDIO Yes, and his ill conditions, and in despite of all, dies for him. 50

DON PEDRO She shall be buried with her face upwards.

BENEDICK Yet is this no charm for the tooth-ache: old signor, walk aside with me, I have studied eight or nine wise words to speak to you, which these hobby-horses must not hear.

[Exeunt Benedick and Leonato]

DON PEDRO For my life, to break with him about Beatrice. 55

CLAUDIO 'Tis even so: Hero and Margaret have by this played their parts with Beatrice, and then the two bears will not bite one another when they meet.

Enter DON JOHN *the Bastard*

DON JOHN My lord and brother, God save you.

DON PEDRO Good den, brother. 60

DON JOHN If your leisure served, I would speak with you.

41–3 Cut from Garrick to Tree, Poel excepted. Saker cut 41–7.

48 In Bridges-Adams's 1933–4 productions Claudio tried to snatch a miniature of Beatrice from Benedick's neck (s87–8).

54 Benedick's exit has often drawn mocking laughter from Claudio and Don Pedro. John Kemble retorted 'I wish, Gentlemen, you would – Pray – Ho! ho! ho!' (s2). Vining pulled a face at his mockers (s12). Sothern repeated 'Hobby-horses!' and went out haughtily (s59, s63). Gielgud fobbed off Don Pedro and Claudio with a superior air (*SR*, NY, 3 Oct. 1959). A harried Sinden rushed off to hoots from Don Pedro (P-1976).

55–8 Cut by Tree and Barton; Craig cut 56–8.

59ff. Irving (1882–7) made the Don John sequence a separate scene in another part of the garden (programmes, s45–7). In Bridges-Adams's productions Don Pedro and Claudio began to study a map of the prince's route to Arragon when interrupted by Don John (s86–8). In most productions his arrival suddenly dampens their hilarity, but in the 1971 and 1976 RSC productions their high spirits continued briefly, Claudio in 1976 offering Don John a jesting foot salute (editor's observation; P-1976).

DON PEDRO In private?

DON JOHN If it please you, yet Count Claudio may hear, for what I
would speak of, concerns him.

DON PEDRO What's the matter?   65

DON JOHN Means your lordship to be married tomorrow?

DON PEDRO You know he does.

DON JOHN I know not that, when he knows what I know.

CLAUDIO If there be any impediment, I pray you discover it.

DON JOHN You may think I love you not, let that appear hereafter, and   70
aim better at me by that I now will manifest, for my brother (I think
he holds you well, and in dearness of heart) hath holp to effect your
ensuing marriage: surely suit ill-spent, and labour ill-bestowed.

DON PEDRO Why what's the matter?

DON JOHN I came hither to tell you, and circumstances shortened (for   75
she has been too long a-talking of), the lady is disloyal.

CLAUDIO Who Hero?

DON JOHN Even she, Leonato's Hero, your Hero, every man's Hero.

CLAUDIO Disloyal?

DON JOHN The word is too good to paint out her wickedness, I could   80
say she were worse, think you of a worse title, and I will fit her to it:
wonder not till further warrant: go but with me tonight, you shall see
her chamber window entered, even the night before her wedding
day: if you love her, then tomorrow wed her: but it would better fit
your honour to change your mind.   85

CLAUDIO May this be so?

DON PEDRO I will not think it.

DON JOHN If you dare not trust that you see, confess not that you know:
if you will follow me, I will show you enough: and when you have
seen more, and heard more, proceed accordingly.   90

63   Claudio has often begun to go.

66   An astonished look passed between Don Pedro and Claudio in Sothern's 1904–5 production
(s59).

68   Branagh's film dissolved to a sequence showing Borachio making love to Margaret at Hero's
window, followed by the words, 'The lady is disloyal. If ... mind' (76, 84–5). Branagh omitted
69–76a, 77–83, 86–100.

70–3 Cut by Creswick (1877 tour) and Saker; abridged by Warren and Wood (1804) and Seale.

76ff. Some directors have tried to make Claudio appear less reprehensible by showing him
affronted at first by Don John's insinuations against Hero: Claudio's hand went to his sword
in Irving and Bridges-Adams's productions; in Fanny Davenport, Sothern and Bridges-
Adams's productions he started angrily towards Don John at 78 (pbks).

CLAUDIO If I see anything tonight, why I should not marry her tomor-
row in the congregation, where I should wed, there will I shame her.
DON PEDRO And as I wooed for thee to obtain her, I will join with thee,
to disgrace her.
DON JOHN I will disparage her no farther, till you are my witnesses: bear   95
it coldly but till midnight, and let the issue show itself.
DON PEDRO Oh day untowardly turned!
CLAUDIO Oh mischief strangely thwarting!
DON JOHN Oh plague right well prevented! So will you say, when you
have seen the sequel.   100

Exeunt

91–2   Spoken with sad solemnity in Irving's productions (s47), which sought, like many nineteenth-
and early twentieth-century performances, to represent Claudio as a sincere, though flawed
character.

97–100   In Eyre's production Don Pedro and Claudio spoke in stunned and hollow tones, Don John
replying with careless indifference. Barton highlighted the gender implications of the
sequence by having Ursula appear on the balcony singing 'Sigh no more, ladies' from 2.3.
At 'men were deceivers ever' Don John waved to her and made his exit; at 'to one thing
constant never' Claudio shattered the night with three shots, followed by a single shot from
Don Pedro (pbk). At the exit Don John smiled maliciously in Fanny Davenport's production,
scowled in Hanford's, laughed in Sothern's, and in Zeffirelli's split the sofa in two with a kick
(pbks). In Seale's production three ominous drum-beats accompanied his exit (*Bolton
Evening News*, 27 Aug. 1958). Lines 97–100 were cut in most productions from Garrick to
the late nineteenth century (not by Macready and Irving).
Borachio's assignation with Margaret. The scene ended with a representation of
Borachio's encounter with Margaret at Hero's window in the productions of Saker, Daly,
Drake (1946), the Brattle Theatre, Cambridge, Mass. (1955), Hutt (Stratford, Ontario, 1971)
and Siletti (NY National Shakespeare Company, 1979) (Saker; Daly; Crosse, 'Performances',
XIX.29; Sprague and Trewin, *Shakespeare's Plays*, 52; SQ 22, 1971, 370; 31, 1980, 213).
Bridges-Adams began 3.3 with Borachio coming as if from Hero's window. Langham
inserted an assignation sequence at 3.3.77, Branagh at line 68 above. In Daly's production
Borachio met a heavily veiled Margaret to the sounds of 'Sigh no more, ladies ... / Men were
deceivers ever' (Daly); in Siletti's production Margaret was disguised as Hero (SQ 31, 1980,
213). The value of such a sequence is an open question. The shallowness of Claudio's
affection and his proneness to jealousy and hasty judgements have already been
established in the first two acts, and in 3.3 Borachio describes in some detail his meeting
with Margaret and Claudio's reaction to it. On the other hand, it is arguable that a visual
representation of the encounter at the window may make Claudio's reactions more
plausible to the audience. The conventions of film tend to invite visual signification.
An over-transparent representation, however, may hinder belief.

ACT 3, SCENE 3

Enter DOGBERRY *and his compartner* [VERGES] *with* [SEACOAL, WATCHMAN 1, WATCHMAN 2 *and the rest of*] *the Watch*

The watch scenes have traditionally been played with much slapstick business. In the nineteenth and early twentieth centuries 3.3 was most commonly set in a Sicilian street or piazza. Charles Kemble dressed Dogberry in coarse grey coat and pantaloons and a 'huge formal black hat' (Cumberland, 8); Macready presented the watch in long grey gowns and tight-fitting hoods pointed like jesters' caps (*ILN*, 4 Mar. 1843, 162; Lacy, iv). See introduction for other representations of Dogberry, Verges and the watch. Sothern (1911) transposed 3.3 to precede 3.2 (S63).

0 SD Daly commenced the scene with townspeople crossing the piazza just before sunset, Flanagan (Queen's, Manchester, 1900–1, 1917) with citizens gathering at the street fountain to sing an evening prayer (*St*, 22 Feb. 1917). In Tree's production the watch knocked at the houses on either side of the stage to wake Dogberry and Verges, who addressed the watch from their respective windows, Dogberry's pulpit-like position reinforcing the comic effect of his self-importance (S69; souvenir programme; *DT*, 26 Jan. 1905). In Bridges-Adams's 1933–4 production the characters entered from an upper level via zig-zag ramps descending between two buildings. Borachio descended first with a rope ladder as if coming from Hero's window, then moved offstage. The watch followed, Verges putting them in line, then knocking at Dogberry's house to wake him (S87–8; pr. photo; *SH*, 21 Apr. 1933). In Gielgud's 1950 production Dogberry shouted and banged his staff offstage as the Watchmen straggled on in disorder. Despite their terror of his authority, his attempts to bully them into order seemed ineffective: they bungled with their pikes, got out of line, and were inattentive as he tried to address them (S93). In Zeffirelli's production an actor armed as a conquistador climbed onto a pedestal to form a bronze statue. The watch then entered arguing loudly, Verges on a bicycle, Dogberry shouting to restore order and throwing his hat on the floor in exasperation (pbk; *TW*, March 1965, 13; *MCT*, 26 Feb. 1965). In Branagh's film Dogberry and Verges were played as psychopaths galloping in and out on imaginary horses.

1–3 In Sothern's 1911 production Dogberry spoke 'in a loud gruff voice', 'very pompous and commanding'; a 'shrivelled and doddering' Verges spoke in 'a piping whistling voice' (S63).

DOGBERRY Are you good men and true?

VERGES Yea, or else it were pity but they should suffer salvation body and soul.

DOGBERRY Nay, that were a punishment too good for them, if they should have any allegiance in them, being chosen for the prince's 5 watch.

VERGES Well, give them their charge, neighbour Dogberry.

DOGBERRY First, who think you the most desartless man to be constable?

WATCHMAN 1 Hugh Oatcake, sir, or George Seacoal, for they can 10 write and read.

DOGBERRY Come hither, neighbour Seacoal, God hath blessed you with a good name: to be a well-favoured man, is the gift of Fortune, but to write and read, comes by nature.

SEACOAL Both which, master constable – 15

DOGBERRY You have: I knew it would be your answer: well, for your favour, sir, why give God thanks, and make no boast of it, and for your writing and reading, let that appear when there is no need of such vanity: you are thought here to be the most senseless and fit man for the constable of the watch: therefore bear you the lantern: 20 this is your charge, you shall comprehend all vagrom men, you are to bid any man stand, in the prince's name.

SEACOAL How if a will not stand?

Verges has traditionally been represented as a wizened little old man.

10ff.   In Q there is some imprecision in the assignment of speeches to the Watchmen. Productions have assigned the speeches in various ways according to the number of Watchmen on stage (see Wells, 'Editorial treatment', 11–12).

12   Jewett (Boston, 1926) made Dogberry's choice of constable seem questionable, representing Seacoal as a dullard who had to be prompted repeatedly by Oatcake (s81).

12b–19a   Irving (1887ff.) and Craig cut Dogberry's observations on Seacoal's ability to write and read. Zeffirelli cut 16b–19a.

16   **You have** In the productions of Garrick and others, Seacoal added after these words 'I have', prompting Dogberry's response, 'I knew ... answer' (Bell, s3, s21).

20   The lantern was a means of signifying darkness in the Renaissance theatre, where stages were lit continuously by daylight (outdoor theatres) or candlelight (indoor theatres).

21ff.   Seacoal held the lantern for Dogberry to read the charge in Sothern's 1911 production (s63). In Barton's Indian Raj production a turbaned Dogberry squatted to deliver the charge to turbaned Watchmen squatted in a semicircle round him (pr. photo). Sothern (1911) cut 21b–36a.

23   In Macready's production Dogberry, baffled by Seacoal's question, looked enquiringly at Verges (s16). In Sothern's 1904–5 production Dogberry stalled for time with a surprised

DOGBERRY Why then take no note of him, but let him go, and presently
call the rest of the watch together, and thank God you are rid of a   25
knave.
VERGES If he will not stand when he is bidden, he is none of the prince's
subjects.
DOGBERRY True, and they are to meddle with none but the prince's
subjects: you shall also make no noise in the streets: for, for the   30
watch to babble and to talk, is most tolerable and not to be endured.
WATCHMAN 2 We will rather sleep than talk, we know what belongs to
a watch.
DOGBERRY Why you speak like an ancient and most quiet watchman,
for I cannot see how sleeping should offend: only have a care that   35
your bills be not stolen: well, you are to call at all the alehouses, and
bid those that are drunk get them to bed.
SEACOAL How if they will not?
DOGBERRY Why then let them alone till they are sober: if they make you
not then the better answer, you may say, they are not the men you   40
took them for.
SEACOAL Well, sir.
DOGBERRY If you meet a thief, you may suspect him, by virtue of your
office, to be no true man: and for such kind of men, the less you
meddle or make with them, why the more is for your honesty.   45
SEACOAL If we know him to be a thief, shall we not lay hands on him?
DOGBERRY Truly by your office you may, but I think they that touch

'Eh?', looked to Verges, who turned away coughing, then collected his thoughts and replied
with a superior gesture (S59). In Zeffirelli's production Verges searched in vain for the
answer in a book of law (pbk).

30   In Barton's production Dogberry accidentally speared himself on one of the watch's pikes
     (*FT*, 1 July 1977).

31   Lightning flashed at several points in Zeffirelli's scene as a prelude to the rain mentioned at
     86–7. Verges and one of the watch here raised umbrellas (pbk).

36a **bills** i.e. halberds. In nineteenth- and early twentieth-century productions the watch were
     usually armed with staves, pikes or halberds. The armaments in subsequent productions
     have been more varied: in Carey's production (1956) Dogberry carried a fishing rod, the
     watch halberds, a rake and a pitchfork; in Zeffirelli's the arms included a musket and a club;
     in Trevis's production the Watchmen carried a shovel, a broom, an oar and a fishing net; in
     Alexander's (1990) halberds and flaming torches (pbks; pr. photos).

36b **call ... alehouses** In Zeffirelli's production the watch rushed upstage to comply, recalled by
     a blast from Dogberry's whistle (pbk).

38   In Sothern's 1904–5 production Dogberry scratched his head at this question and turned in
     vain for Verges' help (S59).

pitch will be defiled: the most peaceable way for you, if you do take a thief, is, to let him show himself what he is, and steal out of your company.　50

VERGES You have been always called a merciful man, partner.

DOGBERRY Truly I would not hang a dog by my will, much more a man who hath any honesty in him.

VERGES If you hear a child cry in the night, you must call to the nurse and bid her still it.　55

WATCHMAN 2 How if the nurse be asleep and will not hear us?

DOGBERRY Why then depart in peace, and let the child wake her with crying, for the ewe that will not hear her lamb when it baas, will never answer a calf when he bleats.

VERGES 'Tis very true.　60

DOGBERRY This is the end of the charge: you, constable, are to present the prince's own person, if you meet the prince in the night, you may stay him.

48–50　Renaissance audiences would have appreciated the ambiguities in Dogberry's social ideology: while insisting on distinctions of rank and power in his relations with Verges, he here subverts conventions of public order and authority. In Sothern's 1904–5 production Dogberry laughed heartily at his own wit, but had to prompt the watch to laughter by poking them with his stick. They were careful to laugh at his next piece of wisdom (line 59). In Sothern's 1911 production Dogberry said 'steal' emphatically 'with a long sweeping gesture of both hands', the watch following his action 'with awed admiration' (s59, s63).

51–60　Cut in Sothern's 1911 production. Daly cut 51–3.

54–5　When Verges tried to express his opinion (St James's, 1898) he was put back by an overbearing Dogberry (Crosse, 'Performances', I.161). Daly and Jewett included similar business at line 60 (Daly, s81).

　56　At Burton's and Daly's Theatres, NY, the question drew a nonplussed 'Ah!' from Verges, who turned to Dogberry for help (s21, Daly). In Jewett's production Verges thought in vain for an answer until Dogberry nudged him aside (s81).

58–9　In Zeffirelli's production Dogberry sang these lines to the drinking song from *La Traviata*, the watch correcting his wrong notes (pbk; *Western Mail*, 20 Feb. 1965; *Ind*, 28 Feb. 1965). In Jewett's production Dogberry, aware by now of Seacoal's limitations, pointed to him at the word 'calf' (s81).

　61a　In Sothern's 1911 production Dogberry rolled up the paper from which he had read the charge and stuck it in his belt, then rose, struck the ground with his staff, and cleared his throat to deliver his final instructions (s63).

61b–9　The discussion about 'present[ing] the prince's own person' and the watch's powers to 'stay him' was cut by Irving (1887ff.), Craig and Zeffirelli.

VERGES Nay by'r Lady that I think a cannot.

DOGBERRY Five shillings to one on't with any man that knows the   65
statutes, he may stay him: marry, not without the prince be willing,
for indeed the watch ought to offend no man, and it is an offence to
stay a man against his will.

VERGES By'r Lady I think it be so.

DOGBERRY Ha, ah ha! Well, masters, good night: and there be any   70
matter of weight chances, call up me: keep your fellows' counsels,
and your own, and good night: come, neighbour.

SEACOAL Well masters, we hear our charge, let us go sit here upon the
church bench till two, and then all to bed.

DOGBERRY One word more, honest neighbours, I pray you watch about   75
Signor Leonato's door, for the wedding being there tomorrow,
there is a great coil tonight: adieu, be vigitant I beseech you.

Exeunt [Dogberry and Verges]

64 In Barton's production Verges produced a book to prove his point (pbk).

66 **statutes** In Tree's production Verges tried again to contradict his partner, but Dogberry cut
him off with the reminder, 'Neighbour, an two men ride of a horse, one must ride behind',
producing a volume of law to prove his point (s69).

72 **come neighbour** Dogberry turned grandly to command Verges in Sothern's 1911 production
(s63). Dogberry and Verges have often made an exit here, returning at 75.

73–4 The Watchmen have generally moved upstage, jumping to attention as Dogberry has turned
or re-entered to deliver his last instructions.

77 **vigitant** Dogberry gave the word explosive emphasis in Sothern's 1911 production, then
repeated it with arms shooting skyward (s63).

77 SD At Burton's and Daly's Theatres, NY, Verges turned at the exit as if to give further instruction
to the watch, but forgot his point and hobbled off after Dogberry (s21, Daly). In Sothern's
1904–5 production Verges began to exit ahead of Dogberry, who hauled him back by the ear
and claimed the right of precedence (s59). Traditionally the watch have retired upstage for
their vigil. In the 1949 and 1982 Stratford productions they settled down to sleep; in
Langham's 1961 production they played cards; in Nunn's 1969 production they hid behind a
rustic handcart; in Warchus's they chatted to each other on mobile phones (pbks; *Ind*, 11 July
1993). Rain began to fall here in many productions from Macready on, the watch in Eyre's
production sheltering under a makeshift cloth awning (pbks; pr. photos).

Langham (RSC 1961) interpolated here a sequence in which Borachio appeared on the
balcony with a heavily cloaked woman, to whom he said 'Good night, sweet Hero', watched
by Don Pedro, Claudio and Don John. Claudio and Don Pedro reacted in words transposed
from 3.2.91b–94 ('Tomorrow ... disgrace her'). After their exit Don John threw a wallet to
Borachio (pbk; *ES*, 5 Apr. 1961).

Enter BORACHIO *and* CONRADE

BORACHIO What, Conrade?
SEACOAL Peace, stir not.
BORACHIO Conrade, I say.   80
CONRADE Here, man, I am at thy elbow.
BORACHIO Mass and my elbow itched, I thought there would a scab
    follow.
CONRADE I will owe thee an answer for that, and now forward with thy
    tale.   85
BORACHIO Stand thee close then under this penthouse, for it drizzles
    rain, and I will, like a true drunkard, utter all to thee.
SEACOAL Some treason, masters, yet stand close.
BORACHIO Therefore know, I have earned of Don John a thousand
    ducats.   90
CONRADE Is it possible that any villainy should be so dear?
BORACHIO Thou shouldst rather ask if it were possible any villainy
    should be so rich. For when rich villains have need of poor ones,
    poor ones may make what price they will.
CONRADE I wonder at it.   95
BORACHIO That shows thou art unconfirmed: thou knowest that the
    fashion of a doublet, or a hat, or a cloak, is nothing to a man.

Branagh's film cut to a shot of Hero and Claudio engrossed with each other at dinner. This
was followed by 2.2.1–17 (Borachio's disclosure to Don John of his plan to defame Hero),
followed by a much abridged version of 3.2, then a sequence showing Borachio making love
to Margaret at Hero's window, then a shot of Hero asleep in her bed.

78ff. Borachio and Conrade have often been represented as partly intoxicated. *UP* omitted the
       Borachio–Conrade sequence (78–147), substituting an adapted version of 4.2. Lines 78–147
       have often been heavily abridged, the passages most commonly cut or shortened being
       82–5, 89–118a, 127–30a, 135–47. Edwin Booth cut the entire sequence.

  78   Spoken offstage in the productions of Macready, Sothern and Bridges-Adams, Borachio
       entering at 80. Line 78, traditionally shouted as a summons, was in Zeffirelli's production
       spoken as a half-whispered question in response to a tap from Conrade (pbks).

79, 81 The assumption that characters on stage might be inaudible or invisible to one another was
        a common convention of Renaissance staging.

  86   **penthouse** In the Renaissance theatre, locations were generally imagined by the audience
       in response to verbal cues. Borachio and Conrade may have sheltered beneath the roofed
       part of the stage or stood close against the tiring-house façade; at the Blackfriars they
       probably stood against the architectural façade at the rear of the stage. Macready, Kean,
       Irving and Daly represented the 'penthouse' by structures mounted on stage (s19; s26; *Time*,
       Nov. 1882, 959; Daly). The references to penthouse and rain (86–7a) have often been cut.

CONRADE Yes, it is apparel.

BORACHIO I mean the fashion.

CONRADE Yes, the fashion is the fashion.   100

BORACHIO Tush, I may as well say the fool's the fool, but seest thou not
  what a deformed thief this fashion is?

WATCHMAN 1 I know that Deformed, a has been a vile thief, this seven
  year, a goes up and down like a gentleman: I remember his name.

BORACHIO Didst thou not hear somebody?   105

CONRADE No, 'twas the vane on the house.

BORACHIO Seest thou not, I say, what a deformed thief this fashion is,
  how giddily a turns about all the hot-bloods, between fourteen and
  five and thirty, sometimes fashioning them like Pharaoh's soldiers in
  the reechy painting, sometime like god Bel's priests in the old   110
  church window, sometime like the shaven Hercules in the smirched
  worm-eaten tapestry, where his cod-piece seems as massy as his
  club?

CONRADE All this I see, and I see that the fashion wears out more
  apparel than the man: but art not thou thyself giddy with the fashion 115
  too, that thou hast shifted out of thy tale into telling me of the
  fashion?

BORACHIO Not so neither, but know that I have tonight wooed
  Margaret, the Lady Hero's gentlewoman, by the name of Hero: she
  leans me out at her mistress' chamber window, bids me a thousand   120
  times good night: I tell this tale vilely, I should first tell thee how the
  prince, Claudio and my master planted, and placed, and possessed,
  by my master Don John, saw afar off in the orchard this amiable
  encounter.

CONRADE And thought they Margaret was Hero?   125

BORACHIO Two of them did, the prince and Claudio, but the devil my
  master knew she was Margaret, and partly by his oaths, which first
  possessed them, partly by the dark night which did deceive them,

105 Borachio's question was provoked in Macready and Kean's productions by the dropping
     of the watch's lantern; at Burton's, NY, 1857 by the watch scurrying behind columns when
     Borachio dropped his staff; in Gielgud's 1955 production by a Watchman's cough (pbks).

120–1 **bids ... good night** In Sothern's productions the drunken Borachio lost his balance while
     leaning over to kiss his hand, and was caught by Conrade. Borachio threw kisses effusively
     in Bridges-Adams's 1933–4 productions (pbks).

125 Spoken disbelievingly in Jewett's production (s81).

126–33 From the Kembles on, the watch have often advanced slowly downstage during this speech.
     At 'away ... enraged' (SMT 1933–4) the tipsy Borachio gave a great gesture which sent the
     Watchmen retreating up the ramps in alarm. In Macready's production Borachio laughed
     at the prospect of Hero's being sent home without a husband (pbks).

but chiefly, by my villainy, which did confirm any slander that Don
John had made – away went Claudio enraged, swore he would meet   130
her as he was appointed next morning at the temple, and there,
before the whole congregation shame her, with what he saw o'er
night, and send her home again without a husband.

SEACOAL We charge you in the prince's name, stand.

WATCHMAN 2 Call up the right master constable, we have here   135
recovered the most dangerous piece of lechery, that ever was known
in the commonwealth.

WATCHMAN 1 And one Deformed is one of them, I know him, a wears
a lock.

CONRADE Masters, masters.   140

WATCHMAN 1 You'll be made bring Deformed forth I warrant you.

SEACOAL Masters, never speak, we charge you, let us obey you to go
with us.

BORACHIO We are like to prove a goodly commodity, being taken up of
these men's bills.   145

CONRADE A commodity in question I warrant you: come, we'll obey
you.

Exeunt

134ff. In Kean's 1858 production the apprehension of Borachio and Conrade 'was so well
contrived, and the semblance of a "street-row" was so efficiently produced, that a situation
which usually passes unnoticed was brought out into relief by the pictorial manner of its
treatment' (*T*, 22 Nov. 1858). As the watch brought Borachio and Conrade to the ground in
Sothern's 1904–5 production, Seacoal ordered, 'We charge you in the prince's name, stand'!
(s59). In Jewett's production a Watchman knocked violently at Dogberry's door while his
companions struggled with the villains; after some delay Dogberry, in his nightcap,
appeared with Verges in the doorway, each holding a pot of ale (s81). The arrest was noisy
and violent in Bridges-Adams's 1933–4 production, Conrade and Borachio plunging in
different directions to avoid capture, and finally dragged off up the ramps with much
shouting (s87–8). There were vigorous struggles in the Stratford productions of 1949, 1961
and 1968 (pbks). Zeffirelli staged a spectacular brawl with umbrellas and other implements
as weapons; a club-wielding Watchman accidentally felled two of his companions before
beating Conrade and Borachio into submission; another Watchman wrenched a sword from
the grip of the 'statue', replacing it with his umbrella, which the 'statue' raised to shelter
from the rain (pbk; *MCT*, 26 Feb. 1965). In the 1981 NT production Conrade and Borachio
held the watch off for a time with drawn swords (pbk).

140 In Trevis's production Borachio attempted to bribe the watch (pbk).

147 SD After the prisoners were taken off in Tree's production, Dogberry and Verges, who had slept
through the fracas despite the watch's efforts to wake them, appeared at their windows with

nightcaps and candles, peered wonderingly into the street, shook their heads, and politely bade each other goodnight (s69). In Gielgud's 1950 production the tipsy Borachio sang 'Sigh no more, ladies' (from 2.3) while hustled off noisily by the watch. In Barton's Indian Raj production Conrade and Borachio kept their dignity as British officers even under arrest, bowing to the watch, who returned the courtesy (pbk). Daly followed this sequence by the examination of the prisoners (4.2).

ACT 3, SCENE 4

Enter HERO *and* MARGARET *and* URSULA

HERO Good Ursula, wake my cousin Beatrice, and desire her to rise.
URSULA I will, lady.
HERO And bid her come hither.
URSULA Well.   [*Exit*]
MARGARET Troth I think your other rebato were better.   5
HERO No pray thee, good Meg, I'll wear this.
MARGARET By my troth's not so good, and I warrant your cousin will
   say so.
HERO My cousin's a fool, and thou art another, I'll wear none but this.
MARGARET I like the new tire within excellently, if the hair were a   10
   thought browner: and your gown's a most rare fashion i'faith. I saw
   the Duchess of Milan's gown that they praise so.
HERO Oh, that exceeds they say.
MARGARET By my troth's but a night-gown in respect of yours, cloth
   o'gold and cuts, and laced with silver, set with pearls, down sleeves,   15

The scene was omitted by Warren and Wood (1804), Charles Kemble, Wood (1829), most
Victorian managers (Macready excepted), Craig, Sothern, Payne (Manchester, 1909), Jewett
and Branagh (film). The scene has often been heavily abridged, the passages most
frequently cut or abbreviated being 10–18, 20–8, 33–7, 41–52, 56, 60b–70. Garrick and
Macready cut about half the scene, J. P. Kemble and Vining about 70 per cent. Hanford
(c.1900) placed it after 3.5. One effect of deleting 3.4 is to place two Dogberry scenes
together (3.3 and 3.5).

0 SD   The scene has often been set in Hero's bedroom or dressing room. In Tree's production
        Hero sat in her window singing with a zither while Margaret and a lady-in-waiting combed
        her hair (s69; property plot, UBTC). Seale showed Hero being laced into her stays, Ursula
        anchoring her arms in front while Margaret strained at the end of three or four feet of cord
        behind (pr. photo). Zeffirelli drew laughter with corset-lacing business at line 14, Nunn
        (1969) at 19 (pbks). In Antoon's production Hero appeared on her wedding morning
        clutching a huge teddy bear (*HR* 26, 1973, 338).

4–28   J. P. Kemble and Vining omitted this sequence between Hero and her maids, Hanford almost
        all of it, focusing the scene on Beatrice.

11–18   Hero's wedding dress was evidently in the tradition of lavish costuming current in the
        principal Renaissance theatres.

side sleeves, and skirts, round underborne with a bluish tinsel – but
for a fine quaint graceful and excellent fashion, yours is worth ten
on't.

HERO God give me joy to wear it, for my heart is exceeding heavy.

MARGARET 'Twill be heavier soon by the weight of a man.   20

HERO Fie upon thee, art not ashamed?

MARGARET Of what, lady? Of speaking honourably? Is not marriage
honourable in a beggar? Is not your lord honourable without marriage? I think you would have me say, saving your reverence, a
husband: and bad thinking do not wrest true speaking, I'll offend   25
nobody: is there any harm in the heavier for a husband? None I
think, and it be the right husband, and the right wife, otherwise 'tis
light and not heavy: ask my Lady Beatrice else, here she comes.

Enter BEATRICE

HERO Good morrow, coz.

BEATRICE Good morrow, sweet Hero.   30

HERO Why how now? Do you speak in the sick tune?

BEATRICE I am out of all other tune, methinks.

MARGARET Clap's into *Light o' Love*: that goes without a burden: do you
sing it and I'll dance it.

BEATRICE Ye light o'love with your heels, then if your husband have   35
stables enough, you'll see he shall lack no barns.

MARGARET Oh illegitimate construction! I scorn that with my heels.

BEATRICE 'Tis almost five o'clock, cousin, 'tis time you were ready: by
my troth I am exceeding ill, heigh ho.

MARGARET For a hawk, a horse, or a husband?   40

BEATRICE For the letter that begins them all, H.

MARGARET Well, and you be not turned Turk, there's no more sailing
by the star.

---

28 SD   Winifred Emery (1905) entered with her face in her hands, nursing a toothache like
        Benedick's in 3.2 (S69). Numerous actresses have made comic capital of Beatrice's cold:
        Maggie Smith (1965) shuffled on bleary-eyed, muffled in an enormous yellow quilt
        concealing a multi-coloured nightdress and a huge green cup of coffee (pbk; *T*, 17 Feb. 1965;
        Sp, 26 Feb. 1965); a 1976 production photo shows a very ill-looking Judi Dench inhaling from
        a basin, a medicine bottle in front of her and a towel over her head.

33ff.   Sybil Thorndike (1927) sat 'glowering and splendid' under the fire of Margaret's chaff
        (Crosse, 'Performances', XI.39).

39, 53 Sinead Cusack (1982) examined herself in the reflective set to confirm how ill she was (pbk).
        Janet Suzman (1969) covered her head with a sheet at 'I am sick' (53), popping out in
        surprise at the jest on '*benedictus*' (54), and withdrawing again (61) at Margaret's
        suggestion that she was in love (pbk).

BEATRICE What means the fool, trow?

MARGARET Nothing I, but God send everyone their heart's desire.   45

HERO These gloves the count sent me, they are an excellent perfume.

BEATRICE I am stuffed, cousin, I cannot smell.

MARGARET A maid and stuffed! There's goodly catching of cold.

BEATRICE Oh God help me, God help me, how long have you professed apprehension?   50

MARGARET Ever since you left it: doth not my wit become me rarely?

BEATRICE It is not seen enough, you should wear it in your cap: by my
troth I am sick.

MARGARET Get you some of this distilled *Carduus benedictus*, and lay it
to your heart, it is the only thing for a qualm.   55

HERO There thou prick'st her with a thistle.

BEATRICE *Benedictus*, why *benedictus*? You have some moral in this
benedictus.

MARGARET Moral? No by my troth, I have no moral meaning, I meant
plain Holy Thistle, you may think perchance that I think you are in   60
love, nay by'r Lady I am not such a fool to think what I list, nor I list
not to think what I can, nor indeed I cannot think, if I would think
my heart out of thinking, that you are in love, or that you will be in
love, or that you can be in love: yet Benedick was such another, and
now is he become a man, he swore he would never marry, and yet   65
now in despite of his heart he eats his meat without grudging, and
how you may be converted I know not, but methinks you look with
your eyes as other women do.

BEATRICE What pace is this that thy tongue keeps?

MARGARET Not a false gallop.   70

Enter URSULA

URSULA Madam, withdraw, the prince, the count, Signor Benedick,
Don John, and all the gallants of the town are come to fetch you to
church.

HERO Help to dress me, good coz, good Meg, good Ursula.

[*Exeunt*]

59–70   Maggie Smith (1965) kept passing things absent-mindedly to Hero during this sequence: a
comb, a mirror, her cup of coffee, the saucer. Hero passed the items on one-by-one to
Margaret, who returned them to Beatrice, who in turn recycled them to Hero; at 66 Beatrice
absent-mindedly used the comb to stir her coffee (pbk).

69   A fierce Maggie Steed (RSC 1988) advanced on her mockers with a hatpin (*T*, 14 Apr. 1988).

74 SD   As the wedding bells began to ring in Tree's production the maids decked Hero with her veil
and bouquet of lilies. Hero kissed the women, crossed herself, looked wistfully at her bed as
in farewell, and moved hesitantly to the door (s69). Hanford (c.1900) and Nunn (1969)

focused the end of the scene on Beatrice, Hanford cutting 71–4, Nunn 71b–73. After
Margaret and Hero in Hanford's production had gone offstage repeating 'Benedictus!
Benedictus! Get you Benedictus', Benedick himself entered, sighing and lost in thought; he
was at first unnoticed by the sighing Beatrice, but their eyes met as the curtain fell (s56).
Nunn ended the scene with the women singing 'Ring a ring of roses' around Beatrice, then
breaking away laughing (P-1969).

Enter LEONATO *and* [DOGBERRY] *the Constable and* [VERGES] *the Headborough*

LEONATO What would you with me, honest neighbour?
DOGBERRY Marry, sir, I would have some confidence with you, that
    decerns you nearly.
LEONATO Brief I pray you, for you see it is a busy time with me.
DOGBERRY Marry this it is, sir.
VERGES Yes in truth it is, sir.   5
LEONATO What is it, my good friends?
DOGBERRY Goodman Verges, sir, speaks a little off the matter, an old

---

The scene was omitted by Irving, Fanny Davenport, Edwin Booth, Daly, Craig, Tree and
Sothern (1911). Jewett transposed an abbreviated version of lines 5–33 to follow 5.1.198a,
cutting the rest of the scene. The scene has often been set in a room in Leonato's house.

1ff. Bridges-Adams suggested the civility of a great house by 'sundry small, unobtrusive touches
      – for instance the grave courtesy of Leonato to Dogberry, and the attention shown to the
      constable by the page' (*DT*, 6 Feb. 1926). In Sothern's 1904–5 production Leonato sat writing
      at a table, receiving and dispatching business papers while interviewing Dogberry and
      Verges, the imminent wedding festivities foreshadowed by music and singing offstage (S59).
      In Gielgud's 1950 production pages crossed with food and drink (S93). In Seale's production
      Leonato signed documents at his desk and selected his wedding clothes while valets
      trimmed his hair (pr. photo). In Eyre's production Leonato, flustered by the approaching
      wedding, studied notes for a speech and tinkered nervously on the piano as he listened to
      Dogberry and Verges. In Hands's production a pre-wedding officers' cocktail party upstage
      established a context of male camaraderie and solidarity for the ensuing wedding scene
      (pbk). In Barton's production Dogberry kowtowed amusingly to Leonato's authority (*PP*,
      June 1976, 21); in Alexander's (1990) he showed his conceit by preening himself in a mirror
      (*PI*, June 1990).

8, 26 At Covent Garden, 1777–94, Quick's 'affected pity at the ignorance of Vergis [*sic*], while he
       glaringly exposes his own, made the audience always regret that the scene was not longer'

man, sir, and his wits are not so blunt, as God help I would desire
they were, but in faith honest, as the skin between his brows.   10
VERGES Yes I thank God, I am honest as any man living, that is an old
man, and no honester than I.
DOGBERRY Comparisons are odorous, palabras, neighbour Verges.
LEONATO Neighbours, you are tedious.
DOGBERRY It pleases your worship to say so, but we are the poor duke's   15
officers, but truly for mine own part, if I were as tedious as a king, I
could find in my heart to bestow it all of your worship.
LEONATO All thy tediousness on me, ah?
DOGBERRY Yea, and 'twere a thousand pound more than 'tis, for I hear
as good exclamation on your worship as of any man in the city, and   20
though I be but a poor man, I am glad to hear it.
VERGES And so am I.
LEONATO I would fain know what you have to say.
VERGES Marry, sir, our watch tonight, excepting your worship's
presence, ha' ta'en a couple of as arrant knaves as any in Messina.   25
DOGBERRY A good old man, sir, he will be talking as they say, when the
age is in, the wit is out, God help us, it is a world to see: well said
i'faith, neighbour Verges, well, God's a good man, and two men ride
of a horse, one must ride behind, an honest soul i'faith, sir, by my

(Taylor, *Records*, II.148–9). Keeley's performance as Verges (CG 1823–32) 'culminated'
when Dogberry 'patted him on the head, and he first bent under the honour, and then
became the taller for it, gazing into his patron's face with an expression of fatuous
contentment perfectly marvellous' (Goodman, *The Keeleys*, 163). The Dogberry of Henry
Compton (1843–63) was admired for his 'senile patronage of senility' in this scene,
especially 'the wonderful smile of amused conceit which broke out gradually over his
countenance' as he referred to Verges (*DT*, 7 Apr. 1863). Dogberry has often put Verges back
as the old man attempted to speak. In Hands's production Dogberry removed the hat from
Verges' head to remind his partner to pay respect to his betters (pbk).

13   In Zeffirelli's production Dogberry hit Verges with Leonato's hat, letting Verges' bicycle fall
     on Leonato (pbk).

14   In Sothern's 1904–5 production Dogberry, 'profoundly pleased' at what he took to be a
     compliment, bowed with a triumphant look at Verges (s59). In Trevis's production
     Dogberry's 'expression of pleasure and satisfaction on hearing that he is tedious seem[ed]
     to catch the essence of the man in one inane and fatuous beam' (*SQ* 40, 1989, 85).

24–5 In Sothern's 1904–5 production Dogberry looked piqued when Verges took over (s59).

26ff. Keeley's Dogberry (Haymarket, 1850) apologised for his partner's dotage while 'astonished
     and amused at his perspicuity and presumption' (*Era*, 17 Mar. 1850). A production photo
     (SMT 1949) shows George Rose as Dogberry pushing Verges aside with one hand and taking
     over in expansive mood, as if prepared to stay forever.

troth he is, as ever broke bread, but God is to be worshipped, all　30
men are not alike, alas, good neighbour.
LEONATO　Indeed, neighbour, he comes too short of you.
DOGBERRY　Gifts that God gives.
LEONATO　I must leave you.
DOGBERRY　One word, sir, our watch, sir, have indeed comprehended　35
two aspitious persons, and we would have them this morning
examined before your worship.
LEONATO　Take their examination yourself, and bring it me, I am now in
great haste, as it may appear unto you.
DOGBERRY　It shall be suffigance.　　　　　　　　　　　　　　40

[*Enter* MESSENGER]

LEONATO　Drink some wine ere you go: fare you well.
MESSENGER　My lord, they stay for you, to give your daughter to her
husband.
LEONATO　I'll wait upon them, I am ready.
　　　　　　　　　　　　　　　　Exit [*Leonato with Messenger*]
DOGBERRY　Go, good partner, go get you to Francis Seacoal, bid him　45
bring his pen and ink-horn to the gaol: we are now to examination
these men.
VERGES　And we must do it wisely.
DOGBERRY　We will spare for no wit I warrant you: here's that shall drive
some of them to a noncome, only get the learned writer to set down　50
our excommunication, and meet me at the gaol.
　　　　　　　　　　　　　　　　　　　　Exeunt

31　Buckstone's Verges (Haymarket, 1850) forgot where he was and pulled faces at Dogberry's
　　conceit (*Era*, 17 Mar. 1850).
35　In Zeffirelli's production Dogberry climbed through Verges' bicycle in his eagerness to
　　deliver this news (pbk).
41ff.　Dogberry has often prevented Verges from getting his share of the wine. At the Arch Street
　　Theatre, Philadelphia (1854), Verges was approaching the wine when Dogberry directed him
　　offstage, saying 'Partner, there lies your way' (S25). Similar business was recorded in
　　Stephens' NY promptbook (P-WHS). In Sothern's 1904–5 production Dogberry took the cup
　　offered to Verges, who looked on crestfallen as the constable sat with a drink in each hand
　　(S59). In Bridges-Adams's 1933–4 production Dogberry stopped Verges from getting any
　　wine by shaking the hand which Verges stretched out to take it (S87–8). Dogberry drank
　　Verges' wine in the Stratford productions of 1950, 1971 and 1988 (pbks). Leonato's offer of
　　wine was omitted, surprisingly, by the Kembles, Vining, Wallack, Burton's Theatre, NY
　　(1857), W. Lacy and Hunt.
42–4　Cut in most productions from Garrick to the late nineteenth century (Macready excepted),
　　and by Sothern (1904–5) and Hunt.

44 SD   After several failed attempts to shake Leonato's hand, David Waller's Dogberry (RSC 1988)
         at last succeeded as the governor made his exit (*SS* 42, 1989, 132). In Warchus's production
         Verges 'long[ed] to be allowed at least to shake hands with Leonato ... but the officious
         Dogberry push[ed] him aside' (*FT*, 9 July 1993).

46   **gaol** In Hanford's production, Dogberry, forgetting the wine in his eagerness to examine the
         prisoners, signalled to Verges to follow him out, but changed his mind when Verges pointed
         back and made signs of drinking (S56).

49–50   **here's that ... noncome** Whereas most actors of Dogberry point to their brains, George
         Rose (SMT 1950) quaffed a noisy draft of wine (S93).

ACT 4, SCENE I

Enter DON PEDRO, DON JOHN, LEONATO, FRIAR [FRANCIS],
CLAUDIO, BENEDICK, HERO *and* BEATRICE[; *Wedding Guests*]

LEONATO Come, Friar Francis, be brief, only to the plain form of
    marriage, and you shall recount their particular duties afterwards.
FRIAR FRANCIS You come hither, my lord, to marry this lady?
CLAUDIO No.

Since the eighteenth century traditionally set in a church or chapel. For Victorian and
Edwardian settings see introduction, pp.26ff. Twentieth-century directors have often
suggested a church by movable properties. Trevis (1988) transformed an alcove behind
the acting area into the apse of a Byzantine basilica set with gold mosaics (pr. photo).

0 SD   Saker, Irving, Alexander (1898), Sothern and Tree featured ecclesiastical processions. The
major Victorian productions crowded the stage for the wedding, Macready using fifty-five
people, Kean about forty, Irving over one hundred (see introduction, p.33). Gielgud showed
two wedding processions entering the church from the piazza; the exterior façade of the
church was then swung back to reveal the processions moving up the aisle within (s92–4;
Punch, 23 Jan. 1952). Langham (Stratford, Ontario, 1958; RSC 1961) gave the scene 'the full
climactic treatment' with organ music, processional, Friar in cloth-of-gold, candles, prayer
stools, and choirboys and townspeople on the balcony (*NYT*, 26 June 1958; *SH*, 7 Apr. 1961;
pbk; pr. photos). Zeffirelli burlesqued the entry, Verges cutting in front of the procession on
a bicycle, Benedick creeping up the line to Beatrice, the clerk moving around the guests with
a collection bag, and the 'toothless, leering old Friar' (*FT*, 22 Mar. 1967) shaking hands with
the guests until Leonato recalled him to the business of the occasion. The collusion of
Claudio, Don Pedro and Don John was signified by their arrival together at a separate
entrance (pbk). Tree lit Don John and his men with a cold blue light, the rest of the stage in
warm yellow tones (*DT*, 26 Jan. 1905). Hands staged the ceremony 'in a dazzling light on a
white carpet', the major characters dressed in white, Don John in black (*CL*, 13 May 1982).

1–2   **plain form of marriage** Suggests simple staging in the Renaissance theatre, despite the
sumptuousness of Hero's wedding gown (3.4.11–18). Tree retained this phrase despite his
lavish staging. Irving, Craig (P-1903a), Seale, and Nunn (1969) cut 1–2.

4   In Daly's 1896 production spoken in an undertone, with intense feeling (Daly). In Sothern's
1904–5 production Hero, slightly surprised, edged closer to her father (s59). In Zeffirelli's,
the guests comically turned their heads in sequence (pbk).

LEONATO To be married to her: friar, you come to marry her.   5
FRIAR FRANCIS Lady, you come hither to be married to this count?
HERO I do.
FRIAR FRANCIS If either of you know any inward impediment why you
should not be conjoined, I charge you on your souls to utter it.
CLAUDIO Know you any, Hero?   10
HERO None, my lord.
FRIAR FRANCIS Know you any, count?
LEONATO I dare make his answer, none.
CLAUDIO Oh what men dare do! What men may do! What men daily
do, not knowing what they do!   15
BENEDICK How now! Interjections? Why then, some be of laughing, as,
ah, ha, he.
CLAUDIO Stand thee by, friar: father, by your leave,
Will you with free and unconstrainèd soul
Give me this maid your daughter?   20
LEONATO As freely, son, as God did give her me.
CLAUDIO And what have I to give you back, whose worth
May counterpoise this rich and precious gift?
DON PEDRO Nothing, unless you render her again.
CLAUDIO Sweet prince, you learn me noble thankfulness: 25

10   In an attempt to play Claudio sympathetically, Stephen Russell (Stratford, Ontario, 1980)
      'began to question Hero almost gently, as if regretting his decision to shame her, before
      becoming violent' (*SS* 34, 1981, 158).

15   In Macready and Kean's productions the crowd reacted with surprise (s15, s26). Crowd
      reactions at different points in this scene have often intensified its effect.

16a   Spoken comically in Zeffirelli and Eyre's productions. 16b–17 have usually been cut.

18   The Friar discreetly motioned the acolytes to leave in Bridges-Adams's 1933–4 production;
      modesty prompted the bridesmaids to leave at 37. In Daly's 1896 production the acolytes
      left at 37, in Irving's at 46 (pbks, Daly).

25–39 Actors have often attempted to soften Claudio's rejection of Hero, Mills (*UP*, 1737) wearing
      mourning to highlight his grief, Whitfield speaking with a 'retired Shew of Tenderness' (*PA*,
      10 Jan. 1784), Forbes-Robertson with tears in his voice (*Soc*, 14 Oct. 1882), his youth and
      impulsiveness seeming partly to condone Claudio's behaviour (*Ac*, 21 Oct. 1882). Terriss
      mingled regret with his indignation (*St*, 6 Jan. 1891), Woodward despair (*SH*, 29 Aug. 1958).
      Guard (SMT 1949) backed away from Hero when she turned to him at 31; at 37 Lander (SMT
      1950) hid his head in grief on the Friar's shoulder (s92–3). Rees (RSC 1971), 'distraught with
      anger and insecurity', spoke with the impetuousness of inexperience (*St*, 22 Dec. 1971;
      editor's observation). Larkin (RTC 1988), 'tense, feverish, gripped by passionate suspicions
      quite out of his control', gave the sequence a 'fierce emotional extremity' (*G*, in *LTR*, 13–26
      Aug. 1988); McAndrew (RSC 1990) 'went pathetically out of control', 'blurting out his

> There, Leonato, take her back again,
> Give not this rotten orange to your friend,
> She's but the sign and semblance of her honour:
> Behold how like a maid she blushes here!
> Oh what authority and show of truth   30
> Can cunning sin cover itself withal!
> Comes not that blood, as modest evidence,
> To witness simple virtue? Would you not swear
> All you that see her, that she were a maid,
> By these exterior shows? But she is none: 35
> She knows the heat of a luxurious bed:
> Her blush is guiltiness, not modesty.
> LEONATO What do you mean, my lord?
> CLAUDIO   Not to be married,
> Not to knit my soul to an approvèd wanton.

accusations between his tears' (*SQ* 42, 1991, 346). On the other hand Lloyd (1968), Fiennes (RSC 1988) and Leonard (Branagh film), denounced Hero with venom (*ST*, 20 Oct. 1968; *TES*, 29 Apr. 1988). Reilly (NYSF 1988) brought out 'the savagery in Claudio's extreme moral righteousness' (*NYr*, 1 Aug. 1988). Claudio has often thrown Hero from him; Warren (1961) exposed her by tearing off her veil; in productions by Sothern (1904–5), Gielgud (1949) and Hands Claudio passed her decorously back to her father. Hero has traditionally sought comfort in Beatrice; in Gielgud's 1949 production she turned vainly to Claudio (pbks). Fernandez as Leonato (Lyceum 1882) struggled between incredulity and dread that Claudio's charges might be true (*St*, 13 Oct. 1882). Helena Faucit described her own reactions to the sequence as follows:

> When Claudio brings forward his accusation against his bride, Beatrice is struck dumb with amazement. Indignation ... is mingled with the keenest sympathy for Leonato as well as for Hero. I never knew exactly for which of the two my sympathy should most be shown, and I found myself by the side now of the one, now of the other ... What a conflict of strong emotions used to come over me when acting this scene! ... When Claudio ... went on with his charge, I could hardly keep still. My feet tingled, my eyes flashed lightning upon the princes and Claudio. (Faucit, 'Female characters', 221–2)

Kate Terry's face 'assumed an appearance of utter disbelief, not unmixed with defiance', and her 'arms went shelteringly around ... Hero's waist' as if to screen her from her accusers (*ST*, 28 July 1867). The passionate resentment welling up in Ellen Terry mingled with looks of the most tender solicitude for Hero (Agate, *Theatre Talks*, 44). At 'wanton' (39) Julia Marlowe exclaimed with indignation, putting her arms around the weeping Hero (s63); Emma Thompson cried 'No!' and rushed to Hero's aid. In Jewett's production Beatrice attempted to go to her, but was stopped by Leonato (s81). In Zeffirelli's production the rejection of Hero was staged with unusual intensity (*Encore*, Mar.–Apr. 1965, 40), patriarchy asserting itself as

LEONATO Dear my lord, if you in your own proof,   40
　　　　Have vanquished the resistance of her youth,
　　　　And made defeat of her virginity –
CLAUDIO I know what you would say: if I have known her,
　　　　You will say, she did embrace me as a husband,
　　　　And so extenuate the forehand sin: no, Leonato,   45
　　　　I never tempted her with word too large,
　　　　But as a brother to his sister, showed
　　　　Bashful sincerity, and comely love.
HERO And seemed I ever otherwise to you?
CLAUDIO Out on thee seeming, I will write against it!   50
　　　　You seem to me as Dian in her orb,
　　　　As chaste as is the bud ere it be blown:
　　　　But you are more intemperate in your blood,
　　　　Than Venus, or those pampered animals,

three men crossing to protest to Claudio were restrained by a lord (pbk). The crowd has traditionally started in astonishment at this sequence, sometimes breaking into commotion. In Barton's production Claudio's denunciation of Hero divided the characters at first into two groups: on the one hand Hero, Leonato, and the women; on the other, in male solidarity, Claudio, Don Pedro, Don John and Benedick. Benedick later moved from his companions to side with Hero and Beatrice (pbk).

27　　*UP* softened 'rotten orange' to 'blemish'd Brillant'. The line was usually cut from Garrick to the first decade of the twentieth century, Poel excepted.

30–6　Cut or abridged in most productions from Garrick to Tree. Abridged by Zeffirelli, Seale and Eyre.

38ff.　A critic of Seale's production (*NS*, 6 Nov. 1958) thought Leonato and Hero's reactions too subdued: 'The family standing around were stiff with middle-class consternation when one expected a Sicilian storm of tongues'; Hero reacted as 'the Victorian girl losing her respectability, not the Sicilian bride losing her honour'. Zeffirelli's production righted all that.

42–5a　Cut or abridged in most productions from the Kembles to Tree, and by Hunt, Carey and Barton.

46–8　In Branagh's film an overwrought Claudio rushed impulsively at Hero at the end of 46, the women screaming for fear he would attack her; standing over her, he shouted lines 47–8 in a tone of denunciation.

50–5　In Langham's 1961 production Claudio slapped Hero's face (pbk; *Liverpool Post*, 5 Apr. 1961); in Branagh's film he spat at her (at 'Venus'), struggling to restrain his tears; in the 1949 SMT and 1969 RSC productions he wept at 55 (pbks). The Benedick of Charles Kemble and others retired upstage to watch with concern (Dolby; *T*, 8 Apr. 1840; S25, Daly); Stephens as Benedick (1965) tried to restrain Claudio (pbk). The crowd began to dwindle away gradually in Irving's productions, only Hero, Beatrice, Benedick, Leonato, Ursula and the Friar

That rage in savage sensuality. 55
HERO Is my lord well, that he doth speak so wide?
LEONATO Sweet prince, why speak not you?
DON PEDRO   What should I speak?
    I stand dishonoured that have gone about
    To link my dear friend to a common stale.
LEONATO Are these things spoken, or do I but dream? 60
DON JOHN Sir, they are spoken, and these things are true.
BENEDICK This looks not like a nuptial.
HERO   True, oh God!
CLAUDIO Leonato, stand I here?
    Is this the prince? Is this the prince's brother?
    Is this face Hero's? Are our eyes our own? 65
LEONATO All this is so, but what of this, my lord?
CLAUDIO Let me but move one question to your daughter,
    And by that fatherly and kindly power,
    That you have in her, bid her answer truly.
LEONATO I charge thee do so, as thou art my child. 70
HERO Oh God defend me, how am I beset!
    What kind of catechising call you this?
CLAUDIO To make you answer truly to your name.
HERO Is it not Hero? Who can blot that name
    With any just reproach?

remaining by line 102 (S47). Lines 53–5 were often cut in Victorian and early twentieth-century productions. *UP* softened 54–5 to 'Than – what I will not say', Creswick (S44) to 'Than Venus' self'.

56   Spoken hysterically in Branagh's film. In Carey's production (1956) Hero knelt at Claudio's feet; in Hands's she went to him, but he broke away from her (pbks).

57b–9   Spoken icily in Branagh's film. Helena Faucit cast her eye at Benedick and from that moment acted as if she had determined he should avenge Hero (Faucit, 'Female characters', 221). Most productions from the Kembles to the first decade of the twentieth century softened 'common stale' to 'wanton here' or a similar euphemism.

61   Glenny's Don John adopted a 'guise of regret and forbearance' (*Std*, 13 Oct. 1882). In Tree's production a shocked crowd echoed 'True!!' (S69).

62a   Often given a comic inflection, but spoken by Gielgud as a rebuke to Claudio (S93). Cut in most productions from the Kembles to the first decade of the twentieth century (Macready and Poel excepted), and by Zeffirelli.

62b   Hero's isolation was emphasised as Viola Tree staggered to the altar and knelt there alone (*English Illustrated*, Apr. 1905). In Barton's production Claudio's smile at Benedick assumed solidarity with an officer friend (pbk).

72   In Barton's production Hero threw down her bouquet in anger and distress (pbk).

CLAUDIO   Marry that can Hero,   75
Hero itself can blot out Hero's virtue.
What man was he, talked with you yesternight,
Out at your window betwixt twelve and one?
Now if you are a maid, answer to this.
HERO I talked with no man at that hour, my lord.   80
DON PEDRO Why then are you no maiden. Leonato,
I am sorry you must hear: upon mine honour,
Myself, my brother, and this grievèd count
Did see her, hear her, at that hour last night,
Talk with a ruffian at her chamber window,   85
Who hath indeed most like a liberal villain,
Confessed the vile encounters they have had
A thousand times in secret.
DON JOHN   Fie, fie, they are
Not to be named my lord, not to be spoke of,
There is not chastity enough in language,   90
Without offence to utter them: thus, pretty lady,
I am sorry for thy much misgovernment.
CLAUDIO Oh Hero! What a hero hadst thou been,

77–9 Irving's covert glance conveyed suspicion of Don John (*Phl*, 19 Mar. 1884). In Zeffirelli and
Trevis's productions Margaret made a swift exit, ashamed of her part in Hero's defamation
(P-1965; *SQ* 40, 1989, 84); in Trevis's production she later appeared scrubbing the steps of
the patio (5.2), 'presumably in self-imposed penance' (*ibid.*).
    80 Geraldine McEwan as Hero (SMT 1958) gave 'considerable power' to her declaration of
innocence (*SH*, 29 Aug. 1958).
   81a Regularly cut from Garrick to the first decade of the twentieth century.
    85 At the Shakespeare Theatre, Washington, 1992, Margaret, who until now had 'stood aside as
the appalling realisation that Hero was being blamed for [her] misdeed gradually dawned
on her … stepped forward impulsively … but Don John quickly stepped in front of her and, in
a brutally threatening gesture, slid open his wooden walking stick to reveal a dagger hidden
inside. Margaret checked herself and gazed at the dagger, wide-eyed with terror. During the
remainder of the scene, she paced back and forth on the sidelines, wringing her hands' (*SQ*
43, 1992, 460–1). Branagh's film showed Margaret aghast with dawning realisation. In
Jewett's production Hero gave a quick cry and buried her face in Beatrice's breast; in
Branagh's film she fainted. Leonato shrank from his daughter in Hanford and Barton's
productions; the crowd shrank from her in the productions of Macready, Kean, Tree and
Branagh (pbks).
 86–92 Prudery motivated the frequent cutting or abridgement of these lines in nineteenth- and
early twentieth-century productions.
    93 Forbes-Robertson spoke the line as a passionate cry (*Th*, 1 Nov. 1882). In Jewett's production

> If half thy outward graces had been placed
> About thy thoughts and counsels of thy heart?   95
> But fare thee well, most foul, most fair, farewell
> Thou pure impiety, and impious purity,
> For thee I'll lock up all the gates of love,
> And on my eyelids shall conjecture hang,
> To turn all beauty into thoughts of harm,   100
> And never shall it more be gracious.
> LEONATO Hath no man's dagger here a point for me?
> [*Hero faints*]

Claudio stretched out his arms in anguish to Hero (s81); Philip Guard (SMT 1949) buried his face in his hands (s92).

93–101   Seale cut 93–5, 99–101. Line 97 was cut in most productions from Garrick to the first decade of the twentieth century, and by Eyre.

96   In Barton's production Hero rushed to Claudio, who pushed her away (pbk). Claudio's anguish and the hurt of Leonato were 'electrifying' (*BWJ*, 15 Apr. 1976). McAndrew's Claudio (1990) was 'hardly able to resist kissing Hero' (*SQ* 42, 1991, 346).

101   In Barton's production Hero looked appealingly to Don Pedro, then to her father, who spat at her. In Tree's production Claudio, Don Pedro and Don John made their exit to the sound of organ and tolling angelus, the ensuing silence intensifying Leonato's request for a dagger (pbks).

102 SD   In Zeffirelli's production Hero cried 'Claudio!' as she fainted, Beatrice, Ursula and Balthasar rushing to her aid. In Nunn's production Claudio showed some lingering feeling for Hero, making a move towards her as she collapsed (*Punch*, 23 Oct. 1968). Leonato has often remained detached from his daughter, giving point to Beatrice's 'help, uncle!' (106). Tears streamed down Ellen Terry's cheeks as she comforted her cousin (*Th*, 1 Oct. 1880, 220; *ILN*, 21 Oct. 1882). Benedick has traditionally shown solicitude for both Hero and Beatrice. Garrick cried 'Look to the lady!' as Hero fainted (Bell). The Kembles, Macready and Irving ran to help raise her (pbks), Charles Kemble scrutinising her countenance as he supported her, his suspicions striving with a growing sense of her innocence (*Kidd's*, 11 Apr. 1840). Macready bent over her with tender and 'chivalrous solicitude' (s19; Pollock, *Macready*, 134). At the Haymarket in the 1850s players used to score cheap laughter in this sequence, Benedick coming over to take Hero's hand and Beatrice striking him away, jealous, as Walter Lacy explained to Ellen Terry, that her man should touch another woman (s32; Terry, *Lectures*, 95–6). Irving showed deep solicitude for Beatrice's distress (*Liverpool Courier*, 27 Sep. 1883). As Fred Terry watched the agonised Beatrice 'there suddenly shone forth an intense sincerity, transforming him into a man one had not seen before' (*MP*, 2 May 1911). The 1981 NT production emphasised Hero's isolation, no-one coming to her aid (*DE*, in *LTR*, 13–26 Aug. 1981). Trevis's production highlighted the polarisation of gender, Hero surrounded by a flock of sympathetic women while the men retired 'to nurse their personal

BEATRICE Why how now, cousin, wherefore sink you down?
DON JOHN Come let us go: these things come thus to light,
       Smother her spirits up.
                    [Exeunt Don Pedro, Don John and Claudio]
BENEDICK   How doth the lady?   105
BEATRICE Dead I think, help, uncle!
       Hero, why Hero: uncle: Signor Benedick: friar!
LEONATO Oh Fate! Take not away thy heavy hand,
       Death is the fairest cover for her shame
       That may be wished for.
BEATRICE   How now, cousin Hero?   110
FRIAR FRANCIS Have comfort, lady.
LEONATO   Dost thou look up?
FRIAR FRANCIS Yea, wherefore should she not?
LEONATO Wherefore? Why doth not every earthly thing

grievances' (*T*, 14 Apr. 1988). Benedick had tried to assist Hero, but had been pushed away by Beatrice and the maids (pbk). Some productions turned Hero's swoon into melodrama, Poel with three wailing chords from the organ (s57), Moshinsky with thunderous sound effects as the lights dimmed and a black curtain moved across the cyclorama (*Listener*, 25 May 1989).

104–5a Cut in most nineteenth-century productions, and by Sothern and Tree.

105 SD In David Richman's American production, 'Benedick began to exit with his friends. Turning for a last look at Beatrice, he saw that she was glaring at him with shock and disappointment. With a troubled expression, he slowly rejoined the forlorn group clustered around the fallen Hero', as if 'leaving forever … the comradely but conventional world of his friends' (Richman, *SC* 18.266). In Gielgud's 1949–50 productions Ursula picked up Hero's bridal tiara which had rolled to the ground, a symbol of her ruin (s92–3).

108ff. Irving and Craig cut Leonato's speech at 108–110a, allowing uninterrupted focus on Beatrice. As Hero regained consciousness, Irving detached himself upstage a little to assess the situation (s47). During Leonato's denunciation (113ff.), Gielgud (1955) soothed Hero with a handkerchief moistened at the font (s94).

113–36 Often abridged considerably. Productions from the eighteenth to the early twentieth century tended to dignify and idealise Leonato in this scene, the cuts to his longer speeches softening his resentment and self-pity and making him a more sympathetic figure than in the full text. In a comment probably reflecting Garrick's staging, Francis Gentleman characterised Leonato as 'a sensible [i.e. sensitive], feeling father', whose responses at the broken wedding 'must affect every heart capable of impression' (*DrC* 2, 1770, 319–20). Fernandez (1882) played Leonato in this scene with 'the pathetic devotion of the grand old father', Vernon (1898) similarly idealising the role (*Th*, 1 Nov. 1882; *Era*, 19 Feb. 1898). Something of the traditional idealisation persisted in Quartermaine's Leonato (SMT 1949),

Cry shame upon her? Could she here deny
The story that is printed in her blood?   115
Do not live, Hero, do not ope thine eyes:
For did I think thou wouldst not quickly die,
Thought I thy spirits were stronger than thy shames,
Myself would on the rearward of reproaches
Strike at thy life. Grieved I, I had but one?   120
Chid I for that at frugal nature's frame?
Oh one too much by thee! Why had I one?
Why ever wast thou lovely in my eyes?
Why had I not with charitable hand,
Took up a beggar's issue at my gates,   125
Who smirchèd thus, and mired with infamy,
I might have said, no part of it is mine,
This shame derives itself from unknown loins:
But mine, and mine I loved, and mine I praised,
And mine that I was proud on, mine so much,   130
That I myself, was to myself not mine,
Valuing of her: why she, oh she is fallen
Into a pit of ink, that the wide sea
Hath drops too few to wash her clean again,
And salt too little, which may season give   135
To her foul tainted flesh.

T. C. Kemp commenting that in the broken-wedding scene he showed 'a gallant old gentleman battling with grief and anger and coming very finely out of the struggle' (broadcast typescript, 3 May 1949). Tony Church (RSC 1971), on the other hand, reacted with 'Victorian paternal outrage' to the supposed infidelity of his daughter (*St*, 22 Dec. 1971). In Branagh's film Leonato dragged Hero about violently by the hair, threw her to the ground (116), and struck her (132).

120 **Strike at thy life** In numerous productions Leonato has threatened to strike Hero, restrained sometimes by Benedick, the Friar or Antonio. In Trevis's production Ursula screamed as Leonato lunged at his daughter (pbk). In some productions Leonato has again threatened Hero at 147b, in others at 184a.

121 In Sothern's 1911 production Leonato struck his breast in self-pity (s63). In Barton's production he knelt by Hero and picked her up in his arms (P-1976), an action in poignant tension with his preceding words.

129 In Carey's production (1956) this line brought a sob from Hero. In Nunn's 1969 production Leonato took Hero in his arms, then at 133 flung her to Beatrice (pbk).

134 In Sothern's 1911 production Leonato buried his face in his hands, sobbing; in Zeffirelli's he slowly sank onto a bench, where Antonio tried to console him (pbks).

BENEDICK Sir, sir, be patient. For my part I am so attired in wonder, I
    know not what to say.
BEATRICE Oh on my soul my cousin is belied.
BENEDICK Lady, were you her bedfellow last night?   140
BEATRICE No truly not, although until last night,
    I have this twelve month been her bedfellow.
LEONATO Confirmed, confirmed, oh that is stronger made,
    Which was before barred up with ribs of iron.
    Would the two princes lie, and Claudio lie,   145
    Who loved her so, that speaking of her foulness,
    Washed it with tears? Hence from her, let her die.
FRIAR FRANCIS Hear me a little, for I have only been
    Silent so long, and given way unto
    This course of fortune, by noting of the lady.   150
    I have marked
    A thousand blushing apparitions,
    To start into her face, a thousand innocent shames,
    In angel whiteness beat away those blushes,
    And in her eye there hath appeared a fire,   155
    To burn the errors that these princes hold
    Against her maiden truth: call me a fool,
    Trust not my reading, nor my observations,
    Which with experimental seal doth warrant
    The tenure of my book: trust not my age,   160
    My reverence, calling, nor divinity,
    If this sweet lady lie not guiltless here,
    Under some biting error.
LEONATO   Friar, it cannot be,
    Thou seest that all the grace that she hath left,

37–93a   Cut by Edwin Booth (s41).
  139   Helena Faucit spoke this line in a voice 'resonant with the energy of assured conviction'
      (Faucit, 'Female characters', 221). Ellen Terry blazed with indignation (Terry, *Lectures*, 89).
  140   Charles Kemble asked the question earnestly (*JB*, 12 Apr. 1840).
141–2   Louisa Nisbett, departing from the Kemble tradition, was criticised for failing to register
      distress at the words 'until last night' (*JB*, 12 Apr. 1840). The gestures of Lewis's Benedick
      expressed 'absolute conviction of Hero's guilt' (*MP*, 10 Oct. 1797).
143–7   Spoken 'in deep grief' at Burton's, NY, 1857 (s21).
148–63   Often heavily abridged.
  163a   As the Friar affirmed his belief in Hero's innocence, Ellen Terry fell to her knees impulsively
      and kissed his hand (*SR*, 18 June 1887), business also adopted by Marie Drofnah (s56) and
      Julia Marlowe (s59).
164–6   This fatuous assertion by Leonato was cut by Macready, Kean, Saker, Irving and Craig.

Is that she will not add to her damnation 165
A sin of perjury, she not denies it:
Why seek'st thou then to cover with excuse,
That which appears in proper nakedness?
FRIAR FRANCIS Lady, what man is he you are accused of?
HERO They know that do accuse me, I know none: 170
If I know more of any man alive
Than that which maiden modesty doth warrant,
Let all my sins lack mercy. Oh my father,
Prove you that any man with me conversed,
At hours unmeet, or that I yesternight 175
Maintained the change of words with any creature,
Refuse me, hate me, torture me to death.
FRIAR FRANCIS There is some strange misprision in the princes.
BENEDICK Two of them have the very bent of honour,
And if their wisdoms be misled in this, 180
The practice of it lives in John the bastard,
Whose spirits toil in frame of villainies.
LEONATO I know not: if they speak but truth of her,
These hands shall tear her, if they wrong her honour,
The proudest of them shall well hear of it. 185
Time hath not yet so dried this blood of mine,
Nor age so eat up my invention,
Nor fortune made such havoc of my means,

171   In Nunn's production Hero took up a Bible, as if affirming under oath the truth of her words
       (P-1969).
173b   In the Kemble productions Hero rushed to Leonato and fell at his feet with an impassioned
       affirmation of her innocence (S6; *JB*, 12 Apr. 1840), business often adopted since. Maria
       Foote (CG 1817) made Hero's appeal 'forcible and affecting' (*T*, 29 Nov. 1817). At Burton's
       and Daly's, NY, Leonato turned away from his daughter's entreaty (S21, Daly).
177   At Burton's and Daly's, NY, Hero fainted, Beatrice and the other ladies raising her and
       conducting her upstage (S21, Daly). Beatrice has often comforted Hero at this point.
       In Zeffirelli's production Beatrice and Ursula wept at her words (pbk).
181–2 Tree pointed to Don John leering through the chapel grille (S69).
184a   Leonato advanced menacingly in Sothern and Bill Alexander's productions (S59; *SS* 44,
       1990, 171); in Gielgud's (1949–50) he threw Hero down (S92–3). Langham and Barton cut
       this threat (183b–4a).
186–93a In Bridges-Adams's 1933–4 production Leonato shook hands with Antonio (192) as if sealing
       a pact of vengeance (S88). Leonato's over-pitched assertions of his powers to avenge Hero
       were cut or abridged in most productions from Garrick to the late nineteenth century (Irving
       excepted), and often since.

Nor my bad life reft me so much of friends,
But they shall find, awaked in such a kind,   190
Both strength of limb, and policy of mind,
Ability in means, and choice of friends,
To quit me of them throughly.
FRIAR FRANCIS   Pause awhile,
And let my counsel sway you in this case:
Your daughter here the princes left for dead,   195
Let her awhile be secretly kept in,
And publish it, that she is dead indeed:
Maintain a mourning ostentation,
And on your family's old monument
Hang mournful epitaphs, and do all rites,   200
That appertain unto a burial.
LEONATO What shall become of this? What will this do?
FRIAR FRANCIS Marry, this well carried, shall on her behalf,
Change slander to remorse, that is some good,
But not for that dream I on this strange course,   205
But on this travail look for greater birth:
She dying, as it must be so maintained,
Upon the instant that she was accused,
Shall be lamented, pitied, and excused
Of every hearer: for it so falls out,   210
That what we have, we prize not to the worth,
Whiles we enjoy it; but being lacked and lost,
Why then we rack the value, then we find
The virtue that possession would not show us
Whiles it was ours: so will it fare with Claudio: 215
When he shall hear she died upon his words
Th'idea of her life shall sweetly creep
Into his study of imagination,
And every lovely organ of her life,
Shall come apparelled in more precious habit,   220
More moving-delicate, and full of life,

193–201   Maggie Smith as Beatrice (1965) sat facing upstage in grief (pbk). Lines 198–201 were cut in most productions from Garrick to the first decade of the twentieth century, and by Hunt, Seale and Barton.

203–36   Often heavily abridged. Ada Rehan as Beatrice prostrated herself on the steps of the altar, weeping (Sprague, *Shakespeare and the Actors*, 16); Judi Dench broke upstage weeping at 223 (P-1976). In Sothern and Gielgud's productions Hero kissed the Friar's hand at 229 (S59, S92–3, P-1952). Jacobi as Benedick moved about the stage cogitating during the Friar's speech, forming the ideas expressed in the speech that follows (P-1982).

Into the eye and prospect of his soul
Than when she lived indeed: then shall he mourn,
If ever love had interest in his liver,
And wish he had not so accusèd her: 225
No, though he thought his accusation true:
Let this be so, and doubt not but success
Will fashion the event in better shape
Than I can lay it down in likelihood.
But if all aim but this be levelled false,   230
The supposition of the lady's death,
Will quench the wonder of her infamy.
And if it sort not well, you may conceal her,
As best befits her wounded reputation,
In some reclusive and religious life,   235
Out of all eyes, tongues, minds and injuries.
BENEDICK Signor Leonato, let the friar advise you,
And though you know my inwardness and love
Is very much unto the prince and Claudio,
Yet, by mine honour, I will deal in this,   240
As secretly and justly as your soul
Should with your body.
LEONATO   Being that I flow in grief,
The smallest twine may lead me.
FRIAR FRANCIS 'Tis well consented, presently away:
For to strange sores, strangely they strain the cure: 245
Come, lady, die to live, this wedding day
Perhaps is but prolonged: have patience and endure.
                          Exeunt [Friar Francis, Leonato and Hero]

237–42a   Louisa Nisbett moved upstage weeping (s20). Peggy Ashcroft gave a start when Benedick
          said his love was 'very much unto the prince and Claudio' (s94).
242b–3   In Sothern's 1904–5 production Leonato struggled inwardly before speaking, then bowed
          resignedly and took Hero's hand as Benedick led him to her (s59). In Murdoch and
          Davenport's productions Leonato waved Hero off and made his exit (s13, s36).
245   Often cut. Garrick substituted 'A grievous wound requires a desperate cure.'
247 SD   Hero has usually been assisted out by the Friar, sometimes by her maids. Hero and Beatrice
          have sometimes embraced in the moments preceding the exit (s6, s92–4, p-1965). In
          Sothern's 1904–5 production Leonato gently drew Hero to him, put his arm about her, and
          led her off; in Hanford's Hero knelt briefly at the altar; in Tree's Leonato was led out sobbing,
          leaning disconsolately on Antonio and Benedick (pbks). Beatrice has traditionally remained
          weeping, Julia Marlowe sinking onto the altar steps, head averted and face in hands (s59,
          s63). Organ music accompanied the exit in the productions of Irving, Fanny Davenport, Daly
          and Sothern; in Poel's a choir sang 'Ave Verum' (pbks). In Tree's production Don John

BENEDICK Lady Beatrice, have you wept all this while?
BEATRICE Yea, and I will weep a while longer.

crossed the stage after the exit, smiling and rubbing his hands in satisfaction (s69).
Some productions have introduced a distinct break between the broken-wedding
sequence and the ensuing Beatrice–Benedick dialogue, *UP* by an act break, Saker by an
elaborate recessional, Flanagan by a high mass, including a choral performance of the Kyrie
from Palestrina's *Missa assumptu est Maria* (*MG*, 22 Jan. 1900; *St*, 22 Feb. 1917). Tree
changed scenes from the church to the cloisters; Fred Terry (King's, Hammersmith, 1920)
lowered a curtain (programmes); Branagh moved from the garden into a chapel. Tree
justified his scene change on the grounds that the Beatrice–Benedick sequence was more
appropriate in the cloisters than the church (programme). Not all reviewers agreed, one
arguing that the charge to 'Kill Claudio' is 'more solemn and serious' when uttered before
the altar than when Benedick is 'fondling [Beatrice] in the cloisters' (*SpT*, 28 Jan. 1905),
another that the change of location broke the 'climaxing tension' of the scene, divorcing the
Beatrice–Benedick dialogue from its motivating circumstances (*DT*, 25 Jan. 1905), a third
that 'the audience [was] chilled by the interval, by the pause before the supreme moment
of the play' (*WG*, 25 Jan. 1905).

In most productions there is a suspenseful pause as Benedick and Beatrice find
themselves alone together for the first time since their mutual change of heart. Baliol
Holloway (SMT 1934) searched for a way to approach Beatrice as she knelt in tears at the
altar (s88). Gielgud and Peggy Ashcroft (1955), inclined at first to leave with the rest of the
wedding party, stopped independently, Gielgud returning to centre stage, Ashcroft
remaining hesitantly at one side (s94). Janet Suzman (1968–9) sank sobbing behind the
front pew, Alan Howard moving down from the shadows upstage and kneeling reticently in
a pew further back. Before the altar, they confessed their love for each other 'in a hushed
wonder, a breathless awe, as if consciously in the solemn presence of God himself' (*EN*, 30
July 1969; pbks). Judi Dench (1976) forestalled an approach from Benedick by picking up
Hero's bouquet, then distractedly sweeping up the scattered flowers left after the broken
wedding and dumping them into a basket (pbk). Sinead Cusack (1982) sank sobbing to the
floor as the rest of the company went off, Jacobi circling her slowly with 'wary devotion',
'almost as if afraid to speak' (*G*, 14 May 1983). As he paced round the stage 'trying to make
sense of the situation', he developed visibly 'from the flippant, almost epicene joker of the
early scenes into a man who could feel genuine love and genuine honour' (*SQ* 34, 1983, 84).
Branagh knelt patiently as Emma Thompson, barely controlling her distress, prayed in the
chapel. There was no such reticence in Vining and Kean's productions. Vining approached
Beatrice purposefully as she filed out with the other guests (s12); Charles Kean 'rush[ed] into
hearty lovemaking', delighted at being relieved from the suspense of uncertainty (*T*, 30 Jan.
1861).

48–316 Garrick played this sequence with a good deal of comedy, *The London Chronicle* (19–22

BENEDICK I will not desire that.   250
BEATRICE You have no reason, I do it freely.
BENEDICK Surely I do believe your fair cousin is wronged.
BEATRICE Ah, how much might the man deserve of me that would right
    her!
BENEDICK Is there any way to show such friendship?   255

March 1757) reporting that he made it one of the most entertaining parts of the play (see
also *DrC* 2, 1770, 315). Comedy and sentiment mingled with intenser feelings in most
Victorian performances. The 1984 BBC-TV production and Branagh's film made the
sequence deeply serious throughout.

248–77 The hesitancy and indirection of much of this dialogue were diminished in *UP*. Walter Lacy
    played the sequence with a 'delicacy' described as 'most artistic' (*BWM*, 14 Apr. 1866). Irving
    and Ellen Terry took the lines rapidly, blending comedy with seriousness (*SR*, 21 Oct. 1882;
    DT, 2 June 1884), Terry brushing tears from her eyes as the dialogue commenced (*BET*, 28
    Feb. 1884), Irving displaying 'the sheepishness of a first affection' (*T*, 24 Oct. 1882), his
    embarrassment and uncertainty 'delicious and enjoyable' (Foss, *What the Author Meant*,
    113). However, some critics thought the comic elements in Irving's performance jarred with
    the solemn cathedral setting (*Quarterly Review* 155, 1883, 382; Fitzgerald, *Irving*, 194–5).
    James Dale and Florence Saunders (SMT 1925) played the sequence 'with exquisite delicacy'
    (*BM*, 18 Apr. 1925), as did Gielgud and Diana Wynyard, 'the intensity of their love mut[ing]
    their voices almost to a whisper' (*Punch*, 23 Jan. 1952). After the bolder drama of Hero's
    humiliation, this 'extreme quietness' came with great effect (*ibid.*). Susan Fleetwood and
    Roger Allam made the passage 'tearful and tense' (*FT*, 12 Apr. 1990).

248 A long look of sympathy passed between Gielgud and Diana Wynyard (*Drama* 25, 1952, 14).

249 Warren and Wood (1804) added, 'for the cause demands it' (s3). Judi Dench answered
    brusquely while compulsively sweeping; in the end Benedick had to declare his love to
    her unyielding back (pbk; *O*, 11 Apr. 1976).

250 Jewett took Beatrice's hand, which she withdrew at once (s81).

252 Helena Faucit and Ellen Terry brushed aside their tears as Benedick affirmed his belief in
    Hero's innocence (Faucit, 'Female characters', 223; *BET*, 28 Feb. 1884).

253–4 Cherie Lunghi (BBC-TV, 1984) said 'Ah' as if a solution had just struck her; then after a pause,
    she proceeded with earnest longing, giving determined emphasis to the words 'right her'.
    After this, the command to kill Claudio came as no surprise. Charlotte Cushman spoke with
    'persuasive sincerity' (*O*, 7 Apr. 1845). At 'right her' Julia Marlowe looked significantly at
    Benedick (s63).

255 Irving raised a laugh as he limped across to Beatrice 'in unusually grotesque fashion'
    (*MN*, Chicago, 21 Jan. 1885), contemplated her hand and quickly kissed it before speaking
    (s45–6).

BEATRICE A very even way, but no such friend.
BENEDICK May a man do it?
BEATRICE It is a man's office, but not yours.
BENEDICK I do love nothing in the world so well as you, is not that
          strange?   260

256   At Beatrice's first phrase Sothern took a quick step towards her, but Julia Marlowe stopped
      him with a gesture (s59).

258   At 'a man's office' Sothern again started towards Beatrice, stayed, however, by her next
      words, 'but not yours' (s59). In the mid-Victorian period some actresses had delivered this
      phrase as a sarcastic slight on Benedick's manhood, a reading rejected by Helena Faucit and
      Ellen Terry (Faucit, 'Female characters', 223; *T*, 24 Oct. 1882). After a pause 'full of exquisite
      humour' in the centre of the line (*LDP*, 16 Dec. 1870), Faucit spoke 'but not yours' merely to
      signify Benedick's ineligibility on account of his not being Hero's kinsman (Faucit, 'Female
      characters', 223). Ellen Terry spoke the phrase as 'the afterthought of a woman ... unwilling
      to expose her lover to the dangers of a duel, even at the risk of his manhood being
      compromised' (*T*, 24 Oct. 1882). She then attempted to leave, hastening Benedick's
      confession of love (Terry, MS note in her copy of Fletcher, *Shakespeare*, 271). While Ada
      Rehan was rehearsing the part, the Shakespearean scholar H. H. Furness sent her the
      following advice on the interpretation of the line:

> This is generally accepted as a bitter sarcasm, which I think is utterly wrong.
>   It is really a confession of love, and should be uttered sadly – almost tenderly. Had it
> been sarcasm, Benedick would have been stung to the quick – whereas it elicits almost a
> declaration of love on his part.
>   It was a man's duty inasmuch as the quarrel should be taken up by a brother – or a
> cousin, or a very near relation. The privilege of that relationship Benedick had not then,
> but were he Beatrice's accepted lover – then he might claim the right of vindicating
> Hero's honor. And in Beatrice's words there should be heard the faint echo of an
> exquisite confession of love. (Reproduced in J. F. Daly, *Augustin Daly*, 605)

      Fanny Davenport's reading was consistent with this view: as she spoke the line she dropped
      her hand by her side for Benedick to take (s36). Sybil Thorndike spoke the words not as a
      taunt, but 'as if checking herself in an appeal for Benedick's help' (Crosse, 'Performances',
      XI.35). Cherie Lunghi's tone (BBC-TV, 1984) indicated that she cared so much for Benedick
      she did not want his life endangered.

259–60 The following business, probably Charles Kemble's, but possibly Walter Lacy's, was
      recorded in Lacy's transcription (s7) of Kemble's promptbook: Benedick, looking full in
      the face of Beatrice, 'gently and very gradually' took her hand in his, raised it 'slowly and
      cautiously until near his lips', and snatched a kiss of it before declaring his love. Charles
      Kean paused expressively before his declaration, then pressed Beatrice's hand tenderly to

BEATRICE As strange as the thing I know not: it were as possible for me to say, I loved nothing so well as you, but believe me not, and yet I lie not, I confess nothing, nor I deny nothing: I am sorry for my cousin.

his lips (s26; *ILN*, 10 July 1852). Belton (Burton's, NY, 1857) played the moment half-teasingly, tickling Beatrice's hand with a feather before snatching it to his lips for a kiss (s21). Irving paused and sighed (s45–6), then affirmed his love 'with a quaint sincerity and recklessness' (*A*, 10 Jan. 1891), his hand delicately touching Beatrice's as it hung by her side (*SR*, 21 Oct. 1882). Then ogling her, he added with abrupt comic awkwardness, 'Is not that strange?' (Foss, *What the Author Meant*, 113; *EN*, Glasgow, 28 Aug. 1883). Sothern turned to Beatrice 'with wide eyes, intent, but tremulous within with feeling', and taking her hand, confessed his love 'in level tones'. At 'Is not that strange?' he paused slightly, then laughed, 'softly, half-ashamed, delighted, pensive' (*RHC*, 28 Sep. 1904; s59). Marie Drofnah turned on Benedick as he confessed his love (s56). Clement McCallin (1947) expressed his with considerable tenderness (*St*, 22 May 1947). Gielgud put 'all the wonderment and earnestness imaginable' into his confession (*MA*, 23 Jan. 1952). A 1965 production photograph shows Stephens wooing Beatrice in demonstrative Sicilian style, caressing her cheek and speaking with extravagant ardour (NT archives). Judi Dench stopped short in her sweeping as Sinden made his declaration (pbk; *O*, 11 Apr. 1976). Jacobi's 'strangled' declaration came as 'the climax to a long process of introspective struggle' (*SS* 36, 1983, 152). Merrison raised laughter as he 'scurrie[d] nervously' into the speech (*SQ* 40, 1989, 85). Rylance was also 'nervous and engagingly awkward' (*SS* 47, 1994, 193).

261–4 *UP* eliminated some of the vacillations in Beatrice's response. Fanny Kemble replied 'half good-humouredly, half peevishly', with 'a spontaneous avowal at first, followed by an attempt at disguise which comes too late; embarrassment, and then an evasion', uttered abruptly and tearfully, 'I am sorry for my cousin' (*Tatler*, 18 Feb. 1831; *O*, 20 Feb. 1831). Faucit smiled in remembrance of what she had overheard in the garden, but found it hard to confess her affection. She twice half yielded and withdrew, then tried to escape her embarrassment by changing the subject, speaking the final phrase 'with tremulous emotion' (Faucit, 'Female characters', 223). As Ellen Terry spoke, Irving moved about awkwardly, interjecting a comical 'Ah' or 'Eh' after each phrase (s45; *Knowledge*, 10 Nov. 1882). Richman (1896) turned the speech to comedy, dropping to his knees at 'love ... you' and rising again immediately at 'believe me not' (Daly). Winifred Emery (1905) spoke the lines coquettishly, making as if to nestle into Benedick's arms, then moving coyly away (s69). Diana Wynyard confessed her love with 'breathless ardour' (*MA*, 23 Jan. 1952). Joan Plowright paused for some time before speaking, her eyes darkening with alarmed tenderness (*O*, 26 Mar. 1967), her features torn between anger at Hero's humiliation and rapture at Benedick's declaration of love (*T*, 22 Mar. 1967). As Janet McTeer spoke, an 'involuntary giggle suddenly cascade[d] through' her sobs (*Ind*, 8 July 1993). At 'sorry ... cousin' Eve Walsh Hall (1926) sat on the altar steps and covered her face (s81); Peggy Ashcroft looked tearfully after the departed Hero (s93).

BENEDICK By my sword, Beatrice, thou lovest me.   265
BEATRICE Do not swear and eat it.
BENEDICK I will swear by it that you love me, and I will make him eat it
    that says I love not you.
BEATRICE Will you not eat your word?
BENEDICK With no sauce that can be devised to it: I protest I love thee.   270
BEATRICE Why then God forgive me.
BENEDICK What offence, sweet Beatrice?
BEATRICE You have stayed me in a happy hour, I was about to protest I
    loved you.
BENEDICK And do it with all thy heart.   275
BEATRICE I love you with so much of my heart, that none is left to
    protest.

265   Jacobi knelt beside Beatrice, who was still sitting on the ground in distress (P-1982).
265–71 Helena Faucit's emotions see-sawed between Benedick and Hero (Faucit, 'Female
       characters', 223).
270b   Judi Dench finished cleaning up the last few flowers, stood up slowly, and grasping the
       chance which Benedick had placed before her, responded with 'awestruck rapture' (*NS*, 16
       Apr. 1976; P-1976). Sinead Cusack rose from the floor (see commentary on 265), Jacobi
       taking both her hands in his (P-1982).
273   Fanny Davenport put her arms around Benedick's neck (P-1886).
276–7 In *UP* the speech corresponding to these lines was given not to Liberia, but to Protheus.
       Liberia made no open confession of love before challenging Protheus to kill Bellario. Only
       when he agreed did she consent to love him, mainly to requite his services. Helena Faucit
       confessed her love half wittily, half earnestly (Faucit, 'Female characters', 223), Ellen Terry
       with 'exquisite grace and faintly reluctant completeness of … surrender' (*BDA*, 28 Feb. 1884).
       Some Victorian actresses, on the other hand, represented Beatrice's confession of love as
       a lure to secure Benedick's agreement to challenge Claudio (*WD*, 13 Sep. 1857). It was
       traditional in the nineteenth century for Beatrice and Benedick to embrace at the end of the
       speech, Fanny Kemble throwing herself impulsively into Benedick's arms (*T*, 18 Feb. 1831),
       Ellen Terry abandoning herself to Irving and sighing with delight as he covered her face with
       kisses (S46–7; *ECG*, 28 Aug. 1883), business which made the Beatrice–Benedick relationship
       seem more settled at this point than the text suggests. In the 1850s some Benedicks at the
       Haymarket strutted about after the embrace in self-congratulation at having won Beatrice,
       business which Walter Lacy rejected as tasteless (S32). Tree sentimentalised the embrace
       more than most previous actors, with 'amorous moans', 'little tender grunts' and 'bleatings
       of inarticulate emotion' (*Speaker*, 28 Jan. 1905). Some other productions have played the
       moment less romantically, Julia Marlowe refusing the offered kiss (S59), Peggy Ashcroft, as
       at 264, looking tearfully after the departed Hero (S93). After the comedy of Clive Merrison's
       declaration of love (RSC 1988), Maggie Steed, with a long pause that stilled the house,
       confessed hers in full seriousness (*SQ* 40, 1989, 85). Branagh and Emma Thompson spoke

BENEDICK Come bid me do anything for thee.
BEATRICE Kill Claudio.
BENEDICK Ha, not for the wide world.   280
BEATRICE You kill me to deny it, farewell.

273–7 with increasing tempo, building to a passionate embrace at 277. In the Lost Theatre
production (Edinburgh Festival, 1993), Beatrice and Benedick found their declaration of
love 'a thrilling and liberating experience' (*SQ* 45, 1994, 349).

278   Spoken 'rapturously' by Belton (S21), in 'ringing tones' by Irving (*PhI*, 19 Mar. 1884), and by
Gielgud (1950) after a charged pause in which he stepped back two paces, giving the words
an added expansiveness (S93). Alan Howard spoke the line in a low key (*ILN*, 9 Aug. 1969).
Lipscomb (Champlain SF, 1975) swaggered upstage, turned, set himself, and 'joyously
proclaim[ed] "Come! Bid me do *anything* for thee!"' (*SQ* 27, 1976, 42). Lindsay (BBC-TV,
1984) invited Beatrice lovingly, with deep sincerity and no hint of extravagance. Branagh,
flushed and excited after embracing her, spoke with unguarded expansiveness.

279   Helena Faucit spoke her 'Kill Claudio' half appealingly, half commandingly, in a voice
earnest, yet startling in its bitterness and force (*ManC*, 11 Apr. 1866; *LDP*, 16 Dec. 1870).
Louisa Nisbett clasped Benedick impulsively about the neck, fell on his shoulder and burst
out sobbing (S19; *MP*, 25 Feb. 1843). Ellen Kean said the words with concentrated
indignation (*ST*, 17 March 1850, 28 Nov. 1858), Louisa Herbert with fiery spirit (*WD*, 8 Apr.
1866). Ellen Terry spoke them less fiercely than some, though with swift impulsiveness,
turning with sudden eagerness on Benedick (*A*, 7 June 1884; *Th*, 1 Nov. 1882; *PhI*, 19 Mar.
1884). As she matured in the role she delivered the line with 'concentrated energy', 'like an
arrow from a full-drawn bow', emphasising the words with 'a gesture like that of a thrusting
lance' (*PhI*, 19 Mar. 1884; *BDA*, 28 Feb. 1884). Fanny Davenport spoke the words intimately,
her lips to Benedick's (P-1886). Helena Modjeska's demand was 'quick and passionate'
(Shattuck, *Shakespeare on the American Stage*, II.132). Tree's stage business softened the
line, he and Winifred Emery holding their embrace while he invited, 'Come bid me do
anything for thee'. 'Anything?' she queried. 'Anything', he assured. She spoke her 'Kill
Claudio' still clasped in his arms (S69; *St*, 25 Jan. 1905). Julia Marlowe turned fiercely at 'Kill
Claudio' (S63), her words ringing out like a clarion (Shattuck, *Shakespeare on the American
Stage*, II.265). Sybil Thorndike's 'Kill Claudio' 'nearly killed everyone in the house' (Casson,
Lewis and Sybil, 142), Crosse describing it as 'quiet but intensely strong' (*Playgoing*, 52).
Marie Ney (Old Vic, 1925) spoke the line in 'a voice as sharp, as clear, as cold as an icicle':
'one froze in one's chair as one listened' (*ST*, 20 Oct. 1946). Claire Luce (SMT 1945) turned
swiftly and spoke as if by a sudden whim, Antony Eustrel falling back a pace or two in
shocked reaction (S91; *T*, 2 Apr. 1945). Diana Wynyard 'paused for a moment in a charged
silence' (Sprague and Trewin, *Shakespeare's Plays*, 75), then hummed the words low
(*Sunday Graphic*, 13 Jan. 1952), with a 'deadly calm' (*Truth*, 18 Jan. 1952). Barbara Jefford
uttered them fiercely (*PP*, Dec. 1956, 15). Googie Withers's words had 'the low-toned

intensity of urgent, passionate, personal appeal – a close-up, with all the force in "Kill"' (*SQ*
9, 1958, 529). In Zeffirelli's hot-blooded Sicilian setting the words were instantly plausible
(*Sc*, 22 Feb. 1965), Maggie Smith delivering them 'with a savage force that ma[de] laughter
unthinkable' (*DT*, 17 Feb. 1965). Joan Plowright spoke them quietly and matter-of-factly (*DT*,
22 Mar. 1967; *FT*, 22 Mar. 1967); Janet Suzman as a quick response, 'with a break in her
voice' signifying 'the terrible nature of her request' (*ILN*, 9 Aug. 1969; *FT*, 30 July 1969).
Elizabeth Spriggs spoke them softly, with a querying intonation; Judi Dench with cool
intensity, the words creating a sudden impact after the stillness of the preceding love
declaration (*FT*, 9 Apr. 1976; David, *Shakespeare*, 219). Barbara Dirickson (American
Conservatory Theatre, San Francisco, 1980) was 'so conscious ... of the terrifying
absoluteness of her command that she could only whisper it' (*SQ* 32, 1981, 266). Penelope
Wilton (NT 1981) made a prolonged pause, as if she were 'flinging down a challenge [to
Benedick] which she kn[ew] might end their relationship' (*G*, in *LTR*, 13–26 Aug. 1981), then
spoke the words 'very matter of factly' (*DE*, in *LTR*, 13–26 Aug. 1981). Joan Stuart-Morris
(Oregon SF, 1983) spoke the line pleadingly (*SQ* 35, 1984, 358). Cherie Lunghi (BBC-TV,
1984) had been waiting for an opportunity to give this command: her words came without
a pause, slow, serious, and deeply intended. Samantha Bond uttered the line 'in a voice of
quiet, controlled venom' (*ES*, 26 Aug. 1988). After a long pause, Emma Thompson spoke
very slowly, with deep, deadly intensity. See introduction, pp.2–3, for a discussion of
audience reactions to lines 279–80.

280 Charles Kemble, Macready, Marston and Irving hesitated before replying, their features
showing a conflict between Benedick's reluctance to quarrel with his friend and his wish to
oblige Beatrice (*JB*, 12 Apr. 1840; S16; *Lloyd's*, 26 Jan. 1851; *ThT*, 25 Nov. 1848; *BWM*, 16 Oct.
1882). George Alexander's reply was slow and deliberate (*MP*, 17 Feb. 1898). Sothern shrank
back as he spoke (S59). James Dale (1936) spoke 'quietly, with a slight smile', as if to say,
'No; I can't do that, even for you' (Crosse, *Playgoing*, 73; Crosse, 'Performances', XV.151). In
1950 Gielgud replied quickly, starting back a pace, his posture inviting laughter (S93; *ThN*, 24
June 1950). In 1952 his reply came in a 'quick, startled undertone' (*Sk*, 30 Jan. 1952), a
'scarcely breathed, horrified refusal' (*ST*, 13 Jan. 1952), 'the almost incredulous exclamation
of a man who had not realised how friendship must struggle with love and honour' (Sprague
and Trewin, *Shakespeare's Plays*, 75). Redgrave paused an instant in 'motionless dismay'
before his astonished reply (*SH*, 29 Aug. 1958; *SQ* 9, 1958, 529). Plummer's refusal was quiet
and matter-of-fact (*TW*, May 1961, 27). Stephens stepped back shocked (P-1965), and after a
long pause replied 'with the utmost gravity' (*St*, 18 Feb. 1965; *DT*, 22 Mar. 1967). Howard,
also after a long pause, declined in a low, gentle voice (*FT*, 30 July 1969; *ILN*, 9 Aug. 1969).
Lipscomb's smile disappeared (Champlain SF, 1975) as 'he realised that he really *was* being
called upon to live up to his lover's hyperbole'. His reply was 'a quiet, hurt, angry
declaration of loyalty to his friend, "not for the *wi-i-de* world"' (*SQ* 27, 1976, 42). Sinden
started away upstage with a 'stricken, low-toned' reply (*Sp*, 17 Apr. 1976; David,
Shakespeare, 219). Jacobi laughed hysterically before replying (P-1982; *Sp*, 28 May 1983).
Donadio's hesitation (Alabama SF, 1981) 'opened a wound of disillusionment' in Beatrice's

BENEDICK Tarry, sweet Beatrice.
BEATRICE I am gone, though I am here, there is no love in you, nay, I
    pray you let me go.
BENEDICK Beatrice. 285
BEATRICE In faith I will go.
BENEDICK We'll be friends first.
BEATRICE You dare easier be friends with me, than fight with mine
    enemy.
BENEDICK Is Claudio thine enemy? 290
BEATRICE Is a not approved in the height a villain, that hath slandered,
    scorned, dishonoured my kinswoman? Oh that I were a man! What,
    bear her in hand, until they come to take hands, and then with
    public accusation, uncovered slander, unmitigated rancour? Oh
    God that I were a man! I would eat his heart in the market place. 295
BENEDICK Hear me, Beatrice.
BEATRICE Talk with a man out at a window, a proper saying.
BENEDICK Nay, but Beatrice.
BEATRICE Sweet Hero, she is wronged, she is slandered, she is undone.
BENEDICK Beat – 300
BEATRICE Princes and counties! Surely a princely testimony, a goodly
    count, Count Comfect, a sweet gallant surely, oh that I were a man

face (*SQ* 33, 1982, 347). Lindsay (BBC-TV, 1984) spoke in an affronted tone, as if to say, 'Of
course not'. Branagh (1988) spoke the line as 'the wounded reaction of a man asked to
betray one set of values for another that he also prizes', the conflict between love and
friendship 'more than usually prominent' (*SS* 42, 1989, 133). In the 1993 film he spoke
the line slowly and agonisingly, after a long, sighing 'Ah'.

281   Emma Thompson replied swiftly, her voice breaking with emotion. In most productions
    Beatrice has attempted to leave, and has been restrained by Benedick. In *UP*'s adaptation of
    Beatrice's attempted departure, Liberia broke into invective: 'Nay, farewell then – love me –
    yes – you love your own dear Carcase indeed – 'tis highly worth preserving I must own.'

283   **there is no love in you** Maggie Smith (Stratford, Ontario, 1980) delivered these words 'with
    a quiet earnestness' (*SS* 34, 1981, 159).

287   Macready said confidentially, 'We'll be friends *first*? Eh?' (s17).

291–307   Often performed with Beatrice striding about the stage pursued by a pleading Benedick. In
    the Renaissance theatre, where Beatrice was played by a male actor, the words 'Oh that I
    were a man' must have carried considerable irony. Frances Abington acted this sequence
    with glowing animation, her mind agitated with 'disdain, rage and pity' (*PA*, 3 Nov. 1785;
    cutting, *European Magazine*, c.1780, Garrick Club). Dorothy Jordan's indignation showed
    'no ill-nature, no malice' (*C*, 16 Nov. 1807), whereas Nanette Johnston's (CG 1807, 1811, 1812)

bordered on malignity (*E*, 3 Jan. 1808) and Louisa Herbert's rose 'almost to malevolence' (*MA*, 7 Apr. 1866). Ellen Kean's indignation was sudden and impetuous (*DT*, 22 Nov. 1858), Kate Terry's 'alternately coaxing, petulant and menacing' (*ST*, 28 July 1867). Some mid-Victorian actresses made Beatrice's outburst 'rather comic' (Terry, *Lectures*, 95–6), 'a mere passionate vexation' (*WD*, 13 Sep. 1857). More percipient players represented her indignation as an expression of deep emotional pain, Helena Faucit describing it as the breaking out of 'all the pent-up passion' that had shaken Beatrice during the broken-wedding sequence ('Female characters', 224). Ellen Terry's marginal gloss on this passage in the manuscript of her *Four Lectures* reads, 'Not *emotion*. A *passion*.' Bram Stoker described the 'surging, choking passion in her voice, as striding to and fro with long paces', she uttered her 'whirling words' (*Irving*, I.101), Irving trying to interject protests at each pause (s47). Her cry 'Oh God that I were a man!' (294–5) was 'a sudden, passionate sob of suppressed emotion'. At 'I would –' (295) she made 'a long pause, as if ... too passionately indignant to give her thoughts utterance, but soon, with a wounded cry, and with rage expressed in the scarcely suppressed tears, [came] the words, "I would eat his heart in the market-place"' (*Th*, 1 Nov. 1882, 300). The words 'oh that I were a man for his sake' (302–3) received 'the full measure of sarcastic bitterness' (*Era*, 7 June 1884). Like Faucit and Marlowe, Terry ended the passage (307) with tears streaming (Faucit, 'Female characters', 224; *LE*, 27 Sep. 1883; s63). Ada Rehan's passion, 'not turbulent, nor combative, nor hysterical', was the expression of an 'outraged mind and suffering heart' (Winter, intro. to Daly acting edition, 9); she looked fixedly at Benedick at 'a man for my sake' (303) (Daly). Julia Marlowe's outburst was 'half despair at her helpless inability, and half the enthusiasm of resentment and coveted revenge' (*NYP*, 1 Nov. 1904). At 'undone' (299) she burst out weeping; then at 'Princes and counties!' turned suddenly on Benedick, and spoke 'oh that I were a man' (302) with both hands raised above her head, fists clenched (s59, s63). 'Princes and counties!' was spoken contemptuously at Burton's, NY, 1857 (s21); Eve Walsh Hall stamped her foot (s81). Sybil Thorndike acted this sequence 'with splendid force and emotion' (Crosse, 'Performances', XI.35). Florence Buckton, on the other hand, merely 'click-clicked about the stage in a pettish temper' (*New Age*, 29 Sep. 1921). Katharine Hepburn (ASF 1957) offended some in the audience by kicking a kneeling cushion over the altar in her fury (*SQ* 8, 1957, 509); Sinead Cusack (302) threw a chair upstage in her anger (P-1982). Maggie Smith's insistence on Claudio's death became 'a Sicilian point of honour' (*NEP*, 30 Mar. 1965): 'I have never seen a Beatrice ride so towering a wave of unself-regarding anger', wrote Harold Hobson (*ST*, 21 Feb. 1965). In a production set in small-town America, Kathleen Widdoes (NY, 1972) 'threw a tantrum like a Yankee shrew' (*NR*, 9 Sep. 1972). Janet Suzman (RSC 1968–9) spoke the lines with 'hard ferocity' (*What's On*, 8 Aug. 1969). Judi Dench 'stormed to and fro on the front of the stage, deaf to [Benedick's] entreaties' (David, *Shakespeare*, 219). Susan Fleetwood's rage was 'furious and frightening' (*FT*, 12 Apr. 1990). Emma Thompson was a lady not to be trifled with: at 'unmitigated rancour' (294) she overturned a bench in her fury, and at the top of her voice threatened to eat Claudio's heart in the marketplace.

for his sake! Or that I had any friend would be a man for my sake! But manhood is melted into curtsies, valour into compliment, and men are only turned into tongue, and trim ones too: he is now as   305 valiant as Hercules, that only tells a lie, and swears it: I cannot be a man with wishing, therefore I will die a woman with grieving.

BENEDICK Tarry, good Beatrice, by this hand I love thee.

BEATRICE Use it for my love some other way than swearing by it.

BENEDICK Think you in your soul the Count Claudio hath wronged   310 Hero?

BEATRICE Yea, as sure as I have a thought, or a soul.

BENEDICK Enough, I am engaged, I will challenge him. I will kiss your hand, and so I leave you: by this hand, Claudio shall render me a dear account: as you hear of me, so think of me: go comfort your   315 cousin, I must say she is dead, and so farewell.

[*Exeunt*]

303   E. L. Davenport and J. H. Barnes interpolated 'Oh, Beatrice!' (S36, P-1886).

309   Helena Faucit spoke in a voice 'still quivering with emotion' (Faucit, 'Female characters', 224). Julia Marlowe threw off Benedick's proffered hand (S63); Eve Walsh Hall slapped it (S81). Maggie Smith placed Benedick's dagger in his outstretched hand (P-1965); Cherie Lunghi (BBC-TV, 1984) thrust her hand indignantly against the hilt of his sword.

310   Lindsay (BBC-TV, 1984) spoke with horror-struck realisation.

312   Faucit spoke the line as a solemn affirmation (Faucit, 'Female characters', 224), Emma Thompson slowly, with intense conviction.

313–16 J. P. Kemble substituted the following dialogue, adopted with variations in most nineteenth-century productions.

Ben. Enough, I am engag'd; I will challenge him.
Beat. Will you?
Ben. Upon my soul I will. I'll kiss your hand, and so leave you. By this hand, Claudio shall render me a dear account.
Beat. You'll be sure to challenge him.
Ben. By those bright eyes, I will.
Beat. My dear friend, kiss my hand again.
Ben. As you hear of me so think of me. Go, comfort your cousin – I must say she is dead & so farewell.
Beat. Benedick, kill him, kill him if you can –
Ben. As sure as he is alive, I will.

(S5; also in S2, S6–7, Inchbald B, Dolby, Oxberry, Cumberland)

Kemble's ending built the scene to a climactic curtain line, significant in the eighteenth- and nineteenth-century theatre where each scene was a discrete unit marked by the fall of the curtain. However, Kemble's dialogue made the developing relationship between Beatrice and Benedick seem less provisional at this point than in the quarto text, and tended to sentimentalise the passage; the repeated assurances sought by Beatrice were also rather heavy-handed.

As Charles Kemble went off he resolutely put on his hat (Cumberland), business adopted in several other productions (s9, s16, s32, s56). Elizabeth Brunton (CG 1817) anticipated later staging tradition in her 'eager delight' at Benedick's resolve to challenge Claudio, the 'transport of joy' with which she called him back to kiss her hand again, and the comic flavour she gave to the passage (*LC*, 29 Nov.–1 Dec. 1817; *T*, 29 Nov. 1817).

Macready heightened the comic effect with an interpolation after lines 310–12 ('Think you ... soul'):

> Ben. – You do?–
> Beat. I do! –
> Ben. – You? – / Beat assents. / Enough! – I am engaged – I'll challenge him! – I will!
>
> (s16)

Macready announced his decision to challenge Claudio with an 'exulting and important air' (*MP*, 24 Jan. 1851), Beatrice looking up at him delightedly, her hand on his shoulder. As their eyes met he smiled, took her hand and kissed it (s16). Macready's text continued as in Q, except for the words 'Kiss my hand again', inserted at 315 (after 'account'). At the end of the passage Macready accompanied Beatrice to the exit, still kissing her hand. When she was off he put on his hat 'with a kind of comic resolution', arranged his costume, drew on his glove, and 'very self-satisfiedly' strutted off, 'inflated with the pride of successful love' (s16; *MP*, 24 Jan. 1851).

The staging of this sequence in the Victorian period followed patterns established by the Kembles and Macready, Beatrice typically responding to Benedick's resolve with joy and affection, inviting him to kiss her hand again, and seeking repeated assurances that he would stand by his promise. Fanny Davenport's response was condescending: 'Benedick, you may kiss my hand again' (s36). Catherine Sinclair (Haymarket, 1857) and E. L. Davenport added melodramatic lines in which Beatrice sought even further assurances that Benedick would kill Claudio (s32, s36). Most productions of the period gave the sequence a comic edge, sentimentalised it to some degree, and loaded it with amorous business. Benedick typically ended the scene in triumph at winning Beatrice. One effect of such staging was to affirm the Beatrice–Benedick relationship prematurely.

Charles and Ellen Kean played the passage comically, separating at the end 'in an ecstasy of mutual delight' (*A*, 27 Nov. 1858; *T*, 22 Nov. 1858). Irving slightly shortened the Kemble dialogue, adopting it much against Ellen Terry's wishes (s45; Terry, *Life*, 163; Terry, *Lectures*, 96). He also subdued the comic flavour given to the closing lines in most Victorian productions, kissing Beatrice's hand 'respectfully but devotedly' (Howard, *Dramatic Notes*, 52), and making his exit 'with a manner reminiscent of triumph on the field, but without a hint of levity or braggadocio' (Pollock, *Irving*, 86). George Alexander and Julia Neilson also played Kemble's ending with less comic emphasis than in most Victorian productions (*Idler*, Apr. 1898, 339).

During the first decade of the twentieth century most directors abandoned Kemble's ending, though Sothern and Benson retained it (s59, s63; *T*, 18 Feb. 1908) and Jewett (Boston Repertory Theatre) used it as late as 1926 (s81). Some of the traditional business also lived on into the twentieth century. Julia Marlowe (1904–5) called 'Benedick!' as Sothern made his exit; 'Beatrice!' he responded, crossing to her, and they embraced and ran off in opposite directions (s59). In 1911 Marlowe kissed Benedick and ran off with a little cry; Sothern stood paralysed a moment, then jumped in the air with a shout of joyous laughter and ran off after her (s63). Winifred Emery (1905) called to Benedick as they went off and held out her hand for him to kiss; Tree kissed both her hands and took her in his arms, she sighing delightedly (s65, s69). Payne (1936) also ended the scene with an embrace (s89). Poel and Bridges-Adams eliminated the traditional passionate embracings, Benedick assuming a soldierly aspect in Bridges-Adams's 1933–4 production, saluting Beatrice as he went off to challenge Claudio (s88). Most twentieth-century productions have played lines 313–16 seriously, though Benson raised laughter with a meditative addition to the final line: 'And I said I would die a bachelor' (*BP*, 18 Apr. 1911). Wilfrid Walter (SMT 1929) invited laughter by a deliberate pause at 'I will kiss – your hand' (*SH*, 26 Apr. 1929). Antony Eustrel and Claire Luce (SMT 1945) also acted the lines for comedy, he making three false exits and she interpolating an 'Ah!' after each sentence (s91).

Sybil Thorndike played for a climactic curtain, uttering a passionate cry of 'Benedick' at the end of the closing line (Crosse, 'Performances', XI.34). Gielgud, however, played the sequence towards a falling close – a 'grave and peaceful ending' held to a 'single sustained note of glowingly romantic tenderness' (Hobson, *Theatre Now*, 37; *T&B*, 23 Jan. 1952). He retreated on 'Enough, I am engaged', and then, 'halting, as if arrested by a premonition ... spoke the words, "I will kiss your hand, and so I leave you" ... About to go, he still hesitated', making a lingering pause before each utterance (Hayman, *Gielgud*, 172). The 1958 SMT production also ended on a note of falling intensity, with Beatrice left alone looking up at the rose window as the lights faded and violins played (*WI*, 31 Aug. 1958). Rita Litton (Champlain SF, 1975) stopped in her exit, 'turned, stared thoughtfully at the flame [of her candle], and blew it out as if blowing out Claudio's life' (*SQ* 27, 1976, 42). Judi Dench showed a conflict between desire for Claudio's death and concern for Benedick's safety (*PP*, June 1976, 21); at 'farewell', 'a long, still look' passed between them, then she picked up her basket of flower petals and went off slowly (P-1976; David, *Shakespeare*, 220). Robert Lindsay (BBC-TV, 1984) spoke his 'farewell' with a long look at Beatrice, conscious that he might not live to see her again. There was something moving and absurd about Merrison's Benedick (1988), a 'little sparrow of a man', going off on the 'patently hopeless task' of fighting Claudio (*SQ* 40, 1989, 85). Susan Fleetwood, 'at last willing to be kissed', 'found herself kissed only on the hand by a Benedick now needing to concentrate solely on the challenge to Claudio' (*SQ* 42,

1991, 347). Mark Rylance was 'soberly reluctant' about the challenge (*Ind*, 11 July 1993). Branagh (1993 film) spoke the final lines quietly, earnestly, with utter determination.

316   *UP* followed this sequence with an adaptation of the Benedick–Beatrice dialogue in 5.2.44–66. Branagh's film followed the sequence with a shot of Don John laughing at his success, a triumph ironically negated in the ensuing examination scene.

ACT 4, SCENE 2

Enter the Constables [DOGBERRY *and* VERGES] *and the* [SEXTON *as*]
Town Clerk in gowns, [CONRADE *and*] BORACHIO

DOGBERRY Is our whole dissembly appeared?
VERGES Oh a stool and a cushion for the sexton.

Most frequently set in a prison (3.5.51). Daly's setting was a street, Seale's a market square,
with Dogberry perched on a vendor's cart before a crowd of citizens (Daly; 1958 pr. photo;
MA, 31 Aug. 1958). Branagh filmed the scene in a cellar, with the prisoners straddling poles
protruding from the wall, feet tied to the floor and hands to the ceiling. Dogberry has often
been seated at a desk or table, sometimes elevated on a dais. In the Renaissance theatre and
in Garrick's productions the examining officers wore gowns (Q, Bell), traditional for
constables and sextons in Shakespeare's England. In Warchus's production (1993) Dogberry
appeared unusually opinionated in a lawyer's gown (*SS* 47, 1994, 192). Since Macready the
Sexton has often been given a large book and inkhorn. Irving omitted the scene in 1887,
restoring it in 1891 (S45; 1891 programme). Fanny Davenport (1886) omitted it; Daly
transposed it to the end of 3.3.
Speech headings. In Q the character named 'Towne clearke' at 0 SD was designated Sexton
in the speech headings. Garrick made the Town Clerk and Sexton separate characters, and
redistributed the speeches to make the Town Clerk the chief interrogator: line 1 Town Clerk;
2 Dogberry; 3 Sexton; 4 Verges; 5 Dogberry; 6 Sexton; 8–48: Town Clerk received all the
speeches attributed to Dogberry in this sequence in the New Cambridge Shakespeare.
Garrick's speech distribution was similar to that in full-text editions from Rowe (1709) to
Capell (1767–8), and in the Smock Alley (c.1750) and Yair (1754) acting editions. Warren
and Wood (1804) assigned to the Town Clerk Dogberry's speeches at 8 and 42, and all the
Sexton's speeches except lines 28–9 (S3). Kemble's acting editions (1797, 1810, 1815) reverted
to a speech distribution similar to Q, except that the First and Second Watchmen were
designated Seacoal and Oatcake. In the London theatres the Town Clerk and Sexton were
cast as separate characters until 1797 at DL and 1798 at CG (playbills).

2 Indicates that in Renaissance performances stage properties were being placed as the
dialogue commenced. Q's speech headings at 2 and 5 identify the original actor of Verges
as Richard Cowley.

SEXTON Which be the malefactors?
DOGBERRY Marry that am I, and my partner.
VERGES Nay that's certain, we have the exhibition to examine.   5
SEXTON But which are the offenders, that are to be examined? Let them
  come before master constable.
DOGBERRY Yea marry, let them come before me: what is your name,
  friend?
BORACHIO Borachio.   10
DOGBERRY Pray write down Borachio. Yours, sirrah?
CONRADE I am a gentleman, sir, and my name is Conrade.
DOGBERRY Write down Master Gentleman Conrade: masters, do you
  serve God?
BORACHIO ⎱
                } Yea, sir, we hope.   15
CONRADE ⎰
DOGBERRY Write down, that they hope they serve God: and write God
  first, for God defend but God should go before such villains: mas-
  ters, it is proved already that you are little better than false knaves,
  and it will go near to be thought so shortly: how answer you for
  yourselves?   20
CONRADE Marry, sir, we say we are none.
DOGBERRY A marvellous witty fellow I assure you, but I will go about
  with him: come you hither, sirrah, a word in your ear, sir: I say to
  you, it is thought you are false knaves.

---

4   Q's speech heading is 'Andrew', indicating that the role of Dogberry was intended for the
    clown or 'merry Andrew' of the Lord Chamberlain's Company, identified as 'Kemp' in Q's
    speech headings at 8ff.

8b–9 A photograph of the 1956 Old Vic production shows Borachio and Conrade looking down on
    a diminutive Dogberry who eyes them defiantly, a contrast with George Rose's mountainous
    Dogberry elevated on his dais in Gielgud's productions of 1949–52 (see illustration 9).

10 Spoken impudently in Sothern's 1904–5 production (s59).

12 **gentleman** Shouted in Sothern's 1911 production, Dogberry, Verges and the Sexton jumping
    with fright (s63). In Branagh's film the watch gave a mocking 'ooo' at 'gentleman'.

15–17 **Yea ... villains** Omitted in F, perhaps reflecting a stage cut made in response to the Act to
    Restrain Abuses of Players (1606) which forbade jesting with the name of God in plays
    (Chambers, *Shakespeare*, I.238–41).

21 Caused a sensation among the Watchmen, SMT 1949 (s92).

23 **come ... hither** In Tree's production Borachio leaned his arm familiarly on Dogberry's table
    (s69).

23–4 **I say ... knaves** In the 1933–4 SMT production spoken in a loud whisper, mimicked in
    Borachio's reply (s88).

BORACHIO Sir, I say to you, we are none.   25
DOGBERRY Well, stand aside, 'fore God they are both in a tale: have you
writ down, that they are none?
SEXTON Master constable, you go not the way to examine, you must call
forth the watch that are their accusers.
DOGBERRY Yea marry, that's the eftest way, let the watch come forth.   30

[*Enter* SEACOAL, WATCHMAN 2 *and the rest of the Watch*]

Masters, I charge you in the prince's name, accuse these men.
SEACOAL This man said, sir, that Don John the prince's brother was a
villain.
DOGBERRY Write down, Prince John a villain: why this is flat perjury, to
call a prince's brother villain.   35
BORACHIO Master constable.
DOGBERRY Pray thee, fellow, peace, I do not like thy look I promise
thee.
SEXTON What heard you him say else?
WATCHMAN 2 Marry that he had received a thousand ducats of Don   40
John, for accusing the Lady Hero wrongfully.
DOGBERRY Flat burglary as ever was committed.
VERGES Yea by mass that it is.
SEXTON What else, fellow?
SEACOAL And that Count Claudio did mean upon his words, to dis-   45
grace Hero before the whole assembly, and not marry her.
DOGBERRY Oh villain! Thou wilt be condemned into everlasting
redemption for this.

25   Dogberry appeared confounded at this in Macready's production (s16).
26   **tale** In Zeffirelli's production Dogberry crashed to the floor while trying to sit on the desk,
     maintaining a 'nonchalant posture as if his descent ha[d] been deliberate' (pbk; *MCT*, 26
     Feb. 1965).
28–9 Whispered confidentially in Tree's production (s69).
32   In Kean's 1858 production Borachio glanced at Conrade with 'insolent contempt for the
     watchmen' (*T*, 22 Nov. 1858). In Daly's 1896 production he lunged at Seacoal with his sword
     (Daly).
35   In Irving's production the prisoners laughed at Dogberry's fatuity (s47).
36   Spoken petulantly at Burton's, NY, 1857. Borachio offered money to Dogberry in the 1968
     and 1988 RSC productions (pbks).
42   In Sothern's 1904–5 production Dogberry slapped the table, startling the sleeping Verges
     (s59).
47–8 In Sothern's productions an indignant Dogberry leaned over the table, but lost his balance
     and fell across it (s59, s63). In the 1968 RSC production he struck the table with a mallet
     (pbk).

SEXTON What else?
SEACOAL This is all. 50
SEXTON And this is more, masters, than you can deny: Prince John is
this morning secretly stolen away: Hero was in this manner accused,
in this very manner refused, and upon the grief of this, suddenly
died: master constable, let these men be bound, and brought to
Leonato's: I will go before and show him their examination. [*Exit*] 55
VERGES Come, let them be opinioned.
CONRADE Let them be in the hands of coxcomb.
DOGBERRY God's my life, where's the sexton? Let him write down the
prince's officer coxcomb: come, bind them, thou naughty varlet.
CONRADE Away, you are an ass, you are an ass. 60
DOGBERRY Dost thou not suspect my place? Dost thou not suspect my

---

54 **died** Borachio and Conrade showed amazement in Sothern's 1904–5 production, dismay at
the SMT in 1933–4, and concern in Gielgud's 1955 production, reactions which prepared the
way for Borachio's later confession (S59, S87–8, S94).

55 In Daly's 1896 production Borachio and Conrade attempted to escape. During the ensuing
fracas the windows and doorways of houses overlooking the street filled with people roused
from sleep by the noise (Daly).

56 Variously assigned to Verges or Dogberry. Q's speech heading is 'Constable', but the stage
direction at the head of the scene designates both Dogberry and Verges as 'Constables'.

56 **opinioned** In most productions the watch have taken this to mean 'pinioned', and have
commenced to bind the prisoners; but in Sothern's 1904–5 production the watch looked on
uncomprehending as Dogberry added 'Opinion them! Opinion them!', then impatiently
clarified the order to 'Bind them! Bind them!' (S59). A struggle has often ensued.

57–9a Often cut from Garrick to Edwin Booth, so that the command 'let them be opinioned' (56)
was followed immediately by the clarification, 'Come, bind them' (59b).

57 Q assigned this speech to 'Couley' (Richard Cowley), F to the Sexton. Nineteenth- and
twentieth-century productions which retained the speech commonly assigned 'Let them
be in the hands' to Verges, amending the next two words to 'Off, coxcomb', assigned to
Conrade (as in most full-text editions since Warburton). The words 'Off, coxcomb' have
been addressed variously to Dogberry, Verges or a Watchman trying to bind Conrade. In
Sothern's 1904–5 production, where they were addressed to Dogberry, the constable
staggered back shocked, almost knocking Verges over (S59).

58 In Sothern's 1911 production Dogberry 'sputter[ed] and puff[ed], almost inarticulate with
anger' (S63).

60 Assigned to 'Couley' in Q and F, but since the eighteenth century regularly given to Conrade.
Dogberry has generally staggered back gasping, often into Verges' arms. George Rose
(1949–52) collapsed like a mountain on top of Verges, knocking him flat (S92–3, P-1952).

61–70 Blanchard (CG 1829) delivered this speech 'with exquisite gusto; it was the perfection of

years? Oh that he were here to write me down an ass! But masters,
remember that I am an ass, though it be not written down, yet forget
not that I am an ass: no, thou villain, thou art full of piety as shall be
proved upon thee by good witness: I am a wise fellow, and which is   65
more, an officer, and which is more, a householder, and which is
more, as pretty a piece of flesh as any is in Messina, and one that
knows the law, go to, and a rich fellow enough, go to, and a fellow
that hath had losses, and one that hath two gowns, and everything
handsome about him: bring him away: oh that I had been writ down   70
an ass!

Exeunt

garrulous imbecility' (*TO*, 16 Dec. 1829). *Windsor Magazine* (May 1909, 768) thought
George Weir's 'outraged vanity' unforgettable. In Sothern's 1911 production Dogberry flew
at Conrade in sputtering rage, advancing on him with increasing volume at every phrase,
dancing up and down in fury at 68–9 (s63). A photograph of the 1956 Old Vic production
(BPL) shows Dogberry, lips pursed in vicious aggression, pointing at Conrade, who is
lunging at him, restrained with difficulty by a Watchman; the rest of the watch are agape
with shock. Frank Finlay's Italianate Dogberry (1965) was tearfully furious about the insult to
his dignity (Gilliatt, *Unholy Fools*, 333). He pushed Conrade to the ground twice (68), but
when he tried to push him again at line 70 the watch pulled Conrade out of reach and
Dogberry fell on his face (P-1965). David Waller (1968–9, 1988) made the speech 'a
marvellous prose aria of self-righteousness' (*SS* 42, 1989, 132); at 'Dost thou not suspect my
place', it was as if 'boiling oil' were about to 'hurtle down' on the hapless Conrade (*ILN*, 9
Aug. 1969). At the end of the speech Dogberry has sometimes collapsed into a chair (s56,
P-1968/9), or into the arms of Verges (s59) or a Watchman (s63).

ACT 5, SCENE I

Enter LEONATO *and his brother* [ANTONIO]

ANTONIO If you go on thus, you will kill yourself,
And 'tis not wisdom thus to second grief,
Against yourself.
LEONATO   I pray thee cease thy counsel,
Which falls into mine ears as profitless,
As water in a sieve: give not me counsel,   5
Nor let no comforter delight mine ear,
But such a one whose wrongs do suit with mine.
Bring me a father that so loved his child,
Whose joy of her is overwhelmed like mine,
And bid him speak of patience,   10
Measure his woe the length and breadth of mine,
And let it answer every strain for strain,
As thus for thus, and such a grief for such,
In every lineament, branch, shape and form:
If such a one will smile and stroke his beard,   15
And sorrow; wag, cry hem, when he should groan;
Patch grief with proverbs, make misfortune drunk

In nineteenth- and early twentieth-century productions set most commonly before Leonato's house or in the garden. Seale's setting was a street.

0 SD Daly began with a glimpse of Hero singing sadly and distractedly, Gielgud with the passing of her supposed funeral procession. Zeffirelli and Barton dressed Leonato and Antonio in mourning. Barton also used the entry to contrast stereotypical gender roles in a patriarchal society, Beatrice and Margaret crossing with a laundry basket as Leonato was served with coffee. Gill (NT 1981) introduced a touch of comedy, Dogberry hovering about looking for an opportunity to tell Leonato about his examination of the prisoners (pbks; Daly; 1965 pr. photo).

1–44 Leonato's grief was heavily abridged in many productions, the most frequent cuts being 4–5a, 11–26, 32, 35–8.

        With candle-wasters: bring him yet to me,
        And I of him will gather patience:
        But there is no such man, for, brother, men   20
        Can counsel and speak comfort to that grief,
        Which they themselves not feel, but tasting it,
        Their counsel turns to passion, which before,
        Would give preceptial medicine to rage,
        Fetter strong madness in a silken thread,   25
        Charm ache with air, and agony with words –
        No, no, 'tis all men's office, to speak patience
        To those that wring under the load of sorrow,
        But no man's virtue nor sufficiency
        To be so moral, when he shall endure   30
        The like himself: therefore give me no counsel,
        My griefs cry louder than advertisement.
ANTONIO Therein do men from children nothing differ.
LEONATO I pray thee peace, I will be flesh and blood,
        For there was never yet philosopher,   35
        That could endure the tooth-ache patiently,
        However they have writ the style of gods,
        And made a push at chance and sufferance.
ANTONIO Yet bend not all the harm upon yourself,
        Make those that do offend you suffer too.   40
LEONATO There thou speak'st reason, nay I will do so,
        My soul doth tell me, Hero is belied,
        And that shall Claudio know, so shall the prince,
        And all of them that thus dishonour her.

Enter DON PEDRO *and* CLAUDIO

ANTONIO Here comes the prince and Claudio hastily.   45
DON PEDRO Good den, good den.
CLAUDIO   Good day to both of you.

---

44 SD   In Macready's production Claudio and Don Pedro strolled on nonchalantly, arm in arm.
       In several productions they walked past Leonato and Antonio, appearing to ignore them
       (Hanford, Eyre, Gill, Branagh film). In Carey's production Don Pedro entered calling
       Benedick's name, as if looking for him (see lines 108, 118) (pbks).
46ff.   Terriss (Lyceum, 1882) spoke his passing 'Good den, good den' 'in accents so cavalier as
       to be, under the circumstances, almost brutal' (*Gl*, 12 Oct. 1882). Richard Easton's Claudio
       (SMT 1955) seemed so young and bitterly hurt as to give an edge of intensity to the quarrel
       sequence (*GH*, 23 July 1955). In Barton's production Don Pedro and Claudio were 'coldly
       frivolous' (*FT*, 9 Apr. 1976), in Hands's production callous (*O*, 25 Apr. 1982). In Trevis's
       production 'the sneering of Fiennes' Claudio and the blandly smiling pity of David Lyon's

LEONATO Hear you, my lords?
DON PEDRO   We have some haste, Leonato.
LEONATO Some haste, my lord! Well, fare you well, my lord,
    Are you so hasty now? Well, all is one.
DON PEDRO Nay do not quarrel with us, good old man.   50
ANTONIO If he could right himself with quarrelling,
    Some of us would lie low.
CLAUDIO   Who wrongs him?
LEONATO Marry thou dost wrong me, thou dissembler, thou:
    Nay, never lay thy hand upon thy sword,
    I fear thee not.
CLAUDIO   Marry beshrew my hand,   55
    If it should give your age such cause of fear,
    In faith my hand meant nothing to my sword.
LEONATO Tush, tush, man, never fleer and jest at me,
    I speak not like a dotard, nor a fool,
    As under privilege of age to brag,   60

poised and elegant Pedro present[ed] nicely complementary versions of contempt' (*SQ* 40, 1989, 84).

48ff. Francis Gentleman, probably reflecting eighteenth-century stage tradition, described Leonato and Antonio in the quarrel sequence as two 'old gentlemen violently agitated with passion' (*DrC* 2, 1770, 316). Egerton and Bartley (CG 1823), like many actors since, gave a comic edge to the old men's irascibility (*TO*, 17 Apr. 1823). Henry Howe (Lyceum, 1882) played Antonio in this sequence as a 'somewhat petulant and peppery old gentleman' (*ILN*, 28 Oct. 1882) angered from the first by the cavalier manner of Don Pedro and Claudio (*GI*, 12 Oct. 1882). In Seale's production citizens gathered in the street to watch the quarrel (pbk).

53 Claudio has traditionally reached for his sword. In Sothern's 1911 production Leonato advanced fiercely on Claudio (s63); in Jewett's he reached for his sword (s81); in Branagh's film he struck Claudio on the shoulder.

54ff. The quarrel sequence has often been cut extensively, the abridgement of Antonio and Leonato's more extravagant outbursts tending to reduce the ludicrous element in the old men's wrath. 54–62: Cut by Craig and Langham. 59–66: Cut by Irving (1887ff.), abridged by several others. 67–76: Cut by Hunt. 68–72, 78b–82: These references to Hero's death were cut in most productions from the Kembles to the late nineteenth century, Macready and Irving excepted. A third reference to Hero's death (86–7) was cut by the Kembles, Vining, Davenport and W. Lacy. 78–100: Cut by Edwin Booth. Fanny Davenport cut 86–99, Craig 91–9, Sothern (1911) 91–8, Hunt 82–100, Nunn 93–100.

58ff. In Zeffirelli's production Claudio backed around the stage as Leonato advanced on him during this speech. In Barton's production Leonato held his sword at Claudio's throat (58); in Nunn's 1968 production Leonato shook him (62) (pbks).

What I have done, being young, or what would do,
Were I not old: know, Claudio, to thy head,
Thou hast so wronged mine innocent child and me,
That I am forced to lay my reverence by,
And with grey hairs and bruise of many days,   65
Do challenge thee to trial of a man:
I say thou hast belied mine innocent child.
Thy slander hath gone through and through her heart,
And she lies buried with her ancestors:
Oh in a tomb where never scandal slept,   70
Save this of hers, framed by thy villainy.
CLAUDIO My villainy?
LEONATO   Thine, Claudio, thine I say.
DON PEDRO You say not right, old man.
LEONATO   My lord, my lord,
I'll prove it on his body if he dare,
Despite his nice fence, and his active practice,   75
His May of youth, and bloom of lustihood.
CLAUDIO Away, I will not have to do with you.
LEONATO Canst thou so daff me? Thou hast killed my child,
If thou kill'st me, boy, thou shalt kill a man.
ANTONIO He shall kill two of us, and men indeed,   80
But that's no matter, let him kill one first:
Win me and wear me, let him answer me,
Come follow me, boy, come, Sir Boy, come follow me,

66 **challenge** In the Kembles' and Jewett's productions Leonato drew his sword (Dolby, Cumberland, s81); in various RSC productions he slapped Claudio's face (1961, 1982, 1988), reached for his dagger (1988) or threw down a glove (1968, 1982). In Hands's production Claudio kicked the glove away at 77 (pbks).

74 In Langham's production Leonato challenged Claudio to a boxing match, which he sulkily declined at line 77 (*Tablet*, 15 July 1961, 678). Sebastian Shaw as Leonato (RSC 1969) underlined the ludicrous aspect of the old man's aggression, his sword becoming stuck in the scabbard as he tried to draw it (pbk; *DM*, 30 July 1969). In Branagh's film there was a scuffle as Leonato struck Claudio and Antonio dragged his brother away.

78ff. As the old men raged in Branagh's film, Don Pedro's face assumed a dark and dangerous look.

80–100 Antonio, who in the preceding sequence attempted in some performances to calm Leonato, now bursts into aggression himself, Leonato trying with difficulty to restrain him. In Sothern's 1911 production Antonio flourished his staff violently at Claudio and Don Pedro (s63); in Zeffirelli's he threw an umbrella at Claudio while chasing him round the stage; in Nunn, Barton and Gill's productions he threatened him with a sword; in Hands's he chased

> Sir Boy, I'll whip you from your foining fence,
> Nay, as I am a gentleman, I will.
> LEONATO   Brother.   85
> ANTONIO Content yourself, God knows, I loved my niece,
> And she is dead, slandered to death by villains,
> That dare as well answer a man indeed,
> As I dare take a serpent by the tongue.
> Boys, apes, braggarts, Jacks, milksops.
> LEONATO   Brother Anthony.   90
> ANTONIO Hold you content, what, man! I know them, yea
> And what they weigh, even to the utmost scruple:
> Scambling, out-facing, fashion-monging boys,
> That lie, and cog, and flout, deprave and slander,
> Go anticly, and show outward hideousness,   95
> And speak off half a dozen dangerous words,
> How they might hurt their enemies, if they durst,
> And this is all.
> LEONATO But brother Anthony –
> ANTONIO   Come 'tis no matter,
> Do not you meddle, let me deal in this.   100
> DON PEDRO Gentlemen both, we will not wake your patience,
> My heart is sorry for your daughter's death:
> But on my honour she was charged with nothing
> But what was true, and very full of proof.
> LEONATO My lord, my lord –
> DON PEDRO   I will not hear you.   105
> LEONATO No come, brother, away, I will be heard.
> ANTONIO And shall, or some of us will smart for it.
> *Exeunt Leonato and Antonio*
> DON PEDRO See, see, here comes the man we went to seek.

> *Enter* BENEDICK

him with a stick 'in transports of senile rage' (*T*, 21 Apr. 1982); in Langham's he collapsed
with a seizure at line 100, Don Pedro helping him up (pbks).

107 SD   In Sothern's 1904–5 production Antonio shouted 'Boys, apes, braggarts, jacks, milksops,
villains, aye villains!' as Leonato dragged him off (S59). After Antonio's 'choleric brow-
mopping' outburst in Seale's production the two old men went off 'muttering indignantly at
each other', Don Pedro, Claudio and the audience tittering as they left (*SH*, 29 Aug. 1958).
In Barton's production Claudio whistled nonchalantly as the old men made their exit; Don
Pedro tossed a pineapple to a servant, sliced it with his sword, and began juggling oranges
(pbk).

108 SD   Irving strode past Claudio with apparent indifference (S46). Jacobi entered with drawn

CLAUDIO Now, signor, what news?
BENEDICK   Good day, my lord.
DON PEDRO Welcome, signor, you are almost come to part almost a   110
fray.
CLAUDIO We had like to have had our two noses snapped off with two

---

sword (P-1982). *UP* omitted the challenge sequence.

109   Sothern as Benedick ignored Claudio's proffered hand, addressing his 'Good day, my lord'
       coldly to Don Pedro (S59, S63). Robert Hardy's Claudio (Phoenix, 1952) kept a worried eye
       on Benedick through the opening lines of the sequence (*JLW*, 1 Feb. 1952).

109ff. Unlike most Benedicks, Garrick delivered his challenge to Claudio as a conscious
       performance, with an air of flippant self-satisfaction. In this sequence, wrote Frederick
       Reynolds, he 'made me laugh more heartily than I ever did before; particularly on his exit,
       when sticking on his hat, and tossing up his head, he seemed to say as he strutted away,
       Now, Beatrice, have I not cut a figure?' (*Life and Times*, I.86–7). Charles Kemble played the
       sequence with 'dignity and determination' (*LC*, 29 Nov.–1 Dec. 1817), seeming to tower
       'above the associates ... of his merrier moods' (*MS*, 21 Apr. 1823, 108–9); he eyed Claudio
       with 'fixed purpose', ignoring his jests with contempt (*T*, 8 Apr. 1840). Macready, cool and
       gentlemanly, spoke quietly, with a bitterness like cold steel (*MP*, 25 Feb. 1843). In shaking off
       the jests of his former companions he 'nicely distinguished the impatience shown by a man
       with a serious purpose on his mind ... from that of the mere butt, who is fidgetty [*sic*] at
       being teased' (*T*, 25 Feb. 1843). Charles Kean also played the sequence as a cool and
       polished gentleman of honour, 'not in the least disposed to be laughed out of his gravity'
       (*T*, 22 Nov. 1858). Irving's manner was 'resolute, dignified, simple ... touched with a tone of
       dangerous menace' (Winter, *Irving*, 61). George Alexander acted with 'cool incisiveness'
       (*Era*, 19 Feb. 1898), Tree with a combination of dignity, severity and self-restraint (*Era*, 28
       Jan. 1905), Oscar Asche (Imperial, 1903) with 'blunt indignation' (Crosse, 'Performances',
       III.110). Casson (1927) was gravely quiet but strong (*ibid.*, XI.34). Redgrave spoke with
       civility, exchanging visiting cards with the prince and Claudio and taking a drink from a
       street vendor's cart (S100; *LDP*, 28 Aug. 1958). In Langham's 1961 production, which
       contemporised the play's actions and manners to some degree, Christopher Plummer was
       'not thinking in terms of swordplay' when he challenged Claudio: 'he [took] off his coat and
       want[ed] to punch the young man's nose' (*DT*, 5 Apr. 1961). Stephens (1965) kept his dignity
       as Don Pedro and Claudio blew cigar smoke superciliously in his face (*ST*, 21 Feb. 1965; pr.
       photo). Sinden (1976) spoke quietly, with a seriousness that showed up the flippancy of
       Claudio and Don Pedro (David, *Shakespeare*, 219). Rylance's awkward little Benedick (*Ind*,
       8 July 1993) was anything but dignified, 'getting his sword in a twist when delivering the
       challenge' (*Ind*, 11 July 1993).

112ff. Francis Gentleman condoned Claudio's flippancy here as 'agreeable raillery' (Bell). Richard

old men without teeth.
DON PEDRO Leonato and his brother: what think'st thou? Had we
fought, I doubt we should have been too young for them.   115
BENEDICK In a false quarrel there is no true valour: I came to seek you
both.
CLAUDIO We have been up and down to seek thee, for we are high
proof melancholy, and would fain have it beaten away, wilt thou use
thy wit?   120
BENEDICK It is in my scabbard, shall I draw it?
DON PEDRO Dost thou wear thy wit by thy side?
CLAUDIO Never any did so, though very many have been beside their
wit: I will bid thee draw, as we do the minstrels, draw to pleasure us.
DON PEDRO As I am an honest man, he looks pale, art thou sick, or   125
angry?
CLAUDIO What, courage, man: what though care killed a cat, thou hast
mettle enough in thee to kill care.
BENEDICK Sir, I shall meet your wit in the career, and you charge it

Riddle's Claudio (Old Vic, 1931) was 'grave and worried, not frivolous and jeering' (Crosse,
Playgoing, 69), and continued to play in serious key until his reconciliation with Hero
(Crosse, 'Performances', XII.135). Richard Easton (SMT 1955) made Claudio's jests 'more a
desperate attempt to keep his spirits up than a heartless forgetfulness of Hero's tragedy'
(*SH*, 9 Dec. 1955). Roger Rees (RSC 1971), on the other hand, seemed frivolous and shallow.

121   The Cruickshank–White engraving of this moment, published in Cumberland's acting
        edition, and probably based on Charles Kemble's performances, contrasts the angry
        determination of Benedick, about to draw his sword, with the facile nonchalance of Claudio
        and Don Pedro. Sothern spoke the line menacingly, slapping the hilt of his sword (s63).

122ff. Extensive cuts to Claudio and Don Pedro's banter in the challenge sequence have often
        made their behaviour seem less flippant and reprehensible than in the full text. 122–4:
        Often cut or abridged. 127–35: Cut by Hunt; often abridged. 141–69a: Cut by Hunt; often
        extensively abridged; lines 143–5 were abbreviated and 147–62 cut in most productions
        from Garrick to Tree, and by Gielgud (s93–4), Langham and Nunn. 179–80: Cut by
        Edwin Booth, Nunn and Eyre. 181–3: Usually cut or abridged.

124   John Fraser's Claudio (Old Vic, 1956) engaged in mock sword-play (s95).

125–6   In Sothern's 1911 production Don Pedro spoke with mock concern for Benedick (s63).

127–8   Claudio slapped Benedick familiarly on the shoulder in the productions of C. Kean, E. L
        Davenport and J. B. Booth Jr (*T*, 30 Jan. 1861; s36, s42); in Sothern's 1904–5 production he
        placed his hand on Benedick's shoulder, Benedick politely but firmly removing it before
        speaking (s59). Basil Gill (His Majesty's, 1905), about to slap Benedick's back, suddenly
        changed his mind as Benedick caught his eye (s69).

against me: I pray you choose another subject. 130
CLAUDIO Nay then, give him another staff, this last was broke cross.
DON PEDRO By this light, he changes more and more, I think he be angry indeed.
CLAUDIO If he be, he knows how to turn his girdle.
BENEDICK Shall I speak a word in your ear? 135
CLAUDIO God bless me from a challenge.
BENEDICK You are a villain, I jest not, I will make it good how you dare, with what you dare, and when you dare: do me right, or I will protest your cowardice: you have killed a sweet lady, and her death shall fall heavy on you: let me hear from you. 140
CLAUDIO Well I will meet you, so I may have good cheer.
DON PEDRO What, a feast, a feast?
CLAUDIO I'faith I thank him, he hath bid me to a calf's head and a capon, the which if I do not carve most curiously, say my knife's naught: shall I not find a woodcock too? 145
BENEDICK Sir, your wit ambles well, it goes easily.
DON PEDRO I'll tell thee how Beatrice praised thy wit the other day: I said thou hadst a fine wit, true said she, a fine little one: no said I, a great wit: right says she, a great gross one: nay said I, a good wit: just said she, it hurts nobody: nay said I, the gentleman is wise: certain 150 said she, a wise gentleman: nay said I, he hath the tongues: that I

130 **subject** Benedick added 'I don't like it' in many productions from Garrick to Daly.

135 Don Pedro moved discreetly aside or upstage in most nineteenth- and early twentieth-century productions.

136 At Burton's and Daly's Theatres, NY, Claudio looked imploringly at Don Pedro (s21, Daly). In Barton's production he crossed himself as Don Pedro nonchalantly poured coffee (pbk).

137 Sothern spoke 'with great force', looking Claudio in the eye (s63). Irving, Gielgud and Plummer struck him with a glove; Michell (1956) slapped his face (*A*, 7 June 1884; s93–4, s101, s95). Branagh (1993) gripped him by the cheeks and thrust him to a wall, speaking with great intensity, his face close to Claudio's. Brian Bedford (Stratford, Ontario, 1980), on the other hand, spoke the words quietly (*SS* 34, 1981, 158–9). In some productions Claudio failed at first to realise Benedick's seriousness, smiling or laughing at 'You are a villain' (s21, s36, Daly, s59, s69); but at Burton's and Daly's, NY, he turned suddenly serious at 'I jest not'.

139 **you ... lady** Spoken by Charles Kemble with 'a tremulous change of voice' (*T*, 8 Apr. 1840).

140 **let ... you** Sothern signified his intent by touching the hilt of his sword (s59).

147 **Beatrice praised thy wit** Maurice Evans's Benedick (1934) reacted with secret self-satisfaction (Crosse, 'Performances', XV.17). Jim McQueen (Stratford, Ontario, 1980) treated this speech (147ff.) 'as an embarrassed attempt to restore' the 'earlier friendly relaxation' with Benedick, rather than as a 'piece of heartless indifference to the news of Hero's apparent death' (*SS* 34, 1981, 159).

believe said she, for he swore a thing to me on Monday night, which
he forswore on Tuesday morning, there's a double tongue, there's
two tongues: thus did she an hour together trans-shape thy particular virtues, yet at last she concluded with a sigh, thou wast the   155
properest man in Italy.

CLAUDIO For the which she wept heartily, and said she cared not.

DON PEDRO Yea that she did, but yet for all that, and if she did not hate
him deadly, she would love him dearly, the old man's daughter told
us all.   160

CLAUDIO All, all, and moreover, God saw him when he was hid in the
garden.

DON PEDRO But when shall we set the savage bull's horns on the
sensible Benedick's head?

CLAUDIO Yea and text underneath, 'Here dwells Benedick the married   165
man'?

BENEDICK Fare you well, boy, you know my mind, I will leave you now
to your gossip-like humour: you break jests as braggarts do their
blades, which God be thanked hurt not: my lord, for your many
courtesies I thank you: I must discontinue your company: your   170
brother the bastard is fled from Messina: you have among you killed
a sweet and innocent lady: for my Lord Lack-beard there, he and I
shall meet, and till then peace be with him.   *[Exit]*

DON PEDRO He is in earnest.

CLAUDIO In most profound earnest, and I'll warrant you, for the love of 175
Beatrice.

DON PEDRO And hath challenged thee?

CLAUDIO Most sincerely.

DON PEDRO What a pretty thing man is, when he goes in his doublet
and hose, and leaves off his wit!   180

167–73 Spoken with courtesy in Wood's production (Baltimore, 1829), Benedick doffing his hat to
Claudio (170) at 'I thank you' (S9). Macready spoke with cool gentlemanliness, bowing as he
repudiated Don Pedro at 169–70 (S16); but beneath the veneer of civility was a hard intent,
indicated in Macready's studybook (S17) by triple underlining at 'he and I shall meet'. Irving
delivered the lines with grim courtesy (*Phl*, 19 Mar. 1884), Sothern quietly, with a
contemptuous emphasis on 'boy' that made Claudio flinch (S63). Waterston's Benedick
(NY, 1972–3) spoke on the verge of tears (*NYT*, 14 Jan. 1973), Allam (1990–1) with 'barely
controlled fury' (*SS* 44, 1991, 171). In Sothern's 1904–5 production Claudio and Don Pedro
exchanged significant glances (171) on hearing of Don John's flight (S59). The words 'Let me
hear from you' were added at the end of 173 by most Benedicks from the Kembles to
Creswick, and by Sothern, who tapped his sword menacingly (S59).

174–8 Jeffery Dench's Don Pedro (1971) affected astonishment at 174, breaking into a guffaw at 178.

179–80 Seale's production, set in the nineteenth century, deleted 'doublet and hose'; Langham

CLAUDIO He is then a giant to an ape, but then is an ape a doctor to such a man.

DON PEDRO But soft you, let me be, pluck up my heart, and be sad, did he not say my brother was fled?

Enter DOGBERRY *and* VERGES, CONRADE *and* BORACHIO [*with Watchmen*]

DOGBERRY Come you, sir, if justice cannot tame you, she shall ne'er   185
weigh more reasons in her balance, nay, and you be a cursing hypocrite once, you must be looked to.

DON PEDRO How now, two of my brother's men bound? Borachio one.

CLAUDIO Hearken after their offence, my lord.

DON PEDRO Officers, what offence have these men done?   190

DOGBERRY Marry, sir, they have committed false report, moreover they have spoken untruths, secondarily, they are slanders, sixth and lastly, they have belied a lady, thirdly they have verified unjust things, and to conclude, they are lying knaves.

DON PEDRO First I ask thee what they have done, thirdly I ask thee   195
what's their offence, sixth and lastly why they are committed, and to conclude, what you lay to their charge?

CLAUDIO Rightly reasoned, and in his own division, and by my troth there's one meaning well suited.

DON PEDRO Who have you offended, masters, that you are thus bound   200
to your answer? This learned constable is too cunning to be under-

---

substituted 'tunic and breeches' for the same reason.

184 SD   Hands contrasted Don Pedro in a white suit with Conrade in black and Borachio in black and dark red (pr. photo).

185–7   Cut by Saker and Gielgud; abridged by Craig, Daly, Tree and Nunn (1969).

189   Cut by Daly, Nunn (1969), Eyre and Trevis.

197   Frank Finlay as Dogberry (NT 1965) moved away confused (pbk).

198–9   Usually cut or shortened.

200–2   Abridged by Craig, Gielgud (1949–50) and Seale.

201–2, 205–6, 233   At 'too cunning ... understood' (201–2) Dogberry, flattered by what he took as a compliment, bowed in Kean and Sothern's productions (*MP*, 22 Nov. 1858; S59), 'smirked with pleasure' in Creswick and Trevis's (S44; *SS* 42, 1989, 132). In Daly and Antoon's productions Dogberry and Verges were similarly flattered at 205–6a: 'what your wisdoms could not discover, these shallow fools have brought to light' (Daly; *NYT*, 19 Nov. 1972). In Zeffirelli's production, on the other hand, a Watchman at 'shallow fools' clubbed Borachio for his impertinence (pbk). Dogberry and Verges were mistakenly flattered at 'Here stand a pair of honourable men' (233) in several nineteenth- and early twentieth-century American productions (S13, S21, S36, S42, S59, S81).

stood: what's your offence?

BORACHIO Sweet prince, let me go no farther to mine answer: do you
hear me, and let this count kill me: I have deceived even your very
eyes: what your wisdoms could not discover, these shallow fools   205
have brought to light, who in the night overheard me confessing to
this man, how Don John your brother incensed me to slander the
Lady Hero, how you were brought into the orchard, and saw me
court Margaret in Hero's garments, how you disgraced her when
you should marry her: my villainy they have upon record, which I   210
had rather seal with my death, than repeat over to my shame: the
lady is dead upon mine and my master's false accusation: and briefly
I desire nothing but the reward of a villain.

DON PEDRO Runs not this speech like iron through your blood?

CLAUDIO I have drunk poison whiles he uttered it.   215

DON PEDRO But did my brother set thee on to this?

BORACHIO Yea, and paid me richly for the practice of it.

DON PEDRO He is composed and framed of treachery,
     And fled he is upon this villainy.

CLAUDIO Sweet Hero, now thy image doth appear   220
     In the rare semblance that I loved it first.

DOGBERRY Come, bring away the plaintiffs, by this time our sexton hath
reformed Signor Leonato of the matter: and masters, do not forget
to specify when time and place shall serve, that I am an ass.

VERGES Here, here comes Master Signor Leonato, and the sexton too. 225

     Enter LEONATO, *his brother* [ANTONIO] *and the Sexton*

203–13   Usually spoken with deep remorse, Borachio sometimes bowing his head or kneeling in
contrition. Everett (Princess's, 1858) spoke with 'chapfallen aspect' (*T*, 22 Nov. 1858). Peck
(RSC 1976) requested death with heartfelt emotion (213), attempting to take Claudio's sword
to kill himself (pbk; *T*, 2 July 1977). At the Shakespeare Theatre, Washington, 1992, Margaret
overheard Borachio's confession from a balcony (*SQ* 43, 1992, 462). In Sothern's
productions Claudio tottered half fainting at Borachio's revelation (S59) or turned away,
hiding his face in his hands (S63), Don Pedro placing his hand sympathetically on Claudio's
shoulder (S63). At 208 Richard Easton's Claudio (SMT 1955) shook Borachio angrily (S94).
In Branagh's film an agonised Claudio wept, 'Sweet Hero!'

216   In Langham's 1961 production Don Pedro dragged Borachio to his feet; in Gill's production
(1981) he grabbed him by the doublet (pbks).

220–1   In Poel's production a long pause before these lines gave a more deeply considered quality
to Claudio's response than in many performances (S57). In Sothern's production Claudio
sank to a bench, burying his face in his hands (S59). Charles Kean cut the lines, perhaps
considering them too facile.

LEONATO Which is the villain? Let me see his eyes,
          That when I note another man like him,
          I may avoid him: which of these is he?
BORACHIO If you would know your wronger, look on me.
LEONATO Art thou the slave that with thy breath hast killed   230
          Mine innocent child?
BORACHIO   Yea, even I alone.
LEONATO No, not so, villain, thou beliest thyself,
          Here stand a pair of honourable men,
          A third is fled that had a hand in it:
          I thank you, princes, for my daughter's death,   235
          Record it with your high and worthy deeds,
          'Twas bravely done, if you bethink you of it.
CLAUDIO I know not how to pray your patience,
          Yet I must speak, choose your revenge yourself,
          Impose me to what penance your invention   240
          Can lay upon my sin, yet sinned I not,
          But in mistaking.
DON PEDRO   By my soul nor I,
          And yet to satisfy this good old man,
          I would bend under any heavy weight,
          That he'll enjoin me to.   245
LEONATO I cannot bid you bid my daughter live,
          That were impossible, but I pray you both,

226 **Which is the villain?** Claudio rose in Sothern's 1904–5 production as if identifying himself as the culprit (s59).

231b Leonato raised his stick to strike Borachio in Gielgud's 1949–50 productions, lowering it again as he caught sight of the prince and Claudio (s92–3); in Barton's he threw Borachio to the ground (pbk).

232–7 Irving (1887ff.) cut Leonato's sarcasm.

238ff. *UP* extended Bellario's remorse to sixty-five lines (see introduction, p.10, on *UP*'s adaptation of Claudio). *The Morning Herald* (26 Jan. 1788) observed that Claudio's conduct in this passage 'should be marked by the gravest regret', a comment probably reflecting late eighteenth-century theatrical tradition. Claudio has often knelt before Leonato in deep penitence.

242b–5 Irving (1887ff.) cut Don Pedro's speech.

246–59a In Branagh's film Claudio struggled to hold back tears during Leonato's speech, replying with breaking voice. The reference to the ritual at Hero's 'tomb' (249b–52) was cut in most productions from Garrick to the 1870s, and by Tree, Payne (1909) and Hunt, as these productions omitted the tomb scene (5.3). Tree and Gielgud (1949–50) cut 257, removing a possible mercenary motive for Claudio's compliance.

Possess the people in Messina here,
How innocent she died, and if your love
Can labour aught in sad invention,　　　　　　　　　250
Hang her an epitaph upon her tomb,
And sing it to her bones, sing it tonight:
Tomorrow morning come you to my house,
And since you could not be my son-in-law,
Be yet my nephew: my brother hath a daughter,　　255
Almost the copy of my child that's dead,
And she alone is heir to both of us,
Give her the right you should have given her cousin,
And so dies my revenge.
CLAUDIO　　　　　　　　　Oh noble sir!
Your over kindness doth wring tears from me,　　260
I do embrace your offer, and dispose
For henceforth of poor Claudio.
LEONATO Tomorrow then I will expect your coming,
Tonight I take my leave: this naughty man
Shall face-to-face be brought to Margaret,　　　　265
Who I believe was packed in all this wrong,
Hired to it by your brother.
BORACHIO　　　　　　　　No by my soul she was not,
Nor knew not what she did when she spoke to me,
But always hath been just and virtuous
In anything that I do know by her.　　　　　　　270
DOGBERRY Moreover, sir, which indeed is not under white and black,
this plaintiff here, the offender, did call me ass, I beseech you let it
be remembered in his punishment: and also the watch heard them
talk of one Deformed, they say he wears a key in his ear, and a lock
hanging by it, and borrows money in God's name, the which he hath　　275
used so long, and never paid, that now men grow hard hearted and

---

255　**my brother hath a daughter** Antonio looked surprised in Gielgud's productions (s93–4);
in the Houseman–Landau production (1957) he did an expert double take (*SR*, NY, 24 Aug.
1957).

s9b–62　In Daly and Sothern's productions Claudio took Leonato's hand in pledge of his sincerity
(Daly; s59); in some productions he has knelt.

264a　Claudio and Don Pedro have often made their exit here. Lines 290–2 have sometimes been
substituted for the farewell at 263–4a.

266–70　Edwin Booth and Poel cut the discussion of Margaret's guilt. Borachio made a vigorous
defence of Margaret in Zeffirelli's production, forcing his way to Leonato by dragging the
Watchman to whom he was chained.

273b–8　Dogberry's comments on 'one Deformed' have often been cut or abridged.

will lend nothing for God's sake: pray you examine him upon that
point.
LEONATO I thank thee for thy care and honest pains.
DOGBERRY Your worship speaks like a most thankful and reverent   280
youth, and I praise God for you.
LEONATO There's for thy pains.
DOGBERRY God save the foundation.
LEONATO Go, I discharge thee of thy prisoner, and I thank thee.
DOGBERRY I leave an arrant knave with your worship, which I beseech   285
your worship to correct yourself, for the example of others: God
keep your worship, I wish your worship well, God restore you to
health, I humbly give you leave to depart, and if a merry meeting
may be wished, God prohibit it: come, neighbour.
                                        Exeunt [Dogberry and Verges]
LEONATO Until tomorrow morning, lords, farewell.   290
ANTONIO Farewell, my lords, we look for you tomorrow.
DON PEDRO We will not fail.
CLAUDIO   Tonight I'll mourn with Hero.
                            [Exeunt Don Pedro and Claudio]
LEONATO Bring you these fellows on, we'll talk with Margaret, how her
acquaintance grew with this lewd fellow.
                                                               Exeunt

282 Leonato has traditionally given Dogberry money. At the Haymarket, 1850, he gave him a
gold chain, which Verges examined in astonishment (*Era*, 17 Mar. 1850). In the productions
of Barton (1976) and Bell (1996), Leonato decorated Dogberry with a service medal (pbk). In
Stephens's NY promptbook (P-WHS) Verges reached to accept the proffered purse, but was
forestalled by Dogberry. In Sothern's 1904–5 production Verges, taking advantage of his
partner's inattention, received the money, but lost it to Dogberry when it fell through a hole
in his hat (S59). David Waller (RSC 1988), more condescending than most, passed some of
the money to Verges (pbk).

285–9 In Barton's production Leonato tried to exit three times during Dogberry's speech. Waller's
Dogberry (1988) made three attempts to shake Leonato's hand, only to find that at 'God
prohibit it', Leonato shook his (pbks). Daly, Craig and Tree abridged the speech.

289 SD In Sothern's 1911 production Verges, prodded by Dogberry, disconsolately followed his
partner offstage, Dogberry, with a gloating chuckle, holding up the purse which Verges
had failed to get (S63).

290–2 Cut or abridged in most productions from Garrick to Tree. Sometimes transposed to follow
262.

293–4 George Foss, who directed *Much Ado* at the Old Vic in 1918, suggested that Margaret should
see Borachio led off to prison, burst into tears, and in the next scene speak her dialogue with
Benedick flippantly to mask her emotion (*What the Author Meant*, 116). Lines 293–4 were
cut by Saker, Irving (1887ff.), Craig, Bridges-Adams (S86), Zeffirelli.

ACT 5, SCENE 2

Enter BENEDICK *and* MARGARET

BENEDICK Pray thee, sweet Mistress Margaret, deserve well at my
hands, by helping me to the speech of Beatrice.
MARGARET Will you then write me a sonnet in praise of my beauty?
BENEDICK In so high a style, Margaret, that no man living shall come
over it, for in most comely truth thou deservest it.   5
MARGARET To have no man come over me, why, shall I always keep
below stairs?
BENEDICK Thy wit is as quick as the greyhound's mouth, it catches.
MARGARET And yours, as blunt as the fencers' foils, which hit, but hurt
not.   10
BENEDICK A most manly wit, Margaret, it will not hurt a woman: and so
I pray thee call Beatrice, I give thee the bucklers.
MARGARET Give us the swords, we have bucklers of our own.
BENEDICK If you use them, Margaret, you must put in the pikes with a

---

Often set in a garden or within Leonato's house. George Alexander (1898) set the scene in a
courtyard before the house, Branagh on a balcony overlooking the Tuscan countryside.
Surprisingly, Francis Gentleman considered the scene 'a very unimportant conference'
(*DrC* 2, 1770, 317). Saker omitted it. Branagh's film reversed the order of 5.2 and 5.3.

0 SD   In Zeffirelli's production Benedick entered in dark glasses, frightening Margaret, who
screamed and dropped her basket of flowers (pbk; *MCT*, 26 Feb. 1965). In Barton's
production Margaret was amused at the sight of Benedick with guitar and music book (pbk,
pr. photo). In Trevis's production Benedick fed the fish in the pond as Margaret scrubbed the
patio (pbk). Some productions have focused on Margaret's shame for her part in Hero's
tragedy. At the Shakespeare Theatre, Washington, 1992, she attempted to sneak away from
the house 'carrying a valise with clothes hastily stuffed inside ... She got only as far as the
gate, however, before she thought better of it and came back to sit down despondently in
the garden, where Benedick found her' (*SQ* 43, 1992, 462). In Warchus's production (1993)
Benedick came upon Margaret 'sitting in mourning outside Hero's monument ... trying to be
witty but crushed by her part in the events' (*SS* 47, 1994, 192).

1ff.   Irving played this scene with a lighter touch than he usually showed in comedy (Crosse,
'Performances', I.59).

1–17   The Benedick–Margaret sequence was omitted by Edwin Booth (s41) and in Branagh's film.

vice, and they are dangerous weapons for maids.   15
MARGARET Well, I will call Beatrice to you, who I think hath legs. *Exit*
BENEDICK And therefore will come.
[*Sings*]   The God of love
                             That sits above,
                             And knows me,   20
                             And knows me:
                             How pitiful I deserve.
I mean in singing, but in loving – Leander the good swimmer,
Troilus, the first employer of panders, and a whole book full of
these quondam carpet-mongers, whose names yet run smoothly in   25
the even road of a blank verse, why they were never so truly turned
over and over as my poor self in love: marry, I cannot show it in
rhyme, I have tried: I can find out no rhyme to lady but baby, an
innocent rhyme: for scorn horn, a hard rhyme: for school fool, a
babbling rhyme: very ominous endings. No, I was not born under a   30
rhyming planet, nor I cannot woo in festival terms.

Enter BEATRICE

Sweet Beatrice, wouldst thou come when I called thee?
BEATRICE Yea, signor, and depart when you bid me.
BENEDICK Oh stay but till then.
BEATRICE Then, is spoken: fare you well now, and yet ere I go, let me   35
go with that I came, which is, with knowing what hath passed

The bawdy at 6–11 was cut by Fanny Davenport, Craig, Poel, Tree, Payne (1909) and Bridges-Adams (s86); most directors deleted the bawdy jests at 12b–15. Lines 16b–17 were cut in most productions from Garrick to the 1850s and by Daly.

18–31 J. P. Kemble's attempts at singing were so amusing that when he asked, 'for which of my bad parts didst thou first fall in love with me?' (44–5), Elizabeth Farren answered, 'Why for your singing, I think' (*Or*, 11 Jan. 1793). Irving and Sothern's voices kept breaking as they attempted to sing (*Daily Star*, Montreal, 3 Oct. 1884; s59, s63). Merrison (1988) examined the paper (27ff.) on which he had tried to compose rhymes, finally screwing it up and throwing it into the pond. Kean cut Benedick's song (18–23a), Edwin Booth (s41) both the song and Benedick's soliloquy (18–31). Prudery may have motivated Poel's omission of 27b–31.

31 SD In Tree's production Beatrice discovered Benedick's poem on the ground and read it with amusement, Benedick trying to snatch it from her. In Nunn's 1968 production Benedick ran off as Beatrice picked up his poem and read it; on his return she ran from hedge to hedge pretending to avoid him (pbk).

35 **fare you well** Maggie Smith (1965), Penelope Wilton (1981) and Sinead Cusack (1982) made false exits, which they repeated at 40 (pbks).

between you and Claudio.

BENEDICK Only foul words, and thereupon I will kiss thee.

BEATRICE Foul words is but foul wind, and foul wind is but foul breath,
and foul breath is noisome, therefore I will depart unkissed.   40

BENEDICK Thou hast frighted the word out of his right sense, so forc-
ible is thy wit: but I must tell thee plainly, Claudio undergoes my
challenge, and either I must shortly hear from him, or I will subscribe him a coward: and I pray thee now tell me, for which of my
bad parts didst thou first fall in love with me?   45

BEATRICE For them all together, which maintained so politic a state of
evil, that they will not admit any good part to intermingle with them:
but for which of my good parts did you first suffer love for me?

BENEDICK Suffer love! A good epithet: I do suffer love indeed, for I
love thee against my will.   50

38ff. Maggie Smith thrust her hat over her face as Benedick tried to kiss her (pbk). Other
Beatrices have dodged away. The jests on foul words/foul breath (38–42a) were cut in most
productions from the Kembles to Bridges-Adams.

44a **subscribe ... coward** Despite Beatrice's witty conceits culminating at 'I will depart unkissed'
(40), Peggy Ashcroft (1955), Barbara Jefford (1956) and Geraldine McEwan (1961) accepted a
kiss at the news of the challenge. Penelope Wilton (1981) initiated the kiss (pbks).

44bff. Helena Faucit's reference to the 'pretty sarcasms and humorous sadness' of the ensuing
dialogue suggests that she gave it a softening radiance, despite her observation that Beatrice
can now 'afford to resume some of her natural gaiety' (Faucit, 'Female characters', 225–6).
Irving and Ellen Terry made the conversation warm and joyous (*Brooklyn Daily Times*, 6
Mar. 1885), Terry 'full of arch happiness', her affection touched at moments with coquetry
and playful defiance (*MN*, Chicago, 16 Jan. 1885; *SR*, 21 Oct. 1882, 537; Terry, *Life*, 230).
Irving still showed some of the sheepishness of a first affection (*T*, 24 Oct. 1882), toying now
and then with Beatrice's fan, or touching her hand as if by accident while contemplating her
face (*ECG*, 28 Aug. 1883). Tree blurred the witty edge of the dialogue by sentimental love-
play (*DN*, 25 Jan. 1905). Sothern and Julia Marlowe took the passage playfully (s63): at
'suffer love!' (49) he looked reproachfully at her, she laughing and drawing her hand away
as he kissed it (50). James Dale (SMT 1925, 1936) blended sincerity and self-mockery
(Crosse, *Playgoing*, 73). Elizabeth Spriggs (1971), who had entered as if from baking in the
kitchen, absent-mindedly placed a flour-covered hand on Benedick's blue jacket. As
Sinden's Benedick (1976) sprawled in a chair, Judi Dench began from long habit to clear the
table. Jacobi (1982), slightly embarrassed, checked that no-one was listening before he
spoke of love (pbks). Except for 'one glorious concluding embrace', Susan Fleetwood and
Roger Allam (1990) conducted their 'barbed, bantering exchange' inclining towards each
other from either end of a park bench, 'minimal contact exert[ing] maximum emotion'
(*What's On*, 25 Apr. 1990).

BEATRICE In spite of your heart I think: alas poor heart, if you spite it
for my sake, I will spite it for yours, for I will never love that which
my friend hates.

BENEDICK Thou and I are too wise to woo peaceably.

BEATRICE It appears not in this confession, there's not one wise man   55
among twenty that will praise himself.

BENEDICK An old, an old instance, Beatrice, that lived in the time of
good neighbours: if a man do not erect in this age his own tomb ere
he dies, he shall live no longer in monument than the bell rings and
the widow weeps.   60

BEATRICE And how long is that think you?

BENEDICK Question: why an hour in clamour and a quarter in rheum,
therefore is it most expedient for the wise, if Don Worm (his conscience) find no impediment to the contrary, to be the trumpet of his
own virtues, as I am to myself; so much for praising myself, who I   65
myself will bear witness is praiseworthy: and now tell me, how doth
your cousin?

BEATRICE Very ill.

BENEDICK And how do you?

BEATRICE Very ill too.   70

BENEDICK Serve God, love me, and mend: there will I leave you too, for
here comes one in haste.

55–66a The discussion of self-praise has often been cut or abridged, especially from Macready to
Bridges-Adams. Craig cut 51–66a.

66 **praiseworthy** Gielgud (1955) almost kissed Beatrice, then changed his mind (s94).

70 Ellen Terry, Fanny Davenport, Julia Marlowe and Winifred Emery (1905) nestled their heads
on Benedick's shoulder (*MN*, Chicago, 16 Jan. 1885; P-1886; s59; s65), Marlowe laughing as
Sothern dolefully imitated her sigh (s63).

71 In Bridges-Adams's productions Beatrice and Benedick were caught kissing as Ursula
entered (s86, s88). In Gielgud, Langham and Hands's productions, Benedick and Beatrice
drew apart as Ursula approached (s93–4, s101, P-1982).

Enter URSULA

URSULA Madam, you must come to your uncle, yonder's old coil at home, it is proved my Lady Hero hath been falsely accused, the prince and Claudio mightily abused, and Don John is the author of   75 all, who is fled and gone: will you come presently?

BEATRICE Will you go hear this news, signor?

BENEDICK I will live in thy heart, die in thy lap, and be buried in thy eyes: and moreover, I will go with thee to thy uncle's.

Exeunt

76   Maggie Smith (1965) embraced Ursula at the news (pbk).

77–9 Peggy Ashcroft (1955) curtsied mockingly at 'signor', ran into Benedick's arms as he vowed to live in her heart, and at his rhetorical climax (79b) gave his face a slap (594). Branagh (1993) spoke 78–9a ('I ... moreover') with a grand rhetorical flourish, modulating to a swift comic naturalism at 'I will go ... uncle's'.

ACT 5, SCENE 3

Enter CLAUDIO, DON PEDRO *and three or four [Attendants] with*
tapers [and music]

This scene was omitted in *UP*, in nearly all productions from Garrick to the late nineteenth
century (Irving and Alexander excepted), and by Fry, Sothern, Tree (after the first night),
Payne (1909), Fred Terry (touring production, 1920), Monck (P-NM) and Hunt. The omission
of the scene removes an important transition between the broken wedding and the closing
festivities. The solemn ritual at the monument, made doubly impressive by music,
movement and (in later times) lighting effects, is a symbolic act of penitence and expiation
(see 5.1.240–1, 251–2), Don Pedro's reference to the coming dawn (24–7) heralding a new
beginning and preparing the audience for the auspicious opening of the final scene. At the
Seattle Repertory Theatre, 1978, the ritual seemed a symbolic exorcism of the darkness of
some of the preceding scenes (*SQ* 30, 1979, 263). In Warchus's production (1993) the earlier
scenes had featured 'a painted cupid with the eyes torn off, an emblem of love blinded that
was only healed when the missing strip of painting was found watching the tomb'. Warchus
heightened the emblematic significance of the tomb scene by setting the monument in 'a
canopied space previously used as the wedding-chapel' (*SS* 47, 1994, 192). The sequence
when movingly played has the potential to present a more sympathetic view of Claudio than
previous episodes, Edward Woodward (SMT 1958), for example, showing 'genuine grief',
John Horton (Stratford, Ontario, 1958) 'a moment of pathetic nobility' (*SQ* 9, 1958, 537; *SH*,
29 Aug. 1958). In the Lost Theatre production (Edinburgh Festival, 1993) 'a disguised Hero
witnessed Claudio's sincerity in the eulogy scene, so we understood her forgiveness' (*SQ*
45, 1994, 349).

0 SD   The tapers in Q's stage direction were a means of signifying darkness on the continuously
lit stages of Renaissance theatres. In nineteenth- and twentieth-century productions the
mourners have usually borne candles, lanterns or flaming torches on a darkened stage.
In Irving's production a torchlit procession of monks, armed vergers and black-robed
mourners entered to a tolling bell as a choir sang 'Pardon, goddess of the night'. The music
continued softly during the spoken lines (S46–7; *Time*, Nov. 1882, 961; *GN*, 30 Aug. 1883;
Joseph Hatton, in Brown, *Effective Theatre*, 200). George Alexander (1898) set the scene in

CLAUDIO Is this the monument of Leonato?
LORD It is, my lord.
　　　　　　　[He reads the] epitaph
Done to death by slanderous tongues,
Was the Hero that here lies:
Death in guerdon of her wrongs,　　　　　　　　　　　5
Gives her fame which never dies:
So the life that died with shame,
Lives in death with glorious fame.
Hang thou there upon the tomb,
Praising her when I am dumb.　　　　　　　　　　　10
CLAUDIO Now music sound and sing your solemn hymn.
　　　　　　　Song
Pardon, goddess of the night,
Those that slew thy virgin knight,
For the which with songs of woe,

the crypt of a church, with massive stone columns and arches and a monumental tomb lit by a blue glimmer as of dawn. Choirboys in red cassocks and white surplices intoned the requiem as black-robed mourners entered with flaming torches (photo, *Sk*, 23 Feb. 1898; cutting, 17 Feb. 1898, SCL; Crosse, 'Performances', I.154). Branagh's film showed a spectacular panorama of a torchlit procession moving in darkness up the mountainside to mourn at Hero's tomb. This dissolved to a close-up of Antonio comforting Hero (Did the viewer really need this assurance that Hero was still alive?). Antoon (1972) staged the scene wistfully with umbrellas under the 'rain' (*NYM*, 4 Sep. 1972).

Speech distribution Lines 3–10 and 22–3 have generally been given to Claudio. Barton redistributed the speeches in lines 1–11 as follows: line 1 Don Pedro; 2 Balthasar; 3–4 Claudio; 5–6 Don Pedro; 7–8 Claudio; 9 Don Pedro; 10 Claudio; 11 Don Pedro.

1　**the monument** The inclusion of a tomb in Henslowe's 1598 inventory of stage properties for the Rose Theatre (*Henslowe's Diary*, ed. Foakes and Rickert, 179) raises the possibility that a property monument may also have been used in Renaissance theatres where *Much Ado* was performed.

3ff.　Barton staged the ritual as a military ceremony, the officers saluting with swords erect. Claudio and Don Pedro placed on the stage a large wreath, in the centre of which Claudio laid the epitaph. A penitent Borachio placed a smaller wreath as 'Pardon, goddess' was sung by a military quartet. During the song Claudio and Don Pedro circled the wreaths in slow march, unsheathing and re-sheathing their swords by numbers. The ceremony ended with the last post (pbk; *YP*, 10 Apr. 1976; *FT*, 1 July 1977; *SunTel*, 3 July 1977; *SS* 30, 1977, 81). The scroll containing the epitaph has usually been hung on the monument. In Branagh's film Claudio read in a voice breaking with grief. Nunn (1969) omitted the epitaph (1–11).

12–21　Until the mid-twentieth century 'Pardon, goddess' was frequently sung solo by Balthasar;

Round about her tomb they go: 15
Midnight assist our moan,
Help us to sigh and groan.
Heavily, heavily.
Graves yawn and yield your dead,
Till death be utterèd,   20
Heavily, heavily.

LORD   Now unto thy bones good night,
Yearly will I do this rite.

DON PEDRO Good morrow, masters, put your torches out,
The wolves have preyed, and look, the gentle day   25
Before the wheels of Phoebus, round about
Dapples the drowsy east with spots of grey:
Thanks to you all, and leave us, fare you well.

CLAUDIO Good morrow, masters, each his several way.

[Exeunt Attendants]

DON PEDRO Come let us hence, and put on other weeds,   30
And then to Leonato's we will go.

CLAUDIO And Hymen now with luckier issue speeds,
Than this for whom we rendered up this woe.

Exeunt

ensemble arrangements have predominated since. In Eyre's production 'Pardon, goddess' was sung *a capella* by a choir of cloaked mourners spread over a darkened stage. In Zeffirelli's production two concentric rings of mourners circled the monument in opposite directions during the song; in Nunn's production soldiers circled the tomb (pbks). Irving and Langham transposed the song to the beginning of the scene. In the 1927 Old Vic production it was sung with stringed accompaniment during the reading of the epitaph (Crosse, 'Performances', XI.40; *O*, 27 Nov. 1927). Poel, in quest of Renaissance 'authenticity', substituted an Elizabethan song by John Dowland on the pretext that the original music for 'Pardon, goddess' had been lost (programme).

24–33 The sense of a new beginning was signalled in Barton's production by a chorus of dawn birds (pbk); in Branagh's film the scene dissolved to a shot of Leonato's villa in bright morning sunlight. In Irving's production the dirge modulated at the end of the scene to a bright measure (S47). The closing moments of the sequence in Barton's production anticipated the reconciliations of the final scene, Claudio placing his hand on Borachio's shoulder and Don Pedro and Borachio shaking hands (pbk). Poel cut 24–9, Gielgud 30–3, Seale 29–33, Nunn (1969) 30b–1.

ACT 5, SCENE 4

Enter LEONATO, BENEDICK, MARGARET, URSULA, ANTONIO,
FRIAR [FRANCIS *and*] HERO

FRIAR FRANCIS Did I not tell you she was innocent?
LEONATO So are the prince and Claudio who accused her,
    Upon the error that you heard debated:
    But Margaret was in some fault for this,
    Although against her will as it appears,   5
    In the true course of all the question.
ANTONIO Well, I am glad that all things sorts so well.
BENEDICK And so am I, being else by faith enforced
    To call young Claudio to a reckoning for it.
LEONATO Well, daughter, and you gentlewomen all,   10
    Withdraw into a chamber by yourselves,
    And when I send for you come hither masked:
    The prince and Claudio promised by this hour
    To visit me: you know your office, brother,
    You must be father to your brother's daughter,   15
    And give her to young Claudio.

                           Exeunt Ladies

In nineteenth-century and Edwardian productions the scene was commonly set in a hall
in Leonato's house, sometimes in the garden. Most productions have suggested a festive
atmosphere from the beginning, often crowding the stage with people (Macready used
sixteen supers in this scene (s16); an engraving of Phelps's production (TM) shows twenty-
seven people on stage). In Barton's production the women clapped as Hero entered;
Leonato kissed Hero and Beatrice; Beatrice and Benedick exchanged significant glances
(pbk). The 1984 BBC-TV version foregrounded the weeping Margaret.

1–9   Several productions heightened the auspicious atmosphere by cutting the references to
        Margaret's guilt (4–6) and Benedick's challenge to Claudio (8–9). Poel cut the whole of 1–9,
        Tree 2–9.

10–17   Sometimes abridged; 13–14a are the lines most frequently cut.

ANTONIO Which I will do with confirmed countenance.
BENEDICK Friar, I must intreat your pains, I think.
FRIAR FRANCIS To do what, signor?
BENEDICK To bind me, or undo me, one of them: 20
    Signor Leonato, truth it is, good signor,
    Your niece regards me with an eye of favour.
LEONATO That eye my daughter lent her, 'tis most true.
BENEDICK And I do with an eye of love requite her.
LEONATO The sight whereof I think you had from me, 25
    From Claudio and the prince, but what's your will?
BENEDICK Your answer, sir, is enigmatical,
    But for my will, my will is, your good will
    May stand with ours, this day to be conjoined,
    In the state of honourable marriage, 30
    In which (good friar) I shall desire your help.
LEONATO My heart is with your liking.
FRIAR FRANCIS   And my help.
    Here comes the prince and Claudio.

        Enter DON PEDRO *and* CLAUDIO, *with Attendants*

DON PEDRO Good morrow to this fair assembly.
LEONATO Good morrow, prince, good morrow, Claudio: 35
    We here attend you, are you yet determined,
    Today to marry with my brother's daughter?
CLAUDIO I'll hold my mind were she an Ethiop.
LEONATO Call her forth, brother, here's the friar ready.
                                [Exit Antonio]

18 Henry Marston called the Friar aside with a 'humourous [*sic*] and rather sheepish look' expressing 'the full consciousness of [Benedick's] bachelor resolutions' (*ThT*, 25 Nov. 1848).

22 Sinden (1976) growled the line, 'spitting out the last word as if it [had] stung him'. He had similar trouble with 'marriage' at line 30 (*NS*, 16 Apr. 1976). So did Kevin Kline (NYSF 1988), who stammered the word (*NR*, 22 Aug. 1988).

23–31 Barton cut 23–8a, Bridges-Adams 25–31.

32 In *LL* the Duke offered Beatrice's hand as a reward for Benedick's exploits in battle.

33 SD In Nunn's 1968 production, where war motifs were frequent, soldiers entered with Don Pedro and Claudio (pbk).

38 Sometimes spoken flippantly, e.g. by Abbott, CG 1823 (*TO*, 17 Apr. 1823; *MS*, 21 Apr. 1823, 109). Gielgud as Benedick (1955) gave a deprecatory 'Ahem' at Claudio's tactlessness (*s94*). Some actors have spoken the line with sincere feeling, Maurice Colbourne (SMT 1922–3, 1925), for example, attempting to soften several of Claudio's utterances in this scene (*Oxford Chronicle*, 26 June 1925).

DON PEDRO Good morrow, Benedick, why what's the matter,   40
    That you have such a February face,
    So full of frost, of storm, and cloudiness?
CLAUDIO I think he thinks upon the savage bull:
    Tush fear not, man, we'll tip thy horns with gold,
    And all Europa shall rejoice at thee,   45
    As once Europa did at lusty Jove,
    When he would play the noble beast in love.
BENEDICK Bull Jove, sir, had an amiable low,
    And some such strange bull leaped your father's cow,
    And got a calf in that same noble feat,   50
    Much like to you, for you have just his bleat.

       Enter ANTONIO, HERO, BEATRICE, MARGARET [*and*]
                    URSULA [*masked*]

CLAUDIO For this I owe you: here comes other reckonings.
    Which is the lady I must seize upon?
LEONATO This same is she, and I do give you her.
CLAUDIO Why then she's mine, sweet, let me see your face.   55

40–51   Cut or abridged in most productions from Kemble to Bridges-Adams, and by Branagh (film).
        The cutting of this passage makes Claudio and Don Pedro appear less frivolous than in the
        full text. From Kemble to the early twentieth century the cuts to the passage were probably
        also motivated by prudery.

51 SD   Helena Faucit hid from Benedick behind the other ladies (*ManC*, 11 Apr. 1866), business also
        used in J. W. Wallack's performances (S8). In Gielgud's 1955 production Hero was disguised
        with a stooping crippled gait and a mask sufficient to have 'frightened off a less penitent
        swain' (Sykes, 'Journal Notes', 1955). In Antoon's production the women, ludicrously
        swathed, entered on carousel horses on the stage revolve (*NYM*, 4 Sep. 1972, 51; *NR*, 9 Sep.
        1972). In Barton's production the women entered as 'black-gowned muslim ladies in strict
        purdah' (David, *Shakespeare*, 218).

52a   Spoken in deadly seriousness in the 1984 BBC-TV production, with a menacing finger at
        Benedick.

53ff.   Zeffirelli added a touch of comedy to the unveiling: when Claudio asked 'Which is the
        lady ...?', Antonio mistakenly indicated Beatrice, who waved him away (pbk). At the Odessa
        Globe production, Texas, 1975, Claudio grimaced 'as he reluctantly joined hands with what
        he thought must be – given the disguised Hero's exaggerated efforts to seem awkward and
        ugly – the world's most undesirable woman' (*SQ* 27, 1976, 74). In the 1990 RSC production
        John McAndrew's apprehension was 'palpable' (*SQ* 42, 1991, 346). In Branagh's film the
        sequence was played with the greatest tenderness, the emotions recorded in intimate
        close-up.

55b   **let ... face** John McAndrew (RSC 1990) made the request 'disingenuously, apparently

LEONATO No that you shall not, till you take her hand,
    Before this friar, and swear to marry her.
CLAUDIO Give me your hand before this holy friar,
    I am your husband if you like of me.
HERO And when I lived I was your other wife,   60
    And when you loved, you were my other husband.
CLAUDIO Another Hero?
HERO   Nothing certainer.
    One Hero died defiled, but I do live,
    And surely as I live, I am a maid.
DON PEDRO The former Hero, Hero that is dead.   65
LEONATO She died, my lord, but whiles her slander lived.
FRIAR FRANCIS All this amazement can I qualify,
    When after that the holy rites are ended,
    I'll tell you largely of fair Hero's death:
    Meantime let wonder seem familiar,   70
    And to the chapel let us presently.
BENEDICK Soft and fair friar, which is Beatrice?

hoping [Hero] wouldn't know the rules. When his inescapable predicament was insisted on
... there was a solemn, deeply apprehensive pause as he looked at the impenetrable veil ...
Taking [her] hand required courage and honor' (*SQ* 42, 1991, 346). Edwin Booth removed
the suspense for Claudio by cutting 55–61.

60–1   In Sothern's 1904–5 production Claudio started back in astonishment as Hero unveiled
     (s59); Roger Rees (RSC 1971) showed 'a compound of puzzled excitement, disbelief and
     pleasure' (*St*, 22 Dec. 1971); Robert Sean Leonard (Branagh film) gasped with emotion.

64   Forbes-Robertson (Lyceum, 1882ff.) received Hero rapturously (*Std*, 6 Jan. 1891). In
     productions by Sothern (1904–5) and Gielgud (1955) Claudio knelt and kissed Hero's
     hand (s59, s94); in other productions they have embraced. At the Shakespeare Theatre,
     Washington, 1992, 'Margaret crossed swiftly over to [Hero] and knelt, kissing the hem of
     [her] dress and murmuring contritely while Hero smiled in token of forgiveness' (*SQ* 43,
     1992, 462). Cherie Lunghi (RSC 1976) informed Claudio emphatically, 'I *am* a *maid*' (*SS* 30,
     1977, 172). Edwin Booth, Daly and Sothern coyly altered 'a maid' to 'innocent'; Warren and
     Wood (1804), Macready, Poel and Payne (1909) cut the reference.

65   In the 1984 BBC-TV production Don Pedro crossed himself as if witnessing a miracle.

71   In the eighteenth century Francis Gentleman saw nothing problematic in Hero's marriage
     to Claudio, describing it as 'a just reward of slandered innocence' (Bell). Stephens' NY
     promptbook had organ music burst forth here.

72   Irving searched eagerly for Beatrice among the veiled ladies. In some earlier productions
     'the old fashion was to make the ladies, clad in horribly gaudy and ill-assorted satins, stand
     in a row, along which Benedick stalked till he reached Beatrice' (*SR*, 10 Jan. 1891). Tree took
     Ursula's hand by mistake, then dropped it with an angry exclamation and rushed from lady

BEATRICE I answer to that name, what is your will?
BENEDICK Do not you love me?
BEATRICE Why no, no more than reason.
BENEDICK Why then your uncle, and the prince, and Claudio, 75
    Have been deceived, they swore you did.
BEATRICE Do not you love me?
BENEDICK Troth no, no more than reason.
BEATRICE Why then my cousin, Margaret and Ursula
    Are much deceived, for they did swear you did.
BENEDICK They swore that you were almost sick for me. 80
BEATRICE They swore that you were wellnigh dead for me.
BENEDICK 'Tis no such matter, then you do not love me?
BEATRICE No truly, but in friendly recompense.
LEONATO Come, cousin, I am sure you love the gentleman.
CLAUDIO And I'll be sworn upon't, that he loves her, 85

to lady lifting veils (s69). In the 1945 SMT production Beatrice kept changing places to foil Benedick (s91).

73   Elizabeth Edwin unveiled with a teasing expression (Carver–Partridge engraving, 1815, TM). Peggy Ashcroft (1955), feigning lameness, hobbled down to Benedick (s94).

73ff. The final encounter between Beatrice and Benedick was played in Garrick's productions 'with very entertaining spirit' (Bell), Frances Abington assuming a comic bashfulness 'which drew applause from every part of the house' (*Gz*, 20 Feb. 1783). Gielgud and Ashcroft played the sequence with the whimsical half-seriousness they had shown at numerous points in the play: 'When they deny their love at the end, it is not to deceive the others, but is a game played out between themselves' (*SH*, 9 Dec. 1955). In the Lost Theatre production (Edinburgh Festival, 1993) Beatrice and Benedick's 'relapse into the habit of joking denial dismayed both of them until they found a way ("friendly recompense," etc.) to be both witty and in love' (*SQ* 45, 1994, 349).

74b In *UP*, Liberia's riposte was blunter than Beatrice's: 'Why no; no more than I love Aukwardness [*sic*] and Ill-nature.' Protheus' response at 77b ('Why no, no more than I love Pride and Pertness') was also harsher than in *Much Ado*. Elizabeth Edwin's denial (74b) was 'full of natural wonderment and simplicity' (*E*, 12 Nov. 1809). There was a subtlety in Dorothy Black's tongue-in-cheek half-rejection of Benedick (*BED*, 19 Apr. 1934).

75   Irving stood for a moment as if dismayed, as did Ellen Terry at 77b (cutting, Fitzgerald's Irving scrapbooks, VIII.23). Jacobi (1982) replaced Beatrice's veil over her face; she at once removed it (pbk).

83   Geraldine McEwan (1961) made as if to exit. In Zeffirelli and Hands's productions Beatrice and Benedick shook hands as if in farewell (pbks). In some productions they have moved away to opposite sides of the stage.

For here's a paper written in his hand,
A halting sonnet of his own pure brain,
Fashioned to Beatrice.
HERO   And here's another,
Writ in my cousin's hand, stol'n from her pocket,
Containing her affection unto Benedick.   90
BENEDICK A miracle, here's our own hands against our hearts: come, I
will have thee, but by this light I take thee for pity.
BEATRICE I would not deny you, but by this good day, I yield upon great
persuasion, and partly to save your life, for I was told, you were in a
consumption.   95
BENEDICK Peace I will stop your mouth.
DON PEDRO How dost thou, Benedick the married man?

86–90   Typically Benedick and Beatrice have each received the sonnet written by the other, often
        snatching it, sometimes in a scuffle, often moving away in opposite directions to devour
        each other's poem. The *NY Mirror* (11 Sep. 1830) described Clara Fisher in this sequence
        (Park Theatre, NY) as follows: 'Watch her looks when she snatches the stanzas from
        Benedick, the joy and triumph beaming in her eyes, and the light of successful vanity and
        love gleaming altogether from her radiant face; then, when her own verses are produced,
        and seized by *Benedick*, mark the change – rapid and complete as the workings of thought –
        and then the gradual yielding, as the archness and merriment break forth again, and she
        accepts him' (cited Sprague, *Shakespeare and the Actors*, 18). At Burton's and Daly's, NY,
        Beatrice and Benedick held up the poems exultantly (S21, Daly). In the 1955 and 1976
        Stratford productions Beatrice got both sonnets (pbks). In Moshinsky's production (1989)
        a short-sighted Beatrice held her poem against her nose while a long-sighted Benedick
        tried to read his at arm's length (*FT*, 15 May 1989).
91–5   Irving said 'I *will* have thee' with comic emphasis, but shrugged his shoulders and assumed
        an air of martyred resignation when Beatrice resumed her old habit of chattering (S45; *Th*,
        Nov. 1882, 299).
96   Ellen Terry surrendered joyously to Benedick (*Evening Times*, Glasgow, 28 Aug. 1883), then
        moved upstage to re-read and kiss his sonnet, hiding it next to her heart (*Spirit of the Times*,
        NY, 5 Apr. 1884). Stephens (1965) stopped Beatrice's mouth with 'a marathon kiss' that left
        the watchers admiringly incredulous and the lovers exhausted (*MCT*, 26 Feb. 1965);
        Stephens at last dropped away into Claudio's arms and Beatrice (Maggie Smith) reached
        for a cup of coffee (pbk). Branagh and Thompson kissed long and tenderly as the crowd
        applauded.
97   In Tree's production Don Pedro snatched Benedick's sonnet and jeeringly read, 'Lady ...
        baby' (S69–70). In Nunn's production the male characters made horns and mooed at
        Benedick's surrender to matrimony (*O*, 20 Oct. 1968).

BENEDICK I'll tell thee what, prince: a college of witcrackers cannot
flout me out of my humour: dost thou think I care for a satire or an
epigram? No, if a man will be beaten with brains, a shall wear   100
nothing handsome about him: in brief, since I do purpose to marry,
I will think nothing to any purpose that the world can say against it,
and therefore never flout at me, for what I have said against it: for
man is a giddy thing, and this is my conclusion: for thy part,
Claudio, I did think to have beaten thee, but in that thou art like to   105
be my kinsman, live unbruised, and love my cousin.

CLAUDIO I had well hoped thou wouldst have denied Beatrice, that I
might have cudgelled thee out of thy single life, to make thee a
double dealer, which out of question thou wilt be, if my cousin do
not look exceeding narrowly to thee.   110

BENEDICK Come, come, we are friends, let's have a dance ere we are
married, that we may lighten our own hearts, and our wives' heels.

LEONATO We'll have dancing afterward.

BENEDICK First, of my word, therefore play music. Prince, thou art sad,
get thee a wife, get thee a wife, there is no staff more reverend than   115
one tipped with horn.

Enter MESSENGER

MESSENGER My lord, your brother John is ta'en in flight,
  And brought with armed men back to Messina.

BENEDICK Think not on him till tomorrow, I'll devise thee brave
  punishments for him: strike up, pipers.   120
  Dance [and exeunt]

3–106   In *UP* Protheus delivered a moralised vindication of matrimony in place of Benedick's light-
hearted, tongue-in-cheek rationale. William Lewis (1777ff.) 'retorted the jeers of his friends
with so much good humour and gaiety, that he fairly turned the laugh in his favour' (intro.
to Cumberland, 6–7). Macready defied his companions' jests with an exhilarating 'outbreak
of spirits' (*T*, 25 Feb. 1843). Benedick's defence of his decision to marry was burlesqued in
Warchus's production (1993), Rylance announcing that 'man is a giddy thing' in 'the earnest
tones of a social anthropologist' (*G*, 8 July 1993). Fanny Davenport and Daly surprisingly cut
98–104a; Edwin Booth and Nugent Monck (P-NM) cut 99b–104a. Lines 104b–6, addressed
to Claudio, were cut in several productions from C. Kean to Sothern, and by Monck (P-NM).

)7–10   After Claudio's 'sneering delivery' of these lines in Alexander's 1990 production, 'only
Beatrice's intervention stopped Benedick [Roger Allam] continuing the quarrel'; the 'barely
controlled fury' shown by Allam in the challenge sequence had 'not at all abated' (*SS* 44,
1991, 171). Lines 108b–10 were cut in most productions from Garrick to Irving (1882). Since
Irving (1887) Claudio's speech (107–10) has frequently been omitted.

111a   There was unusual tenderness (RTC 1988) in Branagh's reconciliation with Claudio (*SS* 42,
1989, 133–4). In contrast, John McAndrew's Claudio (RSC 1990) was 'petulantly reluctant to

take Benedick's hand'; 'one ha[d] the feeling that ... the camaraderie between [them] w[ould] never be quite the same again' (Gay, *As She Likes It*, 177; *DT*, 12 Apr. 1990). In Zeffirelli's production Beatrice and Benedick, Claudio and Hero embraced and kissed one another in demonstrative Sicilian fashion (pbk). Irving (1887ff.), Edwin Booth, Poel and Sothern cut 111a.

111b–14a   Cut in most productions from the Kembles to the 1870s, and by Edwin Booth and Jewett.
114b–16   The Kembles ended the play as follows:

> *Ben.* Prince, thou art sad.
> *Ped.* Yes, I've got the tooth-ake.
> *Ben.* Got the tooth-ake! – Get thee a wife; and all will be well. –
>   Nay, laugh not, laugh not: –
>   Your gibes and mockeries I laugh to scorn;
>   No staff more reverend, than one tipp'd with horn. (s5)

Variations of this ending were adopted in most nineteenth-century productions, and by Jewett. Macready (s15), Irving and Fanny Davenport inserted 'I have got the toothache' after line 114, ending the play with lines 115–16. (The transcription of Macready's promptbook in s16 also included Kemble's line 'Your gibes ... scorn'). After the interpolated line 'I have got the toothache', Saker ended the play with 'Get thee a wife, and all will be well'; Daly with 'Strike up, pipers'; Tree with 'Get thee a wife, get thee a wife. Strike up, pipers.' In Macready and Irving's productions Don Pedro glumly held his hand to his face at the toothache reference (s19; sketch dated 2 Nov. 1882, TM); Ralph Richardson (Old Vic, 1931) mimed toothache without speaking the interpolated line (Crosse, 'Performances', XII.137).

115b–16   **there ... horn** These words, implying cuckoldry as the inevitable fate of husbands, were cut by Saker, Daly, Craig, Poel, Tree, Monck (P-NM), Bridges-Adams, Seale, Langham and Eyre. In Barton's production the characters booed at the words (pbk).

117–20a   The Messenger's announcement of Don John's capture and Benedick's reference to punishments were deleted in most Victorian and Edwardian productions (Poel excepted), and by Atkins (1945) and Seale. The omission of these lines made the ending appear more harmonious than in the full text. Gielgud slid over the lines lightly, dismissing Don John in the surge of a joyous finale: 'think not of him' (*O*, 13 Jan. 1952). Some late twentieth-century productions, on the other hand, have foregrounded the passage as a dissonant element in the play's conclusion. Don John's capture was shown on stage in the Houseman–Landau production (ASF 1957), the watch apprehending him in a 'melodramatic chase across the piazza' (*SR*, NY, 24 Aug. 1957). In Jean-Pierre De Decker's production (Ghent, Belgium, 1983) Don John entered as leader of a *coup d'état*, with warplanes heard overhead; organ pipes which earlier had served for the marriage ceremony were turned to become missiles menacing the audience (*SQ* 35, 1984, 467). Alexandru Darie (Oxford Stage Company, 1992) altered the Messenger's announcement to 'your brother John is turned in flight, / And comes with armed men back to Messina', 'threatening a renewal of the war that had ended as the play began' (*SS* 46, 1993, 168–9). In Warchus's production (1993) Don Pedro was 'deeply shamed by Don John's capture and the public humiliation at his share in the success of his brother's plot' (*SS* 47, 1994, 192). See introduction, p.84, for Branagh's treatment of this moment. The Kembles, Wallack and Jewett transposed 117–20a to 104. The Haymarket productions in the 1850s transposed 117–18 to 104, cutting 119–20 (S32).

120b The play has traditionally ended with music and dancing. Q indicated a dance accompanied by pipers. Garrick's performances usually ended with a country dance by the characters, in which Garrick's agility and grace became proverbial (playbills; Lichtenberg, *Visits*, 7; *MP*, 7 Nov. 1775). Fanny Davenport was roguish to the end, dancing in and out beneath the linked arms of the couples as if evading Benedick, who finally caught her (pbk). Bridges-Adams (1933–4) used the dance for a last piece of comedy at Benedick's expense: when Benedick got his steps muddled, Beatrice paired up with Don Pedro to demonstrate the movements; she and Don Pedro then whirled off together, leaving Benedick practising alone until a page took his hand and danced away with him (S88). Antoon (NY 1972) ended the play with a piñata party, the couples spearing the bull-shaped piñata which 'rained its multi-coloured blessings upon them' (*HR* 26, 1973, 337–8).

Whereas performances of *Much Ado* from the early nineteenth to the mid-twentieth century tended to climax on a note of joyous romantic harmony, many productions since the 1960s have ended more ambiguously. In Zeffirelli's the dance, commencing at 114, was twice interrupted: once when Benedick stopped the revelry to speak his 'Prince, thou art sad', etc. to a pensive and isolated Don Pedro, and again at the announcement of Don John's flight and capture. These stop–start interruptions highlighted the discordant elements cutting across the prevailing festivity. After the 'riotous, orgiastic, fancy-dress celebration' of Zeffirelli's finale, the lights and dancers faded away, leaving Don Pedro seated alone, smoking and gazing wistfully into the distance, the festivities finally 'puffed out into nothingness by a single flicker of [his] sceptical cigar' (*PP*, July 1967, 57; *MCT*, 26 Feb. 1965; *ILN*, 27 Feb. 1965). Don Pedro was left similarly isolated and melancholic in the productions of Knapp (Tokyo, 1979), Gill (NT 1981), Broad (Alabama SF, 1981), Hands (RSC 1982), Moshinsky (Strand, 1989) and Bell (Sydney Opera House, 1996). In Barton's production Benedick encouraged everyone on stage to join in the festivities, leaving Beatrice standing awkwardly with his sword in the middle of the rejoicings (*FT*, 9 Apr. 1976). Don Pedro, who had fired a pistol ominously at the commencement of the dance, left after the announcement of Don John's capture to get more guns and holsters, business suggesting that the merry-making was only a pause in continuing hostilities (pbk). Trevis's production (1988) questioned with bitter scepticism whether marriage was in any sense a happy or a comic outcome (see introduction, p.78). Branagh's film, on the other hand, ended joyously, the players exultantly singing 'Sigh no more' (from 2.3) as they danced from courtyard to garden with confetti whirling from the upper windows, the final reprise of the song augmented with symphony orchestra and operatic chorus. The words 'strike up, pipers' (120b) were cut in most productions from the Kembles to the 1870s, and by Fanny Davenport (1886), Edwin Booth and Craig.

BIBLIOGRAPHY

Periodical sources of reviews are not listed in the bibliography.

1. 'FULL-TEXT' EDITIONS OF WORKS BY SHAKESPEARE

Mr William Shakespeares Comedies, Histories, & Tragedies. Published according to the True Originall Copies (First Folio edition), London, printed Isaac Jaggard and Ed. Blount: 1623.

Much adoe about Nothing. As it hath been sundrie times publikely acted by the right honourable, the Lord Chamberlaine his seruants (first quarto edition), London, printed by V.S. for Andrew Wise and William Aspley: 1600.

Much Ado About Nothing, New Variorum edition, ed. H. H. Furness, New York, J. B. Lippincott: 1899.

Much Ado About Nothing, London, Folio Society: 1976.

Much Ado About Nothing, New Cambridge Shakespeare, ed. F. H. Mares, Cambridge University Press: 1988.

Poems: Written by Wil. Shake-speare, London, Tho. Cotes: 1640.

2. ACTING EDITIONS

Much Ado about Nothing ... As it is acted at the Theatre-Royal in Smock-Alley, Dublin: [c.1750].

Much Ado about Nothing ... As it is Acted at the Theatre in Edinburgh, Edinburgh, J. Yair: 1754.

Much Ado about Nothing ... as performed at the Theatre-Royal, Drury-Lane, London, John Bell: 1773.

Much Ado about Nothing ... As it is Acted at the Theatres-Royal in Drury-Lane and Covent-Garden, London, J. Wenman: 1778.

Shakspeare's Much Ado About Nothing, revised by J. P. Kemble, and acted ... at the Theatre Royal, Drury-Lane, London, C. Lowndes: 1797.

Much Ado About Nothing ... As performed at the Theatres Royal, Drury Lane and Covent Garden ... With remarks by Mrs Inchbald, London, printed for Longman, Hurst, Rees, and Orme, by William Savage: [1808].

Much Ado About Nothing ... As performed at the Theatres Royal, Drury-Lane and Covent Garden ... With remarks by Mrs Inchbald, London, printed for

Longman, Hurst, Rees, Orme and Brown, by James Ballantyne,
    Edinburgh: [1808].
*Shakspeare's Much Ado About Nothing ... Revised by J. P. Kemble ... as it is acted
    at the Theatre Royal in Covent Garden*, London: 1810.
*Shakspeare's Much Ado About Nothing ... revised by J. P. Kemble ... as it is
    performed at the Theatres Royal*, London, John Miller: 1815.
*Dolby's British Theatre. Much Ado About Nothing ... As performed at the
    Theatres-Royal, London*, London, T. Dolby: 1823.
*Much Ado About Nothing ... Marked with the stage business, and stage directions, as
    it is performed at the Theatres Royal, by W. Oxberry, Comedian*, London,
    W. Simpkin and R. Marshall: 1823.
Much Ado About Nothing ... as now performed at the Theatres Royal, London,
    London, John Cumberland: [c.1829].
*Shakespeare's comedy of Much Ado about Nothing. Arranged for representation at
    the Princess's Theatre, with explanatory notes, by Charles Kean*, London,
    J. K. Chapman: [1858].
Much Ado About Nothing. A Comedy, in five acts. By William Shakespeare,
    London, Thomas Hailes Lacy: [c.1858].
*Shakspere's Much Ado About Nothing. As arranged for performance at the Crystal
    Palace* [by William Creswick], Sydenham: 1874.
*William Shakespeare's Much Ado About Nothing produced at The Alexandra
    Theatre, Liverpool ... 1878. Arranged for representation by Edward Saker*,
    Liverpool: [1878].
Much Ado About Nothing, The Memorial Theatre edition, ed. C. E. Flower,
    London, Samuel French: [c.1880–1]. Other editions [c.1880–91], 1891,
    1896.
Much Ado About Nothing ... as arranged for the stage by Henry Irving, London,
    Chiswick Press: 1882 (edition used in s45). Other editions 1882, 1883,
    1887, 1891.
*Much Ado About Nothing ... As arranged for production at Daly's Theatre by
    Augustin Daly*, [New York]: 1897.
*Much Ado About Nothing ... Screenplay, Introduction, and Notes on the Making of
    the Film by Kenneth Branagh*, London, Chatto and Windus: 1993.

3. PROMPTBOOKS

Promptbooks listed in Shattuck, *The Shakespeare Promptbooks* (1965), are
coded s, followed by Shattuck's catalogue number. Promptbooks not listed in
Shattuck are coded P, followed by a date or the initials of a person associated
with the book. In the descriptions of the books the first entry is a person to
whom the book relates; the last entry is the book's location.

Promptbooks listed in Shattuck

s2   J. P. Kemble. Partbook for Benedick, marked in Kemble's hand and
      dated DL, 30 Apr. 1788. Folger.

s3   William Warren and William Wood. Chestnut Street Theatre,
      Philadelphia, 1804. Harvard Theatre Collection.

s5   J. P. Kemble. Partbook for Beatrice, marked in Kemble's hand. Folger.

s6   J. P. and Charles Kemble. Transcription of J. P. Kemble's promptbook.
      Garrick Club Library.

s7   The Kembles and Walter Lacy. Transcription of s6 made by Lacy in
      1859, with some additional notes by Lacy. Harvard Theatre Collection.

s8   J. W. Wallack. Folger.

s9   William Wood. Baltimore, 1829. Folger.

s12   Frederick Vining. Haymarket, 1833. Shattuck erroneously dates this
      book 1832. Harvard Theatre Collection.

s13   James Murdoch. Park Theatre, New York, 1838. University of
      Pennsylvania.

s15   W. C. Macready. Drury Lane, 1843. TM.

s16   Macready. Drury Lane, 1843. Promptbook record of Macready's
      arrangements made by George Ellis in 1845, based mainly on s15.
      Harvard Theatre Collection.

s17   Macready. Drury Lane, 1843. Macready's study copy. Forster
      Collection, V&A.

s18   Charles Kean. Promptbook compiled by George Ellis for Charles Kean
      in 1850. Shattuck relates s18 to Macready, but the book is much closer
      to Kean's s26 than to Macready's arrangements. Folger.

s19   Macready. Drury Lane, 1843. Promptbook record of Macready's
      arrangements made by George Ellis for Hermann Vezin, based mainly
      on s15. University of Illinois Library.

s20   Macready. Drury Lane, 1843. Promptbook record of Macready's
      arrangements prepared by George Becks, based mainly on s15.
      Contains some notations of Charles Kemble's business. NY Public
      Library.

s21   John Moore. Burton's Theatre, New York. Folger.

s24   Barry Sullivan. 1850s. SCL.

s25   T. Agnew Dow. Arch Street Theatre, Philadelphia, 1854. Folger.

s26   Charles Kean. Princess's Theatre, 1858. Folger.

s32   Walter Lacy. Haymarket, 1859. Lacy's transcription of s6, augmented
      with business from the 1859 Haymarket production. Folger.

s35   James H. Taylor. Boston Theatre, c.1860. Harvard Theatre Collection.

s36   Edward L. Davenport. William Seymour Theatre Collection,
      Princeton University Library.

s41   Edwin Booth, c.1889–90. Folger.

s42   Junius Brutus Booth Jr, c.1875. Folger.

s44   William Creswick. Australian tour, 1877. SCL.

s45   Henry Irving. Rehearsal promptbook. Scene descriptions in Lyceum
       programmes suggest that the MS markings in s45 relate to the 1887
       Lyceum production, not the 1882 production as stated in Shattuck.
       Folger.

s46   Irving. Preparation promptbook, probably for the 1882 Lyceum
       production. Folger.

s47   Irving. Promptbook record of Irving's 1884 touring production as
       played at the Star Theatre, New York, 31 Mar. 1884. Shattuck
       erroneously dates this production 31 Mar. 1883. NY Public Library.

s50   Irving, Edward Gordon Craig. Craig's studybook for the Messenger in
       Irving's 1891 Lyceum production. Craig Collection, University of
       California Library, Los Angeles.

s56   Charles B. Hanford, Washington, c.1900. Folger.

s57   William Poel. Court Theatre London and various London halls, 1904.
       TM.

s59   E. H. Sothern and Julia Marlowe, c.1904–5. Folger.

s63   Sothern and Marlowe, 1911. Folger.

s65–8 Herbert Beerbohm Tree. His Majesty's, 1905. UBTC.

s69   Tree. His Majesty's, 1905. Final promptbook record. UBTC.

s70   Tree. His Majesty's, 1905. Seven rehearsal partbooks. UBTC.

s81   Henry Jewett, Boston Repertory Theatre, 1926. Folger.

s86   W. Bridges-Adams. SMT, 1922, 1923, 1925, 1927, 1929. SCL.

s87   Bridges-Adams. Relates to the 1933 SMT production, but not used in
       performances. SCL.

s88   Bridges-Adams. SMT, 1933–4. Other sources suggest that the book
       was not also used in 1929–30, as stated in Shattuck. SCL.

s89   B. Iden Payne. SMT, 1936. SCL.

s91   Robert Atkins. SMT, 1945. SCL.

s92   John Gielgud. SMT, 1949. SCL.

s93   Gielgud. SMT, 1950. SCL.

s94   Gielgud. SMT touring production, 1955. SCL.

s95   Denis Carey. Old Vic, 1956. TM.

s100   Douglas Seale. SMT, 1958. SCL.

s101   Michael Langham. RST, 1961. SCL.

s102   Ellen Terry. Contains notes in Ellen Terry's hand relating to Lyceum
       performances between 1882 and 1891. Ellen Terry Museum, Small
       Hythe, Kent.

Promptbooks not listed in Shattuck

P-1819   A. Bunn. Theatre Royal Birmingham, 1819. BPL.

P-WHS   W. H. Stephens. New York, mid-nineteenth century. Harvard
          Theatre Collection.

P-1886   Fanny Davenport, 1886. Harvard Theatre Collection.

P-ET   Ellen Terry. Irving acting edition (1883), with additional cuts and a
          few notations in Ellen Terry's hand. Bram Stoker Collection, SCL.

P-1903a   Edward Gordon Craig, 1903. Preparation promptbook marked in
          Craig's hand. Bibliothèque Nationale, Paris.

P-1903b   Craig, 1903. Preparation promptbook based on Cassell edition,
          1901. Ellen Terry Museum, Small Hythe, Kent.

P-1904/5 Sothern and Marlowe, 1904–5. Harvard Theatre Collection.

P-NM   Nugent Monck. Favourite Classics edition, Heinemann, 1904,
          pasted in workbook and bound in brown cloth boards. TM.

P-1947   Hugh Hunt. Bristol Old Vic and Embassy Theatre London, 1947.
          UBTC.

P-1952   John Gielgud. Phoenix Theatre London, 1952. TM.

P-1965   Franco Zeffirelli. NT, 1965, 1967. NT archives.

P-1968   Trevor Nunn. RST, 1968. SCL.

P-1969   Trevor Nunn. Aldwych Theatre, London, 1969. SCL.

P-1971   Ronald Eyre. RST, 1971. SCL.

P-1976   John Barton. RST, 1976. SCL.

P-1981   Peter Gill. NT, 1981. NT archives.

P-1982a   Terry Hands. RST, 1982. SCL.

P-1982b   Terry Hands. RST, 1982. SCL.

P-1988   Di Trevis. RST, 1988. SCL.

P-1990   Bill Alexander. RST, 1990. SCL.

4. OTHER WORKS

Agate, James E., *My Theatre Talks*, London, Arthur Barker: 1933.

Alexander, George, *Souvenir, 'Much Ado About Nothing', St James's Theatre 1898*, London: 1898.

Amussen, Susan, *An Ordered Society. Gender and Class in Early Modern England*, Oxford, Basil Blackwell: 1988.

Archer, William, *Henry Irving, Actor and Manager*, London, Field & Tuer: 1883.

William Charles Macready, London, Kegan Paul: 1890.

Arne, Thomas A., *Six Cantatas for a Voice and Instruments Set to Music by Thomas Augustine Arne* (Book 1 of Arne's *Vocal Melody*), London, I. Walsh: c.1749.

Babula, William, *Shakespeare in Production, 1935–1978. A Selective Catalogue*, New York, Garland: 1981.

Bancroft, G. P., *Stage and Bar. Recollections*, London, Faber & Faber: 1939.

Belsey, Catherine, 'Disrupting sexual difference: meaning and gender in the comedies', in John Drakakis (ed.), *Alternative Shakespeares*, London, Methuen: 1985.

Berry, Ralph, *On Directing Shakespeare. Interviews with Contemporary Directors*, London, Croom Helm: 1977.

Boaden, James, *Memoirs of the Life of John Philip Kemble*, 2 vols., London, Longman: 1825.

Memoirs of Mrs Siddons, 2 vols., London, Henry Colburn: 1827.

Brereton, Austin, *The Life of Henry Irving*, 2 vols., London, Longmans: 1908.

Shakespearean Scenes and Characters, London, Cassell: 1886.

Bristol, Michael, *Carnival and Theatre*, London, Methuen: 1985.

Brown, Ivor, Dent, A. H., and Hobson, Harold, 'Critics' Forum', broadcast typescripts for 20 Apr. 1949 and 24 Apr. 1949, Birmingham Public Library.

Brown, John Russell, *Effective Theatre*, London, Heinemann: 1969.

Brownsmith, John, *The Dramatic Time-Piece: or, Perpetual Monitor*, London, J. Almon: 1767.

Burnim, K. A., *David Garrick, Director*, University of Pittsburgh Press: 1961.

Burton, Robert, *The Anatomy of Melancholy*, Oxford, John Lichfield & James Short, for Henry Cripps: 2nd edn, 1624.

Butler, Frances A., *Journal of Frances Anne Butler*, 2 vols., London: 1835.

Campbell, Thomas (ed.), *The Dramatic Works of William Shakespeare. With Remarks on his Life and Writings by T. Campbell*, London, E. Moxon: 1838.

Carlson, Susan, *Women and Comedy*, Ann Arbor, University of Michigan Press: 1991.

Casson, John, *Lewis and Sybil*, London, Collins: 1972.

Chambers, E. K., *The Elizabethan Stage*, 4 vols., Oxford, Clarendon Press: 1923.

William Shakespeare. A Study of Facts and Problems, 2 vols., Oxford, Clarendon Press: 1930.

Cibber, Theophilus, *Theophilus Cibber, to David Garrick, Esq.*, London, W. Reeves and J. Phipps: 1759.

Coffey, Denise, introduction to *Much Ado About Nothing*, London, Folio Society: 1976.

Cook, Judith, *Shakespeare's Players*, London, Harrap: 1983.

Women in Shakespeare, London, Virgin Books: 1980.

Coursen, H. R., *Shakespearean Performance as Interpretation*, Newark, University of Delaware Press: 1992.

Craig, Edward A., *Gordon Craig. The Story of his Life*, London, Victor
 Gollancz: 1968.
Craig, Edward Gordon, *Henry Irving*, London, Dent: 1930.
 On the Art of the Theatre, London, Heinemann: 1911.
Crosse, Gordon, 'Shakespearean performances which I have seen', MS
 notebooks, Birmingham Public Library.
 Shakespearean Playgoing 1890–1952, London, Mowbray: 1953.
Daly, J. F., *The Life of Augustin Daly*, New York, Macmillan: 1917.
Davenant, William, *The Law Against Lovers* (1662), in *The Works of Sr William
 Davenant, K^t*, London, T. N. for Henry Herringman: 1673.
David, Richard, *Shakespeare in the Theatre*, Cambridge University Press:
 1978.
Davies, Thomas, *Memoirs of the Life of David Garrick*, 2 vols., London: 1780.
Dessen, Alan C., *Elizabethan Stage Conventions and Modern Interpreters*,
 Cambridge University Press: 1984.
 'Shakespeare and the theatrical conventions of his time', in Stanley Wells
 (ed.), *The Cambridge Companion to Shakespeare Studies*, Cambridge
 University Press: 1986.
Dickins, Richard, *Forty Years of Shakespeare on the English Stage*: 1907.
Digges, Leonard, 'Upon Master William Shakespeare', in *Poems: Written by
 Wil. Shake-speare*, London, Tho. Cotes: 1640.
Faucit, Helena, 'On some of Shakespeare's female characters', *Blackwood's
 Magazine* 137 (1885): 203–31.
Findlater, Richard, *The Player Kings*, London, Weidenfeld & Nicolson: 1971.
Fitzgerald, Percy H., *Henry Irving. A Record of Twenty Years at the Lyceum*,
 London, Chapman & Hall: 1893.
 'Henry Irving: his life and characters', scrapbooks, Garrick Club, London.
 Shakespearean Representation. Its Laws and Limits, London, Elliot Stock:
 1908.
Fletcher, George, *Studies of Shakespeare*, London: 1847.
Foakes, R. A., 'Playhouses and players', in *The Cambridge Companion to
 Renaissance Drama*, ed. A. R. Braunmuller and Michael Hattaway,
 Cambridge University Press: 1990.
Foote, Samuel, *A Treatise on the Passions as far as they Regard the Stage*,
 London, C. Corbet: [1747].
Foss, George R., *What the Author Meant*, London, Oxford University Press:
 1932.
Gay, Penny, *As She Likes It. Shakespeare's Unruly Women*, London, Routledge:
 1994.
Gielgud, Kate Terry, *Kate Terry Gielgud. An Autobiography*, London,
 Reinhardt: 1953.

Gielgud, John, *An Actor in His Time*, Harmondsworth, Penguin: 1981 (first pub. 1979).

Stage Directions, Westport, Conn., Greenwood Press: 1979 (first pub. 1963).

Gilbert, Sandra M. and Gubar, Susan, *The Madwoman in the Attic. The Woman Writer and the Nineteenth-Century Literary Imagination*, New Haven and London, Yale University Press: 1979.

Gilliatt, Penelope, *Unholy Fools. Wits, Comics, Disturbers of the Peace: Film and Theatre*, London, Viking Press: 1973.

Gilliland, Thomas, *The Dramatic Mirror: Containing the History of the Stage from the Earliest Period, to the Present Time*, 2 vols., London, C. Chapple: 1808.

Goede, C. A. G., *The Stranger in England*, 3 vols., London: 1807.

Goodman, Walter, *The Keeleys on the Stage and at Home*, London, R. Bentley & Son: 1895.

The Green-Room Mirror, London: 1786.

Grein, J. T., *Dramatic Criticism, 1899–1905*, London, J. Long: [1906].

Gurr, Andrew, *The Shakespearean Stage 1574–1642*, 3rd edn, Cambridge University Press: 1992.

Haddon, Archibald, *Green Room Gossip*, London, Stanley Paul & Co: 1922.

Halio, Jay L., *Understanding Shakespeare's Plays in Performance*, Manchester University Press: 1988.

Hattaway, Michael, *Elizabethan Popular Theatre*, London, Routledge: 1982.

Hawkins, William, *Miscellanies in Prose and Verse*, London: 1775.

Hayman, Ronald, *John Gielgud*, London, Heinemann: 1971.

Hazlitt, William, *Characters of Shakespear's Plays*, London, Macmillan: 1903 (first pub. 1817).

A View of the English Stage, London: 1818.

Headlam, S. D., *Shakespeare and the Evening Schools Under the London School Board*, London: 1904.

Henderson, Katherine and McManus, Barbara, *Half Humankind: Contexts and Texts of the Controversy about Women in England, 1540–1640*, Urbana, University of Illinois Press: 1985.

Henry Irving. A Short Account of His Public Life, New York: 1883.

Henslowe, Philip, *Henslowe's Diary*, ed. R. A. Foakes and R. T. Rickert, Cambridge University Press: 1961.

Hobson, Harold, *The Theatre Now*, London, Longmans, Green & Co: 1953.

Holderness, Graham (ed.), *The Shakespeare Myth*, Manchester University Press: 1988.

Hotson, Leslie, *The Commonwealth and Restoration Stage*, Cambridge, Mass., Harvard University Press: 1928.

Howard, Cecil, *Dramatic Notes, 1882*, London: 1883.

Hunt, Leigh, *Critical Essays on the Performers of the London Theatres*, London, John Hunt: 1807.

Ireland, Joseph. N., *Records of the New York Stage, from 1750 to 1860*, 2 vols., New York: 1866–7.

Isaac, Winifred, *Ben Greet and the Old Vic. A Biography of Sir Philip Ben Greet*, London: [1964].

James, Reese D., *Old Drury of Philadelphia. A History of the Philadelphia Stage 1800–1835*, New York, Greenwood Press: 1968 (first pub. 1932).

Jameson, Anna B., *Characteristics of Women*, 2 vols., 2nd edn, London: 1833.

Kemp, T. C., 'The Stratford festival', broadcast typescripts, 3 May 1949 and 14 June 1950, Birmingham Public Library.

Kemp, T. C. and Trewin, J. C., *The Stratford Festival. A History of the Shakespeare Memorial Theatre*, Birmingham, Cornish Bros: 1953.

Kennedy, Dennis, *Looking at Shakespeare. A Visual History of Twentieth Century Performance*, Cambridge University Press: 1993.

King, Margaret L., *Women of the Renaissance*, University of Chicago Press: 1991.

Kitchin, Laurence, *Mid-Century Drama*, London, Faber & Faber: 1960.

Kolin, Philip C. (ed.), *Shakespeare in the South*, Jackson, University of Mississippi Press: 1983.

Kyd, Thomas, *The Spanish Tragedie*, 1615 edition.

Lamb, Charles, *The Art of the Stage as Set Out in Lamb's Dramatic Essays, with a Commentary by Percy Fitzgerald*, London, Remington: 1885.

Larson, Orville K., *Scene Design in the American Theatre from 1915 to 1960*, Fayetteville, University of Arkansas Press: 1989.

Leiter, Samuel L. (ed.), *Shakespeare Around the Globe. A Guide to Notable Postwar Revivals*, New York, Greenwood Press: 1986.

A Letter to David Garrick, on Opening the Theatre, London: 1769.

Letters of an Unsuccessful Actor, London, Cecil Palmer: 1923.

Lichtenberg, G. C., *Lichtenberg's Visits to England as Described in His Letters and Diaries*, tr. M. L. Mare and W. H. Quarrel, Oxford, Clarendon Press: 1938.

Loney, Glen (ed.), *Staging Shakespeare. Seminars on Production Problems*, New York, Garland: 1990.

Malone Society, *Collections*, vol. VI (1961), Oxford University Press: 1962.

Marcus, Leah S., 'Shakespeare's comic heroines, Elizabeth I, and the political uses of androgyny', in *Women in the Middle Ages and the Renaissance*, ed. Mary Beth Rose, Syracuse, New York, Syracuse University Press: 1986.

Marshall, Norman, *The Producer and the Play*, London, Macdonald: 1957.

Marston, J. W., *Our Recent Actors*, 2 vols., London, Sampson Low & Co: 1888.

Martin, Theodore, *Helena Faucit*, London, W. Blackwood: 1900.
Mason, Pamela, *Much Ado About Nothing. Text and Performance*, London, Macmillan: 1992.
Matthews, Bache, *A History of the Birmingham Repertory Theatre*, London, Chatto & Windus: 1924.
Matthews, J. B. and Hutton, L., *Actors and Actresses of Great Britain and the United States*, 5 vols., New York, Cassell: 1886.
Mazer, Cary M., *Shakespeare Refashioned. Elizabethan Plays on Edwardian Stages*, Ann Arbor: UMI Research Press: 1981.
Miller, James, *The Universal Passion. A Comedy. As It Is Acted at the Theatre-Royal in Drury-Lane*, London, J. Watts: 1737.
Molière, Jean Baptiste de, *La Princesse d'Elide*, [Amsterdam]: 1674.
Murphy, Arthur, *The Life of David Garrick, Esq.*, 2 vols., London: 1801.
Odell, G. C. D., *Annals of the New York Stage*, 15 vols., New York, Columbia University Press: 1927–49.
Old Vic Annual Report, 1930–1.
Pedicord, H. W., *The Theatrical Public in the Time of Garrick*, Carbondale, Southern Illinois University Press: 1954.
Pepys, Samuel, *The Diary of Samuel Pepys*, ed. H. B. Wheatley, 8 vols., London, George Bell: 1904–5.
Pollock, Juliet, *Macready as I Knew Him*, London, Remington: 1884.
Pollock, Thomas C., *The Philadelphia Theatre in the Eighteenth Century*, New York, Greenwood Press: 1968 (first pub. 1933).
Pollock, W. H., *Impressions of Henry Irving*, London, Longmans: 1908.
Reynolds, Frederick, *The Life and Times of Frederick Reynolds*, 2 vols., London: 1826.
Robertson, W. G., *Time Was. The Reminiscences of W. Graham Robertson*, London, Hamish Hamilton: 1931.
Robinson, Henry Crabb, *The London Theatre 1811–1866: Selections from the Diary of Henry Crabb Robinson*, ed. Eluned Brown, London, Society for Theatre Research: 1966.
Robson, William, *The Old Play-goer*, London: 1846.
Rothwell, K. S. and Melzer, A. H., *Shakespeare on Screen. An International Filmography and Videography*, London, Mansell: 1990.
Rutter, Carol, *Clamorous Voices: Shakespeare's Women Today*, London, The Women's Press: 1988.
Saintsbury, H. A. and Palmer, Cecil (eds.), *We Saw Him Act. A Symposium on the Art of Sir Henry Irving*, London, Hurst & Blackett: 1939.
Scott, Clement W., *Ellen Terry*, New York, Frederick A. Stokes Co.: 1900.
Seaton, Ethel, *Literary Relations of England and Scandinavia in the Seventeenth Century*, Oxford, Clarendon Press: 1935.

Seilhamer, George O., *History of the American Theatre*, 3 vols., New York, Greenwood Press: 1968 (first pub. 1888–91).

Shakespeare Memorial Theatre 1954–56. A Photographic Record, London, Max Reinhardt: 1956.

Shakespearean Criticism, Detroit, Gale Research: vol. VIII, 1989; vol. XVIII, 1992.

Shattuck, Charles H., *Shakespeare on the American Stage* [vol. I] *from the Hallams to Edwin Booth*, Washington, Folger Shakespeare Library: 1976.

Shakespeare on the American Stage [vol. II] *from Booth and Barrett to Sothern and Marlowe*, Washington, Folger Shakespeare Library: 1987.

The Shakespeare Promptbooks. A Descriptive Catalogue, Urbana, University of Illinois Press: 1965.

Shaw, George Bernard, *The Dying Tongue of Great Elizabeth*, London, London Shakespeare League: 1920.

Speaight, Robert, *Shakespeare on the Stage*, London, Collins: 1973.

Sprague, Arthur C., *Shakespeare and the Actors*, New York, Russell and Russell: 1963.

Sprague, A. C. and Trewin, J. C., *Shakespeare's Plays Today*, London, Sidgwick & Jackson: 1970.

St John, Christopher, *Ellen Terry*, London, John Lane: 1907.

Stoker, Bram, *Personal Reminiscences of Henry Irving*, 2 vols., London, Heinemann: 1906.

Sykes, E. F., 'Journal notes: seventh series', 1955. Typescript, Birmingham Public Library.

Taylor, Gary, *Reinventing Shakespeare. A Cultural History from the Restoration to the Present*, London, Hogarth Press: 1990.

Taylor, John, *Records of My Life*, 2 vols., London, Edward Bull: 1832.

Terry, Ellen, *Ellen Terry's Memoirs*, ed. Edith Craig and Christopher St John, London, Victor Gollancz: 1933.

Four Lectures on Shakespeare, London, Martin Hopkinson: 1932.

MS lecture on *Much Ado About Nothing*, Ellen Terry Museum, Small Hythe, Kent.

The Story of My Life, London, Hutchinson: 1908.

Theatrical Biography: or, Memoirs of the Principal Performers of the Three Theatres Royal, 2 vols., London, S. Bladon: 1772.

Thomson, Peter, *Shakespeare's Theatre*, London, Routledge: 1983.

Towse, J. R., *Sixty Years of the Theater. An Old Critic's Memories*, New York, Funk & Wagnalls: 1916.

Trewin, J. C., *Robert Donat*, London, Heinemann: 1968.

Underdown, D. E., 'The taming of the scold: the enforcement of patriarchal authority in early modern England', in *Order and Disorder in Early Modern*

England, ed. Anthony Fletcher and John Stevenson, Cambridge University Press: 1985.

Van Lennep, W., *et al.*, *The London Stage 1660–1800*, 11 vols., Carbondale, Southern Illinois University Press: 1960–8.

Victor, Benjamin, *The History of the Theatres of London and Dublin from the Year 1730 to the Present Time*, 3 vols., London, T. Davies: 1761–71.

Wells, Stanley, 'Editorial treatment of foul-paper texts: *Much Ado About Nothing* as a test case', *Review of English Studies* 31 (1980): 1–16.

Wiesner, Merry E., *Women and Gender in Early Modern Europe*, Cambridge University Press: 1993.

Wilkes, Thomas, *A General View of the Stage*, London: 1759.

Wilkinson, Tate, *The Wandering Patentee*, 4 vols., York: 1795.

Williamson, Audrey, *Old Vic Drama*, London, Rockliff: 1948.

Winter, William, *Henry Irving*, New York, G. J. Coombes: 1885.

Vagrant Memories, New York, G. H. Doran: 1915.

Woodbridge, Linda, *Women in the English Renaissance. Literature and the Nature of Womankind, 1540–1620*, Brighton, Harvester Press: 1984.

Wrightson, Keith, *English Society 1580–1680*, London, Hutchinson: 1982.

The Year's Work in the Theatre, 1949–50, 1950.

INDEX